A CHANGING TURKEY

A CHANGING TURKEY

The Challenge to Europe and the United States

HEINZ KRAMER

BROOKINGS INSTITUTION PRESS
Washington, D.C.

1775 Massachusetts Avenue, N.W.
Washington, D.C. 20036
www.brookings.edu

Library of Congress Cataloging-in-Publication data

Kramer, Heinz.
A Changing Turkey : the challenge to Europe and the United States / Heinz Kramer.
p. cm.
ISBN 0-8157-5023-4
1. Turkey—Politics and government—20th century. 2. Turkey—Foreign relations. I. Title.
DR576.K73 1999 99-050446
956.103′9—dc21 CIP

9 8 7 6 5 4 3 2 1

The paper used in this publication meets the minimum requirements of the American National Standard for Information Sciences—Permanence of Paper for Printed Library Materials, ANSI Z39.48-1984

Typeset in Minion

Composition by Northeastern Graphic Services
Hackensack, New Jersey

Printed by R. R. Donnelley and Sons
Harrisonburg, Virginia

THE BROOKINGS INSTITUTION

The Brookings Institution is an independent organization devoted to nonpartisan research, education, and publication in economics, government, foreign policy, and the social sciences generally. Its principal purposes are to aid in the development of sound public policies and to promote public understanding of issues of national importance.

The Institution was founded on December 8, 1927, to merge the activities of the Institute for Government Research, founded in 1916, the Institute of Economics, founded in 1922, and the Robert Brookings Graduate School of Economics and Government, founded in 1924.

The general administration of the Institution is the responsibility of a Board of Trustees charged with safeguarding the independence of the staff and fostering the most favorable conditions for scientific research and publication. The immediate direction of the policies, program, and staff is vested in the president, assisted by an advisory committee of the officers and staff.

In publishing a study, the Institution presents it as a competent treatment of a subject worthy of public consideration. The interpretations or conclusions in such publications are those of the author or authors and do not necessarily reflect the views of the other staff members, officers, or trustees of the Brookings Institution.

Foreword

DURING A RECENT visit to Europe, President Clinton emphasized the importance of Turkey, both in Europe and for shaping the future of the critical region that lies between Europe and the wider Middle East and Central Asia. This is nothing new; during the cold war, Turkey played a central role in containing the Soviet drive toward the Middle East and the Mediterranean.

But even before that, Turkey had embarked on a difficult journey. More than 75 years ago, the newly established Turkish Republic set out to gain an undisputed place among the modern, Western, contemporary societies. In so doing, the country distanced itself from its Islamic, eastern past. Since then, Turkey has been pursuing the course prescribed by Atatürk. In the aftermath of World War II, this process was supported and stabilized by Turkey's firm inclusion in the Western alliance.

After the cold war, Turkey has experienced a new wave of change that for the first time in recent history fundamentally questions the established principles of the Kemalist state tradition. In addition, new foreign and security policy challenges have emerged, inducing a domestic debate over Turkey's regional role.

One result is that Europe and the United States are confronted with a changing Turkey whose contours are only dimly visible. Heinz Kramer's analysis endeavors to depict the main forces for change and to evaluate their impact on Turkey's relations with its European and American allies. Internally, his focus is on the ethnic and religious challenges to the Kemalist tradition. He analyses the development of the country's Kurdish problem and the revival of political Islam as the main challenges to the established political elites. He recommends that a stronger emphasis on liberal democratic policies would create a more stable environment for Turkish politics in the first decades of the new century.

Kramer also assesses the different options available to Turkey with the breakup of the Soviet empire. He evaluates Turkey's choices vis-à-vis the new Turkic world of Central Asia, in relations with its regional neighbors of the Middle East, and in its continuing strong links with its allies in Europe and the United States. Kramer, a European, concludes that Europeans and Americans alike will have to take into account a stronger Turkish assertiveness in regional and international affairs. Allied policies toward Turkey must be readjusted accordingly, including the development of a continuous, high-level political dialogue.

This book could not have been written without the assistance and advice of many people to whom the author is grateful for having the time to share their thoughts. This is especially true of Turkish friends and colleagues—scholars, journalists, politicians, and officials—who during the past twenty years have contributed to his education in Turkish social and political life. It goes without saying that none of them can be held responsible for the views expressed in the following pages.

Heinz Kramer would like to thank Richard Haass of the Brookings Institution for suggesting that he write about this subject and for having the patience to wait for its conclusion. He would also like to thank Susan Jackson, Myrna Atalla, and Mohammed Sulaiman for their verification of the manuscript and Karla Nieting for her valuable assistance throughout the project and German language verification. For the Brookings Institution Press, James Schneider edited the manuscript, Helen Winton proofread the pages, and Sherry Smith provided the index. Most importantly, the author would like to thank the German Marshall Fund of the United States for its support of this effort.

The views expressed in this book are of course those of the author and should not be ascribed to any of the persons whose assistance is acknowledged above, or to the trustees, officers, or other staff members of the Brookings Institution.

MICHAEL H. ARMACOST
President

Washington, D.C.
January 2000

Contents

Preface

Turkey is a long-standing ally of the United States and Europe. Since the inception of the cold war it contributed to the effective containment of the Soviet Union by guarding the southeastern flank of the Atlantic alliance. After the demise of the Soviet Empire its strategic importance changed, but it has not diminished. Today it could play an important role in developing the energy resources of the Caspian Sea region. Its contribution to containing Saddam Hussein's regime in Iraq and its strategic cooperation with Israel are important for the future of the Middle East. Turkey is promoting cooperation in the Black Sea area and supporting the newly independent states (NIS) of Central Asia in their drive for national consolidation and independence. Peace and stability in the eastern Mediterranean depend on Turkey's readiness to solve its long-standing disputes with Greece and help resolve the problem of a divided Cyprus. Developing relations with various Balkan states make Turkey a key to establishing cooperative structures there. Finally, the construction of a new European security architecture depends on Turkey's support for NATO's enlargement and restructuring.

It is against this background that President Clinton declared,

> A democratic, secular, stable and Western-oriented Turkey has supported U.S. efforts to enhance stability in Bosnia, the NIS and the Middle East, as well as to contain Iran and Iraq. Its continued ties to

> the West and its support for our overall strategic objectives in one of the world's most sensitive regions is critical. We continue to support Turkey's active, constructive role within NATO and Europe.[1]

This evaluation of Turkey's strategic importance is widely shared by European political leaders. It has been repeatedly emphasized by declarations of the European Council, the meeting of the heads of state and governments of the members of the European Union. Despite the difficulties the EU has in adequately responding to Turkey's wish for membership, the member states have a strong politico-strategic interest in binding the country firmly to its Western allies. This interest has, among others, been expressed by French Minister for European Affairs Alain Lamassoure in his capacity as acting president of the European Council when he, in explaining to the European Parliament the wish of the EU to conclude a customs union agreement with Turkey, stressed the country's importance:

> At the crossroads of the Caucasus, the Balkans, and the Middle East, and at the door of Central Asia, it holds a strategic position which gives it a role of major importance, on the one hand as a pole of stability in this particularly troubled region and, on the other, as a moderating element in the many regional conflicts at its doorstep.[2]

Turkey's ongoing but altered strategic importance coincides with far-reaching domestic and international changes that lead to the question of how far the country's allies can simply continue their established conduct of relations with it. The international changes in the aftermath of the East-West conflict are obvious to everybody, although their exact meaning and long-term consequences are less clear. The outlines of a new world order are only dimly visible. Because Eurasia has been most strongly affected by the upheaval in international politics, Turkey inevitably has experienced its share of change. Turkish and foreign analysts concur that today the country is facing a foreign and security policy environment completely different from what it was only ten years ago.[3] It is hardly imaginable that Turkey's relations with her Western allies will remain untouched by that development.

What is less often realized in the West is that Turkey is also undergoing extraordinary internal changes. As a side effect of the international changes, important developments such as the uneasy relations with the Kurds or the advance of politicized Islam that have long been in the offing but have been restrained by the repercussions of bipolar international relations on Turkish domestic politics could break through. Prime minister Turgut Özal's policy of radically opening the country to the outside world in the 1980s triggered economic and social changes that accelerated domestic political developments in the early 1990s.

Today, many established political truths of the republic's tradition are being questioned by a growing part of Turkey's public. The most obvious examples are the clash of political ideologies between secularists and Islamists and the debate about Turkey's "Kurdish reality." Such discussions would not have been possible without a general liberalization of Turkey's political climate caused by the slow but constant growth of civil society since the second half of the 1980s.

It is far from clear where these developments, characterized by strong internal dynamics, will lead the country. "The Turkey we have known for 70 years is gone. There is a new Turkey underway in developing both geopolitically and domestically," one observer has said.[4] Turkey's allies will have to respond by adapting their policies toward the country. A reevaluation and eventually a reorientation in relations between the United States and Turkey as well as between Europe and Turkey has to be addressed by U.S. and European political leaders if they want to keep the established relationship intact under the new international and domestic conditions.

This book gives a detailed but by no means comprehensive account and analysis of the main internal changes taking place in Turkey and of the country's foreign policy outlook since the end of the cold war. It is written with a policy-oriented perspective, which means that the evaluations and prescriptive parts are also biased by my liberal democratic convictions.

In the first part the focus is on the internal challenges to the Kemalist foundations of the republic, Turkey's established political raison d'être. The discussion of these challenges is guided by the realization that persistent severe domestic problems prevent the country from fully exploiting the new foreign policy opportunities it is facing. The book analyzes the most important elements of the far-reaching social and economic changes Turkey has been experiencing and its inadequate political responses. The fragmentation of the parliamentary system and the fossilization of the Kemalist political practice as a long-term consequence of the 1980 military coup have been the main factors that prevent the political innovation necessary to successfully deal with the country's most pressing political and social problems. Besides the provision of satisfactory living conditions for a fairly young and still growing population of 65 million, a lasting solution to the Kurdish problem and a convincing answer to the Islamist threat in the framework of a solidly based Western liberal democracy stand out among the challenges Ankara faces. Only bold steps in further developing the liberal and democratic elements of Turkey's political system will provide the country with a solid base for successfully mastering the challenges of the ever more globalizing world of the next century.

The second part of the book focuses on Turkey's new foreign and security policy environment, which is complicating the development of a comprehensive design for realizing the country's national interests in international politics. The way political leaders resolve this situation will also determine the country's future relations with its Western partners. The demise of the Soviet Union brought with it new challenges to the east in the geopolitical maneuverings over Caspian Basin energy resources and the long-term establishment of a political order in Central Asia. The Gulf War dragged Ankara more intensely into reshaping the regional political geometry of the Middle East by confronting it with the problem of the future of Iraq and opening the opportunity to establish strategic cooperation with Israel. All these matters are also analyzed from the point of view of American strategic interests in the Middle East.

The centerpiece of Turkey's relations with the West, its European vocation and embedded position in the Atlantic alliance, have also been put to the test by the new international political situation. Turkey is trying to become a regional power in the eastern Mediterranean and with respect to the Balkans, which could further complicate its relations with the European Union but which also, if constructively managed, could contribute to the stabilization of Europe's politically most volatile region. The deterioration of Turkey-EU relations proper plus the country's creeping marginalization in the establishment of a new European security architecture could, however, lead to a lasting alienation from Europe.

Turkey and its European partners seem unable to adequately address the challenges of the new European situation. A simple continuation of past policy seems no longer possible, but promising new avenues have not been opened. If this situation continues, the overall Atlantic framework cannot remain unaffected. Thus the third part of the book analyzes the essence of American and European policies toward Turkey in more detail and proposes ideas for a more constructive management of these relations.

Far from trying to resolve the current and foreseeable problems of American and European relations with Turkey, my analysis presents a warning to Western (and Turkish) political leaders: the future conduct of relations with Turkey needs a thorough conceptual reassessment that takes into account the domestic and external changes influencing the redefinition of its place in the new international, especially the new Eurasian, political order. Otherwise, the management of international security in a region that is crucial to American and European interests could become unnecessarily difficult and expensive.

PART ONE

The Erosion of the Kemalist Model

For three-quarters of a century Kemalism has been the official ideology of the Turkish Republic.[1] But in the past decade, doubts have arisen that this ideology is still capable of serving as the overall guide for the country in the next millennium. The principles that guided Mustafa Kemal's efforts to establish a modern Turkey were functional for the period the country was then passing through. They were instrumental in creating a nation-state according to nineteenth-century European standards in the Anatolian heartland of the former Ottoman Empire. However, gradually they became an obstacle to Turkey's further democratic consolidation because the country's leading circles tended to base their policy more on an authoritarian interpretation of these principles than on a liberal democratic one, both of which are theoretically possible given the conceptual openness of the "six arrows of Kemalism."[2]

Consequently, Turkey's development toward a mature, open society and liberal Western democracy based on an efficient market economy has been punctuated by periods of narrow-minded politics that gave priority to the preservation of a state-centered political system based on a model of a closed society. The history of Turkey's democratic transition and consolidation after its turn to a multiparty parliamentarian system following World War II has been a history of societal development and emancipation from a state elite that was reluctant to give up its tutelage of the masses and that still tends to justify its reluctance with the need to preserve the principles of the republic's founder. In interpreting the republic's founding principles the elite often overlook the originally forward-oriented character of Atatürk's endeavor.

This has led many Turkish and foreign observers, especially since the end of the cold war, to conclude that Kemalism is an outdated ideological base for running an open democratic system and further developing a largely consolidated nation-state with a multiethnic and multicultural society.[3] What seems actually needed, however, is reinterpretation of the Atatürk political legacy according to the requirements of the new domestic and international realities. This is one of the most important political and intellectual tasks facing today's Turkish leadership.

CHAPTER ONE

The Kemalist Model of Shaping Politics and Society

What Mustafa Kemal, later to be named Atatürk, achieved in the fifteen years from the foundation of the republic in 1923 to his death in 1938 was to initiate the complex and comprehensive transformation of a traditional society that had been run by outmoded state institutions. The establishment of the Turkish republic was simultaneously an endeavor in state building, political institutionalization, nation building, cultural revolution, and far-reaching social and economic change. To a certain extent the transformation could be compared to what is happening in the former socialist countries of the Soviet bloc, with the important difference that most European states presently undergoing that transformation have, at least intellectually, certain bonds with pre-Soviet and presocialist Western structures and ideas. For the vast majority of the Turkish republic's population in the 1920s, what happened during the Kemalist transformation was a real revolution.[1]

The incremental reforms in the late Ottoman Empire notwithstanding, it was the Kemalist reform policies that for the first time deeply affected the masses. *Tanzimat* policies in the mid-nineteenth century and the later efforts of the Young Turks mainly aimed at modernizing the superstructure of the state and some of its institutions, but the Kemalist reforms went to the cultural roots of Anatolia's population by abolishing the religious foundations of the state and eradicating most of the cultural symbols by which these foundations were expressed in everyday life. "Taken as a whole, these reforms aimed at destroying the symbols of Ottoman-Islamic civilization, and substituting them with their western counterparts."[2]

The abolition of the caliphate in 1924 would not have had such a far-reaching impact without the parallel abolition of the office of the şeyh'ül-İslâm, the *shar'ia* courts, the Ministry of Religious Affairs and Pious Foundations, and the medrese, which were the centers of religious instruction and learning. The ban on the activities of the religious orders (*tarikat*) in 1925, which formed the backbone of folk Islam in rural Anatolia, together with outlawing of the fez in favor of the western hat, discouraging veils for women, replacing Arabic script with the European Latin script, and substituting the Gregorian calendar for the Muslim calendar constituted the establishment of a radical new cultural framework for citizens of the new republic. This cultural transformation was accompanied by the adoption of new legal foundations for conducting social and economic life: a new constitution, civil code, penal code, and commercial law, all of which were borrowed from Europe.[3]

A self-educated product of European positivism, Kemal founded his state on the principles of modernity and rationality as developed and practised in Europe.[4] However, he never developed a comprehensive ideology that informed his actions. Instead, he developed a pragmatic approach to the problems connected with organizing and leading the struggle for national independence and establishing his new state. What later became known as the "Kemalist principles" was the ex post rationalization of certain loosely defined ideas on which he wanted to found the republic. These also served to legitimize the power of himself and his followers, the new state elite.

These principles, even after their inclusion in the program of his Republican People's Party (Cumhuriyet Halk Partisi, or CHP) in 1931, resemble headlines more than well-elaborated pieces of a consistent ideology. Nevertheless, over the years of republican development, a commonly agreed body of meaning has been given to them by the standard-bearers of the Kemalist movement, who also represented the power elite of the new Turkish state.[5] From the very beginning, then, Kemalism was both a political program for the social, political, and economic modernization of Turkey and an ideological means of justifying political actions undertaken by its rulers.

These actions were directed at creating a nation-state out of the remnants of the defeated Ottoman Empire. Under the prevailing political circumstances, the nation-state model was the only choice for anybody who wanted to keep a sovereign political entity on Anatolian soil. However, for this to happen, a new and rather alien idea of statehood had to be implanted in a population that until then thought of itself as subjects of the sultan, who as caliph was also the accepted spiritual leader of the community of Muslims. Thus along with building the Turkish nation-state, the Turkish nation as such had to be created. People had to be given a new collective identity, and they had to be persuaded to accept it. The Kemalist revolution had to establish simultaneously the Republic of Turkey, the Turkish people as a nation, and the Turk as a citizen with an identity different from being a Muslim subject of the sultan.

This all-encompassing modernization is strongly reflected in the Kemalist model as it is prescribed by the principles of Kemalism. Republicanism, nationalism, and populism are at the core of this ideology. The first two principles were the acknowledgment of the European experiences in building nation-states, whereas the third can be regarded as a tribute to the communitarian ideals of the Muslim world view. Sovereignty should unequivocally belong to the people (republicanism) that were to be united in a common political body, the nation. The nation should not be defined as a coalition of classes, sects, or otherwise segregated groups but be based on a unity that was, if at all, structured along functional divisions, "the people."[6] In this sense, populism is the denial of the idea of a pluralist society in favor of an organic view of society and people.

The Kemalist interpretation of nationalism is ambiguous.[7] It may have originally borrowed its meaning from the French idea of civic nationalism, a predominantly political definition of the term. The political practice of the Turkish republic, however, gave way to a more ethnically defined interpretation of that principle based on Turkishness. "A concept of nationalism developed that rejected ethnic and cultural differences."[8]

The Kemalist concept of state building and nation building could only be implemented if there were no competing ideas of the legitimation of statehood. The only relevant rival to the European republican concept was the traditional legitimation of public activities, Islam. Thus, banning Islam from the political sphere was a natural corollary to the principles of republicanism and nationalism. Secularism or laicism became another cornerstone of the Kemalist ideology and politics.[9] In theory the principle meant the freedom of conscience, worship, and religion on a strict personal basis for all Turkish citizens. In political practice it had to be applied in such a way as to effectively foreclose any attempts at seizing political power in the name of Islam. This was thought possible only by establishing strict control of the state over all institutions of Islam—mosques, pious foundations, and institutions of religious education.

Taken together, republicanism, nationalism, populism, and secularism not only provided the core of the new state ideology but also served as legitimizing elements for securing the power of the new state elites.[10] This became evident very soon after the foundation of the republic when Mustafa Kemal used any available instrument of force to crush political resistance against his conception of a modern Turkey.

An upheaval in the Kurdish provinces led by the Nakşibendi sheik Said in 1925 was used by Kemal to introduce the Law for the Maintenance of Public Order that gave almost absolute power to two so-called Independence Tribunals for the prosecution of political opponents. He was no longer ready to share his power with other social or political groups that had supported his case in the war of independence. Within two years these tribunals sentenced more than 500 people to death and led to the extinction of all opposition forces, including high-level military leaders and Kemal's former comrades-in-arms during the war of independence. The only opposition party, the Progressive Republican Party, founded in November 1924 by "moderate" parliamentarians that broke away from Atatürk's People's Party, was banned in June 1925 because members of the party had supported Sheik Said's rebellion and had tried to exploit religion for political purposes.[11] The tone was set for all later prosecutions of political opposition movements that tried to deviate from the ideological core of the Kemalist republic, although the fragile conditions of the founding period had then long been overcome by the successful consolidation of Atatürk's republic.

The struggle for power in the young republic had been resolved in favor of Kemal and his followers. "By 1927 all opposition to the regime—military, religious, or political—had been silenced, and when elections were held in August and September 1927 for a third Assembly of the Turkish Republic, only one party, the Republican People's Party of Mustafa Kemal, was there to take part in them."[12]

The center of political power clearly rested with Atatürk and the close leadership circle of the party. This circle did not include the military leadership. The army was relegated to an instrument working on behalf of the power center, as was demonstrated by the lack of importance of Marshal Fevzi Çakmak, chief of the general staff. Atatürk and his "second man" and successor, İsmet İnönü, consciously abandoned their military position when they took off their uniforms. The new Turkish state would be led by civilians.

This was also indirectly underlined in Atatürk's famous speech (*nutuk*) in October1927 to the Congress of the CHP, in which he developed his personal view of the events accompanying the establishment of the Turkish republic since 1919 as a vindication for the path he had chosen to impose his authoritarian reign on the new state.[13] In this speech many of his former comrades-in-arms who did not bow to his political opinions after 1923 were portrayed as insignificant minds. Turkish pupils still learn about the establishment of the modern Turkish state from these and other partisan presentations.

In theory the principles of Kemalism are open to interpretation along Western, liberal, and democatic lines of thinking. The idea of republicanism, especially, carries strong incentives for establishing a democratic regime based on true representation of the popular will. The dilemma of the newly created Turkish republic was that a free representation of the popular will tended to undermine the very basis of the young state by reintroducing the forces of the old regime to political activity. Opposition movements did not only embrace political alternatives for establishing a modern Turkish nation-state according to European models but always showed a tendency to bring back religion-based ideas of collective and individual identity as the foundation of statehood.

As an offspring of the autocratic Ottoman state elite, Atatürk never contemplated the idea of forging the new republic out of the free play of different social and political forces. Although he often spoke of democracy as belonging to the republican regime, he preferred the authoritarian political practice of the old system as the best way for reaching his goals. Consequently, liberalism and democracy were not part of the Kemalist principles. From the beginning the reality-oriented interpretation of these principles was authoritarian, as was the political practice of the new leaders. Under the circumstances prevailing in the Turkey of the 1920s, this seems to have been the only way for Atatürk's modernizing policies to succeed.

In the development of Kemalist thinking, democracy is very much equated with secularism in the sense of separation of state and religion. Secularism is a necessary condition for democracy; religion-based political systems have a built-in tendency to authoritarianism because of the integral and exclusive character of all religions. But secularism is not sufficient to establish democracy. What is equally important is the secularization of society, the gradual overcoming of religion-based value systems by secular values based on the ideas of human individuality and self-determination as developed during the Enlightenment. The Kemalist approach to democracy very much concentrates on the first aspect, secularism, while almost totally neglecting the second. However, fighting the political expression of religion does not necessarily coincide with promoting individual liberties.

Consequently, the Kemalist republic imitated the authoritarian Ottoman state tradition in new, nonreligious guise.[14] The new state was established by imposing political, economic, and social modernization from above with little relation with the basis of society. Not surprisingly, the elites of the new state largely corresponded to the elites of the empire but without the religious leadership, the *ulema.* The Turkish republic was run by the state bureaucracy and military-turned-civilian politicians backed by a caste of urban intellectuals with European-influenced education who entertained an organic understanding of state and society. These groups had hardly any relations with the masses. The masses had to be educated by the elites into their new status as citizens with a Turkish national identity. In this respect the establishment of the republic was not only a political task but also an undertaking in national education that still continues.

The traditional dichotomy between center and periphery in Turkish society and politics was not overcome by the republic with its unifying and equalizing rhetoric of the Turkish nation but instead reenforced by its authoritarian political practice.[15] The cleavage was, indeed, deepened because the republican elites did not share the same basic values with the periphery as the Ottoman elites had. The severing of the religious bond between the new state and its citizens further increased the alienation of the masses. It could not come as a surprise that the first free election within the multiparty system after the end of World War II was won by political groups that could be regarded as opponents of the state elites and sympathetic with the real needs of the masses.

The development of a genuine political elite based on party politics and electoral competition after 1950 was, however, limited by the persistence and defense of the Kemalist core values by the state elite and the military. The republican principle, the national and social homogeneity of the Turkish nation, and the secular character of the republic were givens that could not be openly debated or even questioned by any political group. The same was true for Atatürk, who was elevated from being an outstanding historic personality to an untouchable national icon. Consequently, Turkish democracy is characterized by a disequilibrium between its formal institutional elements on the one side and its value-oriented substance on the other. The democratic principles of individual freedom and plurality of values have always been blocked by the organic understanding of state and society as expressed in the prevailing interpretation of the Kemalist principles.

This became especially clear with the drafting of the present constitution after the military coup of 1980. Its core elements are the Kemalist principles of nationalism and secularism. The principle of nationalism is more precisely defined as the indivisibility of the Turkish state's territory and nation. Together with the principle of secularism, the principle of nationalism and the republican character of the state as laid down in the first three articles of the 1982 constitution are not open to amendment nor can an amendment be proposed. Beyond the constitution these principles are also protected in all politically relevant laws—the party law, the law on associations, the press law, and so forth—that have been promulgated since the 1980 coup.[16]

Thus the Turkish republic is based on a constitutional and legal system, the core principles of which are heavily tainted by a historically developed authoritarian understanding of the unitary state and its functioning as well as an organic and homogenous understanding of the nation. This prevailing understanding of the Turkish republic was, for instance, expressed by President Süleyman Demirel at a July 1997 opening ceremony of a new center of the Turkish Hearths, a nationalist organization that promotes Turkish culture and dates back to the prerepublican period of the rule of the Young Turks. During the ceremony, in which many other leading politicians participated, Demirel declared,

> The country which was established through the genius of Atatürk is the Turkish Republic. The people who established this republic are the Turks. Where this country was established is Turkey, and the official language of this country is Turkish. Everyone should pay the utmost attention to the four concepts I have mentioned: they are the guarantee of peace, trust and happiness in this country.[17]

It is obvious that such an attitude and system run into difficulties in attempting to resolve political and social problems of a society that cannot be regarded as strongly homogenous in cultural (ethnic and religious), political, economic, and social terms, especially under conditions of tremendous economic and social change. Any attempt to strictly uphold the ideological bases of the modern Turkish state as exemplified in the constitution of 1982 can only contribute to an undermining of the democratic process and initiate a vicious circle of authoritarian interventions by the guardians of the Kemalist republic.

This has become all too obvious in the developments since the early 1990s when the military leadership with the support of the Kemalist circles in the state bureaucracy, the intellectuals, and the media tried to roll back the political consequences of softening the strict respect of the Kemalist principles that had occured during the government of Turgut Özal in the second half of the 1980s. The growing maturity of Turkish society as exemplified by the continuous growth of civil society and the freeing of Islam and of the Kurdish identity from the Kemalist Pandora's box created a new challenge for Turkey's political and state elite, including the military, for which the definite answer has not yet been found.

CHAPTER TWO

The Awakening of Society: Between Tradition and Modernity

AT THE OPENING of the twenty-first century, Turkey is characterized by a growing awareness of social cleavages that have been insufficiently bridged by past state policy. The most important are the resurrection of the ideological battle between Kemalist secularists and Islamists, the reawakening of the ethnic and cultural divide between Turks and Kurds with its important implications for the long-term political stability of the country, and as a brand new issue a growing divide between the established political class and civil society at large. These cleavages have become important again as a consequence of pressure on Turkey's polity that has resulted on the one hand from the internal changes produced by the opening up of the country's economy during the 1980s and on the other hand from the far-reaching rearrangement of Turkey's international environment after the end of the cold war.

Social and economic change accelerated tremendously and put heavy strains on Turkish society. The long-retarded process of social modernization gained a critical momentum. The quick expansion of modern transport and communication infrastructure opened even the remotest areas of the country to the achievements of modern civilization. The industrialization efforts that had started after World War II now bore full fruit. The Turkey that had remained a largely rural and traditionally structured society until the 1970s was increasingly becoming an urban and industrialized society in which the patterns of Western consumerism started to take hold outside the industrial centers in the western part of the country.[1] Today, about one-third of the Turkish electorate lives in the country's five largest urban areas.

This still unfinished process of social modernization is accompanied by social uprooting as large parts of the population migrate from the rural areas to urban centers. Today the typical Turk is not the Anatolian villager but a member of the urban lower or middle class who struggles to earn a living under the new conditions of a society that is ever more characterized by industrial and white-collar occupations.

The demographic situation aids this urbanization; more than half of Turkey's population is younger than 30 years old, and about a third is younger than age 15.[2] A majority of Turks who will decide the country's orientation during the next half century will have been brought up under conditions of urbanization, industrialization, and mediazation that tend to question traditional social and political patterns.[3]

A basic flaw of the new social developments is the lack of a firm and guiding value system. The globalizing Western civilization is characterized by a certain openess with regard to guiding values and tends to encourage individualization within societies. All this contrasts sharply with both the traditional religion-based Turkish codes of behavior and the equally community-oriented pattern of Kemalist principles. Consequently, well-established value systems and behavioral patterns in Turkey are increasingly challenged by new modes usually introduced from abroad via the media that tend to undermine the prevailing organic world view.

Three interrelated factors will decisively influence the social change: economic development, political guidance, and ideological modernization. Economic development and industrialization have to provide the basis for continuous growth in the welfare of a vast majority of the people to convince them that the brave new world of a globalized economy is not limited to the profit of a happy few. The political class not only has to design an adequate economic and social policy, but it also has to transmit to the electorate the conviction that it can steer the country through the difficulties of the new age. This will be possible only if the modernizing elites can renovate the country's ideological foundations to make them more compatible with the challenges of social change. A highly dynamic development can hardly be adequately supported by a basically static political and social world view.

The Unfinished Liberalization of the Economy

Turkey has undergone tremendous economic development since the foundation of the modern republic. Recurring growth and stabilization crises notwithstanding, its basically growth-oriented economic policy has succeeded in significantly closing the gap with the developed economies. Today, Turkey's economic capability surpasses that of all its neighbors with, perhaps, the exception of Israel.

Since the mid-1950s, in a politically motivated sequence of liberal and statist development policies, Turkey has become a varied industrial economy based on a richness in important raw materials.[4] However, the country has only small oil and natural gas reserves. To sustain its economic growth, it will have to make enormous efforts to increase its energy imports as well as develop its own resources and improve energy efficiency.[5] The proposal to build a nuclear power plant on its southern shore that had been dormant for some years has reemerged, causing alarm calls by Turkish and international environmentalists.

As a result of the liberalizing economic policies of the 1980s under Prime Minister Turgut Özal, Turkey's economy considerably improved its international competitiveness in construction and in textile, clothing, and houshold equipment manufacturing.[6] Turkish exports continued to flourish during the 1990s, and after the opening of the former socialist economies, Turkish industrialists and businessmen established themselves in Central Asian markets and also in Russia, Romania, and other neighboring countries. Industry increasingly spread to the Anatolian hinterland, creating a new class of businessmen outside the industrial centers of western Turkey. Not content with establishing themselves in the Turkish home market, these "Anatolian tigers" have shown a strong interest in foreign economic activities.[7] The Turkish private sector would be able to establish the country firmly within the ranks of middle-income industrialized states if it could get the necessary support of a rational and balanced government economic policy.

But in spite of its strong progress, Turkey "is still in the transitional stage in that some of the key structural problems that one tends to associate with semi-industrial, semiperipheral economies continue to manifest themselves."[8] These problems have become more obvious as the effects of globalization have become felt more intensely. Some severe structural weaknesses of the economy became evident in the 1990s: an overextended and inefficient public sector, persistent high inflation, inadequate investment in manufacturing, too little technology generation, and a continuing overemphasis on the state's role in the economy. To this, one has to add on the social side deep income inequality, high unemployment, a continuing inequality of economic development between the country's western section and the far less developed east and southeast, and weak institutions of public welfare such as unemployment insurance and old age pension plans.

The persistence of these deficiencies is mainly due to a dramatic failure of Turkey's politicians to design and execute an economic policy that could bring about structural changes and guarantee macroeconomic stability. This is the clear conclusion from reading the Organization for Economic Cooperation and Development's regular economic surveys on the country. In its 1991–92 *Survey* the OECD stated that stricter macroeconomic discipline and further structural reforms "should enable the Turkish economy to achieve high and balanced growth in the decade to come."[9] Growth was high but unbalanced and accompanied by high inflation, a constantly increasing public deficit, and deteriorating income distribution. In its 1997 *Survey* the OECD still strongly urged the necessity of a program of consistent structural economic and social reforms.[10] Thus in terms of economic reform policy, the 1990s can be largely regarded as a lost decade.

This evaluation remains valid even after the efforts of the minority coalition government under Mesut Yılmaz in the summer of 1997 are taken into account. Under that government, privatization took on some momentum, tax reform was brought another step forward, inflation was held below 70 percent, and an agreement was reached with the International Monetary Fund on a staff-monitored accord on Turkey's further economic reform policy. This progress slowed, however, in the second half of 1998 when political instability grew; the harmful effects of the international economic climate, especially the new Russian crisis, began to be felt; and more traditional social democrat and center-right economic policies were applied again with considerable wage increases for public employees and rising agricultural subsidies.[11]

The results of the early parliamentary elections of April 18, 1999, necessitated the formation of another coalition government of parties with divergent economic policies. Both winners of the elections, Bülent Ecevit's Democratic Left Party (Demokratik Sol Partisi, or DSP) and the shooting star of these elections, the Nationalist Action Party (Milliyetçi Hareket Partisi, or MHP) of Devlet Bahçeli, prefer strong state participation in the economy. This contrasts to the market orientation of their coalition partner, the Motherland Party (Anavatan Partisi, or ANAP). This party tends to represent the more dynamic parts of Turkish society, whereas the strength of the DSP and the MHP is among public employees and the rural middle class, the more traditional segments of society.

Nevertheless, based on its sound parliamentary majority, this coalition of uneven partners has been able to design and carry out an economic policy that has prospects of tackling at least some of Turkey's long neglected structural problems. In the first weeks after taking office the coalition managed to pass a reform of the banking sector, further streamline the tax system, change the constitution to introduce rules for international arbitration of disputes over privatization of public companies, and most important raise the age of retirement as the cornerstone of a fundamental reform of Turkey's social security system. Much of this was carried through against the strong resistance of trade unions and public concerns of giving up too much of Turkey's sovereignty. It remains to be seen if the coalition can keep this momentum for much needed reform in even more sensitive matters such as cutting back red tape in public administration or restricting the generous agricultural subsidies. Such measures would severely hurt large parts of the coalition's electorate.

The syndrome of the populist state has remained the basic characteristic of Turkey's economic policymaking since the end of the 1980s.[12] This is mainly the result of the functioning of democratic politics in a weak political environment. The instability of the party system that emerged after the last military coup and the return to civil politics in the second half of the 1980s led politicians to give in to pressures from social interest groups to secure their political survival. The state became more a distributional machine in favor of the electoral (and sometimes also personal) interests of those in government than an institution for devising and implementing political principles for the development of the country. The severe fragmentation of the party system continuously fueled political instability and led to frequent changes of governments, which in turn favored populist economic policymaking that resulted in persistent macroeconomic distortions.[13]

Turkish economic policy during the 1990s has primarily been monetary and exchange rate policy conducted by the financial and economic bureaucracy in the Central Bank and the Treasury. Its imperatives have been to maintain the country's ability to contract foreign and domestic loans. This would secure the flow of money needed to keep the relatively high growth rate that is the basic prerequisite for the continuation of Turkey's development. The annual average growth of Turkey's GNP during the 1990s was about 4.8 percent, one of the highest among members of the Organization for Economic Cooperation and Development. The growth not only created the environment in which Turkey's business community could prosper but also provided the means for large parts of the population to earn a living in the equally flourishing underground economy.

In this way many Turkish families, especially in the fast-growing urban agglomerations of western Turkey, were able to make ends meet and cope with the constant high inflation. Consumer price increases never fell below 60 percent annually, and wage increases could not compensate for the losses to family income. According to a Central Bank analysis, inflation robbed the Turks of one-third of their purchasing power between 1992 and 1997.[14] Thus ever more of them have to find a second (or third) income, preferably from an activity that is not registered and not taxed.

Another consequence was a deteriorating income distribution due to the considerably varying ability of people to cope with inflation. A minority profited from the high economic growth and the accompanying high interest rates, either by engaging in business or earning a considerable income from interest on state bonds. But a growing number of people had to face reductions of their real wealth because they had to rely mainly on fixed incomes to meet costs of living.[15] This situation has caused a significant increase of poverty and child labor, especially in the parts of the large towns where most migrants from rural areas or the southeast live in *gecekondu*, illegal and quickly built housing, most of which has later been legalized and linked to public services. Turkey's largest confederation of trade unions has estimated that more than 10 percent of the population is living with a regular income below the subsistence level.[16]

The driving force behind the high inflation is the government's inability to balance its budget. Public expenditures constantly outgrow public revenues, forcing the state to borrow and pushing interest rates beyond any reasonable level. The main expenditures are for an oversized public sector, including many unprofitable state economic enterprises and a social security and health care system on the verge of bankruptcy.[17] Further contributing to the burden are policies of subsidizing such groups as farmers and state employees and a large military that has been engaged in long and costly warfare against Kurdish separatists in Turkey's southeastern provinces and northern Iraq. As to public revenues, consecutive governments have failed to broaden the tax base by including large parts of rural income and the underground economy. The governments have also failed to level the rates of taxation. Tax fraud and tax evasion is widespread. The three-party coalition government of Mesut Yılmaz finally took a first step on tax reform in 1998; it is too early to judge the long-term structural implications for state revenues, but the early results are fairly promising.

Remedies for Turkey's unsatisfactory economic policy are obvious and have been under discussion for years to no avail. The state must continue the economic liberalization started in the first half of the 1980s by reducing its share in the overall economy and simultaneously increasing the efficiency and effectiveness of its public economic and social actions. Contrary to a widespread assumption, the Turkish state does not act as a strong state in setting the rules in economic affairs and looking after their observance by the private sector. Instead, it engages directly in manifold economic activities and has developed myriad detailed regulations concerning almost any economic activity that can hardly be overseen, much less enforced, by state officials, not to speak of the private sector. Producing red tape is still characteristic of the bureaucracy.[18] Thus privatization of state economic enterprises and reduction of the overextended state bureaucracy, including the burden of the military on public income, is of tantamount importance. It has to be accompanied by growth in and more rational use of public expenditures in education, health care, and social security. Such a policy package could become more likely if the 1998 tax reform could provide the necessary fiscal base for such undertakings.

A glance at the various government programs since the early 1990s reveals that Turkey's politicians are well aware of the necessary policies for improving the country's economic and social conditions. After taking office, however, they have been unable or unwilling to do what they promised. As a consequence, public confidence in the established political class has deteriorated, and the gap between the masses and their political representatives has considerably widened. Today, politicians rank among the least trusted people in Turkey and are mainly regarded as dishonest and corrupt. Without a quick and fundamental remedy, the economic and social policy failures of the established parties and their representatives can prepare the way to a more severe erosion of the foundations of the political system.

The Emerging Civil Society

When in early 1993 the renowned secularist journalist Uğur Mumcu fell victim to a bomb attempt on his life presumably carried out by Islamist terrorists, a crowd took to the streets of Ankara to protest what they condemned as the re-Islamization of Turkey's public life. On the other side, Islamic forces recurringly staged large public protests after Friday prayers in Istanbul and elsewhere against the ban of the *turban,* headscarfs worn in a typical religious way, for female students. In early 1997 a concerted public action called "one minute of darkness for a bright future" spread throughout Turkey's large cities: people switched off their home lights for a minute every evening at 9:00 pm to protest the inability or unwillingness of the state authorities and the governing politicians to clear a series of political and criminal scandals.[19] State security circles and leading politicians were accused of having been engaged in organized crime for political or monetary gain.[20] Spring 1997 also saw public demonstrations either by supporters of Kemalism to bring down the Islamist-led coalition government or by government supporters of Islamic leaning to secure what they called the real freedom of religion.

All these activities, to which others could be added, are witness to the growing ability of Turkey's urban populations to express political and social discontent in an effective but peaceful manner. As a consequence of the economic and social modernization that started in the 1980s, a civil society has developed. The people, accustomed to a ready-made state tradition, have begun to organize to protect their rights against economic and political power and have taken first steps for a transformation of society from bottom to top in contradiction to the established practice of top-down social engineering by the state. The public perception of the state's role in structuring society is about to undergo a fundamental change from the pre-1980s years. A new understanding has grown among parts of the population that "the dynamism of social actors is impeded by the bureaucratic state."[21]

This attitude can mainly be found in the urban centers, although human rights, environmental problems, and other concerns have attracted attention all over Turkey. Forty percent of all Turkish nongovernmental organizations (NGOs) are located in Istanbul, 25 percent in Ankara, and the rest distributed throughout the country but mainly in urban areas. Two-thirds of these organizations have been founded since 1980 and especially after 1990.[22]

As in other countries, civil society consists of a large number of organizations of varying size, institutional strength, and political purpose. There are about 2,700 foundations, 50,000 associations, and 1,200 unions, cooperatives, and business chambers, many of which qualify as part of civil society, depending on the definition of the term. For many in Turkey the idea of civil society is strongly connected with opposition to the ruling state elite and sometimes even the ruling political elite.[23] Others tend to include in the term every NGO that engages in public-oriented activities. An important qualification in the discussion about civil society seems to be the "civil" behavior of associations toward each other as well as an open and democratic inner structure. In short, pluralist values and tolerance are regarded as indispensable ingredients of any element of civil society.[24]

What seems, however, to be more important in Turkey are the strong state barriers and regulations for any form of organized social activity, be it politically oriented or of a more private character. The constitution of 1982 and the Turkish Law on Associations derived from it set strict barriers against any "political activity" of associations and imposed close state control on their activities, including their internal regulations.[25] The state can restrict or even dissolve any association for violating a clause in the law. The Kemalist fundamentals of the Turkish state as laid down in the constitution also have to be respected. Thus it is, for instance, nearly impossible to establish private organizations that support such matters as Kurdish culture or language. More recently, associations that support an Islamic way of public life have also come under attack by state authorities.

These barriers and restrictions notwithstanding, a civil society "culture" is about to develop in Turkey. Some areas and institutions stand out in this respect: human rights issues, environmental issues, business associations, and, most recently, Islamic civil movements. The large group of organizations for the support of Kemalism that have become more lively during the recent battle between secularists and Islamists are of a somewhat mixed character because many are sponsored by the state although formally they are civil associations.

The public-oriented activities of the main human rights organizations, the Turkish Human Rights Association (Türkiye İnsan Hakları Derneği, or İHD) and the Turkish Human Rights Foundation (İnsan Hakları Vakfı, or İHV), which have been able to attract international support, have contributed considerably to public awareness of human rights violations in Turkey. They have openly criticized the widespread practice of torture as standard police behavior with apprehended suspects, especially those involved in so-called political cases, and have made public the human rights violations of the military and security forces that occurred as a by-product of their fight against Kurdish terrorists in the southeastern provinces.[26]

As a consequence of their activity and the constant foreign criticism of the state of human rights in Turkey, the government appointed a state minister for human rights and established a Human Rights Council in which in addition to state officials and experts there are also representatives of the main human rights organizations. The Turkish parliament had already created a Human Rights Commission from within its ranks in 1990.

The state security apparatus, however, still strongly resists taking human rights issues more seriously, as can be deduced from the recurring prosecution of human rights activists by the judiciary, mainly for their criticizing state authorities' behavior in the southeast.[27] The severe risks involved in human rights activism on behalf of Kurds have become evident by the attempt on the life of the chairman of the İHD in May 1998. Akın Birdal was shot in his office by two ultranationalist gunmen after newspapers had published allegations that he was a follower of the Kurdish Workers' Party (PKK) made by a former PKK leader who had been captured by Turkish security forces in northern Iraq. The allegations were reportedly made during interrogations by the security forces that had been leaked to the press.[28] This incident did not prevent the state prosecutor from opening a case against Birdal for having made separatist propaganda in two speeches. He was sentenced to a prison term that he started to serve on June 3, 1999, after having barely recovered from the assault.

Thus the protection of human rights in Turkey needs improvement, as regular reports by Turkish and foreign organizations have shown.[29] Nevertheless, slow progress has been made, and any government that is ready to start enforcing the observance of human rights by state institutions can rely on the backing of a developing civil rights movement.

Civil organizations focusing on environmental problems have also emerged in the past decade.[30] Although Turkey's Greens and the Turkish branch of Greenpeace remain fairly small groups concentrated in the big cities, their activity has contributed to a continuous increase in public awareness of environmental issues. Among the most prominent campaigns in Turkey has been the successful fight against a large tourist establishment in the Dalyan area on the Aegean shore, which is one of the rare breeding places of the endangered sea turtle Caretta-Caretta. The internationally backed protest of the environmental activists not only prevented the construction of the resort but also led the government to declare the coastal strip a protected natural reservation.

Other prominent actions for the protection of the environment in which local people were involved have been the fight against a lignite-run thermal power station at the rim of the famous tourist destination of Gökova Bay and the revived fight against the construction of Turkey's first nuclear power plant on the southern Mediterranean shore near Akkuyu.[31] In these instances as well as in the resistance of a group of villages near the Aegean town of Bergama that are fighting against the operation of a gold mine run by an international firm that will use cyanide for washing the gold, state political interests are directly contested by environmentalists. These activities have involved expanded tourism, energy generation, and the attraction of foreign capital, all of which rank high in the list of economic policy priorities of any Turkish government.

Official şensitivity to environmental issues has grown considerably in the past decade, and today the Ministry of Environment is active in protecting and improving the environment all over Turkey.[32] However, general environmental education needs much improvement, and regulations need much stronger enforcement by the state bureaucracy to reduce the serious environmental damage from waste treatment practices, air and water pollution, and soil erosion.[33] In meeting these challenges, state authorities can increasingly rely on the support of organizations that keep pressure on local administrations and business to take more seriously into account the protection of rare environmental resources.

Trade unions and business associations have also become an important part of Turkish civil society. They increasingly move beyond economic and social affairs to make public statements concerning matters of Turkey's political development. The Istanbul-based Association of Turkish Industrialists and Businessmen (Türk Sanayicileri ve İşadamları Derneği, or TÜSİAD) has become famous for its critical reports on strategic weaknesses of the country's political and social fabric.[34] Its report on democratization in Turkey, published in early 1997, caused a lot of public debate and criticism by the state elite because of its liberal propositions on the role of the military in politics, protection of human rights, including those of the Kurdish population, and other sensitive matters.[35] Another example of extraprofessional engagement of business and trade unions was the common public appeal of five trade and employer unions in May 1997 for an end of the Necmettin Erbakan-Tansu Çiller coalition government—the Welfare Party (Refah Partisi, or RP) and the True Path Party (Doğru Yol Partisi, or DYP)—to stop its Islamization of Turkish politics.[36]

Political reactions to such activities have been mixed. Public resonance in the media has been widespread, but acceptance by political participants has been much less forthcoming. The Turkish political system is still rather insulated against outside influence. Thus the greatest success for business associations or trade unions remains in their area of interest, the guarantee of a free market economy or labor rights and wage policy. However, the public debate over possible reforms of the established system continues to benefit much from the social and political commitment that business and labor organizations developed in the 1990s.

Turkey's civil society also benefited from the liberalization of radio and television broadcasting in the early 1990s. Private stations have mushroomed, and the state-run Turkish Radio and Television (TRT) has been forced into the background.[37] News broadcasts, political magazines, and talk shows have become important parts of the public political debate in which almost any subject—the founder of the republic and the role of the military being the most prominent exceptions—can be widely discussed by journalists, politicians, and scholars. The political impact of these fairly new forms of public discourse seems, however, to be limited. At least, there is no obvious spillover to discussions in forums such as political parties or the parliament. And the public seems to regard talk shows and television debates as political entertainment rather than serious contributions to the formation of informed opinions on crucial national problems.

Unlike the almost nonexistent Kurdish civil society in Turkey, Islamic and Islamist groups and organizations mushroomed in the 1990s, so that one can speak of a parallel society of Islamic institutions.[38] Besides the historic religious orders and communities, there is now an Islamic trade union umbrella organization, Hak-İş; an Islamic human rights organization, Mazlum-Der; an Islamic business association, MÜSİAD; and thousands of foundations of religious background with various purposes.[39] An Islamic media sector with several daily newspapers, weeklies, and other magazines has also developed. And dozens of national and local TV and radio stations are run by Islamist groups, the influence of which can hardly be controlled or curbed by the state's Supreme Board of Radio and Television.[40]

If and how far these organizations can be regarded as part of Turkey's civil society is debated between secularists and liberals within the the nonreligious part of Turkey's civil society. Without any doubt the new Islamic sector is an expression of the existing political and ideological pluralism. For instance, some scholars regard the new Muslim female movement that focuses mainly on whether women should wear religiously influenced female dress as a part of the process of women's emancipation.[41] Indeed, it cannot be questioned that the Muslim women's movement of the 1990s brought a new quality to the face of Islam as well as to the Turkish feminist movement in general.

Like its secular counterpart, which can be regarded as an integral part of the Kemalist reformation of Turkey's social traditions, Muslim feminism is a typically urban and largely middle-class phenomenon.[42] This generally holds true for the more politically conscious part of Turkey's civil society in general. The rural population normally is only engaged in civil activities for or against specific measures of the state or economic organization such as the protest actions against Eurogold in the Bergama region or the Akkuyu power plant that directly affect their living conditions. Civic activities that go beyond single-issue protest actions do not have a tradition in Turkish society. However, the situation is changing in urban areas and will spread to the countryside as well. This takes time, but it seems to be an irresistable development.

The growing civil society, like the booming free enterprise private business sector, is an indicator of the enormous social change under way in the country since the early 1980s. It received additional impetus from the international repercussions of the end of the East-West antagonism that were expressed in growing economic globalization, another wave of worldwide democratization, and the ever greater shrinking of the globe by the Internet, satellite TV, and other international communication systems. As a country that opened up to the outside world with economic reform in the early 1980s, Turkey is unable to isolate itself from the far-reaching social and political consequences of comprehensive globalization. This situation has created one of the greatest challenges to the country's political and state elite, which still shows difficulties in adequately meeting them.

CHAPTER THREE

The Slow Adaptation of the Political System

If the military coup of September 1980 was instrumental in accelerating Turkey's far-reaching economic and social change by providing the circumstances under which Turgut Özal could develop and execute his fundamental economic reforms, it was also instrumental in creating the political system's inability to cope with the consequences of this change. The military leadership of the time failed in its effort to create a new political system with new political participants who would act according to new rules. The constitution of 1982 was devised for guiding political dynamics that never occurred in the intended manner because the generals underestimated the extent of politicization that Turkish society had reached after three decades of parliamentary democracy. Consequently, the new constitution was hardly useful in guiding the political process that emerged after the 1983 elections.

Turkey's political system after the establishment of multiparty parliamentary democracy in 1950 tended toward a bifocal configuration, with the political parties and their leaders forming one focus and the military leadership (plus the state elite) the other. These did not coexist in peace because the question of primacy was never adequately addressed and never solved. Nor could a lasting balance of power between the two be established.

Four times since the establishment of the multiparty system the military has proved its de facto primacy by ousting the government in power. In 1960 it staged a coup against what it regarded as a dictatorial right-wing government. In 1971 the "coup of memorandum" was leveled against a center-right government that seemed too weak to manage the growing political and social turmoil. In 1980 another coup was intended to correct what was regarded—and not only by the military—as widespread political anarchy and violence. And in spring 1997 the military orchestrated the ousting of the first Islamist-led government, which was regarded as a serious threat to the secularist-Kemalist character of the republic.[1]

However, the military leadership never succeeded in bringing about a fundamental change of the political system, the inherent dynamics of which proved miraculously resilient. Time and again the old elements (and often the old personalities) of the multiparty system reemerged and a new cycle of party politics *à la Turca* began, although on the surface, at least after the 1980 coup, some important changes seemed to have occurred. These changes have not led to a new type of political dynamic nor to a new system stability. Consequently, the role and influence of the military in politics remains unchanged because the civilian politicians seem unable to provide long-term political stability and guidance.

The Party System: Old Dynamics in a New Guise

After the September 1980 coup the military leadership tried to stabilize Turkey's political system by introducing a new constitution and reshaping the party system. What the military had in mind was to establish a two-party system consisting of a strong center-right and a strong center-left party that would compete for power. In parliament a stable majority-based government would be controlled by a strong opposition that would have a real chance of replacing the government in elections. Banning and dissolving all old parties and prohibiting any political activity for the old party leadership would pave the way for a new system with new political leaders.[2] But the military leadership itself created a barrier to the realization of its ideas by keeping the traditional electoral system of proportional representation. For the establishment and functioning of the intended two-party system, a majority voting system would have been much more effective.

The result of the November 1983 elections was the surprise success of Turgut Özal's Motherland Party (Anavatan Partisi, or ANAP), and the March 1984 local elections quickly proved that the military's intentions had not been realized. The military-backed, newly created center-right and center-left were politically dead after less than six months. The old dynamics of the party system and politics prevailed, although they were somewhat modified by the new constitution and the legal framework devised under military influence. Old parties were reestablished under new names and with new (temporary) leaders. They had, however, to cope with not being represented in parliament because of the machinations of the military leadership in the run-up to the November elections.[3]

The main consequence of this situation was a rapid fragmentation of Turkey's traditional political camps. Özal's party would make a decisive inroad into the center-right groups and establish itself in the longer term as the only new party in the post-1980 system. As the party in power, it could consolidate itself through the classic mechanisms of Turkish party politics—clientelism and favoritism. Thus it was able to survive the return to politics of Süleyman Demirel, the old leader of the Turkish center-right, who took over the leadership of the True Path Party (Doğru Yol Partisi, or DYP) after a referendum in 1987 that led to prematurely lifting the ban on former political leaders.[4]

Today two parties are vying for the primacy of Turkey's moderate-right political camp. Their political programs and ideologies are hardly distinguishable, and they are separated only by deep personal animosities between their respective leaders.[5] Both are made up of a kind of intraparty coalition of political groups representing bourgeois Westernizers, nationalists, and moderate Islamists. Thus both parties lean toward the more radical right if that seems appropriate for gaining or holding power. In this perspective, Mesut Yılmaz's attempt at forming a coalition with the Islamist Welfare Party after the December 1995 elections, which was aborted at the last minute by an intervention of the military leadership, as well as the more successful try of Tansu Çiller to the same end in June 1996 can by no means be regarded as totally unexpected.[6] The competition between Yılmaz and Çiller, which has been accompanied by mutual allegations of political and personal corruption, contributed to the decline of the center-right: the combined share of votes for ANAP and DYP was halved from 51.04 percent in 1991 to 25.23 percent in the national elections of April 18, 1999. Within a decade, the central pillar of Turkey's political development in the multiparty era has been considerably weakened.

A similar development caused by a division of political forces can be found in the moderate-left political camp. Bülent Ecevit, the veteran leader of Turkey's social-democracy, stubbornly stuck to the idea of being the only legitimate representative of the Turkish left and kept his Democratic Left Party (Demokratik Sol Partisi, or DSP) separated from the revived Republican People's Party (Cumhuriyet Halk Partisi, or CHP) led by Deniz Baykal, which had remained victorious in the complicated process of regrouping the various social-democratic parties that had emerged in connection with or after the 1983 elections.[7] Instead of trying to establish a convincing political alternative to the center-right camp, then, Turkey's social democracy cultivated a tradition of leadership rivalries that had started in the 1960s when Ecevit successfully ousted İsmet İnönü from the top of the old Republican People's Party.

Despite frequent participation in various coalition governments during the 1990s, Turkish social democracy has lost much of its influence over the direction of the country's course. Even Ecevit's convincing success in the national elections of April 18, 1999, when his party came in first with 22.19 percent of the vote, was not so much a confirmation of the political attractiveness of social-democratic ideas as an acknowledgement of Ecevit's personal qualities as an honest, clean, humble, nationalist politician and his reputation as an uncompromising secularist.[8] The decline of Turkey's social democracy was emphasized in the same elections when the CHP under Deniz Baykal could not pass the national threshold of 10 percent necessary to be represented in parliament. Its 8.71 percent of the vote was an all-time low for the republic's oldest political party. As a consequence, Baykal had to abandon the party's leadership and was replaced by Altan Öymen. It remains to be seen if this step and the parallel change in party officials will help unite the moderate left.

The enduring fragmentation of the political center has led to a general weakening of decisive political leadership since the end of the 1980s. This in turn has fostered the rise of more extreme political forces like the Nationalist Action Party under the late veteran ultranationalist Alparslan Türkeş or the now legally banned Islamist Welfare Party under its "eternal" leader Necmettin Erbakan. Both parties had been important in Turkish politics during the crisis-ridden 1970s and contributed to the breakdown of the political system that led to the military coup of September 1980.[9] The rise of antisystemic, politically extremist forces also culminated in the elections of April 18, 1999, when the MHP, the Virtue Party (Fazilet Partisi, or FP), which is to be regarded as the successor to the Welfare Party, and the pro-Kurdish People's Democracy Party (Halkın Demokrasi Partisi, or HADEP) together gained 38.14 percent of the national vote.

Contrary to the generals' expectations, less than a decade after the passing of the new constitution the old dynamics of party politics had taken over the system designed by the military leadership after the 1980 coup. The initiatives toward creating a growing democratization and civilianization of

Turkish politics that had accompanied the rule of Prime Minister Özal between 1983 and 1989 did not lead to a consolidation and stabilization of the political system.[10] Instead, the new constitutional and legal framework contributed to the fragmentation of the political center and greater political instability. This became especially evident after the return to the practice of coalition governments in 1991, which also marked the return of the old political elites to the controls. At the end of its term the parliament elected in 1995 counted representatives of ten different parties, and the last two governments before the 1999 early elections were minority governments that could survive only by the support of other parties.

New political forces that can be regarded as an expression of the consequences of the rapid economic and social change have not established themselves on a lasting nationwide basis. The failure to establish a liberal party in the European understanding of the term is especially proof of the inertia of the traditional dynamics of Turkey's political system.[11] This leaves the growing modern urban social groups without adequate political representation, and the organizations of civil society are but a weak compensation.

It is, however, difficult for the parties to adapt to the changing needs and attitudes of Turkey's electorate. The tremendous economic and social changes of the past decades also led to a breakup of old political allegiances and furthered changes in attitudes that expressed themselves in highly volatile voting, especially in urban areas.[12] The fragmented party system with hardly distinguishable competitors in the center-right and the center-left further contributed to voters' confusion. Votes were split across the political spectrum, leaving no party with more than 25 percent of the total. Today, no party or leading politician can claim to have majority support from the Turkish electorate.

Veteran politicians and new party leaders alike show great difficulties in interpreting these socioeconomic changes and adapting party politics and party programs. The only exception seems to be the Welfare Party and its successor, the Virtue Party, which, according to the results of the local elections of 1994 and 1999, successfully established themselves as representatives at the local level of the masses in the urban shantytowns (*gecekondu*). Social democrats and center-right parties alike proved unable to develop adequate political reactions to integrate the wave of rural immigrants into existing urban communal structures or to provide new ones.[13] The challenge of increased social diversification and interests that results from the economic and social change within a highly mobile society has not been met by Turkey's leading politicians.

The character of Turkey's political parties as patronage mechanisms together with historically oligarchic structures of party leadership have often undermined the political expression of pluralism in intraparty processes and party organization.[14] The parties are strongly leader oriented and directed. Sometimes all the candidates for national parliamentary elections are hand picked by the party leader and his or her closest aides. As a consequence a politician's career does not normally depend on his or her ideological or social position nor on a personal political posture. It depends mostly on the favoritism of the party leader. Nor are local constituencies or embeddedness in local or regional party organizations important for a politician's position in the national party organization. The only exception to this portrait are politicians from the southeast where, because of the still strong influences of the tribal structure of the local society, leadership often also guarantees a certain share of the local vote.

One consequence of this situation is the frequent change of party membership by parliamentarians who often hope to gain greater rewards from their new party leader after having run into troubles with the leadership of their former party. Because of the fragmentation of the party system and the hardly distinguishable programatic differences between the parties of the center, the 1990s became the heyday of party switching among deputies whose party allegiance was weak.[15] Thus Turkey's political instability is also furthered by parties' structural peculiarities that are difficult to change because they are part of the safeguards of party leaders against intraparty political rivals.

At present the old dynamics of Turkish party politics prevail, which means that the parties and their leaders seem absorbed by tactical and personal power games and the yearning for positions of influence for the satisfaction of their personal, often material, interest and that of their followers.

One validation of this observation is the accusations of corruption or financial mismanagement against three of Turkey's prime ministers, Çiller, Yılmaz, and Erbakan, plus other leading politicians that have been made by various parties in the parliament since the mid-1990s. These allegations have not led to much in terms of opening judicial trials. Parliamentary commissions of enquiry, too, have remained without consequences because tactical considerations of power politics in the fragmented parliament have often resulted in a mutual whitewashing of past or prospective coalition partners. Tansu Çiller is a special case in point: she survived various attempts to bring her before the Supreme Court by forging the right alliances in time.

This behavior of the representatives of the political center has led to growing disappointment of the masses, who have seen the pressing problems of their daily lives as well as the severe structural problems of the country being relegated to secondary importance. This disappointment has encouraged the spreading of radical nationalistic or Islamist political ideologies. Not surprisingly, the national elections in December 1995 and April 1999 saw a strong showing of these parties. In 1995 the Islamist Welfare Party came in first with a plurality of 21.4 percent of the vote, and in 1999 the nationalist MHP came in second with 18 percent. This development has alarmed the military leadership, who see the very foundations of the secular Kemalist republic endangered. Thus the generals of the 1980 coup, with their attempt to prescribe a strong legal and institutional framework for Turkey's post-1980 development, laid the groundwork for a major return to politics of their successors in the late 1990s.

Guardians on Alert: The Role of the Military

The Turkish military leadership, by tradition and by legal texts based on that tradition, is designated the task of defending the security of the republic. In this context, security implies defending against domestic as well as external threats. Developments that can be regarded as undermining the domestic stability of the country fall within the responsibility of the military. Therefore, the General Staff should be considered not only a professional military institution but a core element of Turkey's political system.

As such, the military orchestrated the ousting of the Islamist-led coalition government of Prime Minister Necmettin Erbakan in spring 1997. Reacting to a surge of what it regarded as fundamentalist demands and moves by the Welfare Party, which was part of the government, the General Staff presented to the government at the February 28 meeting of the National Security Council (Millî Güvenlik Kurulu, or MGK) eighteen measures designed to drastically curb the power of Islamic movements and elements. But Erbakan stalled the implementation of these measures, and his party organized huge public demonstrations against the main element of the measures, the introduction of an uninterrupted eight-year compulsory primary education to dissolve the religious junior high schools. In response the military managed a wave of public protest against the coalition that finally led to Erbakan's resignation. Observers among Turkish journalists used the term "postmodern coup" for evaluating these developments.

The importance the military assigns to its domestic mission became apparent again in March 1998. Prime Minister Mesut Yılmaz, who had replaced Erbakan in June 1997 by forming a three-party minority coalition of two center-right parties (ANAP and DTP) and the pro-Kemalist Democratic Left Party (DSP) of Bülent Ecevit, was heavily critized by the Turkish armed forces command for having asked the military to mind its own business and leave the fight against Islamic fundamentalism to the political and judicial institutions that are constitutionally endowed with the task. In a harsh reaction, the armed forces command, after a meeting of the Joint Chiefs of Staff, declared in a written statement,

> no matter what position or task is represented, no one, for the sake of his personal interest or aspirations, can display an attitude or make any suggestions or comment that will discourage, confuse, weaken or overshadow the determination of the Turkish Armed Forces [TSK] to struggle against separatist or fundamentalist activities that target the country's security. The TSK also believes that the continuation of such discussions will harm the country's democratic structure and national interest.[16]

With this statement the military leadership also tried to end a political debate that had been started ten days earlier by remarks from Deniz Baykal, the leader of the CHP. He had alleged that the military was seeking to establish an "interim government" to replace the governing minority coalition, which was considered too weak to carry out the necessary measures for lastingly curbing the fundamentalist threat. After this remark a lively political debate and a wave of public speculation erupted as to whether a new military intervention was in the offing and what might be the military's immediate political intentions. It was in the course of this debate that Prime Minister Yılmaz made the remark that caused the statement by the armed forces command.[17]

The statement was another confirmation of the military's strong position in the politics of the country. Yılmaz, who had been hesitant in following the army's lead in the struggle against Islamist forces for fear of problems with the religious-oriented wing of his party, had to give in. In the following weeks the dress code in universitites was again enforced by banning female students with headscarves and male students with beards from entering the campuses or taking exams. The mayor of Istanbul, Recep Tayyip Erdoğan of the former Welfare Party who, like most former RP politicians, had become a member of its successor, the Virtue Party, was sentenced to a ten-month prison term for "inciting hatred among the people" in a speech given in the southeastern city of Siirt in December 1997. He had quoted a poem of Ziya Gökalp, the leading ideologue of Turkish nationalism at the time of the republic's foundation. The poem says that "the mosques are our barracks, the domes are our helmets, the minarets are our bayonets, and the faithful are our army." For the Diyarbakır State Security Court this was a sign of Erdoğan's intention of provoking enmity and hatred among the people by alluding to an armed struggle of Islamists.[18] Some days later a group of Muslim businessmen was detained and their houses searched under the suspicion of illegally financing Islamic groups. These measures against Islamist fundamentalism went unhindered by the government. The third wave of fighting "reactionaryism" after the expulsion of the Erbakan government and the banning of the Welfare Party was another step in the army's program of eradicating the danger of Islamism and securing the integrity of the secular republic.[19]

It was, however, also a sign of the military's disappointment with and disdain for the politicians whom it regarded as unable and unwilling to subordinate their petty political and personal interests to the national interest of preserving the Kemalist republic. The military leadership shows only limited understanding of the complexities of democratic party politics and its parliamentarian power games. For the military, the nation and its survival in the Kemalist sense is of tantamount importance and cannot be left to the political class, which more than once in the past has shown its inability and incompetence in fulfilling its national duty. The armed forces see themselves legitimized to interfere more or less discreetly in political developments if they see their mission of preserving the national security endangered by the political bickering of civilian politicians.[20] This attitude was behind the General Staff's message of January 4, 1999, that indirectly urged the politicians to end the political vacuum that had occurred with the resignation of Yılmaz's minority coalition government on November 29, 1998, after Baykal's Social Democrats had withdrawn their external support for the government. In the same message the military leadership once again stressed its determination to continue the fight against Islamic fundamentalism.[21]

Despite its overbearing behavior, the Turkish military enjoys the support of the vast majority of the public. Since the 1980s, polls have consistently shown that it is the most trusted institution of the Turkish state. Criticism of the political role of the military is only sporadically forthcoming, although a growing part of civil society believes that the Turkish situation is a somewhat deviant case among Western democracies and may not be the correct model of civilian-military relationship in a "contemporary" Turkish democracy at the threshold of the third millennium.[22] However,

> a systemwide consensus on what the appropriate role and place for the military is in a democracy does not exist. The current situation shows once again that the lack of consensus among ordinary political actors on the nature of the regime and its rules, a lack of agreement on what the major problems the country is facing are and the range of possible measures to overcome them create a political vacuum which the military moves in to fill.[23]

Most recently, this moving in has also involved increasing engagement in the conduct of Turkish foreign policy. Since the early 1990s the military has been instrumental in defining the parameters of Turkish policy in the Middle East as it had long done for Greek-Turkish relations. In both areas the security policy prerogatives as defined by the military command set the priorities for foreign policy behavior. The extension of the fight against the Kurdish Workers' Party (PKK) across the Turkish border into northern Iraq was a decision made by the military without much consultation with the civilian government. This could be observed when, in March 1998, Turkish special forces captured Şemdin Sakık, a former close aid of PKK leader Abdullah Öcalan, who after having abandoned relations with the PKK had sought refuge in northern Iraq with Massoud Barzani and his Kurdish Democrat Party, one of the leading factions of Iraqi Kurds. The military did not inform the cabinet nor even Prime Minister Yılmaz of this action in advance. The army justified its behavior with their suspicion that civilian politicians would not be able to keep the necessary secrecy for such a risky operation.

The military also dominates reshaping Turkish-Israeli security relations. The General Staff forced even Islamist Prime Minister Erbakan to sign far-reaching agreements for military cooperation with Israel's armed forces, which led to strong protests among Erbakan's followers and from the Arab states and Iran with which he had tried to establish better relations.[24] The Turkish military is eager to broaden the cooperation with Israel to weapons procurement, as can be seen from plans to develop an antitactical ballistic missile (ATBM) system together.[25]

The latest foreign policy move of the Turkish military seems to aim at the Transcaucasian and Caspian regions where in spring 1998 the chief of the Turkish General Staff, General İsmail Hakkı Karadayı, consecutively visited Azerbaijan, Georgia, and, as a first visit after the end of the cold war,

Russia to hold important political consultations with their governments. He, rather than the relevant agencies of Turkey's foreign policy establishment, concluded an agreement on military cooperation with Georgia.[26] One could get the impression that the armed forces command not only has a prerogative over the Ministry of Defence, which is the normal constitutional situation, but also tries to lead the foreign ministry in an area of vital importance for Turkey's foreign relations. An unnamed senior general commented to the *Turkish Daily News* in 1998 that

> None of us are willing to take control of this country or to become involved in politics. But while some bodies within the Turkish government are in a continuing state of ignorance and negligence, we have no other option. . . . Of course, we respect the Constitution and the laws by which we receive our responsibility and power. . . . But there are vital issues for us on which we cannot make any concession.[27]

This statement falls just short of declaring that the armed forces is a government within the government and is another expression of the military's negligence or ignorance of established rules of policymaking within Western democratic political systems.

Turkey's military, in fact, has a special role in the political system that binds it more intricately than other NATO armed forces to political tasks and decisions. The most important institution to this respect is the National Security Council (MGK), the highest advisory body to the Turkish government. It consists of the president of the republic (the chair); the chief of the General Staff and the respective chiefs of the army, navy, air force, and gendarmery from the military side; and the prime minister, the minister of defense, the interior minister, and the foreign affairs minister from the civilian side. Although it can issue only recommendations, the military normally considers them binding demands on the civilian side of the government, which can hardly dare not to respond to them. Thus via the MGK "the military has actually become part of the constitutionally based state executive power without formally being legitimized to such a position."[28]

Another area of overlapping civilian and military authority is the judiciary, especially the state security courts and the military courts of the state of emergency authority. The state security courts not only cover classical crimes against the state but also try all cases related to the Anti-Terror Law—distributing propaganda for separatism and so forth—that are regarded as "crimes of conviction" in most Western democracies. The activity of the state security courts is regarded as one of the strongest impediments to the full realization of the principle of freedom of thought and expression in the Turkish democracy.[29] Until early 1999 a military judge belonged to each chamber of the courts.

The military courts of the state of emergency authority try certain crimes committed by civilians that are enumerated in the Law of the State of Emergency Authority (Sıkıyönetim Kanunu), mainly "crimes against the state."[30] Both types of courts are prominent in the fight of the state against separatist terrorism and other attacks on the national integrity. In the 1990s they became, willingly or unwillingly, among the most potent instruments in the fight of the state elite and military leadership against any movement to undermine the secular Kemalist republic. In both types of court the military enjoys a considerable influence through the military judges who, although formally independent, are part of the military hierarchy and are consequently influenced by nonjudicial considerations.[31]

In a 1998 judgment the European Court of Human Rights declared that for this reason trials before and sentences of the state security courts are not in compliance with the relevant European conventions.[32] To prevent a similar criticism from European institutions concerning the trial of the PKK leader, Abdullah Öcalan, that took place before the Ankara State Security Court on the small island of İmralı in the Sea of Marmara in spring 1999, the Turkish parliament changed the constitution and the law in such a way as to replace the military judge with a civilan one.[33] This move should not, however, be interpreted as an attempt to curtail the political influence of the military. Indeed, it can be regarded as a step to prevent this influence from being unduly criticized by the Europeans.

With the MGK, its position within the branches of judiciary that deal with internal security issues, and the complete independence of the General Staff from the Ministry of Defence, the military enjoys a position within Turkey's political system that can be regarded as ideal for following a political agenda of its own. Given its historic weight and reputation within Turkish society, the military leadership is also able to see that its agenda is carried out in spite of most civilian resistance. This power has been proven often enough when the civilian side of government has tried to follow a course in domestic politics that ran counter to the military's agenda of defending secularist Kemalism.

The political dilemma of this situation lies in the stabilizing presence of the military on the one hand and on the other the simultaneous preservation and defense of social ideas and constructs that no longer coincide with the social reality of the country. By defending the idea of Westernization as developed by Atatürk through the imposition of narrow limits on the democratic right of freedom of thought and expression, the military distances Turkey ever more from modern Western political systems. Thus the dilemma of Turkey's Westernization is to be seen in the military's attempt to further democracy through nondemocratic measures. Such an attempt can only fail in the longer run, as is clearly shown by Turkey's experience of military-guided democratization. The more fundamental political problem beneath this dilemma is whether the country's society and politicians will be able to devise a course of development along contemporary Western political standards that can ultimately reconcile the divergent domestic social and ideological forces without recurrent recourse to indirect or direct military intervention.

There is some reason to believe that such an experiment can be started only after the role of the military within the political system has been fundamentally changed. For this to happen, the social realities brought about by the economic and social changes since the 1980s have to be acknowledged: that is, some myths inherited from the pure Kemalist ideology have to be questioned, foremost the idea of the one and undivided Turkish nation and its state as well as the notion of secularism as defined by the Kemalist ideology. Without accepting the Kurdish reality and the widespread social implantation of Islam as valid political phenomenons of today's Turkey, an escape from the dilemma of political participation by the military leadership will hardly be possible.

CHAPTER FOUR

The Myth of National Homogeneity and the "Kurdish Reality"

WHEN IN AUGUST 1984 the Kurdistan Workers' Party (Partiya Karkaren Kurdistan, or PKK) attacked two stations of the Turkish gendarmerie, nobody thought it would be the beginning of a protracted military confrontation between the state's forces and Kurdish guerillas that would lead to a deep rift in Turkish society, serious political controversies with Turkey's Western allies, and increased foreign policy problems with regard to the country's situation in the Middle East.[1] Until the beginning of the 1990s the fight against the PKK in the southeastern provinces could be regarded as an internal affair with only marginal repercussions beyond Turkey's borders. But since the end of the cold war, Turkey's struggle to keep its national and territorial integrity by fighting the separatist Kurdish rebels has become an international affair that reverberates through the country's domestic developments.[2] How best to cope with the Kurdish challenge has become an ongoing controversy between Kemalist and nationalist groups on one side and more open-minded liberals on the other plus a small group of Kurdish politicians of various political leanings who try to make their voice heard despite strong state repression of any form of Kurdish political expression.[3]

Until the 1990s, mentioning the words "Kurd" or "Kurdish" in public was generally regarded as breaking a taboo. The person who did it consciously ran the risk of being taken into custody and prosecuted for propagating separatism. In early 1991 President Turgut Özal took the first steps to change Turkey's political approach to the Kurds as part of his more comprehensive policy directing Turkey's role in and after the Gulf War.[4] In November 1991 when Prime Minister Süleyman Demirel first acknowledged the existence of a "Kurdish reality" in the country, the situation had already changed.[5] In April 1991, Law 2932 of 1983, which had effectively banned the use of the Kurdish language in public, was repealed, and later that year the Turkish government started a dialogue with the Kurdish groups in northern Iraq. A general debate about changes of policy toward the Kurds was initiated in the media. Today, the Kurdish question is a matter of public debate that includes even the Islamic part of the Turkish public.[6] This is not to say, however, that anybody at any time can discuss the problem without risk of being taken by the security forces. Spreading "separatist propaganda" is still a severe crime, although the official view of what constitutes such an offense has become less rigid over the years.

In October 1995 the Turkish parliament changed article 8 of the infamous Anti-Terror Law so that discussion of the Kurdish problem did not almost automatically constitute a legal offense. However, there remain many other legal devices in the constitution, party law, and other laws that preclude open and unrestricted public debate of the subject. Politicians, journalists, artists, and human rights activists still face trials and imprisonment for expressing opinions on the Kurdish issue that deviate from the official view, even if they do not make any reference to the PKK or the use of violence for reaching Kurdish goals.[7]

The change in Turkey's official approach toward the Kurds was not only a consequence of the Gulf War and its precarious results with regard to northern Iraq, which led to the establishment of the U.S.-led operation Poised Hammer for the protection of Iraqi Kurds against assaults from Saddam Hussein's army (see chapter 8). It was also caused by the consequences of years of merciless terrorism by the PKK in Turkey's southeast and of the no less merciless reaction of the state security forces.[8] Kurdish separatism thus has turned from a Turkish regional affair into a national political problem, although its direct impact has been largely restricted to the southeast.

Over time the campaign against the separatist PKK guerillas changed to low-level warfare in southeastern Anatolia. After the Turkish General Staff took over the command of fighting the separatists, regular military forces increasingly replaced the gendarmery. About a quarter of Turkey's total land forces became engaged in the effort to crush the PKK and its sympathizers.[9] Air raids against guerilla strongholds became common, and attack helicopters were increasingly used in developing a mobile warfare in rough and otherwise difficult mountain terrain.

Casualties have been high: before September 1997 there were about 23,000 deaths and 13,700 injuries. Among the deaths, some 4,000 were civilians, 4,400 were security forces, and 14,800 were what in common Turkish nomenclature are called "separatists" or "terrorists." Today one speaks of more than 30,000 people that have been killed in the fight between the PKK and Turkish troops. It is remarkable how few PKK fighters have been taken prisoner or have been reported injured in the clashes with the security forces. In the course of military action, especially after 1992, more than 3,000 villages and smaller settlements have been evacuated, and most have been destroyed, causing the forced resettlement of 400,000 persons.[10]

But migration from the Kurdish areas has been much higher because many people have also left their rural homes to escape harassment by both the PKK and the Turkish security forces. They have normally migrated to Diyarbakır, Urfa, Van, or other urban centers in the southeast where they have added to the already large numbers of urban unemployed. Even more people seem to have migrated from the Kurdish provinces to other parts of Turkey to escape the fighting and its side effects as well as the hopeless economic and social situation in the southeast. Most have settled in the more prosperous urban centers of western Anatolia such as Istanbul or İzmir. As a consequence of this internal migration of an estimated 3 million persons, more Kurds are said to live outside the southeastern and eastern provinces than in the original Kurdish homelands of Turkey.[11]

Turkey's domestic Kurdish problem is a mixture of interlinked issues. Predominant is how to resolve the official state doctrine of the "one and indivisible nation and state" with the undeniable existence of 10 to 12 million persons of different ethnic origin and cultural background, a considerable part of whom claim distinct rights because of these differences.[12] A second problem is the economic and social backwardness of the Kurdish areas and the insufficient efforts of the state to improve this situation. As a consequence of the first two problems, there is the struggle with PKK terrorism. These three problems are linked together in such a manner that they have blocked any solution. It is important, however, to realize that the core of the problem, at least for the proponents of Kurdish nationalist claims, is a political issue: the recognition of a Kurdish identity in the state's policy toward the region.

Turkey: One State, One People?

"Had the Kurds not been treated as only a nomadic people in need of being assimilated, the situation could have been different."[13] This statement by a

Turkish journalist who had to quit his profession in Turkey for having become too closely involved in the Kurdish issue, touches on the central problem.

Since the founding of the republic—which had been brought about with the significant assistance of Kurdish tribes during Atatürk's war of independence—the Kemalist state elite has stubbornly defended the doctrine of the unity and indivisibility of the Turkish state, its territory, and its people. It has become a central element of modern Turkey's raison d'être, firmly inscribed in the constitution drafted under military supervision after the coup of 1980 and accepted with a large majority in a referendum in 1982. According to the doctrine, there is only one people in Turkey, and it comprises the totality of the country's citizens, who all enjoy the same rights and have the same obligations. Claims based on ethnic difference are unjustified because every Turkish citizen is a first-class citizen, a sentiment that has become the established reason for politicians and state officials to refuse Kurdish demands for minority rights. Only those groups are recognized as minorities in Turkey that were explicitly assigned minority status in the Treaty of Lausanne by which the Republic of Turkey was internationally recognized in 1923. Thus the only minorities are Armenian Christians, Orthodox Greeks, and Jews.[14]

The original Kemalist doctrine of "civic nationalism" would, indeed, make a differentiation based on ethnicity unnecessary if it had been pursued diligently by the state authorities. But early in the history of the republic sporadic but continuous Kurdish resistance against the new state and its secular and national ideology as well as a state policy of severe indoctrination of the people with the new ideology led to a gradual growth of an "ethnic nationalism" based on Turkishness. The existence of different ethnic groups in the republic was simply denied. Kurds were regarded as ancient Turks who had lost the awareness of their real ethnic roots and who had to be reeducated about their Turkishness.[15] To that end the use of the Kurdish language (or dialects) was forbidden, as were Kurdish names for children, and tens of thousands of Kurdish villages and hamlets got new Turkish names. The state policy of spreading Kemalist norms among the people of Anatolia slowly but constantly deviated from creating a "new Turkish citizen" to assimilating members of different ethnic backgrounds, that is, creating "new Turks."[16]

Many Kurds followed the path prescribed by the state elites, became Turks, and even rose to prominence in the new republic. Thus today it is easy for the advocates of the ideology of a unified Turkish people to name many successful Turks of Kurdish origin who are cited as examples of the nondiscriminatory nature of the Turkish state. The late president Turgut Özal ranks prominently among the contemporary Turks of that kind, but one can also mention many prominent politicians such as Hikmet Çetin, the former Speaker of the Turkish Grand National Assembly and former leader of the reestablished social-democratic Republican People's Party. The Turkish armed forces are especially proud of their nondiscriminatory approach concerning the ethnic background of their officers, as long as they do not make an issue of their ethnicity.

Another way of coping with the requirements of the Turkish state regarding the unity of the Turkish people was chosen by leaders of Kurdish tribes who entered into active cooperation with state authorities, completely leaving open the question if they did this as representatives of a group of Kurdish people or as responsible Turkish citizens. Such behavior is the result of still existing semifeudal structures within the Kurdish population where social organization according to tribe affiliation remains common and tribal leaders can demand undisputed allegiance from their tribesmen.[17] In this way the leaders can extract material advantages from the state—for instance, public procurements for companies run by their families, who offer loyalty to the Turkish state from their tribe members in return. This can sometimes even take the form of uniform voting behavior in favor of a certain party. In this symbiotic relationship Kurdish ethnicity is irrelevant as long as both sides keep their commitments.

However, anyone who insists on keeping his or her identity as a Kurd or who simply has not had the chance to sufficiently "Turkeyfy" because of adverse living conditions in the southeast continues to suffer from state repression. This especially holds true for all who openly demonstrate their Kurdishness or advocate the official recognition of a Kurdish identity in Turkey with cultural and perhaps even political rights of their own.

Prominent contemporary examples of such persons are the Turkish social scientist İsmail Beşikçi, who has been sentenced to 200 years in prison for defending the Kurdish case in his sociological writings, or the greatest living Turkish author, Yaşar Kemal, who has several times faced trial for "making separatist propaganda" in press articles. The case of seven deputies of the banned Democracy Party (Demokrasi Partisi, or DEP), among them Leyla Zana, who were imprisoned for alleged connections with the outlawed PKK, led to international protests in the United States and Europe.[18]

This situation makes it very difficult to establish social or political organizations that promote the Kurdish case. If they do so openly, they will be closed by the state authorities or court verdicts. This happened three times to parties that had been established by Kurdish politicians of social-democratic background. The People's Democracy Party (Halkın Demokrasi Partisi, or HADEP) is constantly faced with the threat of closure, and its leadership has been taken to court several times for charges of having connections with the PKK and of violating the unity of the nation.[19]

It is true that none of these pro-Kurdish political parties, with the exception of the small, more center-oriented Democratic Party of the Masses (Demokrat Kitle Partisi, or DKP), explicitly distanced themselves from the PKK. This was, however, difficult for them, "given the extensive support for the organization within the politicized Kurdish population of Turkey. . . . However, these parties never developed, contrary to the government's claims, the kind of organic relationship which exists between the [Irish Republican Army] and the Sinn Fein in Northern Ireland, where the latter does not hide the fact that it is the political arm of the armed militants."[20]

HADEP has gained an unequivocal political legitimacy among the Kurdish population in the southeastern and eastern provinces. In the national election of 1995 the party came in second after the Islamist Welfare Party in the Kurdish region, and in 1999 it was the strongest party in eleven provinces in the region. It won important mayoral positions in the region in the April 18, 1999, local elections that were held alongside the national elections. Of special importance was its victory in Diyarbakır, the largest city of Turkey's Kurdish region.

HADEP's electoral success is a clear signal that there is a strong popular sentiment for Kurdish nationalism in the southeast. It is important to note, however, that this sentiment is restricted to the region because on the national level HADEP gained less than 5 percent of the vote in the 1995 and 1999 elections. The party also failed to attract the majority of Kurdish people living in the huge west Anatolian urban agglomerations such as Istanbul and Ankara.

A number of politically relevant conclusions can be drawn from this situation. First, there is a deep political cleavage between the Kurdish region and the rest of Turkey. Second, the Kurdish national claims are not recognized by the vast majority of Turkey's population. Third, the unity of the state and nation can only be preserved by bridging the cleavage. Fourth, banning HADEP would hardly change the political attitude in the Kurdish provinces. It would, however, eliminate another representative of Kurdish interests and leave the state with the task of doing all the bridge building by itself.

As long as Kemalist hard-liners in the military and judiciary leadership and nationalist groups in the center-right and rightist parties dominate the state's policy toward the Kurds, the development of a political middle ground will be hampered. This has been proven on various occasions when Turkish governments tried to develop a more forthcoming policy on the Kurdish question. Neither Turgut Özal nor the highly respected Süleyman Demirel, in coalition with the social-democratic leader Erdal İnönü, have been able to overcome the deep-seated doubts of the nationalist-cum-Kemalist front.[21] Necmettin Erbakan, the leader of the Islamist Welfare Party, at the beginning of his premiership in summer 1996 also tried in vain to develop a political solution of the Kurdish question.[22]

For Turkey's hard-liners the recognition of the Kurdish question and possible expressions of Kurdish cultural rights is the beginning of the end of the unified Turkish nation-state. Cultural rights such as the official use of the Kurdish language on certain occasions would, they would contend, inevitably lead to demands for political rights that would trigger demands for reorganizing the republic along the lines of a federation. From there to separation would only be a small step, thus finally bringing about what had been foreseen by the Western powers in the Treaty of Sèvres at the end of World War I and what had been so successfully fought by the Turks in the war of independence.[23]

Every stalled attempt of Turkish governments or politicians to overcome the stalemate on the Kurdish question as well as every crackdown of the state authorities on Kurdish political and social organizations that try to promote consideration of the issue with nonviolent and nonradical means bolsters the position of the PKK and its terrorist tactics. Unfortunately, hard-liners and radicals on both sides have carried the day, providing each other the justification for continuing their policies of harsh action and barring the moderates on both sides from effectively participating.

Recently, however, things have slowly begun to change. As a result of the violence in the southeast but also the growing discrimination in the western urban centers, many Kurds are rediscovering their ethnic origins.[24] "By the mid-1990s a significant proportion of the population in Turkey considered themselves to be Kurds and they have been increasingly demanding the recognition of the right to express their identity."[25] At the same time, it has become clear that the vast majority of these people have no intention of dividing Turkey. What they are overwhelmingly aiming at is the recognition of their identity by the state and the allowance of its expression within the borders of that state. This is also realized by an increasing number of Turkish politicians and representatives of civil society, especially businesses. A variety of reports and opinions have been issued, all of which argue in favor of a political solution of the Kurdish question. Meanwhile, most political leaders of the center-right and the center-left as well as the military leadership are convinced that the main drive to resolve the Kurdish problem has to come from the political sphere.[26] But few results have materialized so far.

The main reason for the lack of progress is the prevailing indecision and discord among the Turkish politicians about what the elements of a political solution should be. Ideas range from economic and social measures to combat economic underdevelopment in the region to measures of general devolution of state authority to indirectly enable a kind of Kurdish self-governance at the local level. Other ideas would be to promote Kurdish cultural identity by enabling Kurdish radio and TV programs or even granting the possibility of teaching Kurdish in schools on a voluntary basis. Nobody is thinking of formally recognizing a Kurdish minority status from which special minority rights could be derived. Above all is the common concern of keeping Turkey's national unity untouched, which the military leadership regards as its most honorable task.[27]

But as long as the PKK's terrorist activities continue and as long as the resistance of orthodox Kemalists and Turkish nationalists against any change in policy toward the Kurds persists, any Turkish government will be very careful in promoting far-fetched political solutions, even more so if it is a weak government based on a shaky coalition as has been the case for most of the 1990s. Turks may thus increasingly realize that they are a multiethnic and multicultural society, but they are far from officially acknowledging that fact, not to speak of drawing the necessary political consequences from it.

Economic and Social Backwardness and the Kurds

The Kurdish problem has another dimension besides state ideology. That is the connection between economic and social backwardness and political resistance plus the economic and political fallout of the continuous warfare in the southeast. As a Turkish observer commented, "had billions of dollars spent defending the region against countless separatist attacks and launching cross-border incursions into neighboring countries instead been spent on investment in the region, the situation could have been different. . . . The PKK . . . has exploited a regional reaction to economic hardships and human rights abuses to the fullest."[28]

The continuous erosion of state authority and the tacit support of the PKK among large parts of the Kurdish population in the southeast, especially among young people, is a result of official repression of any form of Kurdishness and of decades-long neglect of the region in the state's economic policy. Attempts at developing the region have been undertaken halfheartedly and too late. One has to admit, however, that the natural conditions in the region are not favorable to industrial development, and the semifeudal social organization of Kurdish society has posed another impediment to speedy, large-scale economic development. Private investment can only be attracted by offering considerable incentives in the form of indirect or direct subsidies. In this respect the more promising west Anatolian provinces have been preferred by state policies.

Today the southeast is Turkey's economically and socially most backward region. Income per capita is the lowest, unemployment is the highest, the share of industrial firms in economic activity is the smallest, and agricultural productivity is the weakest in the country. Birthrates and the rate of illiteracy are the highest. The numbers of educational facilities and health care institutions are totally inadequate, as is the regional transport and communication infrastructure outside the provincial urban centers. Many villages and small townships are often difficult to reach in winter.

The situation has been aggravated by the continuous fighting between the PKK and the state security forces. Systematic PKK attacks against teachers and schools in rural areas together with the evacuation policy of the state authorities have left 1.5 million children without education. About 500 medical care centers are closed.[29] Those schools and hospitals that still function are hopelessly understaffed and ill equipped.

Because of the fighting, economic activity in the southeast has come to a halt. Those who have been forced to leave their rural homes not only have had to give up their occupation but also have often had to abandon their herds or flocks. Animal husbandry as one of the main sources of rural income has deteriorated badly. Private investment, which was never strong, has almost stopped due to the prevailing insecurity and the weak purchasing power in the region. Prosperous inner-Turkish markets are some hundred miles to the west, and potential markets in neighboring Iraq, Syria, or Iran have lost much of their attractiveness because of the critical regional political situation. The breakdown of trade with Iraq after 1990 has been a severe blow to the economy in Turkey's southeast. The resulting losses could not be compensated by the small-scale irregular border trade that developed after the creation of the safe haven for the Kurds of northern Iraq.

Changing the economic and social underdevelopment of the southeast is a difficult task and will take time. Although public investment in the region has been three times higher than the national average for all regions since the early 1980s, the effect on development has been minimal.[30] Even the Southeast Anatolia Project (Güneydoğu Anadolu Projesi, or GAP), a huge development effort combining hydropower generation and irrigation agriculture in five provinces, will take decades to fully realize its intended effects on economic development. And experiences elsewhere have shown that the economic and social effects of such huge projects are at best mixed.[31]

The basic problem for the development of the region is, however, the lack of adequate human capital. Even if the state could provide the necessary numbers of schools, universities, hospitals, and medical care stations, the problem of staffing them with qualified personnel would remain. These people are not available in the region, and qualified personnel in other regions, especially in the west of Turkey, normally refuse to move to the east and southeast even if the state offers them considerable material incentives. This is not a new phenomenon caused by the regional violence but a long-standing experience of Turkish regional development policy.

It also largely applies to those people of Kurdish background who as migrants to western Turkey have received a good education. They also prefer to stay in the more prosperous areas. This is an indication of the functioning of assimilation processes under conducive economic and social conditions. Economic and social development could, thus, become a strong element of a solution of the Kurdish question if accompanied by tension-reducing political measures in the Kurdish provinces.

A comprehensive development program with a chance of quick results would be difficult to establish, and it would cost sums that most likely would surpass the financial capabilities of Turkey. Yet a diversified, long-term endeavor is needed for a promising economic takeoff in the region. The effort would have to encompass everything from a thorough rebuilding and expansion of the educational and medical infrastructure to the establishment of industrial workplaces that are able to generate an economic surplus. Some progress in this direction could be made if a change in the official approach to the Kurdish question would lead to a reassignment of at least part of the state expenditures of about $6 billion to $8 billion a year that until now has been spent fighting the PKK in Turkey and northern Iraq. Despite the considerable developmental efforts of the state since the mid-1980s, the disproportion between the money spent fighting terrorist separatism and that spent developing the region remains tremendous. A change in politics could also lead to a change in spending purposes. Together, both could also slow down or even reverse the out-migration from the southeast.

The Fight against the PKK

The prerequisite for changing the Kurdish situation is to stop the regional insecurity. This is easier said than done. Over the years the fight against the PKK has considerably changed. What began as isolated countermeasures of state security forces against PKK hit-and-run actions has turned into a regional low-level warfare that transgresses the Turkish border and permanently involves large parts of the regular armed forces. In this process a subculture of the PKK, Kurdish criminal elements, nationalist Turkish outlaws, Kurdish tribal leaders, Turkish politicians, and parts of the state security forces form an almost impenetrable tangle of partly cross-cutting, partly mutual interests and relations. Disentangling these elements could prove to pose the most difficult part of a solution to the problem.

The continuous increase in manpower and material used by the state security forces in actions against the PKK has borne fruit. The organization is now clearly on the defensive, and it has become increasingly difficult for its fighters to establish themselves in larger numbers on Turkish territory. The early 1990s, when the PKK could claim to have "liberated" certain areas in the southeastern provinces, are gone. That is not to say that its military arm is completely defeated, but it has definitely lost its ability to wage larger military operations against state security forces or Kurdish villages that are left in the area of operations.

But it will be difficult to bring the fighting to an end. As long as the PKK fighters can retreat into northern Iraq or Syria and find shelter, they can regroup. Developments since 1991, when a safe haven for Iraqi Kurds was established north of the 36th parallel under the pressure of the international anti-Saddam alliance, have shown that nobody can prevent PKK fighters from seeking refuge in the areas near the Iraqi-Turkish border.[32]

However, various large military incursions of the Turkish armed forces into northern Iraq since 1993 as well as a difficult and always hazy cooperation between the Turkish state and the two dominant Kurdish groups in the region have resulted in a considerable weakening of the PKK position there.[33] As a consequence, Turkish armed forces are actually able to control PKK activities in the southeast and across the Iraqi border to such an extent that the terrorists can no longer be regarded as a real separatist threat to

Turkey's national integrity. That repeated declarations of a unilateral ceasefire by the PKK leadership in 1993 and again since 1995 have never been answered by the Turkish military are an indication of this.[34]

The PKK's position deteriorated further with the capture of its leader, Abdullah Öcalan, by the Turkish authorities in February 1999. Öcalan had been driven out of his longtime Syrian hideout in Damascus in October 1998 when Turkey forced the Syrian government, by threat of a military intervention, to expel Öcalan. After apparently having spent some time in Russia, the PKK leader suddenly surfaced in Rome on November 12, 1998. He sought political asylum in Italy while being faced with a Turkish demand to the Italian government to extradite him. Although the Italian government rejected the Turkish demand because Italian law forbids extradition to a country where a person may face capital punishment, Öcalan's position in Rome became more insecure as the Italian government tried to get rid of him. Rome saw itself left alone with this hot potato, especially after the German government ceased to implement a warrant the German state prosecutor had issued for Öcalan to try him for several murders that had been committed by PKK killers in Germany.

On January 16, 1999, the PKK chief disappeared for a second time when he left Rome on a private Italian plane with an unknown destination. His itinerary is largely unknown, but on February 16 he was captured by a commando team of Turkish security forces in Nairobi on his way from the Greek embassy to the airport. It became known afterward that he had gone to Kenya on the insistence and with the help of the Greek Foreign Ministry, which had desperately tried to get him out of Greece where he had been brought on January 30 with the assistance of a retired Greek admiral who sympathized with the Kurdish cause.[35] Öcalan was brought to custody on the island of İmralı in the Sea of Marmara where his trial before a state security court started on May 31.

Although in his defense the PKK leader contended that he and his organization have abandoned terrorism in favor of a political solution to the Kurdish problem within the boundaries of a democratic and pluralistic Turkish republic, this statement did not impress the judges. On June 29, 1999, the court declared Öcalan guilty of separatist treason and sentenced him to death, causing jubilant reactions in the Turkish public and media and harsh criticism from many European political circles, especially from leftist groups.[36]

The execution of Öcalan's sentence depends on various procedural steps that have to be taken. First, Turkey's Supreme Court of Appeal has to confirm the verdict, which then will be sent to the Justice Commission of the Turkish parliament. The commission has to prepare a report recommending the execution of the sentence, and the report has to be voted on by the General Assembly of the parliament. If the death penalty is approved, the decision will have to be signed by the president and published in the Official Journal before the execution can take place. Since 1984 about 400 death sentences have been passed by Turkish courts, but none has ever been presented to parliament for decision. No executions have taken place in Turkey since then. The question is if Öcalan will be the first exception to this tradition.

After the verdict of the Court of Appeal, Öcalan can bring his case before the European Court of Human Rights (ECHR) to check if any stipulations of the European Convention of Human Rights and its additional protocols to which Turkey is a party have been violated by the Turkish authorities' handling of his case. If the ECHR would declare any such violation to have taken place, Turkey would face great difficulties in carrying out the sentence.

Since his trial Öcalan and the PKK have kept strictly to the new political line of ending terrorist activities. Öcalan asked his fighters to end the violence and withdraw from Turkish soil. To show the sincerity of the new policy, he even urged some of his fighters to surrender to the Turkish authorities. His orders, issued from his prison cell via his lawyers, have been followed by the organization. Other PKK spokespersons also declared the armed fight against the Turkish state finished and asked for a fresh start of political endeavors to solve Turkey's Kurdish problem.

The new coalition government of Bülent Ecevit and the military leadership have not reacted favorably to this change of PKK policy. They have continued to assert that the fight against the separatist terrorism would go on. This attitude risks the resurgence of PKK violence if there is no sign from the Turkish state of a change in its attitude toward Kurdish nationalist demands. A continuation of the special state of emergency in the southeastern provinces accompanied by strong military presence and the prosecution of separatist tendencies by the courts could frustrate the PKK cadres to such an extent that they would take up arms again.

Under such circumstances, the PKK could count on the continuing sympathy of European political groups that have supported the Kurdish cause in the past. General criticism of Turkey would again appear in the European Parliament and other European institutions, and Turkey's relations with most of its European partners would sour again. This would nurture Turkish suspicions of ulterior European motives in relations with Ankara.

There can be no doubt that the PKK's performance in the war was and continues to be influenced by international factors as well as domestic situations. Since its early days, the Kurdish problem has attracted the interest of foreign powers. This was already the case with the Sheik Said rebellion of 1925 in which the British supported the rebellious Kurdish leader.[37] And the PKK has relied not only on Syria but also on various other governments such as the former Soviet Union, Iran, Iraq, Greece, and more recently probably also Armenia that were interested in seeing Turkey in trouble. Ankara's relations with its neighbors in the region, Greece, and the European Union have been damaged by such pro-PKK activities.

It would, however, be misleading to interpret the problem as only the result of foreign intrigues that "are being conducted by those who are afraid of Turkey's power in the future,"[38] as can often be read in Turkish nationalist analyses of the issue. If there had been no severe Kurdish problem in Turkey, its foreign rivals and enemies would not have been able to use Kurdish resistance for their own anti-Turkish intentions.

A considerable part of the internationalization of Turkey's Kurdish problem is the direct result of Ankara's repressive approach toward it. Many of those who try to draw the European public's interest toward the Kurdish cause can do so only because Turkey's authorities have forced them to flee the country to avoid prosecution for propagating separatist ideas. Kemal Burkay, the leader of the Socialist Party of Kurdistan, who has for years lived in exile in Sweden, or Yılmaz Güney, the Kurdish film director who died in European exile, are two well-known victims. There are, however, thousands of others living in Europe who by no means can be said to have gone there to work against Turkey because of foreign powers' influences or anti-Turkish designs.

The internationalization of the Kurdish problem will become more important as long as the situation in Turkey does not change. The globalization of information flows and satellite TV and Internet communication increasingly penetrates national borders and almost automatically renders domestic problems of a certain order international issues. The PKK has successfully made use of this trend to raise foreign public support for the Kurdish cause. Turkey's efforts to stall this development by counterpropaganda and appeals to European governments to put an end to the PKK's propaganda and other activities in European countries seem bound to fail, as Turkey's own experiences in its Kurdish provinces reveal.[39]

It is always preferable to try to change the political and social circumstances that give rise to the dispersion of such propaganda. "Turkey can no longer maintain the fiction that reduces the southeast problem to a matter of public order or economic development. It cannot try to eradicate or to intimidate everyone who disagrees with this view, and then expect the international community to understand and even support it. . . . Turkey cannot . . . continue to believe that she is right and the entire world wrong."[40]

However, there are obstacles to a swift end of the warfare. The protracted fighting has given some groups vested interests in the situation as it stands. Parts of the state security forces have become implicated in illegal activities that have accompanied the fight against the PKK. "Mysterious murders" of PKK sympathizers but also of critical Kurdish journalists and of members of Kurdish parties such as DEP occurred frequently in the early 1990s. Members of the state security forces are said to have been engaged in these incidents.[41] PKK engagement in drug trafficking is hardly possible without the cooperation of other Kurdish and Turkish organizations, especially in the western parts of Turkey. As investigations connected with the so-called Susurluk scandal have shown, the state authorities in the early 1990s cooperated with nationalist outlaws to fight the Kurdish mafia in Istanbul that was suspected to be connected with the drug trafficking and arms sales activities of the PKK.[42] Consequently, there is reason to assume that the Turkish illegal drug business is not only associated with the situation in the southeast but implies a national network of which the PKK is only one part, albeit an important one.

The village guard system installed by the Özal government in 1985 to support the fight against the PKK has developed into another obstacle for ending the fighting.[43] In this system, certain Kurdish tribes are hired by the state to secure their villages against attacks and infiltration of the PKK and support the Turkish armed forces in their operations against the PKK in the tribal area. For this purpose the state not only pays considerable sums to the tribe's leader but also provides the necessary weapons. Tens of thousands of Kurds in the rural areas of the southeast have been armed and have become dependent on this state salary. Because any ending of the state of emergency will be accompanied by a dissolution of the village guards, the Turkish state will have to provide other sources of income for them.

Parts of armed groups, together with other government agents, have become engaged in drug trafficking, arms sales, and other illegal activities, as has been shown by the so-called Yüksekova scandal.[44] Some village guards have used their weapons in the intertribal feuds that are still common in the southeast. The most prominent abuse of the village guards was by Sedat Buçak, a tribe leader and parliamentarian of the True Path Party of former Prime Minister Tansu Çiller. He was directly involved in the Susurluk incident and used his guards to protect him while in the hospital. When confronted with demands for a quick clear-up of the situation, he threatened to make use of his 10,000 men armed by the state. Dissolution of the village guard system may therefore become difficult because of the resistance of some tribal leaders to give up what has become a convenient state-sponsored private army.

The Kurdish Question in a Stalemate

The Kurdish problem is a major fault line within Turkish democracy. Despite the growing awareness among the public that the Kurdish issue is more than just a problem of terrorist separatism or economic and social underdevelopment and despite the threat to national unity that results from keeping the problem in its present unsatisfactory state, a solution is not on the horizon.

> One reason is that the Turkish political actors share different views about its origins. Second, officials do not feel that all alternatives have been fully explored. Third, economic hardships have not caused a total breakdown of the economy. Finally, national identity crises which emerged during the period of the RP/DYP government have resulted in the overdomination of a Kemalist nationalist ideology based on monocultural understanding of nationhood and the principle of protecting the unity of the existing Turkish state.[45]

The last point has convincingly been confirmed by the rise of the ultranationalist MHP in the last parliamentarian elections of April 18, 1999.

It must, however, be admitted that most political solutions of the problem put forward so far affect the unitary character of the Turkish republic. The principle of a unitary state can hardly be upheld unmodified if special treatment is granted to the Kurdish population in the southeastern provinces, even if the Kurds are not formally designated a minority. Legalizing Kurdish radio and television programs, making the teaching of the Kurdish language and culture a voluntary part of school curriculum, establishing departments of Kurdish studies at universities in the southeast and perhaps elsewhere, and allowing the use of Kurdish in official affairs in the southeast would constitute a recognition of political consequences due to ethnic and cultural differentiation within the one and undivided Turkish nation.

It is, however, questionable that a policy that only offers a serious attempt to overcome the economic and social underdevelopment of the southeast, accompanied by a complete abolishing of special measures such as the emergency status, the special regional governor, and the village guard system, as well as redirecting the task of fighting the PKK to the gendarmery by relocating most of the military out of the region would be sufficient in calming down the newly gained feeling of Kurdish pride. The alienation from the state seemingly has progressed too far to be redressed without any sign of recognition of the existence of a Kurdish identity as distinct from the Turkish majority.

There seems to be growing awareness of this fact among parts of the Turkish urban civil society and even among small minorities within the center-right and center-left parties. These liberal forces are, however, far too small and weak to initiate political reevaluation of the problem among the political elite. And the interests of the business community, which knows very well that the economic potential of regional development can only be fully realized if a lasting and self-sustaining stability is created, does not carry enough clout to induce the political majority and the military leadership to accept a fundamental change in policy.

The best one can hope for is that the military actions really have succeeded in encapsulating the PKK terror well enough that economic, social, and some carefully designed political development measures can be undertaken. This should be much easier now that Öcalan has been tried and the PKK further weakened, at least in the short run. The Turkish government has a chance to show magnanimity toward the Kurds, as many foreign and some Turkish observers have tried to suggest in the wake of Öcalan's capture.[46]

This magnanimity may be regarded by a majority of the southeast Kurdish people as a sign that there is some realistic hope for a normalization of the situation in the region. A slow but progressive return to normal living conditions that can already be seen in some areas and cities may also spread to the more rural districts, especially if accompanied by a thorough and generous policy of resettlement. All this can, however, at best lead to a shaky stability for which a lasting basis will also have to be created by more fundamental general change in Turkey's institutional and ideological political cosmos.

Turkey's Kurdish problem is more than just socioeconomic underdevelopment or the separatist terrorism of the PKK. It has to do with the difficult question of how to politically organize a multiethnic and multicultural society without endangering the legitimacy of the polity and its state. Even after the defeat of the PKK, the question will not go away as long as the state answers it in an unsatisfactory manner. The solution will not come in the southeastern and eastern Anatolian provinces unless it starts in the minds of Turkey's elites.

CHAPTER FIVE

The Revival of Political Islam

THE RISE TO POWER of the Welfare Party (Refah Partisi, or RP) and its leader Necmettin Erbakan in June 1996 sent shockwaves through the Turkish establishment and its Western allies. For the first time in its history the republic was governed by a party and a leader that had openly propagated a deviation from the established norms of Kemalism. Political Islam had taken over the helm of the government.

This event was not totally unexpected. For years the party had been on the rise. In fact, it had been the only party that constantly increased its voting share since 1984 when it had been allowed to participate in local elections for the first time after the reconstruction of Turkish democracy in 1983. The results of the general elections of December 24, 1995, when the RP came out as the leading party with a plurality of 21.4 percent of the vote, could be regarded as a harbinger of what happened in June 1996. Given the serious disagreements between the so-called secularist parties of the center-left and the center-right, it was evident that the formation of a stable and lasting government without the participation of RP would be very difficult. It took less than six months to reveal that it was impossible.

The retreat of Erbakan from power in June 1997 because of strong military and public pressure came as a relief to Turkey's Western-oriented elite. The Kemalist core group among the country's leadership then initiated a judicial process that ended with the dissolution of the party by a ruling of the Constitutional Court on January 16, 1998. This was regarded by the Kemalist elite, especially in the military and the judiciary, as the appropriate way to deal a strong blow to political Islam in Turkey to keep the country on its secularist and Western track. Considering the history of Turkey over the past thirty years, there is, however, ample reason to doubt the appropriateness and efficiency of such a measure in dealing with fundamental political and social developments that are regarded as deviations from the right path by the state.

The rise of the Welfare Party to power was the most obvious sign of the revival of political Islam in Turkey that took place, especially since the mid-1980s. Political Islam as such, however, is not a new phenomenon for republican Turkey, although the state was founded in clear contrast to the Ottoman past, which was strongly characterized by religious influences on politics and society. But beneath the secular surface of the republic, religious sentiments and entities have always been politically active.

What is new is the establishment of a far-reaching counterelite with a comprehensive alternative political program based on Islamic ideas.[1] Secularist Kemalism has lost its undisputed position in political ideology and practice. It is, however, doubtful that this development will lead to the creation of another Turkish republic characterized by the predominance of Islamic values and policies. There is more than just the clear-cut choice between Islamic fundamentalism and secular Kemalism, between East and West, or between Europe and the Islamic world.[2] The reality is more complex and developments are more undeterminable than is suggested by the political antagonism that prevailed in Turkish public life during the reign of the Welfare Party and that continues even after its dissolution.

Islam and the Turkish state or Turkish politics have never been as clearly separated as the Kemalist orthodox would like the public to believe. Political Islam in Turkey is far from being a unified and homogenous political movement centered on one party. The Welfare Party, in political and social terms, was much more than just the organizational face of political Islam. Finally, the real choice for the Turks in designing a modern state that is able to face the challenges of the twenty-first century is not between secularist Kemalism and fundamentalist political Islam. The real choice is between a more authoritarian, state-centered way of organizing a fast-changing society, of which Islam is an inexterminable social factor, and a more democratic, civic society–oriented way of dealing with change.

The Interplay of State Politics and Islam

Although the Turkish republic was conceived as a secularist nation-state by Mustafa Kemal, a conception that has become one of the cornerstones of modern Turkey's state ideology, Islam never ceased to be important in the country's public and political life. From the beginning there has been a contingent relationship between state politics and Islam. Even the success of Atatürk's war of independence would hardly have been possible without the mobilization of the religious sentiments of Anatolia's rural masses against the government of the sultan that acted under allied tutelage in Istanbul after the defeat of the Ottoman Empire in World War I.[3] For instance, Said Nursi, the leader of the influential Islamist Nurculuk movement, first propagated the cause of the Kemalist movement and only dissociated himself from Atatürk and his followers after he came into personal contact with them and their ideas.[4] Later on, state policy and party politics were instrumental in determining the political role of Islam in Turkey and thereby also in creating opportunities for political Islam to become an element of Turkish politics. "Islamic politics and movements . . . have been in large part shaped by the changing structure and ideology of the state and the centralist elites."[5]

Official and Unofficial Organization of Islam

Even Atatürk's attitude toward Islam was ambivalent. On the one hand, it symbolized backwardness that had to be overcome to make Turkey a modern nation-state. On the other hand, the new republic could not eradicate Islam overnight, and religion could be useful for establishing republican order.[6] Thus the Directorate for Religious Affairs (Diyanet, as shorthand for Diyanet İşleri Reisliği) was created and endowed with the task of controlling religious institutions by running the mosques and providing personnel for leading prayer and preaching. Although Islam as the official religion of the state was eradicated from the constitution in 1928, it became and remained a state affair via the directorate. The main task of the directorate and its officials was to "make Islam compatible with the modern nation-state."[7] Consequently, from the beginning, state and Islam in modern Turkey have never been separated, although state policies were to be designed and conducted without any relation to religious factors and the official ideology aimed at making religion a totally private affair.[8]

What developed instead was the continuation of the Ottoman situation with a dychotomized religion: an official, purist state Islam and a traditional folk Islam, sometimes mixed with mystical elements. They existed and developed under completely different political circumstances. State Islam was deprived of its powerful political representation, the national class of priests (*ulema),* which had been turned into officials of the Kemalist state. The activities of all institutions of folk Islam became illegal as a consequence of the Kemalist reforms.

Another dychotomy also existed: the schism between official Sunni Islam of the Hanefi school of Islamic thought as represented by the Diyanet, and the special variant of Shi'ism of Turkey's Alewite community that was more or less regarded as heretic by the forces of official Islam. Turkey's Alewites, who are said to constitute about a quarter of the population, show a pronounced secular leaning and a political tendency toward leftism or social-democratic orientation.[9] Given the Shi'ites' century-old discrimination by the Sunni majority of Anatolia, the secular Kemalist republic seemed to be the best guarantor for keeping their different religious identity and for practicing undisturbed their special interpretation of Islamic rites, although the new state did nothing to officially end their social and political discrimination.

Alewites are especially frightened by the idea of a growing Islamization of Turkey, given their experiences with Sunni radicalism and violence as had, for instance, been shown in the 1993 Sivas event and the 1995 Gaziosmanpaşa riots. In Sivas a group of Alewite intellectuals who had gathered in a hotel to commemorate a famous historical Alewite poet fell victim to an arson attack instigated by furious fundamentalist Sunni Muslims. The special political importance of this incident is to be seen in the hidden support given to the arsonists by the Islamist city administration, which did nothing to prevent the attack or capture the culprits.[10]

In the Istanbul city district of Gaziosmanpaşa where large groups of Alewites live, in March 1995 unknown assassins fired at coffeehouses, killing two men and wounding fifteen others. Afterward riots broke out when rumor spread that the attempt had an anti-Alewite religious background. People took to the street and clashed with police forces who used their weapons to disperse the rioters. Finally, the situation was brought under control by bringing in ordinary military because the enraged Alewites did not trust the police force, which is said to be strongly infiltrated by fundamentalist-nationalist elements.[11]

The events at Sivas and Gaziosmanpaşa contributed to a political awakening of Turkey's Alewites, who have since tried to better organize themselves to end their social and political ostracism. These efforts have resulted in a certain official recognition of the Alewites through granting some of their foundation's money from the state budget.[12] The Alewite awakening has, however, not led to a more pronounced political organization. Thus Alewite discontent with Turkey's social and political situation is restricted to either civil society or violent leftist political terrorism. Many of the remaining leftist splinter groups, such as Devrimçi Sol (or "Dev Sol," Revolutionary Left) or TIKKO (Workers and Peasants Liberation Army in Turkey), that arose in the late 1970s have a base among Alewite youth.

The introduction of a state-controlled official Islam by the republican authorities not only did not prevent the continuation of the Alewites, but folk Islam and its institutions, the religious orders (*tarikatler*) and communities (*cemaatler*), also clandestinely continued their activities among the rural masses of Anatolia. This went almost unnoticed and undisturbed by the state as long as the groups refrained from open political opposition. The harsh and violent repression of any such opposition to Atatürk's policy induced the peripheral Islam to turn deeply inwards.

Islam is more heterogeneous in Turkey than in many other Islamic states.[13] There is a great variety of religious orders and communities. All of them advocate Islam as the leading principle for personal and public life, but they differ considerably in their organizational structure and strength, the social composition of their followers, relations with official institutions, and policies for promoting their goals. As the organized "survivors" of the Kemalist struggle against the public influence of Islam, they constitute the source of today's political Islam in Turkey. Besides them, there are some small radical Islamic organizations that are prone to violence in pursuing their cause.[14] And finally, there are so-called Islamic intellectuals who exert considerable influence in academic and student circles but who are not directly linked to Islamic orders or communities.[15] These diversified Islamic groups and persons who claim Islam to be more than just a private affair and who actively promote their version of a true Islamic life make it difficult to perceive political Islam in Turkey as a monolithic and predominantly agressive force.

The broad base of political Islam is formed by the various religious orders and communities.[16] Among them, two are of special importance: the Nakşibendi order and its numerous suborganizations, and the Nurcu movement and its suborganizations that can be regarded as derived from the Nakşibendis.[17] These conceive of themselves as predominantly religious, nonpublic organizations, the basic goal of which is to educate their followers and the Turkish population in general in the conduct of a correct Islamic life. For them, Islam is the only recipe for organizing personal affairs and public affairs as well.

> Tarikats are functional in contemporary Turkey because they offer people a sense of belonging to a community, human companionship, a set of guiding rules, identity, and organization. They also respond to the needs of people concretely by offering financial support, accommodation, and a network for improving professional contacts. They function as social welfare institutions in Turkey where almost 30 percent of the population have no social protection.[18]

They work through society rather than the state. Their aim is a cultural revolution rather than direct political revolution or an armed uprising. Their means are education and networking rather than open political organization. Their goal, however, is to replace the Kemalist state by a political system that obeys religious rules. Many in Turkey regard this indirect attack on the republic to be more dangerous than the open political work of Islamist parties.

The continuation of religious orders and communities was not really countered by a state policy of a nationwide spreading of the Kemalist ideology. The restructuring of the national economy after the almost total eradication of the former business elites of Greeks and Armenians and the restructuring of the state apparatus on the basis of the new republican secular values and habits clearly dominated the official agenda in the formative period of the republic. The vast rural areas were very much left to their own as were the Kurdish areas in the east and southeast. "Republican institutions and values trailed off into the solitary relations of ascriptive groups when they reached the periphery."[19] For many years the Kemalist principles remained alien to the majority of Turkey's population.

The officials of the Directorate of Religious Affairs (DRA) never became convinced Kemalists, although they normally tried to fulfil the duty they had been charged with by the state authorities. The institution developed a split loyalty toward the republic and its ideology and toward Islam as the subject of its activities. This led, for instance, to the somewhat paradoxical situation that the directorate and its subordinate institutions as agents of the secularist state continued to issue legal opinions (*fetwas*) that are based on Islamic law (*shar'ia*). Although the institution as such carefully refrains from commenting on political matters, at the local community level its representatives do express political views, mainly during Friday prayers, that often deviate from the official state ideology.[20]

Whereas the role and size of the directorate was limited until 1950, "the size, activities, and responsibilities of the department have expanded enormously. The DRA has a central apparatus in Ankara, with local branches in all provinces and sub-provinces throughout Turkey, and 63,053 chaplains and preachers in the 68,675 mosques under its control."[21] It is estimated that allocations in the 1999 draft budget that directly or indirectly serve the state religious interests are about TL 300 trillion, a sum that is not much less than that foreseen for education.

Education and İmam Hatip Schools

The development of state-formatted Islam was accompanied by an extension of religious education after 1950. Theological faculties have been established in many universities, and vocational high schools for the training of prayer leaders and preachers (*İmam Hatip Lisesi*) have been established in growing numbers all over the country. In certain periods of center-right party governments the establishment of such religious-oriented schools even outnumbered the establishment of normal high schools, not to speak of vocational high schools for more mundane purposes. "In 1963, there were forty-five 'schools of preachers and imams' (*imam-hatip okullari*) with 9,248 students; fifteen years later, in 1978 . . . the number of pupils had grown to 135,000."[22] More than 500,000 students have graduated from these schools.

Originally conceived as institutions for the limited purpose of raising the necessary numbers of religious experts needed by the directorate to fulfill its functions, the number of İmam Hatip Schools has grown out of proportion. Even female students have been admitted, although there is little need for female personnel in Islamic religious institutions. Over the years İmam Hatip Schools have developed into a parallel education system for all those who do not want to let their children pass through the secular education system. In this way a growing number of high school graduates with an explicit religious background has entered all professional strata of Turkey's public and private sectors; a military career is the single exception.[23] Today, many bureaucrats in public administration, the judiciary, and especially in education have a religious educational background, according to Turkish press reports.

Educational activities in a broad sense are a speciality of today's most prominent religious movement, the Fethullahcılar, named after the leader Fethullah Gülen, a former follower of Said Nursi and employee of the Diyanet, who established his own community.[24] His educational program tries to reconcile religious and secular elements in a common concept that combines Islam with modern logic, religious education with positivist science. With the financial contributions of his followers, Gülen established an empire of secondary schools, preparatory schools, boarding houses, and meeting houses for students that not only furnish the needs of the Fethullahcılar but are open to public attendance as well and now help Gülen earn money for the further expansion of his community's activities.

In recent years the movement has opened a large number of private secondary schools in Central Asia and other parts of the former Soviet Union and also in some Balkan states. Their aim is to provide high-quality modern education for the future elites of the newly independent republics together with teaching a kind of Turkish-Islamic philosophy. In a certain way, Gülen and his movement can be regarded as the most contemporary representation of the idea of a Turkish-Islamic synthesis. This secures him even the sympathy of Democratic Left Party (DSP) leader and prime minister Bülent Ecevit, who has a reputation as a staunch defender of Turkey's secularist principles.

Because of this development in the policy of Islamic groups, education has become a subject of contention between secular and religious forces in Turkey. This has clearly been demonstrated by the circumstances that led to the resignation of the Erbakan government. The resistance against complying with the demand of the military leadership for the introduction of an uninterrupted secular elementary education of eight years was the main issue leading to the fierce military-led public campaign against Erbakan's coalition government in spring 1997.

The haste with which his successor, Mesut Yılmaz, introduced the educational reform against strong resistance from traditional forces immediately after having taken office emphasizes the urgency that the Turkish General Staff ascribed to the issue.[25] The abolition of the middle-school level of İmam Hatip High Schools as a consequence of the reform was of paramount importance for the military in order to deal a lasting and severe blow to the spread of Islamic ideas in the country's educational system. Now Turkish children have to follow the official secularist curriculum until the ninth grade and can only become exposed to a more religious education about the age of fourteen. In this way the military and their civilian supporters in the state elite and general public hope to effectively stop the "creeping Islamization" of Turkey's future elite.[26]

Center-Right Parties and Political Islam

The success of this measure seems, however, arguable, given the interplay between politics and religion that has become one characteristic of Turkey's party politics since 1950 when the single-party reign of the Kemalist Republican People's Party finally came to an end. The center-right parties that have been in power almost uninterruptedly since then tried to promote "the incorporation of Islam as a living cultural tradition into the mainstream of Turkish politics."[27] Simultaneously, they opened up politics to the social forces of the periphery that had been excluded from public affairs by the Kemalist state elite.[28] Thus the public sphere was opened to the forces of traditional folk Islam that had been excluded from public influence by the representatives of state Islam. All this definitely ended the separation of the religious and the public spheres of Turkish society. The coexistence between political and religious organizations has led to an incremental reestablishment of Islam in the Turkish public. Already in the 1950s, observers started to speak of an Islamic revival.[29]

This development did not, however, lead to a pronounced Islamization of Turkey and Turkish politics. All center-right parties are firmly entrenched in the relatively young republican and the even younger democratic tradition of modern Turkey. The softening of Kemalist principles and the use of religion for political purposes in no way meant for the parties a basic deviation from the foundations of the republic. The leadership of the Democrat Party (1950–60) as well as the leadership of the Justice Party (1961–80) under Süleyman Demirel categorically rejected religious fanaticism.[30] This even holds true for Turgut Özal, who became known as the first Turkish prime minister to publicly fulfill the religious obligation of pilgrimage to Mecca.

All the leaders established good relations with the leaders of influential religious orders such as the Nurcular movement or the Nakşibendi order that helped organize the traditional vote in the rural areas. In this way a considerable number of the religious organizations became involved in the patron-client networks characteristic of Turkish politics.[31] Given the fragmented party system and fluid party affiliations, the competition for electoral support of the various religious groups has become an element of electioneering. The center-right parties vie with each other and with the Islamist Party for the "tarikat vote," the organized support of religious orders and communities. Even the icon of left secular politics, veteran politician Bülent Ecevit, openly has displayed his sympathies for the "moderate" Islamist Fetullah Gülen.[32]

During the 1960s, members of the influential İskender Pasha Convent of the Nakşibendi order, under their leader Mehmet Zait Kotku, systematically tried to infiltrate agencies such as the State Planning Organization, the

Ministry of Education, and the Ministry of Internal Affairs. Most Nurculuk groups tended to have lasting relations with the leading center-right party of the 1950s, the Democrat Party, and its various successors. Another religious community with a Nakşibendi orientation, the Süleymancılar, has "always had connections with bureaucrats, deputies, and big capitalists."[33] The political success of Süleyman Demirel's Justice Party in the 1960s was, among other things, a result of its close connections with the leading Islamic orders.

Members of religious organizations are said to have become deputies, especially after the Motherland Party of Turgut Özal came to power in the 1983 elections. Özal and his brother Korkut, the leader of the (insignificant) reestablished Democrat Party, are said to have been or to be members of the Nakşibendi order themselves. The political success of Özal's Motherland Party in the 1980s depended to a considerable extent on the support of this important Islamic order. The same applies to the National Salvation Party that is said to be actually a brainchild of Nakşibendi Sheik Kotku, and its successor, the Welfare Party, both under the leadership of Necmettin Erbakan.[34] Welfare's rise to power is also a result of the political reorientation of the Nakşibendi leadership after Özal's retreat from his post as party leader of ANAP when he was elected president of the republic in 1989. His successors in the party leadership, Yıldırım Akbulut and Mesut Yılmaz, were of a more secular leaning and tried to diminish the influence of ANAP's Islamic wing.[35]

This inclusion of Islamic organizations into the political system proved to be an effective means in preventing the political radicalization of Islam in Turkey. At the same time, the inclusion united the center-right parties, the Islamist groups, and the military leadership in the struggle against leftists and communists, who were regarded as a serious threat to the republican order during the 1960s and 1970s. A dose of religion was considered by all groups to be an effective vaccination against leftism.

The opening of politics to religious influence, however, also paved the way for the establishment of an Islamic party. With the appearance of the National Order Party (Millî Nizâm Partisi, or MNP) under the leadership of Necmettin Erbakan in 1970, the Turkish Islamic movement was no longer limited to providing a value system for organizing and guiding the personal and social life of the more traditional parts of Turkey's society. It now also became an ideology for gaining political power. In that respect it was and is bound to clash with the official secularist doctrine of the republic. Thus it was no surprise when the new party "was disbanded by the

Constitutional Court a year later for violating the Law on the Organization of Political Parties, which forbade the exploitation of religion for political purposes."[36] The same fate was experienced by its successor, the National Salvation Party (Millî Selamet Partisi, or MSP), that had been established in 1972, again by Erbakan, after the third military coup in 1980.

The Islamization of Secularism and the Rise of the Fethullahcılar

The first half of the 1980s marked a new stage in the interplay between state politics and Islam, the "Islamization of secularism."[37] The military leadership that de facto ran politics until 1983 now openly relied on religion as a means of reeducating the people. The concept of a Turkish-Islamic synthesis linking Turkish nationalism to moderate Islam as a modern ideological basis for the Turkish state became the unofficial basis for reconstructing state and society after the coup.[38] This political-philosophical idea was first developed by a group of conservative intellectuals, the Aydınlar Ocağı (Intellectual Hearth) in the early 1970s. In a somewhat simplified description, the main goal of this Islamically revamped secularism has been termed as the creation of "an unmistakable Sunni Muslim identity accompanied by all the personal freedom of a Western democracy, with a heavy dose of Turkish nationalism and pride thrown in for 'solidarity.'"[39]

As a result, the teaching of Islam was made obligatory in primary and secondary schools by the new constitution of 1982, and international Islamic organizations under the dominant influence of Saudi Arabia, such as the World Islamic League, were allowed to become involved in Turkish public affairs. They provided salaries for functionaries of the Directorate for Religious Affairs who were sent to Germany and Belgium to organize religious instruction and services for Turkish migrants in Europe. The league was also engaged in constructing a small mosque for the Turkish parliament and establishing mosques and Islamic centers at various universities, among them the prestigious Middle East Technical University in Ankara. Alongside these activities, Saudi financial institutions such as Faisal Finance Corporation and al-Baraka Financial Corporation established Turkish affiliates under preferential conditions.[40]

The military under General Kenan Evren, the leader of the 1980 coup who was president of the republic until 1989, wanted to use Islam to reconsolidate the foundations of the Kemalist republic that, in the view of the armed forces, had been severely shaken by leftist violence. This impetus went so far as to rewrite secondary schoolbooks to reconcile Islamic and national values following the slogan, "The best Turk is a Muslim Turk—the best Muslim is a Turkish Muslim."[41] However, the military had to realize, especially after the surprise victory of Turgut Özal and his Motherland Party in the elections of 1983, that under the newly adopted policy of economic liberalization and opening toward the outside world the traditional state control of society became much more difficult to maintain.

The Islamic revival flourished under the tutelage of the religious-oriented wing of ANAP and a prime minister who did not give much credit to political ideology, including the official ideology of Kemalism, if it ran counter to his ideas of making Turkey a leading economic and political regional power by the turn of the century. The Motherland Party "mobilized Turkey's traditionally conservative constituencies and some Islamic platforms around the cause of economic liberalism, integrating them with the existing order in the process."[42] Although Özal had no intentions of undermining the secularist order of the state, his seemingly laissez-faire approach to political Islam gave rise to growing concerns of the Kemalist elites who, by the end of the decade, used to evoke the danger of *irtica*, religious reactionaryism and obscurantism, due to the growth of Islamic activities of all kinds, including the militancy of some small organizations.[43]

During these years and especially since the early 1990s Fethullah Gülen and his followers have become the most prominent Islamic representatives of the Turkish-Islamic synthesis and have achieved widespread political prominence as a moderate Islamic counterforce to the seemingly more radical positions of Erbakan's Welfare Party. Gülen's movement has taken an explicit state-oriented and nonconflictual position in the political debate about the preservation of the secular republic.[44] This brought him into especially close connection with Tansu Çiller and her DYP. However, more orthodox Islamists criticize him for treason to the Islamic cause.

Indeed, Gülen's almost total accommodation to the state structures and policies and his equally strong emphasis on Islam as the true path for conducting a correct life and organizing society is sometimes difficult to understand.[45] For some observers, this is simply an especially skillful demonstration of *takkiye*, a permitted behavior of disguise for the sake of promoting the cause of Islam, whereas others see in his approach to furthering Islam in Turkey and elsewhere a modern way of reconciling Islam with democracy.[46] Still, Gülen's strong emphasis on tolerance as a guiding principle of life in and among nations as well as among religions is a remarkable stance in an otherwise sometimes highly politicized public debate about the right path for Turkey and its people.[47] This does not, however, prevent him from exercising an authoritarian leadership within his community.

The Fethullahcılar's moderate and pro-state approach to sensitive political issues has not prevented the military leadership from putting Gülen and his movement high on its list of organizations that wanted to undermine the republic. As a result, most expulsions from the military during the past four years have been officers who were accused of being members or followers of Gülen's community. The movement is accused of pursuing a long-term strategy by seeking to place graduates from its various schools in positions within the state administration. Here they can not only further the Islamic cause but may also influence the award of public tenders and contracts, including the approval of private schools, in favor of companies and organizations that belong to Gülen's "empire."[48]

Such suspicions seemed to have been confirmed by a videotape that was shown on a private television channel in June 1999 in which Gülen made antisecularist remarks, speaking of his strategy to overtake the system in the long run and advising his audience to act cautiously, because "if [Muslims] . . . come out early, the world will squash their heads."[49] These revelations caused some political unrest because of Gülen's well-known friendly relations with many leading politicians. They may have been the start of another round in the state's fight against Islamist tendencies.[50]

The Growth of an Islamic Business Community

The growth in the number of Islamic businesses in the Turkish economy is another result of the more open and nonspiritual activity of religious orders and communities.[51] Some of these businesses, such as İhlas Holding or Kombassan Holding, surpass the level of traditional small and medium-sized companies and are ranked among Turkey's large holding companies. In 1990 the Islamic businesses founded their own organization, the Independent Industrialists and Businessmen's Association (MÜSİAD), which has become the fastest-growing and largest business organization in the country. Among its members are many companies that have been labeled "Anatolian tigers" because of their highly successful effort to mobilize the industrial activities in rural centers such as Denizli, Çorum, and Gaziantep.[52]

Islamic business tends to make use of religion for economic purposes. In doing so it stresses the Eastern and Islamic values of more communitarian societies that contradict the Western capitalist separation of industrialists and employees as well as the need to defend one's country's indigenous culture and social order against a superficial Westernization.[53] This economic philosophy with its strong Islamic connotations is, however, put to the service of economic success of the individual firm and of Turkey in the globalized economy.

In this sense the evolution of the Islamic economic sector is another sign of a certain secularization of Islam in Turkey. It fits very well into this picture of "modern Turkish Islam" that MÜSİAD and its member companies have tried to profit as much as possible from the governmental activities of the Welfare Party. Erbakan tried to turn away from the established channels with the Istanbul-dominated Turkish business and industrial community activities such as tenders, public procurement, and privatization of state economic enterprises. Thus Islamic business in Turkey does not want to have a different state with Islamic structures but the actual state structures to be run by a different social elite that is more congenial to its own ideas and economic interests.

This vision coincides with that of the most prominent religious orders and communities, with which the Islamic sector of the economy is linked by a network of personal relations. This linkage also supports the generally moderate attitude of the orders and communities toward the modern Turkish state and its policies. Together with their intensive relations with various traditional political forces and their nonagressive way of promoting their Islamic belief, the linkage is an important contribution to the preservation of overall political stability in Turkey.

The Beginnings of Turkey's Kulturkampf

Through their involvement in Turkish society the religious orders and communities prevent the sometimes sharp ideological controversies between Kemalists and Islamists from turning into politically motivated violence. And they prevent antisystemic Islamic groups and forces from gaining dominance among Muslim believers. That is not to say that some of them such as the Nakşibendi do not severely criticize various political actions taken by state institutions and political forces. But in the end most large religious orders and communities support the idea of a strong nation-state based on Islam and republicanism, which is the reality of today's republic. What they despise is the emphasis on Kemalist secular values as displayed by the state elite.

This position cannot satisfy the defenders of the Kemalist secular republic. Thus since the political success of the Welfare Party, the military leadership, the Kemalist-inspired parts of the high judiciary, and a majority of Turkey's leading journalists have tried to stem what they regard as an Islamic tide aimed at changing the basic character of the republic.[54] But the economic, social, and political situation of Turkey changed considerably during the 1980s, becoming more open and pluralistic. Consequently, state action against Islamic activities has given rise to passionate public debates in which proponents of Islamic positions openly defended their case. The most prominent example of this was the "headscarf debate" over the official ban in universities of what was regarded as religious dress of female students.[55]

These political debates were accompanied by the growth of ideological Islamic discourse in intellectual circles, and Islamist journals and books poured forth in a hitherto unknown quantity.[56] The resurgence of the Welfare Party was a logical consequence of this development. At the same time, the Kemalist part of the state elite, especially the military leadership, intensified efforts to contain the Islamist movement, which was again regarded as a serious threat to the republic. After the end of the cold war and the demise of the Soviet Union, Islam was no longer needed to stop communist and other leftist attempts to undermine Turkish society.

However, the self-inflicted weakness of the center-right parties together with increased political infighting among the political elites after the death of Turgut Özal in 1993 led to greater alienation of the established representatives of the political system from large parts of the population. This created an environment in which, for the first time in the republic's history, political Islam and its various proponents fully established themselves as an undisputed, legitimate part of Turkish politics: political pluralism in Turkey today includes political Islam.

The Welfare Party: More Than Just a Political Interlude

The importance of political Islam could not have been better proved than by the coming to power of Turkey's first Islamist-led government in June 1996 when Necmettin Erbakan, leader of the Welfare Party, became prime minister of a coalition government formed with Tansu Çiller's True Path Party. This event had been foreshadowed by RP's victory at the municipal elections of March 1994, when the party gained the mayorship in six out of Turkey's fifteen largest cities, among them Greater Istanbul and Ankara. This surprise success was followed by an equally powerful showing in the general elections of December 24, 1995, in which the Welfare Party came out with 21.4 percent of the total vote.[57]

The Kemalist elite from the military leadership to the top-level state officials to the leading newspapers and private associations were not ready to accept this change. After a short interlude of digesting the unexpected, they started a political campaign to reverse the results. As a consequence, since autumn 1996 Turkey has experienced a battle for political hegemony. It mainly took the form of *kulturkampf* between the Islamist elite and the Kemalists about the continuation of the secularist outlook of the republic as defined by the old elites. This battle came to a temporary end with the banning of the Welfare Party in January 1998 by the verdict of the Constitutional Court.

The problems of dealing with the representatives of political Islam are clearly shown by the elites' recourse to legal responses. Upon a more distant and less agitated inspection the political practice of the Welfare-led government does not reveal such a disruption of established politics that elimination of the party at almost all costs seemed to be justified. And this practice was not only caused by consideration for the interests of its secular coalition partner. The behavior of the RP's representatives in government and parliament hardly revealed a strong impetus in the direction of establishing an Islamic republic. What cannot, however, be excluded was a strategy of furthering the creeping Islamization of Turkey by low-profile government activities that aimed at a long-term change of the basic tenets of the republic toward more pronounced Islamic values and practices.

This change has been under way for some time and has even been furthered by the very groups that since 1996 have been fighting the battle against "reactionaryism," the official term for Islamism or political Islam. Creeping Islamization had already occurred under Erbakan when his National Salvation Party (Millî Selamet Partisi, or MSP) was a partner in Demirel's national front coalition governments in the second half of the 1970s. One long-term consequence of the policy of departmentalizing public institutions according to party preferences has been the movement of Turkey's educational system toward providing greater attention to religion. This development has mainly been aided by officials who had been implanted in the system, first during the MSP's period in government and later under the influence of the military's policy of "religious vaccination" against leftism after the 1980 coup. Thus the political practice of the RP-led administrations of the 1990s at the local and national level met with a public that had increasingly become aquainted with such practices and the social values they represented.

This led to the political problem Turkey's secularist circles are facing today of how to deal with an antisystemic political force under the conditions of democratic pluralism. The task is to separate legitimate political competition from illegal political activities. The challenge is especially difficult if the political group or party under suspicion refrains from any action or political propaganda advocating the abolition of the existing political order by violent means. How far should political rhetoric be tolerated that openly or in metaphorical terms asks for another political system to be introduced? Are there limits to the freedom of expression of one's political ideas, and where are these limits?

The answer has been to narrow the limits of political competition and expand the definition of illegal political activity by sticking to a purist interpretation of the Kemalist bases of the republic. In this way the political confrontation of divergent ideologies is largely replaced by legal acts of the state's authorities. The defense of the existing system is conducted less by political argument and more by authoritative actions of state agencies.[58] The more far-reaching question, however, is what will be the long-term effects for Turkish democracy of this heavy-handed way of dealing with fundamental political difference. Will the enforced limitation of Islamist tendencies permanently curb the influence of political Islam in Turkey or could it create a growing class of political outcasts who are waiting for revenge? The answer is unclear. But the experience of dealing with political Islam in power and as an important contender for power demonstrates the difficulties connected with the attempt to eradicate a political force that can build upon well-entrenched social values and habits of a considerable part of the country's population.

The Practice of Welfare Party Government

The Islamist-led coalition government did not deviate far from Turkish mainstream politics. It followed the practices of political patronage. Erbakan tried to secure his position by a large-scale reshuffling of government officials that traditionally takes place after a change in government. The secular newspapers condemned a practice that until then had been regarded as normal because this time it was RP members and followers suspected of fundamentalist leanings who got hold of many, sometimes influential, state offices. A reshuffling of some hundred judicial personnel initiated by Welfare Minister of Justice Şevket Kazan, a veteran aid to Erbakan, was heavily criticized by the media and later stopped by the intervention of administrative courts.[59]

In foreign policy Çiller and Erbakan developed a kind of division of labor, with the deputy prime minister taking care of relations with Europe and the Western allies, while the prime minister tried to establish the first elements of what could be termed a more Islamic foreign policy. His overtures to Iran and Libya were, however, much criticized by the public and the foreign policy establishment. In essentials of security policy, Erbakan completely bowed to the demands of the military, be it with regard to the continuation of the fight against the PKK and the allied supervision of the Kurdish safe haven in northern Iraq or strengthening ties with Israel. Interestingly enough, forging closer ties with Turkish kin in the newly established republics of Central Asia and in the Transcaucasus did not rank prominently among Erbakan's foreign policy activities.[60]

In domestic affairs the Welfare Party made few attempts to leave its imprint. After having been stiffly rebuffed by the military in the National Security Council, Erbakan refrained from trying to bring about an "Islamic solution" of the Kurdish question, although the party received a lot of support in Kurdish areas because of the party's nonnationalistic, religious-inspired approach to the problem.[61] The RP also abstained from any efforts at furthering the democratization of Turkey. It went, however, some way to rescue Tansu Çiller from parliament's investigations of corruption allegations that had been brought forward not least by Erbakan himself when he was in opposition in spring 1996. In the same manner the party cooperated with its coalition partner in shelving the so-called Susurluk scandal, in which again Mrs. Çiller and some of her closest political aides were accused of close links with organized crime. One can therefore argue that Erbakan, too, did not stand the test of political ethics, contrary to the image that he and his followers might have created by their propagation of a "just order" (*adil düzen*).

Partly as a consequence of growing party criticism of his political record, partly in following their deep convictions, Erbakan and his closest aides tried to establish an agenda of soft policy proposals that could be regarded as an effort at furthering the silent Islamization of Turkey. During the Islamic holy month of Ramadan (mainly in January 1997) they advocated building mosques on Istanbul's Taksim Square and in Ankara's Çankaya district, which both have certain republican associations, the one decorated with an Atatürk monument commemorating the war of independence, the other the official residential area of the republic's president.[62] They advocated lifting the ban on wearing head scarves in public buildings and proposed to take away from the Turkish Civil Aviation Foundation the right of collecting and selling the hides of sacrificial sheep and give the right to religious foundations. They also wanted to change working hours during Ramadan to bring them more into line with religious requirements and were in favor of loosening the control of the Directorate of Religious Affairs over the organization of the pilgrimage by allowing overland travel to Mecca.[63]

Although not very spectacular to a Western observer, the realization of these proposals would have meant a clear break with the established cultural tradition of the Kemalist republic and, in some cases, would have contravened constitutional law. It remained, however, unclear how determined Erbakan really was to achieve his plans because he made no strong attempts to get the necessary parliamentary process going for their implementation.[64]

The Kemalist elite nevertheless reacted with indignation and severe criticism that was further fueled by provocative events caused by RP politicians. On November 10, 1996, the mayor of Kayseri, a central Anatolian business center under RP control, publicly announced that he did not like to have to participate in the traditional Atatürk commemoration on that day.[65] In mid-January 1997, amidst a lively public debate about the role and practices of religious orders, Prime Minister Erbakan invited several leaders of such orders whose activity had been banned by Atatürk to his official residence for a meal to break the fast. Finally, on February 2, 1997, the RP mayor of Sincan, a small town near Ankara, and the Iranian ambassador to Turkey, who had been invited to celebrate the remembrance of the Palestinian *intifada* with a so-called Jerusalem night, made speeches that could be understood as appeals to overthrow the republican order.[66] The next day the Turkish army sent tanks through the streets of Sincan. The mayor was imprisoned, and Iran had to withdraw its ambassador.

The Kemalist Elite Strikes Back

After these events, and perhaps stimulated by strong public protests against political corruption, alleged mafia links of politicians and state security officials, and growing signs of Islamic fundamentalism in the RP, the military leadership decided to demand an ultimatum from the Erbakan-Çiller government announcing decisive political measures against the spread of fundamentalism. On February 28, 1997, the military confronted the prime minister in a routine meeting of the National Security Council with a program of eighteen points that were aimed at making impossible the realization of the proposals that had been circulated by RP's leadership in the preceding months. The military also asked for measures that would prevent any new attempts of Islamist forces to weaken the Kemalist principles. The military demanded, for instance, enforcing the existing constitutional prohibitions concerning the activities of religious orders and the official dress code. Above all, they demanded the introduction of compulsory uninterrupted eight-year elementary education, strict control of Koran courses by the Ministry of Education, a reduction in the number of İmam Hatip Schools, and several measures aimed at curtailing the Welfare Party's maneuvering room, for instance, by restricting its financial support from Islamic associations abroad such as the Germany-based National View Association (Millî Görüş Teşkilatı).[67]

When Erbakan tried to stall by not calling a meeting of the cabinet for weeks, the military began a public campaign to end the coalition. It kept the pressure on the prime minister during the monthly meetings of the National Security Council; provided comprehensive, publicized briefing meetings by the General Staff for judicial personnel, journalists, and other professional groups on the dangers of Islamic fundamentalism; and established a special West Working Group within the General Staff for monitoring Islamist activities in Turkey.[68] Public concern grew about the Islamist danger and expressed itself most notably in a common public appeal by the most prominent business and trade union organizations for an end of the coalition.[69]

After pressure on his coalition partner had been increased by the resignation of some fifteen DYP deputies, Erbakan had no choice but to resign with the hope of engineering an intracoalition reshuffle of the post of prime minister to Tansu Çiller. This plan did not work because president Süleyman Demirel installed the minority three-party coalition government of Mesut Yılmaz, who secured a majority in parliament with the assistance of the Republican People's Party. The experiment of an Islamist-influenced government had come to an end after less than a year.

Ousting the RP from government was not regarded by the leading representatives of the Kemalist elite as enough to seriously fight Islamic fundamentalism. The military continued to point to the risk constituted by Turkey's various Islamic movements.[70] The Constitutional Court remained busy in the petition for Welfare's abolition filed by the state prosecutor of the Ankara Court of Appeals on May 21, 1997, on the grounds that the party had become the focal point of antisecular activity. After months of deliberations and procedural haggling with the party leadership and its legal representatives, the Constitutional Court dissolved the party on January 16, 1998, because of, among other things, violations of articles 68 and 69 of the constitution that forbid antisecular activities by political parties. This also meant the end of the party in the Turkish Grand National Assembly, the members of which formally became independent members of parliament. When the verdict took effect after the publication of its reasoning in the *Resmi Gazete* (Official Gazette) on February 22, 1998, Erbakan together with five other RP parliamentarians, three of whom meanwhile had been expelled from the party, lost their seats in parliament and their parliamentary immunity. This enabled the judiciary to take up personal charges against them for violating laws protecting the secular character of the republic.[71]

After fourteen years of increasing influence in politics and after having become the strongest political party, the Welfare Party was disbanded.[72] But this did not mean that political Islam in Turkey had ceased to exist nor that its representation in party politics had ended. Political Islam always had a much broader base than the Welfare Party and even it had already found a successor when the Constitutional Court put an end to its existence: on December 17, 1997, the Virtue Party (Fazilet Partisi, or FP) had been founded by one of Erbakan's close aides to take in the remnants of RP in case the party should be dissolved.

On February 23, 1998, forty-one former RP and now formally independent deputies joined the FP, which immediately formed a new parliamentary group that grew over the next few days to the strength of the former RP parliamentary group.[73] Over the next weeks, almost all RP mayors and their backers in the local assemblies also became members of the FP. Erbakan managed to put his loyal aides into the leading positions of the new party by curbing an attempt of the so-called young guard of the Welfare Party to gain more influence in the Virtue Party.[74] Thus the Welfare Party's ideology and its electoral constituency would continue to be represented in Turkey's political landscape.

The FP followed the established Welfare Party practice of keeping a fairly low profile with regard to decidedly Islamist political demands and views. The party was, however, handicapped. First, although legally banned from taking any office in the party, Erbakan continued his efforts to control all important political and organizational decisions. This hindered the official leadership around Recai Kutan from establishing itself as the decisive institution within the party. Second, the internal dispute between the traditionalists around Erbakan and his long-time companions and the modernizers around Recep Tayyip Erdoğan continued.[75] To followers and outsiders the party's image was no longer that of a homogenous political grouping.

Another hinderance to Virtue's political effectiveness was the unabated fight of the Kemalist elites against Islamist tendencies on all fronts. The Supreme Board of Higher Education (YÖK) enforced a dress code for university personnel and students that was intended to eliminate any Islamic appearance from campuses, especially head scarves for women and beards cut in a "religious manner" for men.[76] Students rebelled at many universities, especially in Istanbul. The rebellions reached a peak at the beginning of the universities' term in October 1998 when thousands of pious Muslim students could not continue their studies because they were forced to apply with documents, the photographs of which had to show them without head scarves or beards.

Organized political Islam endured another severe blow when Tayyip Erdoğan, the mayor of Greater Istanbul, was sentenced to a ten-month prison term by the State Security Court of Diyarbakır in April 1998 on charges of "having incited hatred among the people" with a speech he had given in Siirt in late 1997. The sentence was upheld by the court of appeals, and Erdoğan was removed from office. An implication of the sentence was that he would never again be allowed to take a public office or run for parliament. Unless the political situation changes, the most promising representative of the younger generation of Islamist politicians has ended his political career.[77]

Another target of the war of attrition against Islamists was the so-called green capital, the Islamic business sector. In April 1998 a group of prominent Islamic businessmen were searched and interrogated about money laundering and illegal financing of the Welfare Party.[78] And in May the chairman of MÜSİAD, Erol Yarar, was charged by the Ankara State Security Court with "having incited hatred among the people" in a speech he had delivered at a closed meeting in October 1997. The prosecutor also demanded that the organization be banned.[79] In April 1999 the Ankara State Security Court sentenced Yarar to sixteen months imprisonment, but it postponed the sentence for five years' probation. The demand for the dissolution of MÜSİAD was rejected.[80] A serious warning signal had been given to Islamist business not to overstep the limits of its professional realm.

Meanwhile, the parliament enacted legislation by which the building and running of mosques would be brought under the full control of the Diyanet. This measure should curb the influence of Islamic orders and communities by preventing them from having their own mosques.[81] At the same time, the Supreme Board of Radio and Television (RTÜK) issued a warning against Islamist television and radio stations not to misuse religion and discussed technical measures to be taken against stations if they disobeyed.[82]

All these actions were said to be part of another military-led campaign against the spread of Islamic fundamentalism. In principle they had been decided on in a meeting of the National Security Council on March 29, 1998, to follow up the banning of the Welfare Party. In that meeting the NSC declared that "there are still people and organizations which are trying to exploit religion for their own gains and the activities of these will not be tolerated."[83]

The Virtue Party tried to avoid becoming an explicit target of the anti-Islamist policies by maintaining a low profile and refraining from pro-Islamic rhetoric. The party gained public attention again when, after the resignation of Mesut Yılmaz as prime minister in November 1998, the task of forming a new government raised the question of the role of the largest group in parliament, Virtue itself. President Demirel and the military leadership made it clear to anybody that inclusion of Virtue in a government formula was out of the question.[84] In January 1999 this resulted in Bülent Ecevit's forming a one-party DSP minority government, the main task of which was to take the country to early elections in April 1999.

Political Islam suffered a severe setback in the election when the Virtue Party could gather only 15.41 percent of the vote, which translated into 111 seats in the National Assembly. With this result it became only the third largest party in Turkey. It fared better, however, than any of the traditional center-right parties. Although the secular Kemalist vote seemed to have rallied around Ecevit and his DSP, that part of the traditional Anatolian vote that could not warm itself to Virtue selected the nationalist MHP as its representative.[85]

The electoral setback may also have been caused by the court case that had been filed against the party only weeks before the election.[86] This confirmation of the Kemalist elite's firm intention to curb the rise of political Islam may have induced some of the Anatolian electorate to switch to the MHP, which had campaigned on a platform stressing traditional religion-influenced values.

Virtue's chances of avoiding being closed down for the same reasons as the Welfare Party have been diminished by the "turban scandal" in parliament. For the swearing-in ceremony of the newly elected deputies, Merve Kavakçı, one of Virtue's three women deputies, showed up wearing a head scarf, which caused such an uproar among the DSP group that the ceremony had to be interrupted. In the wake of this it was revealed that she had taken American citizenship only weeks before without giving notice to the Turkish authorities. She was stripped of her Turkish citizenship, which would lead to the loss of her parliamentary mandate. The turban scandal induced the chief prosecutor at the court of appeal to open another closure case against Virtue to be added to the one already pending. This time, however, the dismissal from parliament of all elected Virtue deputies was included in the charge.[87] All this does not bode well for the fate of the Virtue Party.

The Kemalist campaign against Islamic fundamentalism seems to have been effective in curbing the Islamist drive. It did not, however, return to the Kemalist camp the large group of volatile voters who are disappointed by the record of the established secular parties. Political Islam has been confirmed as a minoritarian element of Turkish political life, but one of considerable importance under a fragmented party system. The reasons that favored the rise of the Welfare Party in the 1990s are still valid and the Virtue Party (or a successor party) may be able to build on them if it can overcome some of its internal problems.

Reasons behind the Welfare and Virtue Parties' Rise

Many of the causes for the rise of organized political Islam as represented by the Welfare Party have only indirectly to do with the party's religious outlook. The ascent was strongly influenced by the political and economic changes that took place in Turkey after 1980 and by the way in which, especially since the beginning of the 1990s, the party responded to them.

The opening of the country to the outside world that took place mainly after the 1980 military coup through liberalizing and internationalizing the economy and modernizing the infrastructure, especially in communication technology, accentuated economic and social change and differentiation. At the same time, the attempts of the military leadership in the first half of the 1980s to reestablish stability by restructuring society after the concept of the Turkish-Islamic synthesis and eradicating the established political parties abetted a realignment of the political landscape that strengthened the legitimacy of political Islam. When, at the end of the decade, economic liberalization and internationalization led to greater social inequality and increasing migration from the rural areas to the periphery of the cities, it was the forces of political Islam that best took care of the losers to modernization. And it was the Welfare Party that gained politically.[88]

Welfare's ideology of a just order also provided a convincing countermodel to the "unjust" results of the prevailing policies of liberalization and internationalization. It stressed solidarity, harmony, and justice, strongly appealing to well-established communitarian traditions of Turkish society.[89] It based politics on the activities of a strong and homogeneous state, an idea well embedded in the political traditions of the Turkish people. But the ideology of a just order did not propagate a simple return to the good old days. It asked that modern technology be used to establish a better society. Prospects of modernity and progress were not foreclosed but presented in a different context. In this sense the concept was introduced as "a new presentation and a original definition of the universal Islamic system."[90]

Although at a closer look the ideology of the just order shows many logical flaws, it became ever more convincing for a growing number of voters the less the established secular parties proved able to cope with the disruptive effects of economic and social modernization. The more the center-right and center-left became synonymous with political corruption, conspicuous consumption, and ideological poverty, the more Welfare's ideas appealed. The party presented itself as the guarantor of good governance and honest politics.

The RP can be regarded as the country's first modern mass party. It employed an efficient mix of technology and grassroots orientation within a clearly structured hierarchical organization. "Enormous attention has been given to step-by-step mobilization at the local level, with party militants or representatives diligently coming into contact and gradually building support by establishing close, personalized relationships with potential voters."[91] The party established computerized lists of voters and sympathizers on a street-by-street basis or on the level of living quarters. Special representatives looked after their immediate streets or quarters and, if necessary, mobilized support for people who were unable to take care of themselves or who encountered other difficulties. This grassroots element has been summarized in the typical "Welfare language" by one of its leading figures, Yasın Hatipoğlu, former deputy speaker of the parliament, as "who remains with the people, who understands the people and feels with them, receives the trust and the support of the people."[92]

The record of the majority of RP mayors who "are responsible for the local affairs of two-thirds of the population, some 40 million people"[93] after the great success at the local elections in March 1994, initially contributed to the good image of the party and its successor. They became known for delivering much wanted public services, showing efficient organization and relatively modest cronyism and doing away with the widespread corruption of many of their predecessors. They generally had a pragmatic approach to the realization of typical Islamic policies. Such measures may be much more easily realized in smaller central or east Anatolian towns than in the large urban centers of western Turkey.

Everyday public life in Istanbul or Ankara has not changed drastically after the RP mayors took office there, except that everybody agrees that Istanbul, especially, has become much cleaner.

In a subtle way these mayors have, however, tried to introduce a more religiously influenced policy, for instance, by employing followers in the ranks of municipal inspectors whose judgments on what is acceptable as public order differ considerably from the judgments of their Kemalist colleagues.[94] Some municipalities controlled by the Welfare and Virtue Parties have tried to abolish houses and shelter places for women who had left their families due to harassment by their husband. Others have tried to replace Western sculptures and other decorative art in public places by religiously conforming art. Municipal employees in RP-led town halls normally do not follow the official dress code of the republic; women often wear the religious head scarf and men have beards cut in a way that display affiliation with certain religious groups.[95] But all this has been done in a low-profile manner so as not to disturb the people who had voted for the RP more out of a desire for general change than a desire to establish Islamic politics.

Nevertheless, the RP's politics at the local level have been closely followed by Turkey's secular-oriented media, which have carefully reported on every deviation from the secular path and any return to practices of cronyism and patronage. This, undoubtedly, has contributed to a more realistic image of the party's political practice in the eyes of the public. That RP administrations displayed the same flaws as their secular counterparts did not, however, prevent a large part of the voters from reelecting their RP-FP administration in the local elections of April 1999. The Virtue Party kept many of the mayoral seats that had been won by its predecessor five years before and reached a better overall result in the local elections than in the national parliamentary elections that took place at the same time. The renewed victories of Islamist candidates in the mayoral elections of Greater Istanbul and Greater Ankara can be regarded as a special Islamist political success.

A special feature of Welfare's activities was the mobilization of women.[96] For this purpose it established female representatives who were organized in "women commissions," the main task of which was to spread party propaganda among housewives who normally could not be approached by male party militants. Welfare's women's movement was, however, not restricted to activities concerning female rural migrants in the large cities. As a consequence of the general emancipatory movement of female Muslim students in the late 1980s, modern, educated Muslim middle-class women started to be important in the party.[97]

Although their activities contributed considerably to the modern image of the party, they were excluded from influential positions within the party and the public offices that became available for RP members after the election victories. Even the representatives of the so-called younger, modern generation within the party, such as Recep Tayyip Erdoğan, the former mayor of Greater Istanbul, proved to be fairly traditional Muslims, arguing that women cannot enter important public positions because this is against Creation.[98] Despite its latent gender conflict the Welfare Party, unlike the traditional religious orders, provided a welcome avenue for Muslim women to have an effect on public affairs. And, giving in to pressures from the young guard, the party has elected some women to prominent party positions and nominated female candidates for the national elections of April 1999, three of which were elected to parliament.[99]

Women were not the only group within the RP that questioned traditional Islamic politics. Despite its efficient organization and its unified look, the party was, and the FP continues to be, a coalition of groups and ideological orientations within the broad stream of political Islam that was tied together mainly by the undisputed leadership of Necmettin Erbakan. The basic intraparty difference was between traditionalists and modernists.[100]

The traditionalists, also called the "old guard," are the long-time companions of Erbakan in the party leadership and their followers. To them belong, for instance, Recai Kutan, the official party leader, and Oğuzhan Asıltürk, the former chairman of the RP parliamentary group. They cherish the national Islamic tradition and national values in general; they stress the rights of the Islamic community and the state against the rights of the individual; and they display a conservative, center-right worldview and normally are from a rural background. For them, Islamic identity equals Turkish identity, and personal piety is largely identical with a traditional lifestyle. However, they are not against modernization as expressed in technological development, industrialization, and a strong state, as long as these developments are put to the use of keeping the traditional structure of society and politics unchanged.

The modernists are inspired by the Islamist discourse that took place after 1980 and propagate Islamist ideas that stress concepts such as the *ümmet* (the community of Muslims) or the "golden age of Islam" when the prophet and the first caliphs ruled the Islamic community. Their discourse is inspired by Western social thinking, especially by postmodern criticism of modernization, and they tend to support the individual vis-à-vis the community and the state. They reinterpret Islam along lines of modern thinking without putting the religion outside the religious sphere. On economic and social issues, they support the have-nots against the haves. They come from an urban background and favor modern forms of organization and discourse against the tradition of community and of silent followership. Because many of the younger generation leaders of the RP-FP belong to this group, such as Tayyip Erdoğan or Abdullah Gül, a leading foreign policy expert and former vice chairman of the party, they are referred to as the young guard of the Virtue Party.

Under the influence of factors such as rapid urbanization, spreading audiovisual media, and increasing contact with the outside world that are typical of Turkey's social development since 1980, the Welfare Party succeeded in amalgamizing the traditional and the modernist currents into a party with a contemporary Islamist outlook. Islam, not as a theological phenomenon but as the ideological expression of a certain contemporary social reality, provided the uniting bond, the common social-moral context, and the common language that enabled the coexistence and cooperation of different groups within the same political organization: urban migrants and rural villagers, Turkish nationalists and traditional Kurds, young educated professionals and small traders and artisans of the central Anatolian townships.[101]

Islam is also the common bond that unites the representatives of the different geographical centers that were represented within the Welfare Party: the Kurdish provinces of eastern Anatolia, the rural and business centers such as Kayseri or Konya in central Anatolia, and the vast suburban slums of Istanbul and Ankara.[102] Erbakan's party never managed to become an important political force in the more developed rural provinces of western Anatolia, the Black Sea coastal region, and the tourist areas on the Mediterranean coast where one can find the political strongholds of the traditional center-right parties, which also have their more religious-oriented currents.

Thus the Welfare Party and its successor did not represent the totality of political Islam in Turkey nor did it represent the commonly accepted interpretation of Islamic practice. But it did represent more than just political Islam. It was also the contemporary representative of social and political protest of those parts of Turkish society that have difficulties in coping with the socioeconomic change. It clearly represented the urban losers of that process irrespective of the depth of their religious belief: "only around seven percent of the voters who cast their votes for the RP in [the national elections of December 1995] did so because the latter was a religiously oriented party."[103] The Welfare Party–Virtue Party therefore has to be regarded as an established part of Turkish democratic political life with a strong if clearly limited electoral appeal outside the confines of religious movements and other traditional circles.

This leads to the question of the democratic credentials of the party. Are Welfare-Virtue Islamists also democrats? Does the party accept the principle of political pluralism? Is it ready to cede power after an electoral defeat? It is in respect to these and similar questions that many Westernized Turks raise doubts. An answer is not easy.

First, democracy in Turkey is inextricably linked with secularism. For Kemalists the confession of secularism is identical with democratic conviction, and any nonsecular political force has automatically to be regarded as nondemocratic. This position is arguable from a liberal democratic viewpoint that includes more than secularism under the idea of democracy. Even in the Turkish political context there are secular forces on the far right whose democratic credentials can be questioned. And even the democratic orientation of the strongest secular force in Turkey, the military, can be questioned from a specific liberal democratic viewpoint, as I have argued earlier in this study.

Second, the RP never was very clear on its stance toward democracy. "Some Islamists (including some members of Welfare) define democracy simply as majority rule. . . . Given the ethnic and sectarian pluralism that characterizes Turkish society, the question to be asked about Welfare concerns tolerance; being majoritarian is not the same as a commitment to pluralism."[104] All party leaders paid lip service to secularism and to democracy, sometimes enthusiastically. They even purported to propagate the secular view by leaving it to the individual to decide how significant religion should be in private and public life. But the ideology of the just order and the national way displays an organic understanding of state and society that is hardly compatible with conceptions of Western liberal democracy. Furthermore, the party's organization and intraparty political process is very much leader-oriented like that of all other Turkish parties and all religious orders and communities. Open debate, dissenting views, and competitive elections for leadership positions do not belong to established RP-FP practice, which can best be labeled paternalistic authoritarianism.

Third, in government the RP's Islamic political practice was moderate in every respect. It observed the rules of the system and did not openly advocate changes that would have abolished the democratic institutions and procedures established by republican tradition. It did not react in a radical way to its ousting from government and stuck to the procedural roles of the judicial process in its fight against the charges of the chief prosecutor. The Virtue Party keeps strictly to the same line and even tries to give itself a more modern and open outlook through an even stronger emphasis on democratic and republican principles.

However, when in power the Welfare Party did not seek fundamental political changes in the direction of a rapid and strong democratization of the political system. Its government was not a vigilant fighter for improving the observance of human rights, either. All this leads to the conclusion that the RP-FP may be a moderate Islamic political force but that does not at all mean it is also a convincing advocate of democracy. If the party again comes to power, its victory should not be regarded as improving the chances of further democratization in Turkey. A lasting establishment of the RP-FP at the top of the government would most likely be possible only in a new coalition with a nonreligious party and would at best lead to another type of autocratic rule if it were not countered by another military coup, real or postmodern, as was the case in spring 1997.

CHAPTER SIX

Toward a New Sociopolitical Synthesis

THE TURKISH POLITY is confronted with the challenge of finding solutions for problems that will tear apart the social fabric of society if not addressed properly: How to deal with the consequences of far-reaching and rapid economic and social change for employment, urbanization, education, social security, and income distribution? How to deal with the growing awareness of ethnic and religious diversity? How to treat the aspirations of political Islam? How to accommodate the demands of a growing civil society? How to modernize a political system that officially stands by to a state ideology spelled out three-quarters of a century ago and little changed since then?

These problems bear a considerable similarity to those of other countries of a similar level of sociopolitical development in other parts of Europe and the world. And consolidating democracy in industrializing societies or in so-called transitional democracies raises similar questions.[1] But each country has its own context that must be taken into account in designing possible solutions.

For Turkey one specific aspect of development is that the transition to democracy started immediately after World War II and has continued almost uninterruptedly. The military coups in 1960, 1971, and 1980 were never intended to end Turkish democracy for the sake of establishing a lasting military regime. The return to a civilian democratic political regime was always an integral part of the coups' program.[2] What was under attack were deviations from the designated path of Turkish democracy: the secular Kemalist republic and its principles as understood by the military leadership who were the self-declared custodians of the Kemalist heritage. What has taken place in Turkey's transition to or consolidation of democracy was less the replacement of an authoritarian regime by a democratic one and more a struggle for the "right" democratic order.

This struggle has recurrently erupted because of three sociopolitical cleavages: Kemalist modernizers (secularists) versus religious traditionalists (Islamists), Turks versus Kurds, and Sunni Muslims versus Alewites. The cleavages are the direct result of the original republican sociopolitical synthesis, or social contract, based on Kemalist secularism, Turkish nationalism, and moderate Sunni Islam. In its most prominent form this sociopolitical basis of the republic is represented by the ideology of the Turkish-Islamic synthesis as understood by the military leadership that managed the 1980 coup.

The synthesis deliberately excludes three large and important parts of Turkey's population: the nationally conscious Kurds, the politically aware Muslims, and the religiously heterodox Alewites. These groups partly overlap and would add up to a quarter of the total population. Exclusion is not at all a phenomenon alien to democratic societies, but the exclusion of such a large proportion of a country's population would be bound to create problems.[3] This is especially so in a relatively developed society that is principally based on a market economy and characterized by growing internal mobilization. Under such conditions, excluding a large part of society from being able to fully participate in all relevant political and societal processes becomes an obstacle to further democatic development. To overcome this obstacle is the overriding challenge to Turkey's political class.

There is a widespread consensus that to solve these problems, to which one has to add some serious foreign policy issues, the Turkish political system needs a fundamental overhaul. The centrifugal political fragmentation has to be reversed, and the capacity of the government to make decisions and carry out plans has to be considerably improved.

One way to reach these goals is to minimize the influence of splinter party groups and strengthen the political center to create the necessary conditions for establishing single-party majority government rule.[4] Another way could be to radically change the system in the direction of presidential democracy after the American or the French model. Either approach to creating the necessary conditions for a lasting cure of Turkey's political illnesses would, however, be difficult to realize.

Nor do these technical adjustments guarantee to provide the necessary change in the political system that is needed to meet the challenges. Turkey is not going to get out of its current dilemma "by the amalgamation of the two right-wing parties or the two left-wing parties. It is going to get out of it because it has a reform movement which takes a fundamental look at the way the system is operating."[5] The establishment of stable and sound governance has to be accompanied by a convincing political conception of how to deal with the problems mentioned, which are more the result of inadequate policies than of inadequate governance. Inadequate governance has aggravated the difficulties that have been created by inadequate policies.

A reorganization of Turkey's political center could only be brought about by a merger of the parties on the center-right and center-left. But there is "little hope of reunification within either camp."[6] Although programmatic and ideological differences do not seem to be important between, for instance, the Motherland Party and the True Path Party on the right or the Republican People's Party and the Democratic Left Party on the left, mergers are prevented by personal animosities between party leaders and problems of how to distribute power and influence in a merged party. As long as the differences in public appeal between possible candidates for unification remain as small as in the past, there will be no incentive for giving up organizational and political independence. The merger of the Social Democratic Populist Party (Sosyal Demokrat Halkçı Partisi, or SHP) and the re-created Republican People's Party in 1995 under the umbrella of the CHP was an exception mainly caused by a temporary weakness and disorientation of the SHP after the unexpected stepping-down of its longtime leader Erdal İnönü.

The deleterious effect of the fragmentation of the political center on Turkish politics is aggravated by the center's loss of public support. In the 1995 general elections the combined vote of radical and antisystemic parties was about one-third of the total. If one adds to that the number of nonvoters and invalid votes, which can also be regarded as an expression of political protest in a system in which voting is obligatory, the share of open or indirect protest votes among Turkish voters adds up to more than 40 percent.[7] The elections of April 18, 1999, confirmed this observation, which could be regarded as a signal that Turkish democracy is facing a systemic challenge. This view is also supported by the continued deterioration of the center-right, which once had been the backbone of Turkey's democratic consolidation.

If the electoral system is not drastically changed to bring about rule by a majority party, Turkey will be governed by coalitions of fairly incompatible partners because no party will be able to win a majority of seats in general elections. The coalition governments since the early 1990s have turned out to be "short-lived, incompetent regimes, having difficulty in governing as partners start bickering and break up."[8] But a drastic change of electoral rules would be difficult to bring about because of the very fragmentation and political weakness of the center parties. Discussions about a "fundamental system change," which have taken place time and again in recent years, have produced no action.[9]

Under present circumstances, only a change from the system of moderated proportional representation to a clear-cut system of majority voting could result in majority-party government. This would, however, exclude most of the existing parties from parliamentary politics and the resulting material benefits for politicians and their clientele, so there is great reluctance to consider any change in the electoral system that could lead to such a result. Although one could assume that under the conditions of majority voting rule and majority-party government merger in the political center would be greatly hastened, as long as too many active politicians fear to be among the losers of a drastic change, there is little likelihood that parliament will fundamentally reform the electoral system. The public and Turkey's allies and partners will have to adapt themselves to a continuation of coalition governments in Ankara.

Some circles have suggested replacing the parliamentary system with a presidential system. The idea is that the concentration of political and governmental power would be better able to solve pressing political problems. The transition to a presidential system might also contribute to a reconcentration of the many parties because a governing president needs strong and coherent backing in the legislature. Furthermore, only large and unified parties will be able to offer presidential candidates that can enter elections with some chance of success.

But a presidential system is alien to the tradition of Turkish democracy, which from its beginning in the late 1940s has been guided by the idea of parliamentary democracy. Even the Atatürk period could hardly be interpreted as presidential; it was an era of autocratic leadership, and Atatürk is not normally referred to as Turkey's first president but as the country's "glorious leader." The debate about establishing a presidential system is not completely free of this leadership mentality, which continues to be a characteristic element of Turkish political life. Lately, one of the strongest supporters of this system is the actual president, Süleyman Demirel.[10] The fact does add to the abstract debate a personal element that Demirel is looking for a way to prolong his term of office and, above that, improve his influence in politics by reentering as an active participant. Because all other political leaders sense this personal, selfish element of the debate, there is little chance that the political system will be fundamentally changed in the near future.

At any rate, there are good reasons to doubt that changes in the system or system elements are the right way to address Turkey's urgent political problems. Of course, effective government is an important element of successful politics, and systemic changes that improve political management and problem solving could go far to improve overall political efficiency and stability. However, Turkey's political problem goes beyond achieving effective government. It is directly connected with the perception of political legitimacy, the growing lack of public confidence in the political class, whether because of its disappointing track record or as a result of the actual or feared exclusion of large parts of the population from the political process.

Turkey's people lack the political forces they can trust in order to have a stable continuation of the successful social and political developments of the past. For most of the public there are no politicians who offer convincing conceptual approaches to the most urgent development problems, not to speak of a comprehensive political way of tackling these problems. This public malaise has been confirmed by the results of the 1999 national elections: Ecevit won because he is the only, and last, trusted representative of the established political class, and the MHP was successful because it is the last established party that had not been tried by the people. The elections were less of a show of confidence in the political class than an expression of the people's desperation.

Furthermore, under the prevailing uncertainty about the future, there is a lack of clear and convincing social and political values that allow people to orient themselves amid the growing complexities of everyday life. Only the representatives of political Islam and the military seem to have such an overall view. In difficult situations, people often prefer the easy solutions offered to them, such as Islam or other radical but seemingly well-structured and logical ideologies. But both the Islamic solution and the military's traditional republican one with its strong national undercurrents have severe flaws. They are mainly based on closed idelogies that do not very well fit the complexities and dynamics of modern open societies. Both are basically state centered, which reflects a strong trace of Turkish political tradition that still has a lot of appeal for many people. Nevertheless, such an emphasis on state-centered politics imposed from above neglects the dynamic social processes that have been created by opening the country to the outside world and that are going to be reinforced by international political and economic developments.

Thus the way out of Turkey's domestic political dilemma cannot be the preservation of the Kemalist state tradition. Like all state-oriented and latently authoritarian conceptions of modernization, Kemalism becomes dysfunctional if the stage of social development has crossed a threshold beyond which the majority of the population is no longer ready to follow but demands to become the master of its own fate. Turkey has reached this point. What, then, is needed is a political conception that can accommodate the dynamics of an open society with a plurality of sometimes divergent social interests and groups. In short, the Turkish state has to anchor itself in the acceptance of societal pluralism and the dynamics that mark successful economic and political modernization.

It is admittedly not an easy task to give up long-standing visions of the ideal society and polity that have been used to guide the political education of Turkey's masses for decades. However, sticking with the myth of a homogenous nation and a society that functions within clearly defined but hardly adaptable boundaries of Kemalism will not successfully lead the way into the twenty-first century. Democracy cannot grow within a people if it is suspended or forced into the background every time its results are not acceptable to the powers that be.

This is a lesson that should by now have been learned by Turkey's military leadership. It is no contradiction to such a view that the armed forces remain the social organization trusted most by the people. This esteem is predominantly an expression of the prevailing insecurity and should not be taken as widespread agreement with the direction of the military's domestic political activities. Turkey's generals were taught the impressive lesson in the 1983 elections that the people prefer to decide on their political fate themselves. And in the April 1999 elections the defenders of the military's conception of a strictly laicist Kemalist republic could gain only a bare majority of the total vote if one adds the votes for the DSP, ANAP, DYP, and CHP.

The challenge facing all political forces in Turkey is to develop a new sociopolitical synthesis, a social contract that builds upon the great achievements of the past seventy-five years but at the same time is able to transcend them. The leitmotiv of this synthesis can no longer be exclusive secularism and nationalism; it has to be the inclusive conception of a liberal democracy. Kemalism needs to be reinterpreted from such a perspective to accentuate the democratic ingredients of its ideological components at the cost of its more authoritarian elements. This would require a stronger emphasis on its much neglected principle of reformism (*inkılâpcilik*). Only a convincing proof that the values of liberal democracy are suited to keep and develop the progress and positive results of past modernization policies can, in the longer term, prevent a creeping political Islam from coming to power. Turkey's secular democrats have to prove that they can provide better solutions for the problems of industrialization, market economy competition, consumerism, party pluralism, an open society with growing social mobility, an information society, and globalization.

The new sociopolitical synthesis should not demonize Islam. Any great religion will not only be a guide to the spiritual well-being of people but will also have a certain political importance in the modern societies in which it is embedded. To deny Islam such a role in Turkey would mean to deny a fundamental social reality and would be utterly unpolitical. The secular forces that still represent most of the population face the challenge of developing a political framework that can accommodate political Islam without being overtaken by it. This will in the longer term be possible only if a nonreligiously defined system of democratic values proves, in political practice, its superiority to political Islam. Such a system should also be able to coexist with a political minority that advocates Islamic modes and values as its way of solving the problems mentioned.

Developing and implementing a future-oriented sociopolitical synthesis will not be easy. To be sure, one has to admit that presently the organized forces of Turkey's civil society seem to have better realized the new social challenges and the necessary political consequences than the representatives of Turkey's political and state elite. In any case, recent contributions to the political debate from business circles, trade unions, and other parts of Turkey's civil society seem to be more forward looking than the debates that dominate party discourses, not to speak of the contributions from the military leadership.[11] The three-party coalition government of DSP, MHP, and ANAP established after the April 1999 elections and led by Bülent Ecevit also seems to be more oriented toward the status quo than it is a promoter of far-reaching structural political reforms.

Further strengthening the elements of liberal democracy in the Turkish polity would also have favorable effects in dealing with its more urgent foreign policy problems. Relations with the rest of Europe, especially with the European Union, could only benefit from a fundamental democratization and civilianization of politics and society. The Kurdish question, the state of human rights enforcement, the role of the military in politics, and other matters would lose their chilling effect on EU-Turkey relations. In addition, the position of the U.S. administration in carrying through its policy that Turkey is an important regional partner could be strengthened against congressional resistance, which is mainly nourished by "ethnic policies" from the Greek and Armenian lobbies.

A less strained relationship with its most important Western partners and allies would help Ankara to better meet the challenges it is facing in its relations with neighboring states. The more Turkey presents itself as a mainstream society, the more it can benefit from its inclusion in the system of Western democracies. Moreover, there are many reasons to assume that, in the longer term, greater democratization would also lead to greater political and economic stability under conditions of growing globalization. Greater domestic strength is the most important condition for a successful foreign and security policy.

PART TWO

Turkish Foreign and Security Policy after the Cold War

THE INTERNATIONAL SEA CHANGE following the end of the cold war vastly altered Turkey's foreign and security policy environment, weakening Ankara's bonds with its Western allies and forcing assertiveness in relations with neighboring countries and in regional developments.[1] The old, predominantly passive approach to foreign policy that had been based on the Kemalist maxim "Peace at home. Peace in the world" slowly is giving way to a more self-conscious foreign policy that includes a certain readiness to wage well-calculated conflicts with neighboring countries if they are deemed necessary for the realization of Turkey's national interests.

The definition of these interests is mainly determined by a perception of multidimensional threat that has replaced the traditional perspective of East-West antagonism. Some important elements of this perception include the internationalization of the Kurdish problem, the menace of being excluded from building Europe's new political and security architecture, and the denial of regional influence in Central Asia, especially with regard to the development of the energy-rich Caspian Basin. Turkey's perception is constantly being conditioned by fears of a conspiracy of foreign, mainly European, forces that are trying to dismantle the country to get rid of an unwanted rival.

Within this context, Turkey's foreign policy is undergoing tentative changes on two fronts. First, the country is seeking a new balance between cooperative engagements in old and new multinational frameworks and the more or less single-handed pursuit of national interests based on a greatly strengthened and still growing military capability. As a Turkish observer has said, "Watch out for Turkey's assertive actions in the Middle East, Transcaucasus, and the Balkans to protect its national security interests more vigorously than before. Its cooperation can neither be taken for granted, nor can its legitimate security concerns be sidestepped or subdued."[2]

Second, Turkey's political establishment is increasingly on the lookout for foreign relations beyond the country's traditional exclusive orientation toward the West. Ankara is not severing its relations with Western allies but redefining them while reaching out for a larger Eurasian role. Its wish to become a model for the newly independent states (NIS) of Central Asia as well as for reformist Islamic regimes still is important, although its success has been limited. Nevertheless, important parts of Turkey's political elite still are convinced that the West "needs the help of Turkey in this rough neighborhood to protect fundamental Western security interests and also as a living example of how it is possible to be Muslim and have a pluralistic democracy and free-market economy at the same time."[3]

These changes have not yet led to a new grand strategy for the international position of the country.[4] This is mainly the result of diverging views on what a desirable foreign policy may be. The emergence of new domestic political forces and the continuing uncertainty about the new international order have led to a growing and lively domestic debate about Turkey's course in foreign and security policy. This debate has not yet reached a new national consensus.

The continuation of the established Western orientation as the backbone of foreign policy is most strongly favored by the military, the business elite, the traditional Westernizers of the political center who can mainly be found within the ranks of the CHP, DYP, and ANAP, and most of the country's leading journalists. These political forces disagree, however, on whether Turkey has a right to membership in the European Union, which the EU unjustly withholds, or if it must make severe political efforts to meet criteria for membership that have been established by the EU for any candidate country. The first view is generally adopted by the military and the party politicians; the business elite usually hold that more effort is needed. All these Western-oriented groups agree that there is no viable alternative to joining the European Union. They regard the regional opening of Turkey's foreign policy as a welcome addition to but not a replacement of the European orientation.

A different position is taken by traditional and new nationalists, who are mainly represented by the MHP and the DSP leadership and some of Turkey's influential journalists but who can also be found within the ranks of DYP and ANAP. These people advocate a foreign policy that concentrates on Turkey's national interests as defined by its status as an emerging regional power. Relations with Europe are not considered a necessary basis for Turkey's foreign and security policy but as being instrumental in improving the country's international status.[5] In this perspective relations with Israel or securing a crucial position in transporting Caspian energy are equally important to becoming an EU member. EU membership is, then, only acceptable if it is not contingent upon sacrificing important national interests and if it is not accompanied by a limitation of political sovereignty. Whereas the DSP stresses Turkey's regional position in general, the MHP advocates establishing a special relationship with the Turkic people in Central Asia, which could ultimately culminate in a commonwealth of Turkish states under Turkey's leadership.

Westernizers and nationalists agree that continuing Turkey's NATO membership is the best guarantee for the country's security. This includes maintaining close relations with the United States, but both groups would like to see a better American understanding of Turkey's political needs.

A much different position is taken by Turkey's Islamists. They advocate a preference for relations with the Islamic world, which has, for instance, been expressed in Necmettin Erbakan's D-8 policy, which aimed to establish close relations between Turkey and seven other large or economically strong Muslim states: Iran, Egypt, Pakistan, Bangladesh, Indonesia, Malaysia, and Nigeria. In the long run the Islamists, as represented by the Virtue Party and its followers in the media and intellectual circles, aim at dissociating Turkey from the West and turning the country into a leading power of the Islamic world. As their term in government has shown, however, they are ready and able to adapt to international and domestic realities. Close relations with the European Union and a continuing NATO commitment are thus not foreclosed as long as they are required by the international environment. This can only, however, be regarded as a temporary, if long-lasting, compromise and should not be taken as a reversal of the fundamental foreign policy orientation, at least as long as there is no discussion about this orientation in Islamist circles.

Under the international and domestic political circumstances of the past decade, Turkey's foreign and security policy has been a complex mix of Westernization and nationalism. It is undeniable that the demise of the Soviet Union and the end of the East-West antagonism has opened new avenues for Ankara's regional foreign policy. It has taken its chances and is about to establish itself as a main regional power. Simultaneously, relations with the West have undergone considerable changes that are mainly the result of Turkey's changed importance to Europe. The United States has been able only partly to offer a counterweight to Ankara's rapidly deteriorating relations with the European Union countries. As a consequence, the focus of Turkey's foreign policy is slowly but constantly shifting to a nationalist emphasis. This can, for instance, clearly be concluded from the program of Turkey's fifty-seventh government, Ecevit's three-party nationalist-left coalition, that took office on May 30, 1999.[6] Unless a reorientation of domestic political emphasis toward the values of liberal democracy takes place and is accompanied by the EU's relaxation of its membership policy, this Western-oriented strong nationalism could become the trademark of Turkey's foreign policy at the beginning of the twenty-first century.

CHAPTER SEVEN

Central Asia and the Caspian Basin: Energy, Business, and Kinship

THE ADMITTEDLY SHORT history of Ankara's relations with the newly independent states (NIS) of Central Asia and the Transcaucasus provides a good example of how political leaders in Turkey and its Western allies have misinterpreted the meaning of the demise of the Soviet Empire. Immediately after the end of the cold war, its allies pushed Ankara to seek a special part in the development of the NIS. This policy was mainly driven by the unfounded fear of a rapid and deep Islamization of the region by Iranian fundamentalism. Turkey was promoted as a Western countermodel for Central Asia. Ankara eagerly seized this opportunity to reestablish its strategic importance for the West by designing and promoting a far-reaching Central Asia policy that aimed at turning the region into a sphere of special Turkish influence.[1]

This scheme, however, faltered fairly quickly because Turkey lacked sufficient material support from the Western allies, lacked sufficient indigenous means for pursuing such an ambitious policy, and met growing and determined Russian resistance against losing influence in its "near abroad." Today, for Turkey the main problems concerning Central Asia and the Transcaucasus are not the spread of Iranian fundamentalism but Russia's attempts to reestablish its dominance in the region and to secure a major share in marketing the energy resources of the Caspian Basin.[2]

The Discovery of a "New World": From Euphoria to Realism

The unravelling of the Soviet Union confronted Ankara with a "new world" in Central Asia that it wanted to influence and where it confronted certain demands.[3] For the Turkish public and large parts of the country's elite, the new republics and "new cousins" in what is regarded as the original Turkish homelands was very welcome. Now there are other sovereign states in which "Turks" are the dominant political group, where a related language is officially spoken, and the culture has much in common with that of Anatolia. Turkey's relative isolation between Europe, to which its people strongly want to belong but often have been rejected, and the Arab world, of which the Turks never considered themselves an integral part and that maintained a strong reserve toward Turkey, suddenly seemed to have come to an end.

The relative lack of economic and political development in the new republics gave many Turks a feeling of superiority and offered Ankara an opportunity to take regional leadership.[4] Turkey could never expect to realize such opportunities in its relations with its Western partners. Thus the conditions were set for high expectations concerning the importance, dimension, and scope of relations with Central Asia.[5]

The expectations were especially nurtured by such ultranationalist circles as the pan-Turkish-oriented Nationalist Action Party (Milliyetçi Hareket Partisi, or MHP) of the late Alparslan Türkeş and its followers. There was open talk of the development of a bloc or union of Turkic nations under Turkey's leadership that eventually would become a powerful and recognized political force in forging the new international order.[6]

Mainstream Turkish politicians were also quick in painting a bright picture of a new Turkic world stretching from the Adriatic Sea to the Chinese border with Turkey at its center. President Turgut Özal told his countrymen and the world that the twenty-first century would be the "Turkish century."[7] Turkish politicians were encouraged in the propagation of such visions by Western media and the United States. In early 1992 during a trip to Central Asian capitals, U.S. Secretary of State James Baker recommended that the new republics adopt the Turkish model for their political and economic development.[8] European politicians and media agreed.

This coincidence of political outlooks of Turkey and the West was, however, based on different motivations. For Turkey's political leaders the situation in the former Soviet Union offered another opportunity to restore the country's political and strategic importance for the West—after Turkey's importance during the Gulf War.[9] Western politicians saw Ankara's new mission as an important part of a containment policy against the strategic threat of Islamic fundamentalism, especially in its Iranian-sponsored version. For them, it was urgent to prevent the spreading of fundamentalist Islam into a politically unstable region, and one that could become the site of an uncontrolled proliferation of weapons of mass destruction, including nuclear missiles.

It was a more or less forgone conclusion that Central Asia not only would but should become Turkey's sphere of influence. Turkey was regarded as one of the new regional powers "with influence in Central Asia, the Caucasus, the Black Sea Region, the Balkans and the Middle East."[10] Such ideas were strengthened by American geopolitical analysts in connection with the development of the energy potential of the Caspian Basin.[11] In these considerations Turkey is pivotal, a position that is also part of the prevailing foreign policy philosophy of Prime Minister Bülent Ecevit and Foreign Minister İsmail Cem.[12]

That Turkey should be a model was supported by the political orientation of the Central Asian states at the time the Soviet Union collapsed. In September 1991 President Nursultan Nazarbayev of Kazakhstan visited Ankara. On November 9, 1991, Turkey officially recognized the Republic of Azerbaijan, and in December 1991 the presidents of Turkmenistan, Uzbekistan, and Kyrgyzstan followed one another on official visits. They returned home with a bundle of agreements with Turkey establishing cooperation in various economic and cultural endeavors.[13] On December 16 Turkey officially recognized all other new republics in the area of the former Soviet Union, thus formalizing its relations with Central Asia and the Transcaucasus.

There were, however, some serious obstacles to the realization of Turkish ambitions. Turkey was not the only contender for primacy in Central Asia. At the least, Iran and Russia had to be reckoned with. Iran had historic-cultural justifications for the establishment of a special relationship that were similar to those of Turkey. As heir to the former dominant power of the region, Russia had a continuing interest in keeping the new republics economically and politically dependent. The leaders of the Central Asian states wanted to prevent the replacement of the Soviet big brother by a new Turkish *ağabey*. They wanted to reap the fruits of their countries' newly won political sovereignty by stabilizing their political and economic independence as far as possible and at the same time securing their own positions of undisputed domestic leadership. All of this quickly resulted in a more realistic attitude toward Central Asia in Turkish official circles.

But it was sometimes difficult for Ankara to keep the balance between a realistic foreign policy (without any pretence of regional leadership) in its relations with the new republics and its hopes of establishing a special relationship with some kind of Turkish preferential position in the foreign relations of Central Asian states. Turkish leaders could hardly prevent their words from sounding ambiguous and being misinterpreted. This happened, for instance, when in April 1992 Prime Minister Süleyman Demirel, during a visit to various Central Asian states, declared that Turkey did not have any intention of patronizing the new republics but at the same time spoke of the possibility of establishing an association of sovereign Turkic republics and of Turkey's having taken the responsibility of representing the Turkic world in international forums.[14]

Political circles in Moscow and the Russian military elite took such language as proof of Turkey's intention to replace the Russian influence in the region. This view became even more prominent in Moscow the more the concept of the near abroad became a crucial element of Russia's foreign policy thinking. As a consequence, Turkey's policy toward Central Asia and the Transcaucasus is not only impeded by the various latent and open conflicts in the region but also by the forceful reemergence of Russia as an influential regional power.[15]

Russian suspicion was deepened by the 1992 election of Ebulfez Elchibey as president of Azerbaijan. Elchibey was well known for his strong anti-Russian and equally strong pro-Turkish attitudes. This led Moscow to redouble its efforts at regaining strongholds in the Transcaucasus. In effectively manipulating the conflicts between Azerbaijan and Armenia over Nagorno-Karabakh and between Georgia and its secessionist Abkhazian province, Moscow finally could reestablish its military presence at the Georgian and Armenian borders with Turkey. Elchibey's successor, Haydar Aliyev, tried to steer a more independent political course. First, he tried to keep equal distance from Ankara and Moscow.[16] Later he sought to base his Western-oriented policy on the establishment of sound relations with the United States in order to create a security umbrella for forging special relations with Turkey in pipeline policy.[17]

The Actual Situation: Energy, Business and Kinship

Turkey's relations with the independent states of Central Asia and the Transcaucasus are mainly driven by energy and business possibilities and kinship. Ankara has not totally abandoned the idea of being or becoming a role model, but it has been much more in the background than it was in the early 1990s. It remains to be seen if the conception will experience a political revival under the new, more nationalist, Ecevit coalition government with the MHP.

Energy

Turkey's main regional interest has shifted from the vision of creating a group of Turkic states as a new power in regional politics to more mundane political and economic considerations about how to get its share of the regional energy cake to be distributed over the next decades. It wants to participate in developing and marketing the large oil and gas resources located in the Caspian Sea region, mainly in Turkmenistan, Kazakhstan, and Azerbaijan.[18] In the tapping of these resources Turkish leaders see a means to deal with the country's rising energy demands, gain considerable economic advantages from pipelines and downstream installations, and strengthen the strategic importance of the country for the Central Asian states as well as for traditional allies in the West.[19] Turkey possesses, however, only very limited means of its own to bring about the realization of its interests. The success of its Caspian oil policy mainly depends on the U.S. government's political support.

Turkey is and will remain for the foreseeable future an importer of oil and gas. In 1995 it imported 25.8 million tons of crude oil and will reach more than 40 million tons by 2010, according to energy demand projections. The increase in its consumption of natural gas will be even more striking: from slightly less than 10 billion cubic meters in 1998 it is expected to use 54 billion cubic meters by 2010 and 81 billion cubic meters by 2020. The main reason for this increasing demand is the substitution of natural gas for low-quality Turkish coal for heating the fast-growing metropolitan areas and the increasing use of gas as a pollution-free fuel for power stations and other industrial uses.[20] All this makes Turkey an attractive market for Caspian oil and gas, and it gives a special importance to Turkey's relations with the region that could become its main energy supplier in the early twenty-first century.

Of far greater importance, however, are the pipelines by which the energy resources of the landlocked states around the Caspian Sea will be transported to the world market. From the very beginning Turkey tried to capitalize on the interest of the new republics in pipelines to loosen their dependence on Russia. Since December 1994 Ankara has officially advocated the construction of an oil pipeline from Baku to the Turkish oil terminal on the Mediterranean coast near Ceyhan for the transportation of Azerbaijani offshore oil.[21] The realization of "Baku-Ceyhan" has become one of Turkey's undisputed national interests, and the construction has been vigorously pursued by all the coalition governments whatever their political views.

In the original Turkish position this pipeline could be connected with another one along the Caspian coast for transporting crude from Kazakhstan's Tengiz oil field in the northeastern Caspian region.[22] The pipeline from Baku would have an annual transport capacity of 50 million metric tons and would have a length of about 2,000 kilometers. In January 1995 the U.S. administration declared its backing of the Turkish project within its favorite framework of an east-west energy transportation corridor from the Caspian region.

In the seemingly endless game that evolved between the main actors engaged in the Caspian oil business (the United States, Russia, Iran, Turkey, the new republics, and the international oil firms), Turkey had to adapt its plan several times.[23] It became clear very early that the only viable routing for the Baku-Ceyhan pipeline would be through Georgia; more economical routes via Iran or Armenia were not feasible due to American resistance and the unsolved conflict over Nagorno-Karabakh, respectively. It became equally clear that the Turkish plan could hardly prevent realization of an alternative Russian pipeline from Kazakhstan's Tengiz oil field to the Russian Black Sea harbor of Novorossiisk. For this project Russia, Kazakhstan, and Oman formed the Caspian Pipeline Consortium (CPC) in 1992. It was reconfigured in 1996 by including important international oil firms, especially Chevron, the main developer of Tengiz, to broaden its composition and improve the speed and probability of its realization.[24] Today there is the likelihood of a multiple-track pipeline system that would include a northern option (Russia) and a western option (Georgia-Turkey). A southern option via Iran, which seems to be preferred by some oil companies, is prevented by the American policy of maintaining Tehran's international isolation. Both the CPC project and Baku-Ceyhan are awaiting the final approval of the parties concerned.

Production and transport of a projected 5 million metric tons of oil a year from Azerbaijani fields started in November 1997 via an overhauled northern pipeline from Baku to Novorossiisk through the Chechen capital of Grozny. Another western route of the same capacity between Baku and the Georgian Black Sea terminal of Supsa became operational in April 1999 after its construction had faced some unexpected delays. This route has also been promoted by Turkey, which even offered financial participation in its construction. In doing so, "the Turkish government always made it clear that its support for the western route was linked to the realization ultimately of the Baku-Ceyhan pipeline."[25] When this linkage was rejected by the Azerbaijan International Operating Company (AIOC) in early 1996, Turkey withdrew its support and left the construction of the pipeline to the oil companies and the states concerned.[26] At present, all Azerbaijani early oil that is not sold to Turkey or to other customers in the Black Sea region has to be transported through the Turkish Straits.

The final decision on the main exporting pipeline has still to be taken by the AIOC, the international oil consortium that is the main developer of Azerbaijani offshore fields, that would have to shoulder the risk of an investment in the range of U.S.$2.3 billion to $4 billion, with an amortization period of about twenty years in a tension-ridden and politically explosive region. Officially, the decision on the pipeline route will be made by the Azerbaijani government, that is, President Aliyev. The AIOC can only make a recommendation to him, but this recommendation carries special weight because it will be the oil companies that will be financing the pipeline.

Too many noneconomic factors are in play; they render economic calculations very difficult and caution the international business participants against a hasty decision. First, the Caucasian region has many simmering tensions, of which the conflict over Nagorno-Karabakh between Azerbaijan and Armenia and the unresolved issue of Abkhazian irredentism in Georgia are but the most obvious. Second, the internal stability of the new states in the region is precarious.[27] Third, the involvement of Russia, Turkey, Iran, and the United States in the ongoing strategic game bears the danger of local conflicts spilling over into regional crises. An example is the recent Azerbaijani reflections on the possible establishment of a foreign military base in the country to counter the heavy buildup of the Russian military in neighboring Armenia.[28]

Under these circumstances the main advantage of Turkey's Baku-Ceyhan proposal is that it can be an alternative to a Russian or a theoretically possible and economically very attractive Iranian pipeline, both of which would strengthen already existing monopolies of market access. Its main problem is its likely economic disadvantage because to become profitable, it would have to transport not only Azerbaijan's oil but also a considerable amount of other Caspian oil, which cannot at all be guaranteed at present.[29]

Therefore, the U.S. administration conceived a trans-Caspian and east-west energy transportation corridor that would combine the oil pipeline with a parallel gas pipeline running from Turkmenistan through the Caspian Sea to join Baku-Ceyhan on the Azerbaijani shore. An interagency working group for Caspian energy, chaired by Deputy Secretary of State Strobe Talbott, has been established to coordinate U.S. policy.

The basic idea behind this ambitious and costly scheme is to establish the United States as a dominant strategic force in Central Asia. An effective energy outlet from the area to the West via Turkey would severely diminish the power of Russia and Iran, especially if one takes into consideration that the energy corridor would also include other transportation and communication infrastructure. Officially this U.S. policy has the following objectives:

—Strengthen the viability of these new states as market-based democracies by steadfastly supporting their independence, territorial integrity, and prosperity.
—Enhance business opportunities for U.S. and other companies.
—Mitigate regional conflicts and foster cooperation in order to encourage the integration of the NIS into the global community of democratic nations.
—Ensure that Caspian energy resources bolster the energy security of the United States and its allies, as well as the energy independence of the Caspian NIS, by guaranteeing the free flow of Caspian oil and gas to world markets.[30]

The Clinton administration has put a high priority on this policy because American strategists are convinced that developments in the Caspian region will have a decisive impact in shaping the postcommunist world and consequently on the American influence in this process. This strategic importance was stressed by Energy Secretary Bill Richardson when he declared: "This is about America's energy security, which depends on diversifying our sources of oil and gas worldwide." And "it's also about preventing strategic inroads by those who don't share our values."[31]

This observation is directed mainly against Iran, which is still regarded as the main destabilizing factor in the greater Middle East by sponsoring terrorism, spreading Islamic fundamentalism, and attempting to build or acquire nuclear weapons. As Undersecretary of State Stuart Eizenstat said after a visit to Paris in February 1998 during which he tried to secure European support for America's policy, "We feel very strongly there should be no pipeline across Iran. No ifs, ands, or buts." Iran shall not be given "a chokehold over energy development in the Caspian going west." Instead the

United States is "trying to encourage . . . the creation of an east-west transportation corridor that goes through the Caspian Sea and through the Caucasus," of which Baku-Ceyhan would be an important part.[32]

However, developments in Iran after the election of President Mohammad Khatami and growing American and international criticism of Washington's anti-Iran policy, especially the economic sanctions applied, could eventually lead to a change in U.S. policy. This development would depend on a fundamental and lasting change of the Iranian regime and its foreign policy, which is marked by deep suspicion of American hegemonic interests in the region.

The United States used its leverage on important political participants to prevent the construction of a pipeline from Tengiz to the Persian Gulf in 1994, promote the twin-pipeline solution for transporting Azerbaijani early oil in October 1995, get the consent of President Saparmurat Niyazov of Turkmenistan for the trans-Caspian gas pipeline project, and prevent an anti-Baku-Ceyhan decision by the AIOC in October 1998.

To establish leverage in Caspian Basin development, Washington intensified relations with all regional countries concerned. Since the mid-1990s the presidents of these nations have more or less regularly visited Washington, and many high-level U.S. delegations have toured the region with the purpose of securing "the commitment of Turkey, Azerbaijan, Georgia, Turkmenistan, and Kazakhstan to accelerate development of the trans-Caspian and Baku-Ceyhan pipeline routes. . . ."[33] The American administration promoted the establishment of expert groups in the relevant countries to investigate the technical, financial, and bureaucratic details that are part of constructing a pipeline. Since late 1997 a U.S.-Turkish joint working group has made great efforts to speed up the Baku-Ceyhan project. The most important U.S. institutions involved with financial support for investments abroad, the Export-Import Bank, the Overseas Private Investment Corporation, and the Trade and Development Agency were combined in a Caspian Sea Initiative that was presented at the "Crossroads of the World" international conference in Istanbul in May 1998.[34] On various occasions Washington has also sought support and cooperation of its European allies for its energy transportation corridor plan.

The initial Turkish contribution to the development consisted mainly of engaging Turkey's state-owned petroleum producing company, TPAO, in the Azerbaijani and, to a lesser degree, Kazakh oil business and of constant and intense diplomatic efforts in Baku, Washington, Moscow, Almaty, and Tehran to promote the Turkish option or find compromises with competing plans. But domestic political problems and bureaucratic infighting have prevented Ankara from developing a comprehensive and decisive policy on the pipeline.[35] Potential investors have had to deal with five or six administrations in Ankara in the past five years, which often brought with them repeated changes of top bureaucrats as well as the top personnel of the most important state-run agencies involved with energy policy. Furthermore, Turkish interests did not always agree on what line of policy to follow, as was exemplified by the argument between Emre Gönensay, former chief adviser in energy affairs to Prime Minister Tansu Çiller and short-time foreign minister, and the top administrators of BOTAŞ, Turkey's state-owned pipeline company over the advisability of the Baku-Ceyhan pipeline for the transport of early oil from Azerbaijan.[36]

This infighting changed only after the coalition government under Prime Minister Mesut Yılmaz took office in July 1997. He visited Azerbaijan, Kazakhstan, and Georgia during his first months in power to show his personal interest in the pipeline. In Tbilisi he and Georgian President Eduard Shevardnadze signed an accord for pipeline transport of Azerbaijani oil in March 1998. The Turkish Ministry of Energy established close contacts with Caspian partners that in May 1998 led to the signing of a principal agreement on the pipeline and a common working program for clearing the details of selling procedures, financing, and other technical matters that had been left open by the first feasibility study on the project.[37] Even the military leaders made efforts to bolster Turkey's position in the region by concluding cooperation agreements with Azerbaijan and Georgia during visits of Chief of General Staff General İsmail Hakkı Karadayı in spring 1998.

Foreign Minister İsmail Cem also traveled the region and on March 1, 1998, convened a conference on Baku-Ceyhan and related Caspian energy questions that was attended by the foreign ministers of Kazakhstan, Georgia, Turkmenistan, and Azerbaijan. Their agreement to continue with studies on the Baku-Ceyhan plan was backed in late April when the Turkish, Georgian, and Azerbaijani presidents met in northeast Turkey.[38] This commitment was reiterated in a more solemn form at a meeting of the presidents of Turkey, Georgia, Azerbaijan, Kazakhstan, and Uzbekistan on the occasion marking the seventy-fifth anniversary of the Turkish Republic on October 29, 1998. The presidents signed the Ankara Declaration in which they expressed their political commitment to Baku-Ceyhan as the main export pipeline.[39]

All these were, however, only political commitments; they did not impose any legal or financial obligation on the states concerned. Bilateral and multilateral groups of experts tried to negotiate the difficult details of the construction of the pipeline, the sharing of costs among the states involved and the oil companies that will have to build the pipeline, and the sharing of revenues. These negotations have been complicated by a continuing quarrel between Turkish experts and the AIOC about the cost estimations of the project. Turkish studies put the costs at about U.S.$2.3 billion, whereas estimations of the oil companies are U.S.$4 billion to $4.5 billion, which would make the pipeline economically unattractive. Negotiations are mainly concerned with a Turkish guarantee for settling the cost overrun beyond its own estimated figure.[40]

In following its interests concerning the Baku-Ceyhan pipeline, Ankara did not abstain from playing the card of the Turkish Straits. Although the Montreux Convention of 1936 stipulates that Turkey has to concede free passage through the straits to anybody at any time, except times of war, the Turkish government made it very clear that it was not ready to allow the foreseeable increase in traffic of large oil tankers that would result from shipments of all future Caspian crude from the Russian harbor of Novorossiisk or from Georgia's port of Supsa. The main reason Ankara gave was the environmental and catastrophic risk that would result for the 12 million people of Istanbul.[41]

In 1994 Ankara introduced a new Safety of Passage Act for the straits that restricts traffic of ships carrying combustible and other dangerous material. Ankara intends to uphold this regulation despite severe criticism from Russia, Bulgaria, Romania, Greece, and Cyprus that first erupted at the general meeting of the International Maritime Organization (IMO) in London in November 1997.[42] But the safety of passage will be improved by the introduction of a Vessel Traffic Services System that has been developed by a task force headed by the former naval forces commander, Admiral Güven Erkaya, who was also special advisor to Prime Minister Mesut Yılmaz on maritime affairs. With the new system in place by 2000, the straits should be much better able to cope with the expected traffic.[43] In view of Turkey's efforts the International Maritime Organization's Safety Committee abstained from dealing with the Russian complaints about traffic conditions in its May 1998 session, which did not, however, prevent the Russians from bringing the matter up again at the 1999 meeting of the IMO's committee.[44]

Turkish concerns regarding the risks of greater oil traffic through the straits cannot easily be neglected given the past record of accidents in the Bosporus.[45] The possibility of completely closing the straits to large oil shipments after an accident with heavy consequences for the inhabitants of

Istanbul cannot be totally excluded. But it was not only environmental concern that drove Turkey's policy. In late 1998 the AIOC members further postponed a decision about the main export pipeline due to the unsolved question of its commercial viability. As a reaction, the former Turkish minister of maritime affairs, Burhan Kara, threatened to raise the transit fees for the straits fivefold, commenting "then they will see what happens to their dreams of cheap oil." And in an uncontrolled reaction the Turkish government declared a virtual boycott of British Petroleum and Amoco, which it considered the driving forces behind the AIOC's reluctance.[46]

The boardroom decisionmakers of the international oil consortia have not been very much impressed by the political maneuvering of the Turkish and American governments. For them, economic and financial considerations are the decisive factors; only a profitable plan will be chosen. Growing uncertainties about the magnitude of the Caspian oil potential and the speed of oil production compel the companies to be cautious. It seems likely that for a considerable time the existing pipelines could cope with the expected production, especially if their capacity were upgraded.[47] This throws doubt on the necessity for a new main exporting pipeline, be it Baku-Supsa or Baku-Ceyhan.

Estimations of economic profitability are also influenced by politics, especially in this volatile region with its high potential for intra- and interstate conflicts. The weight of these factors has been increased by the politicization of regional energy development by the American and Turkish governments. Thus it cannot come as a surprise that the oil companies are asking these governments to shoulder a considerable part of the pipeline costs. This would diminish the expected direct economic benefits for Turkey.

Oil investors react to difficult-to-calculate political costs and risks, the possibility of a lastingly low price for crude, and uncertain production prospects by extending their investment periods. According to its spokeswoman the AIOC has reduced its budget for 1999 to U.S.$315 million as compared to a budget of U.S.$700 million in 1998.[48] Moreover, the international oil companies that finally will have to bear the risk of any investment in the regional pipeline project are not under pressure. An oil shortage is unlikely in the near future. Iraq's eventual return to the oil market would mean additional proven reserves of a magnitude that would be roughly equal to the Caspian potential. Caspian oil will not be needed until the beginning of the twenty-first century when increasing demand in East and South Asia will add considerably to world demand.

There is, however, pressure on regional governments to build the pipelines to get the funds needed to improve severely depressed social conditions that threaten the long-term social and political stability of their countries.[49] This may explain, besides their wish to couple their countries more closely with the international economic structures, the recent strong commitment of the Azerbaijani and Georgian leaders to the construction of the Baku-Ceyhan pipeline. If the U.S. government would maintain its pressure in the interest of realizing the east-west energy transportation corridor, if the Turkish government would come up soon with a generous financing plan for Baku-Ceyhan, and if there would not be another outbreak of violent conflict in the region, there may be a good chance to get a decision in principle on the main export pipeline for Azerbaijani oil until 2001. This would not, however, mean that construction would be started immediately. It will not begin until there is reason to believe enough oil, besides the already existing outlets for the early oil, will be available to ensure the profitability of the project.

The situation is further complicated by combining the issue of oil pipelines with those of gas pipelines in the east-west corridor scheme. At present, Turkey satisfies its increasing demand for natural gas by deliveries from Russia that reach the country via Bulgaria. To increase the deliveries, Turkey and Russia have agreed to build a gas pipeline through the Black Sea to the Turkish port of Samsun from where the gas could be pumped into the Anatolian grid. To realize this Blue Stream project, the Russian energy giant Gazprom has concluded a joint venture with the Italian ENI, but the venture has suffered severely from the latest financial crisis in Russia. Nevertheless, dependence on Russian gas will last for some time, which means Ankara cannot ignore Russian interests with respect to the planned oil pipelines. Therefore the Turkish government does not oppose the delivery of Azerbaijani early oil to Novorossiisk and has declared that it will not impede its transport through the straits. Even an increase in oil traffic due to the operation of the CPC's Tengiz-Novorossiisk pipeline will be tolerated if it does not lead to the abolition of the Baku-Ceyhan project.

To loosen dependence on Russia, Turkey has engaged in securing alternative gas supply, but these deals too are not without problems. A big gas deal concluded with Iran in 1996 by Prime Minister Necmettin Erbakan of the Islamist Welfare Party severely annoyed the U.S. administration. Turkey tried to soften the American anger by restricting its financial participation to the Turkish part of the planned pipeline and by combining the Iran-Turkey pipeline with plans for a larger project that aims to bring Turkmen natural gas to Europe via Iran and Turkey (work has already started on the Iran-Turkmenistan leg).

Although Washington finally came to the conclusion that Turkey's Iran gas deal does not violate the Iran-Libya Sanctions Act, the Clinton administration continues its efforts to persuade Turkey that a trans-Caspian gas pipeline from Turkmenistan to Baku and on to Turkey as part of the east-west energy transportation corridor would be at least equally attractive.[50] Ankara has proved to be open to such American suggestions, and on October 29, 1998, a preliminary gas purchase agreement was signed by President Süleyman Demirel and his Turkmen counterpart Saparmurat Niyazov. This agreement was turned into a final purchase agreement in May 1999 when the Turkish minister for energy and natural resources, Ziya Aktaş, signed another agreement that foresees the construction of a 2,000-kilometer gas pipeline through the Caspian Sea, Azerbaijan, and Georgia to Turkey. It could be linked to the European pipeline grid to provide Turkmen gas to European consumers. The pipeline has a capacity of 20 billion cubic meters a year, of which Turkey plans to buy 16 billion. Gas delivery is expected to start by 2002.[51] With this move, Turkey and Turkmenistan now have agreements on natural gas that could either be delivered via Iran or via the trans-Caspian route. Of these options the one through Iran is far more developed; the trans-Caspian one exists only on paper. It remains to be seen which will finally be realized.

In following its oil pipeline interests Ankara has to take into consideration American hostility toward Tehran and has to avoid the impression that its gas pipeline plans run counter to American regional policy goals. But Turkey has no interest in antagonizing Iran with which, for various reasons, it must have functioning and neighborly relations.[52]

As a consequence, to reap the fruits of its pipeline plans, Turkey has to design a policy that will keep the American support for the Baku-Ceyhan plan without antagonizing Russia and Iran too much. This asks for skillful energy diplomacy, but in the end Ankara may have to make clear choices if it wants to get a share of Central Asian energy at all.

This complicated pattern of energy relations that not only affects Turkey's regional policy in the Caspian Basin but also its relations with the United States and Russia imposes on Turkish foreign policy a delicate balancing act that far transcends its regional policy in the (greater) Middle East. This situation, which is full of contradictory elements, contributes to an awareness of high risk among the security and foreign policy elite in Ankara.[53] It adds to the general feeling of uneasiness and insecurity that has led to stronger demands for cooperation by Turkey's Western allies and to a simultaneous upgrading of Turkish efforts at defending its perceived national interests, if necessary unilaterally.

Business

Turkish industry and business undertake many efforts to consolidate and expand their position in Central Asia. The Turkish government lends as much support as it can to these efforts by providing financial and technical assistance to the Central Asian states. These combined efforts have shown mixed results: Turkey has developed a fairly dense network of communications with the region (telecommunication, traffic lines, transport). Its main financial institutions are operating in all important countries. Business relations have been successful, although not without some mutual disappointments. And political support of economic activities has shown a lack of momentum because of domestic political instability, especially during the RP-DYP coalition government in 1996–97. Economic relations with the new republics are by far outdone by economic relations with Russia. Nevertheless, Turkey is becoming the regional hub of economic activities of European and American multinationals in Central Asian, Transcaucasian, and Middle Eastern markets. Economic relations with the newly independent states would profit from a solution to the various regional conflicts in the Transcaucasus, some of which directly affect Turkey's regional policy.

From the very beginning of their political independence, Turkey made great efforts to help the Central Asian states become economically independent by developing their national economies and the structural basis of functioning market economies.[54] Ankara has signed more than 200 agreements with the republics in the economic, cultural, educational, communications and transport, technical assistance, and training fields. The Turkish Eximbank has provided US$1.1 billion as program and investment credits and subsidies for Turkish foodstuffs to the new republics. Further credit engagements sometimes have been hampered by difficulties in timely repayment by some of the Turkic states, for example, Azerbaijan.

Technical assistance, training, and cultural cooperation have mainly been conducted under the umbrella of the Turkish International Cooperation Agency (TICA), an institution founded in 1992 for these purposes that is affiliated with the Turkish Ministry of Foreign Affairs. TICA organizes and supports training managers and state officials, preparing a "Turkic" dictionary, developing university curricula, and transferring Turkey's highly successful national program of developing small-enterprise industrial sites to the Central Asian states.[55] TICA was also instrumental in creating the Eurasian Union of Chambers and Bourses as well as the News Agencies Union of the Turkish Speaking Countries. The organization often also acts as the Turkish liaison to other international organizations that are active in the same area and fields.

The Turkish business and trade community is also active in the Central Asian states. Turkish companies have invested more than US$6 billion in the region. Besides some of Turkey's large construction companies that are building hotels, airports, and other infrastructural complexes, hundreds of smaller industrial and trading firms are active in almost all branches of the Central Asian economies.[56] They take advantage of the fairly well developed communication infrastructure between Turkey and most of the new republics. Istanbul has become an air transport hub for flights to the region, and a considerable part of telecommunication from Central Asia to the world is conducted via satellite through Turkish installations.

Many of the international firms that have subsidiaries in Turkey use these facilities for expanding their activities in Central Asia and the Transcaucasus. In doing so they profit from both the lower costs in Turkey compared with European countries and from the easier access Turks generally have to the new republics due to linguistic and cultural affinities.

Mutual expectations, however, have had to be tempered from euphoric exaggerations in the early period of relations to more sober evaluations of possibilities.[57] Turkish businesses had to learn to come to terms with Central Asian bureaucracies, which have often stuck to old Soviet habits, and with nepotism and corruption as well as professional inexperience. The Central Asian administrations and new business people have had to realize that kinship not always implies the fair behavior of their new Turkish cousins. What contributed more to realign exaggerated expectations has been the endemic shortage of hard currency in the Central Asian states that has severely inhibited business expansion.

This can be seen from trade figures. Exports to the five Turkic republics in 1998 reached U.S.$831.3 million. Although this is more than double the figure for 1993, it is only one-third the value of Turkish exports to all members of the Commonwealth of Independent States (CIS), which stood at U.S.$2.66 billion. The same holds true for Turkish imports from the region: U.S.$448.8 million accounts for a bit over one-tenth of imports from the whole CIS. Turkey's total trade volume of U.S.$1.28 billion with the Turkic republics equals that of its trade with Ukraine (U.S.$1.26 billion). Of all Turkic republics, only Kazakhstan ranked among Turkey's top forty trading partners with a trade volume of U.S.$466.62 million.[58]

The breakup of the Soviet Union boosted Russian-Turkish trade and other economic relations. Officially, Russia ranks sixth among Turkey's trading partners with a volume of U.S.$4.230 billion in 1998, but actual trade has been much greater in recent years if one takes into account the nonregistered "suitcase trade," which only started to decline in the second half of 1998 after Russia's renewed financial crisis. Suitcase trade has little to do with its name but is managed by way of trucks and even vessels carrying "everything from boxes of tangerines to Korean four-wheel drive cars and ironing boards."[59]

Nevertheless, Turkey and its business community have managed to establish themselves firmly in the economic life of the Turkic republics in Central Asia and the Trancaucasus. The low level of economic activity and exchange is mainly caused by the lack of economic and political development of the new republics.[60] There is, however, potential for improvement if and when the energy problems have been resolved, which would also imply that most of the actual or potential crises and tensions in the region would have come to an end. As in other parts of post–cold war Eurasia, economic development in Central Asia and the Transcaucasus very much depends on regional political stability. Turkey's potential contributions to reaching that goal are, however, severely restricted by its limited economic, military, and political capabilities.

Kinship

The Turkish government has toned down its political rhetoric of creating a community of Turkic nations to embrace the more realistic aim of assisting the new republics to develop their Turkic identity if they so wish. However, quieter official efforts at creating a sense of commonality between Turkey and the new republics continue unabated. Nongovernmental organizations are also active in creating links to the Turkic republics. These activities sometimes create problems for the government, especially if they are directed at supporting the cause of opposition groups in the new republics or if they are openly advocating the assembly of all Turkic people under Turkey's leadership. Nevertheless, in the long term, cultural relations of any kind seem to carry the most promising prospects for establishing Turkey's permanent influence in the new republics. This presence is increased by the spreading of Turkish media throughout Central Asia and Transcaucasia.

The Turkish government has tried to underwrite the newly established relationship by offering 10,000 scholarships for students from these countries. Besides that, Turkey is cooperating with the republics in establishing vocational training schools, high schools, and even universities, as in Kazakhstan and Kyrgyzstan.[61] The Ministry of Culture and the Ministry of Education provide personnel, equipment, and training materials. Many of these activities are coordinated by TICA. In addition to these public efforts, a division of the religious order Nurcular under the leadership of Fethullah Gülen, the so-called Fethullahcıları, has opened about one hundred privately run schools in the new republics that place a strong emphasis on high-quality modern education, although the organizational background is a religious one. Generally, these activities are regarded as a welcome supplement to Turkey's official endeavors in cultural and educational cooperation with the Turkic states.[62]

Of a much different kind are the activities of the various solidarity groups and cultural associations where Turks of Caucasian ethnic background gather. They normally support the drive for independence of their kin in the region, whether in Russia or some of the newly established states in the Caucasus. Groups that supported the Chechnian cause and those that support Abkhazian independence from Georgia have become most prominent. Their activity often creates problems for the Turkish government in relations with the countries concerned. It also constitutes a new factor in devising Turkey's foreign policy, which is much more open to public pressure and influence than it was ten years ago.[63]

Sometimes these organizations also display pan-Turkic leanings, although this is much more pronounced in the activities of other private organizations that direct their interest toward the Central Asian states. The Turkic States and Communities Friendship, Brotherhood and Cooperation Foundation (TUDEV) that was strongly influenced by Alparslan Türkeş, the late leader of the pan-Turkic Nationalist Action Party (MHP), has organized six so-called Turkic states and communities assemblies gathering delegations from the whole Turkish world, including Northern Cyprus and "Turkic" republics of the Russian Federation.[64] These events have been regularly attended by high-level Turkish politicians, including Presidents Özal and Demirel and Prime Minister Çiller. These and other openly pan-Turkic activities that have been sponsored by the Ministry of Education and the Directorate of Religious Affairs have contributed to Russian concerns regarding Turkey's political goals in the region.[65]

The pan-Turkic lobby has made few inroads on the formulation of Turkey's foreign policy toward Central Asia and the Transcaucasus. Even when the MHP became a partner in Ecevit's coalition government after the 1999 elections, Turkish foreign policy carefully avoided any pan-Turkic twist, although the emphasis on relations with the NIS was somewhat upgraded.

Perspectives: Functional Regime Building or Classic Political Games?

Turkey has quickly learned to take into account the conflicting interests and superior resources of other participants in the regional political and economic affairs in Central Asia and the Transcaucasus. This holds especially true of Russia, which has established itself again as an important regional power, although clearly not as dominant as the Soviet Union. Russia constitutes the main obstacle to the realization of Turkey's energy-related regional interests and also has succeeded in regaining military positions in Turkey's immediate vicinity.[66] Turkey's dependence on Iran for its energy needs also restricts Ankara's room to maneuver in the region when Iranian interests come into play, for instance regarding the Caspian Sea or gas pipeline proposals.

Turkey cannot realize its goals concerning Central Asia and the Caspian Basin by relying only on its own resources and capabilities. Ankara has to develop a long-term policy that is coordinated with the political interests of its American and, to a lesser extent, European allies. This policy should not only concentrate on developing bilateral relations and on energy matters but should also aim at a multilateralization of Central Asian political and economic patterns and furthering the development of nonenergy businesses. Making use of a division of labor between various parties and establishing a regional infrastructural network is the best long-term guarantee for relative political and economic autonomy of all states in Central Asia and the Transcaucasus. In such a plan Turkey can be an important catalyst, especially if it can secure the long-term support of its Western allies.

Given its limited resources for following a far-reaching national Central Asia policy, Turkey should continue to develop multilateral political and economic plans into platforms for the discussion and realization of commonly agreed policies for the long-term development of the region. This holds especially true for the "Turkic summits," the meetings of the heads of states of Turkey, Azerbaijan, Kazakhstan, Uzbekistan, Turkmenistan, and Kyrgyzstan, that have been initiated by Ankara. Four such meetings have taken place since 1992, but Turkish and Central Asian interest in such events of a wider scope seemingly has diminished. Turkey could try to revive them, not as a platform for establishing some special relationship with the NIS but as a high-level event for the gradual development of regional regimes that would link the various Central Asian states to each other and to important extraregional forces and institutions. This would, however, require a certain readjustment of the Central Asian policies of Turkey and the United States, which in the past few years have become dominated by pipeline considerations and their strategic implications.

New strategic "great games" in the region will, however, create winners and losers and contribute to lasting instability. Such games always bear the risk of becoming militarized, especially if some of the losers feel strong enough to turn their luck by resorting to force. Armenia may become such a case if it were denied participation in the gains of the east-west energy transport corridor. A regionally isolated and relatively impoverished Armenia could try to invoke Russian or Iranian support to undermine Azerbaijan's privileged position by refueling the conflict over Nagorno-Karabakh. Such a development would not leave Turkey unaffected, especially after construction of the Baku-Ceyhan pipeline. This can be understood from Turkey's past involvement in the conflict, which has complicated relations with both Azerbaijan and Armenia.[67]

Ankara is thus interested in helping to bring about a Caspian and even a Central Asian configuration that would enable it to profit from its advantages in relations with the Central Asian and Transcaucasian states without being sucked into regional conflicts. To realize such interests under the conditions of growing globalization, policies based on the functional requirements of the world energy situation and following market forces may be more successful in the long term than classic geopolitics and power games. For Turkey this could mean basing its energy-related Caspian and Central Asian policy less on the Baku-Ceyhan pipeline and more on developing its potential as a natural gas hub between east and west.

CHAPTER EIGHT

The Middle East: Between Involvement and Active Engagement

TURKISH SCHOLAR Soli Özel has concisely described the change that has taken place in Turkey's relations with its Middle Eastern neighbors in the 1990s: "As Turkey undergoes the most profound economic, social, and political crisis of the republican period, Ankara also finds itself involved in the affairs of the Middle East with unprecedented intensity."[1] The demise of the Soviet Empire left the United States as the only major outside power with leverage on Middle Eastern developments. The Gulf War in 1991 changed the balance of power among the regional nations by eliminating Iraq as a regional power for some time to come. The peace talks between Israel and the Palestinians that began in the aftermath of the Gulf War brought further changes to the political landscape of the Middle East. These developments and Turkey's involvement in them strongly influenced its perception of its national interests in the region.

But contrary to expectations that prevailed at the beginning of the decade, no "new world order" and no "new Middle East" emerged. The Palestinian-Israeli peace process slowed down after the Netanyahu government took over in Tel Aviv. Saddam Hussein could consolidate his reign over Iraq and establish the country as a continuous troublemaker in the region by regularly provoking the United Nations as well as the United States. None of the conservative regimes on the Arab peninsula was able to stabilize its precarious internal situation. And Iran continued to support Islamist forces in the region, contributing to instability in many countries and a continued terrorist threat against Israel. Any attempts at creating some type of regionwide, multinational security, political, or economic regime have been unsuccessful.

Under these conditions Turkey has had difficulties developing a comprehensive and consistent policy that would serve its national interests in the region. Although the bases of its foreign policy—preservation of national integrity, modernization along Western standards, and noninvolvement in domestic issues of neighboring countries that could endanger peace and stability—have not changed, policies for their realization in the Middle East have had to be adapted to fit their context. [2]

A much debated problem has been if and how far Turkey should use its unavoidable involvement in crucial issues of Middle Eastern politics to actively influence the course of regional developments in the wake of the 1991 Persian Gulf War. Political evidence suggests that President Turgut Özal favored an active approach to regional affairs, using Turkey's economic potential as a catalyst for forging a new cooperative regional political structure.[3] He hoped to replace the traditional contest between the contenders for regional hegemonic leadership with a more modern pattern of political order in which Turkey could also be more prominent. As a by-product of such a development, Özal hoped, Turkey's standing with its Western allies would improve.[4] These aspirations came to an end after the 1991 elections returned the old political guard to power.

Özal's successors preferred a return to traditional Turkish Middle Eastern policy, one that kept its distance from regional affairs and tried to establish equal relations with all important states in the region.[5] Many observers doubt, however, if and how far such a position is any longer feasible. These doubts are even nourished by some elements of Turkey's regional policy itself that can only be interpreted as moves toward stronger regional engagement, such as the growing relationship with Israel.

One cannot see anything like a grand design behind Turkey's political activity in the Middle East. Özal might have dreamt of his country becoming the Japan or South Korea of the region. But the country's more active engagement in some matters is mostly motivated by political reactions to changes that have occurred in the region since the beginning of the 1990s and that directly affect national security. This caution is in line with the traditional leitmotiv of Turkish foreign policy.[6]

Four challenges are focal points of Turkey's Middle Eastern policy in the 1990s.[7] First, the unwelcome but unavoidable deep involvement in northern Iraq has had repercussions not only for Turkish-Iraqi relations but also for relations with two other immediate neighbors, Iran and Syria. Second, a recently forged special relationship with Israel is dominated by rapidly growing cooperation in military matters that tends to complicate relations with the Arab countries. Third, Turkey has experienced persistent problems with Syria and Iraq over the use of the water in the Euphrates-Tigris basin. Finally, the nation has found it difficult to balance relations with Iran between ideological delimitation and neighborly behavior born of strong economic incentives in energy imports. These matters also affect Ankara's relations with the United States and, to a somewhat lesser extent, its European partners. Thus it must balance its Middle Eastern policy with its Western foreign policy.

Northern Iraq and the Future of the Iraqi Regime

When President Özal firmly positioned Turkey at the side of the U.S.-led alliance in the 1991 Gulf War, he hoped his policy might contribute to a more important Turkish role in the region. To reach this goal, he was ready to override considerable domestic resistance.[8] He even risked a conflict with the military leadership that culminated in the resignation of the chief of the General Staff, General Necip Torumtay, in December 1990 because of serious policy differences over the crisis.[9] By bringing the parliament to pass an extended war powers bill on January 17, 1991, Özal even opened the way for the establishment of a second front by enabling U.S. fighter aircraft to fly sorties against Iraq from the Turkish air base of İncirlik. For the first time in republican history, Arab neighbors were attacked from Turkish soil, although Turkish forces did not participate in military actions.[10]

Özal took the risks because, besides some strong domestic policy considerations, he was interested in changing a regime in Iraq whose policies he regarded as very possibly dangerous for Turkey's fundamental national interests.[11] Some months before the invasion of Kuwait, Saddam Hussein had threatened the visiting Turkish prime minister, Yıldırım Akbulut, that diminishing U.S. Middle East involvement would leave Turkey without an ally in the region. Thus "the war neutralized one of Ankara's most serious potential security problems and consequently broadened its room for maneuver in pursuit of a new regional and international strategy."[12] In designing his policy with respect to the Gulf crisis, Özal had expected "a quick war and a decisive allied victory, followed by the replacement of Saddam Hussein's regime by a democratic system in Iraq."[13]

Özal's policy quickly faltered when it became obvious that the alliance would not actively pursue removing Saddam Hussein from power. The situation became worse when the U.S. government refused to support the Shi'ite and Kurdish uprisings in southern and northern Iraq, respectively, immediately after the military defeat of Saddam. The establishment of a safe haven north of the 36th parallel to protect the Kurds against further persecution by Saddam's troops created a very uncomfortable situation for Turkey, as did the prospect of having to get along with the Iraqi dictator.[14]

The Gulf War caused direct Turkish involvement in determining the unresolved fate of the Iraqi Kurds and in Saddam Hussein's struggle with the United Nations and the United States. Ankara had to develop a delicate balance between Turkish national security interests and alliance solidarity with regard to Washington's halfhearted efforts to eliminate Hussein as a political force in the Middle East. Turkey's involvement also complicated its relations with Syria and Iran.

The establishment of the safe haven south of the Turkish-Iraqi border and the larger no-fly zone north of the 36th parallel under the aegis of the allied Operation Provide Comfort (OPC) that mainly operated out of Turkey's İncirlik NATO airbase proved inadequate in providing lasting stability for the Kurdish-inhabited northern Iraq.[15] The attempt to establish autonomous Kurdish rule in the region based on a careful balance of competences and official positions between the two rival Kurdish groups, the Kurdistan Democratic Party (KDP) of Massoud Barzani and the Patriotic Union of Kurdistan (PUK) under the leadership of Jalal Talabani, lasted for only two years. In 1993 the rivalry between them erupted in military clashes that finally ended in partitioning of the region among the parties.[16] Barzani and his KDP controlled the northwestern part of the region, including the border with Turkey. The more southern and eastern parts, including the "capital" of Erbil and the border with Iran, came under the control of the PUK.[17] American and French attempts at mediating between them in conferences in Ireland and France failed to generate a lasting détente, as had been the fate of an earlier Turkish effort.

For Turkey these developments constituted a continuous source of concern because of the growing political and security vacuum in northern Iraq and its effect on the precarious situation in Turkey's southeast. Already the creation of the safe haven and the ensuing establishment of the autonomous Kurdish authority had disturbed many in Ankara's security circles. They feared that this could be the first step in dismembering Iraq and establishing an autonomous Kurdish state from which bad effects would spread not only into Turkey's southeast but to the entire Middle East. Thus in late 1992 the government established regular high-level contact with Iran and Syria, the other two countries that have been affected by the development of the Kurdish issue in the regional context. Five meetings, some at the level of foreign ministers, took place from 1992 to February 1994, when the endeavor came to an end because of growing political differences among the three countries.[18]

Turkey itself had contributed to the creation of the situation that caused so much concern to its political and security establishment. In April 1991 it needed to get the international community, especially the United States and the United Nations, to do something to stop the flood of Kurdish refugees that had approached the Turkish border after Iraqi troops had invaded the Kurdish area in northern Iraq. Turkish authorities did not want to repeat the experience of refugee camps in the southeastern border provinces that they endured after a previous Iraqi incursion into the Kurdish region. Under the post–Gulf War circumstances such a situation could take on a Palestinian-like permanence with unforeseeable consequences for Turkey's domestic stability and its international relations. "Operation Provide Comfort" was the only logical solution for this problem, however reluctantly the Turkish political leadership might have accepted the idea of leaving developments in northern Iraq to the political skills and ambitions of the Iraqi Kurds and of providing Turkish NATO facilities for allied air control.

Turkey was not, however, without influence on developments in northern Iraq. The mandate for the allied air force in İncirlik had to be renewed by the Turkish parliament every six months. After Saddam Hussein imposed a de facto embargo on the Kurdish area, all deliveries for the Kurds had to pass through Turkish border gates; personnel of international relief organizations could also enter the area only through Turkey. The viability and durability of the Kurdish autonomous region thus depended on Turkish benevolence. As Massoud Barzani admitted in 1994, "We consider our relations with Turkey to be extremely vital. It is our gateway to the outside world."[19]

Turkey was dependent on Kurdish cooperation in its fight against the PKK. Barzani's KDP controls areas in northern Iraq near the Turkish border that are important to the guerrillas in preparing for terrorist activities on Turkish soil or in being used as logistic and recreation bases. As early as October 1991, when Barzani was unable or unwilling to keep a cooperation agreement with Turkey for the control of the PKK in that area, the Turkish military started air strikes and low-level military incursions into northern Iraq to destroy PKK forces and bases.

The situation deteriorated after the outbreak of fighting between the Barzani and Talabani factions in 1994. As a result, Turkish leaders believed the PKK could take almost unhindered advantage of room to maneuver in the border areas.[20] Finally, in March 1995 Turkey staged a large military invasion of northern Iraq to clear the area of PKK presence. This caused a lot of criticism from the Iraqi Kurds, who had not been informed of Ankara's intentions, from the Iraqi government, which complained of the violation of its territory, and from Turkey's Western, especially European, allies, who urged a quick withdrawal of the 35,000 Turkish troops from the region.[21]

No lasting stabilization could be achieved, and Turkey was confronted with another challenge in summer 1996 when Barzani invited Iraqi troops to help him drive Talabani from Erbil and most of northern Iraq. Barzani felt threatened by an Iranian military presence that Talabani had allegedly called into the area controlled by him to fight Iranian Kurdish opposition groups there. Barzani saw no alternative to asking support from Saddam to hold his position against the perceived Talabani-Tehran coalition. However, under pressure from the United States, which started cruise missile attacks on Iraqi military installations in southern Iraq, Saddam Hussein withdrew his troops from the area, and in October 1996 Talabani was able to recapture much of his lost territory. A preliminary cease-fire was established under the guidance of the United States, Turkey, and Great Britain that was turned into the so-called Ankara process aimed at brokering a new arrangement between the two Kurdish groups.[22] In the meantime the U.S. Central Intelligence Agency scheme to organize a domestic uprising against Saddam Hussein had suffered severe damage, and Washington had been forced to precipitately evacuate some thousand Kurdish collaborators from northern Iraq.

By then some facts had become clear for Ankara. Saddam Hussein was still a force in northern Iraq since the Kurds did not dissociate themselves completely from him, his past atrocities against them notwithstanding. The U.S. government had proven unable to devise a convincing policy of containing the Iraqi dictator, not to speak of ousting him. Operation Provide Comfort had lost its meaning after the Kurdish groups had reestablished their old habit of drawing in outside support from Baghdad or Tehran.[23] And because the plan had never been fully supported by Turkey's political circles, it came to an end on December 31, 1996, when the Turkish parliament refused to renew the allied mandate.

The plan was, however, replaced by a similar operation, Northern Watch, that continued the activities of OPC under a somewhat reduced mandate and without further French participation.[24] Paris, meanwhile, had become weary of U.S. policy toward the Iraqi regime and wanted to restore its former good relations with Baghdad, especially after UN Security Council resolution 968 had allowed the sale of a limited amount of Iraqi oil for the purchase of food for the country's starving population. This move also enabled the reopening of the pipeline between Iraq's oil fields in the north and the Turkish Mediterranean oil harbor of Yumurtalık.[25]

These events changed the constellation of forces with respect to developments in northern Iraq. It further undermined Turkish trust in the ability of Iraq's Kurdish leaders to establish effective control in the area by themselves. This inability was confirmed by the slow progress of the Ankara process. Despite some headway on procedures and organizational structures, only a control regime for monitoring the cease-fire with representatives from non-Kurdish northern Iraqi minorities, the Turkoman and Assyrians, was in place by May 1997 when Turkey started another of its large spring invasions to destroy PKK bases in northern Iraq. This time, KDP fighters were involved in activities against PKK targets because the latent KDP-PKK differences had flared up again.[26]

Despite strong criticism from the Iraqi government and various Arab countries as well as from its main European partners, Turkey continued the operation with about 50,000 troops and strong air support for more than six weeks. It can be assumed that since then a small number of Turkish troops has stayed in Iraqi territory and from time to time have been reinforced for operations against PKK bases. In any case the Turkish military staged large operations in northern Iraq in September 1997, December 1997, and May 1998. In these operations the military often cooperated with KDP forces, which had come under attack by the PKK and sometimes by the PUK, which sought to regain the position stipulated by the cease-fire agreement of October 1996. Because the PUK seemingly cooperated with PKK forces that had established a stronghold on PUK-controlled territory, the Turkish military believed that supporting KDP counterattacks was legitimate.

In September 1998 the U.S. administration succeeded in ending the feud between the KDP and the PUK. Meeting in Washington for the first time in four years, Barzani and Talabani reached an agreement to end the fighting and again try to establish a functioning common Kurdish administration in northeren Iraq. The so-called Washington Agreement called for a commitment to a federative Kurdish political entity within a "united, pluralistic, and democratic Iraq" that "would maintain the nation's unity and territorial integrity." The agreement also delineated a transitional period during which, under the guidance of the Higher Coordination Committee that had been established by the Ankara Agreement of October 1996, full normalization of political and other living conditions in the region should be achieved, including the formation of an interim joint regional government. The Kurds agreed on the organization of "free and fair elections for a new regional assembly" that were to take place by July 1999. In this assembly the Kurdish, Turkoman, Assyrian, and Chaldean populations would be represented. The agreement contained an understanding of revenue sharing between KDP and PUK areas plus a firm commitment of both groups to deny sanctuary to the PKK throughout the Iraqi Kurdish region and to "prevent the PKK from destabilizing and undermining the peace or from violating the Turkish border."[27]

The Washington Agreement caused some irritation and concern in Ankara, although the U.S. administration and the Kurdish leaders were quick to declare that it had to be regarded as a further result of the Ankara process. Turkish political leaders, especially Deputy Prime Minister Bülent Ecevit, were embarrassed that Turkey had been left out of the final rounds of negotiation and the signing of the agreement. They had the barely concealed suspicion that the agreement would open the way to eventual establishment of a separate Kurdish state in northern Iraq and would complicate future Turkish military incursions across the border.[28] To demonstrate its differing evaluation and its political independence, Ankara announced relations with Baghdad would be upgraded to the ambassadorial level, and it staged another military cross-border operation in November 1998.

Turkey also demonstrated its resolve to pursue its own policy on the Kurdish problem when it threatened Syria with a military invasion if the PKK leader, Abdullah Öcalan, were not expelled from his longtime refuge there. The quick and large Turkish military buildup along the border in early October 1998 convinced the Syrian leadership that Ankara meant business. Having located most of its troops toward the Israeli border, Syria would have been unable to withstand a large Turkish invasion. Because Damascus feared an Israeli plot to engage it in a two-theater war, although the Israelis were quick to deny any involvement in the Turkish move, it quickly gave in and accepted an understanding with Turkey that had been brokered by the Egyptian government. On October 19, representatives of both governments signed an agreement in which Damascus pledged to end all support for the PKK.[29] Öcalan's odyssey ended with his capture by Turkish special forces in Nairobi, Kenya, on February 16, 1999.

Turkish concerns about northern Iraq relaxed somewhat as it became clear, especially after a meeting of Talabani and Barzani in Ankara in early November 1998, that nobody really wanted to lastingly dissociate Turkey from the developments in northern Iraq and that the implementation of the Washington Agreement did not go as smoothly as foreseen on paper. In a midterm perspective, however, successful implementation cannot be totally foreclosed, and if a functioning Kurdish administration in the three northern Iraqi provinces of Erbil, Dohuk, and Süleymaniye can be established, a spillover into Turkey's Kurdish question cannot be excluded by encouraging Turkey's Kurds to increase their efforts to reach some type of political autonomy within the Turkish state.

Turkish-American cooperation and unity with regard to Iraq was further strained by the American military reaction to Baghdad's renunciation of cooperation with the UN arms inspection teams. First, at the end of December 1998, immediately before the beginning of the Islamic holy month of Ramadan, the United States and Great Britain punished Saddam with Operation Desert Fox, the bombing of Baghdad, for his repeated nonfulfillment of UN resolutions concerning the control and dismantlement of Iraqi weapons of mass destruction and their production facilities. This ended the UN control regime in Iraq. The ensuing deepening rift between Washington and Baghdad was not at all to the pleasure of Turkey's political leadership, which feared negative repercussions on Turkish-Iraqi relations.

In the following months the United States regularly reacted to Iraq's noncompliance to the restrictions of the no-fly zone in the north by attacking Iraqi military installations and fighter planes in the area. The use of İncirlik air base for this purpose was allowed by the Turkish government because it shared the American analysis that Saddam's regime had once again become a threat to neighboring countries. Turkish security concerns were taken into account by the American delivery of Patriot missile systems in January 1999.[30]

Nevertheless, the Turkish government of Prime Minister Ecevit was concerned at the growing militarization of America's attitude toward Iraq, and Ecevit accused Washington of not having a policy.[31] Turkey clearly preferred a political negotiation in dealing with the Iraqi regime, but it was restricted in its activity by the necessity of keeping good relations with Washington because of other vital Turkish interests such as the Baku-Ceyhan pipeline, continued military cooperation, American understanding with regard to the Cyprus problem, and American understanding of Ankara's heavy-handed approach toward its internal Kurdish problem.

Ecevit, however, tried to signal his differing opinion by inviting the Iraqi deputy prime minister, Tariq Aziz, to Ankara in February 1999. This not only annoyed Washington but also failed to produce any political results because it coincided with Öcalan's capture in Nairobi, which totally preoccupied Turkey's government and the Turkish public.[32]

Another element of Turkish irritation about American policy toward Baghdad was the Iraq Liberation Act passed by the U.S. Congress in autumn 1998. This legislation provided aid of U.S.$97 million for the Iraqi National Congress (INC), an umbrella organization of Iraqi opposition groups in exile, for a policy of toppling Saddam Hussein and replacing him with a democratic government. The U.S. administration approved of this move and appointed an official representative for relations with the Iraqi opposition. With this step the U.S. government for the first time openly was developing a policy of overthrowing Iraq's regime.

This move was followed with great concern in Turkey and other countries in the region. Ankara feared that the Iraqi opposition would not be able to establish a functioning political organization that could take over after the end of Saddam's regime. Such concerns may have been bolstered by the visible reluctance of Iraqi Kurdish leaders and the most prominent Iraqi Shi'ite organization to engage in too close a relationship with the INC.[33] As long as the oppositon groups cannot convincingly prove their ability to effectively replace the Iraqi regime, Ankara prefers Saddam to stay, which would, at least for the time being, foreclose a breakup of the regional political balance and give some security for the realization of Turkish national interests in developments in and around Iraq.

Developments in northern Iraq after the 1991 Gulf War left Turkey with mixed and somewhat contradictory interests. The establishment of a Kurdish state as a result of the weakening of Saddam Hussein's regime had to be prevented because of its possible consequences for Turkey's own Kurdish population. But major Iraqi assaults on the Kurds to restore Iraqi rule in the area were not welcome either because of the likelihood of invoking large refugee movements toward Turkey. Kurdish autonomous political authority in northern Iraq also had to be kept weak to prevent the creation of a Kurdish state but strong enough to be able to prevent the PKK from getting a lasting foothold south of the Turkish border. American interests in keeping Saddam ineffective by enforcing the UN sanctions and UN-led elimination of Iraq's potential of weapons of mass destruction also had to be duly taken into account by Ankara. In addition, Turkish economic interests demanded that Ankara keep relatively continuous and harmonious relations with Baghdad. Finally, all these elements could not hinder Turkey's maneuverability in following its security interests in its fight against the PKK terror in the southeast.

These conflicting concerns were characterized by a Turkish diplomat in late 1997: "If the KDP and the PUK agree, they risk creating a Kurdish entity, which is unacceptable to us. If they destroy each other, as is the case at the moment, the fighting will allow the PKK to strengthen its presence in the zone. We would hope for the return of Baghdad into the region, but the U.S. is totally opposed."[34]

Because the ideal solution—the establishment of a democratic Iraqi regime that would give a sufficient degree of autonomy to its Kurdish population, prevent the PKK from using Iraqi territory for its activities, and refrain from building up a large military arsenal—was out of question, Ankara was faced with difficult choices. Not surprisingly, it tried to realize all of its interests to some extent with different degrees of success at different times. The continuous renewal of the mandate for Operation Provide Comfort as well as its replacement by Northern Watch should accommodate the United States. Keeping political contact with both Iraqi Kurdish groups should provide their support against the PKK and ensure Turkish control over developments in northern Iraq. It should also enable relatively unhindered Turkish military operations against the PKK along the Iraqi border. Reestablishment of official relations with Baghdad at a lower diplomatic level relatively soon after the Gulf War, the more recent upgrading of diplomatic representation to the ambassadorial level, and the invitation of Tariq Aziz in February 1999 were aimed at preventing complete alienation between the neighboring states in order to secure a considerable share of possible economic benefits for Turkey from a lifting of the UN sanctions, especially in the context of the UN's oil-for-food program, that led also to the reopening of the twin oil pipeline between Kirkuk and Yumurtalık.[35]

The only exception to this policy of delicately balancing differing interests was the straightforward military activity against PKK strongholds. The Turkish armed forces made its decisions concerning the relevant actions fairly autonomously and with little regard to the Ankara process or the balance of intra-Kurdish relations between the KDP and PUK. Its basic rationale was to prevent a lasting establishment of PKK forces across the Turkish border, to protect Turkish military actions in the country's southeast from hostile interference, and to cut off PKK fighters in Turkey from possible areas of refuge in northern Iraq. If it was regarded as instrumental to that end, the Turkish armed forces were also ready to engage in limited cooperation with Barzani's KDP because their area of control partly overlapped the PKK's area of operation in northern Iraq. Such cooperation with Iraqi Kurds was, however, never allowed to restrict the military's freedom of action. The expulsion of Öcalan from Syria by threat of military intervention also served as an indirect warning to Baghdad and the Iraqi Kurdish leaders to take seriously Turkey's determination to fight the PKK wherever it could be reached.

Turkey's policy of not completely distancing itself from the Iraqi regime caused some problems in its relations with the United States. Turkey's political and military leadership never really accepted the U.S. policy of isolating Iraq and promoting the overthrow of Saddam Hussein for fear of threatening regional stability. There are also many in Ankara's leading circles who believe that the United States and other Western powers, willingly or unwillingly, are furthering the creation of a separate Kurdish state in northern Iraq, a development Turkey will never be ready to accept.[36]

Turkish support for Operation Provide Comfort was always guarded, and debates in the parliament over its prolongation were full of suggestions for abandoning it.[37] However, the Turkish military was able to convince the politicians that prolongation was in Turkey's interest. Even the Islamist Prime Minister Necmettin Erbakan made a U-turn and secured the support of his Welfare Party parliamentary group in July 1996, although when in opposition he had been one of the most ardent opposers of OPC. The Turkish armed forces welcomed the operation because the constant allied military involvement in northern Iraq could help soften public international reactions, especially American ones, to Turkish military incursions into the area.

Suspicions about OPC were but a special expression of a more general feeling of Turkey's people that "owing to the internationalized nature of the Iraqi problem, Turkey has lost its freedom of action in the region. Turkey's current dilemma is that while it is participating in the UN embargo against Iraq, in order to cooperate with U.S. and UN policies, it is actually working against its own interests."[38]

This is evident with respect to economic interests. Turkey suffered severe losses as a consequence of the sanctions imposed on Iraq. Iraq had been an important trade partner and Turkey's most important oil supplier. The economy in the southeast had been dependent on trade relations with Iraq and on income from the transit traffic to Iraq that mostly passed through that region.[39] The semilegal trade that developed with the Kurdish enclave over the years, especially the sometimes interrupted transport of diesel oil from the Kurdish area to Turkey's southeast, could not compensate the losses incurred from the breakdown of normal Turkish-Iraqi business. Turkey thus has a strong economic and, for some, political interest in seeing the UN sanctions lifted.

The Turkish political dilemma and the special position of the country came to the fore whenever tensions arose between the UN and the Iraqi government over the UN demands for controlling the destruction of Iraq's weapons of mass destruction. When such tensions escalated to a point where the United States took military actions against Iraq to enforce UN regulations, Turkey has been caught between its solidarity with the United States and the United Nations on the one hand and its interest in keeping smooth relations with Baghdad on the other. Furthermore, such situations have tended to create domestic political problems because of the divergent views of Turkey's various political forces. This was clear, for instance, during the crisis in early 1998 when the coalition government of Mesut Yılmaz had difficulties in forming a united position. The prime minister's ideas were more in line with the harsh U.S. approach toward Saddam, whereas his deputy and foreign policy coordinator, Bülent Ecevit from the DSP, seemed to display a more sympathetic attitude toward the Iraqi leader.[40] Even after the break between Baghdad and the United Nations and the start of American air strikes, the Ecevit government tried to keep open lines of friendly communication with the Iraqi leadership, although it also emphasized the necessity of Iraq's compliance with the UN resolution.

This overview of Turkey's complex involvement in Iraqi affairs after the Gulf War leads to the conclusion that Ankara is interested in a lasting settlement of the Iraq problem without, however, having the means to bring about such a settlement on its own or to induce its main ally to work for a settlement that would satisfy Turkish interests. There is a growing feeling in Turkey's political circles that sanctions against Iraq should end because the country does not pose a danger to the regional balance any longer. Such an attitude clearly contradicts American policy, which increasingly seeks ways of toppling Saddam's regime. Thus Turkey will continue to be in a situation in which "conflicting pressures from the allies, and Turkey's basic need to have good relations with Iraq, give rise to a perplexing foreign policy dilemma."[41]

The New Turkish-Israeli Strategic Cooperation

The signing of the Oslo agreement of September 1993 between Israel and the Palestine Liberation Organization (PLO) gave a boost to Turkey's relations with Israel. The PLO's recognition of Israel lessened the necessity of following an agonizingly balanced approach toward the Arab states and Israel. The cautious improvement of bilateral relations that had been under way for some years could be turned into the rapid development of a broad and far-reaching military, economic, and political cooperation.[42] While bilateral relations flourished, especially in the military field, expectations of possible Turkish or common contributions to the establishment of a new regional cooperative system could not be realized because of the change of government in Israel and the breakdown of Israeli-Syrian peace talks.

What in the beginning could have been regarded as a cooperative undertaking of the two most powerful states in the region to encourage the establishment of a new regional order developed into a special relationship with unclear perspectives. Syria, Iran, and Iraq felt directly threatened, and most other Arab states were wary about a new "military front" developing in the area that would be "ultimately protecting Israeli and American interests, and containing those states that opposed their policies."[43] This has mainly been the result of Ankara's firm stand on its new relationship with Israel during the Netanyahu era with its de facto freeze of the peace process. It remains to be seen if the return of the new Israeli Barak government to the earlier, more cooperative approach toward the peace process will also mollify Arab concerns about Turkish-Israeli cooperation. If so, the stabilizing effects of the cooperation on regional developments may become more visible.

After Oslo, high-level Turkish-Israeli visits took place that were accompanied by the signing of important bilateral agreements organizing cooperation in various areas. Between November 1993 and November 1994 Turkish Foreign Minister Hikmet Çetin, Israeli President Ezer Weizman, Israeli Foreign Minister Shimon Peres, and Turkish Prime Minister Tansu Çiller visited one another's countries. Çetin signed a memorandum of understanding that envisioned far-reaching cooperation, including military cooperation. Mrs. Çiller tried to pave the way for more intense economic relations. When Turkish President Süleyman Demirel visited Israel in March 1996, a free trade agreement was signed that complemented an agreement on military training cooperation signed in February and going unnoticed for some time.[44] With these agreements the two strongest economies and two of the most potent military forces of the region promised long-term cooperation to each other's benefit. Since then, regular diplomatic traffic of various members of government and other important political persons have accompanied the economic and military cooperation, emphasizing the importance that is attached to it by both sides.

With the Free Trade Agreement, Turkey seeks to align itself in a more indirect manner with the Israeli free trade agreements with the United States and the European Union, thus adding important elements to its own customs union with the European Union that took effect on January 1, 1996.[45] The relatively advanced state of both countries' industrial sectors is also a positive sign for a considerable growth potential in bilateral trade after the Free Trade Agreement has become fully operational. The trade balance has so far been in Turkey's favor. Turkey exports textiles, electronics, food products, and grain to Israel, while Israel sells chemicals, plastics, computers and telecommunication equipment, and irrigation equipment. Trade volume reached U.S.$760 million in 1998, an increase of 20 percent over 1997, and both sides hope that it may grow to US$1 billion by 2000.[46] Another improvement of economic ties could become Turkey's eventual provision of drinking water to Israel, although such ideas can, most likely, only be realized within a broader scheme of regional water policy after a lasting peace settlement between Israel and its Arab neighbors has been reached.

Trade and commercial relations have been accompanied by a surge in Israeli tourists going to Turkey, especially after 1993. For them, Turkey's southern shore not only is a fairly inexpensive nearby holiday area but also, with its casinos, until recently offered a welcome possibility for gambling, which is forbidden in Israel. The ban on casinos imposed in Turkey during the follow-up of the Susurluk affair in 1997 closed this outlet for Israelis. Nevertheless, in 1997 Israeli tourism grew 3.7 percent over that of 1996. Many of the 263,000 Jewish tourists came to Istanbul, which has been home to a Jewish community since Sephardic Jews were expelled from Spain in 1492 during the Catholic Reconquista. After the foundation of Israel many of these Jews emigrated from Istanbul but have kept some bonds with the Turkish metropolis.[47]

Economic relations were put into the background of public interest after the Free Trade Agreement took effect in May 1997. The military dimension of Turkish-Israeli relations has almost completely monopolized the political discussion as a consequence of its scope and speed of development. What started with the military training agreement of February 1996 has quickly developed into a broad cooperation including almost any type of military-related activity.[48] Judged by the intensity of visits of top brass and high-level defense ministry personnel, the focus of decisionmaking in the relation's military sector in Ankara is clearly situated in the Turkish general staff.

At the core of the relationship is a semiannual strategic dialogue, an Israeli idea, that started in Ankara in December 1996. With the participation of a large number of high-ranking military officers, the talks normally concentrate on regional threat assessment as seen by both sides and include an exchange of intelligence information. Such undertakings not only help improve the personal acquaintances of leading military personnel but are an indispensable prerequisite of any eventual common military action. Such an eventuality cannot be ruled out, given missile acquisition by Iran, Iraq, and Syria, which is regarded as a threatening action by both Turkey and Israel.[49]

According to press reports, Jordanian participants were also present during some parts of the meetings.[50] This would have been the second alignment of Jordan with Turkish-Israeli relations after the participation of a high-ranking Jordanian military observer in the U.S.-Israeli-Turkish naval exercise "Reliant Mermaid" that took place in Israeli waters in early January 1998. It seems, however, too early to speculate about an extension of the talks or even of the cooperation into a trilateral undertaking, although the Turkish military would welcome such a development. In any case there have been bilateral training exercises of small land force units in Turkey and Jordan in spring 1998 with the aim of exchanging experiences, gaining knowledge of national practices and training methods, and bolstering military cooperation in general.[51] During a visit to Washington, however, the late King Hussein strongly denied any Jordanian intentions of joining the Turkish-Israeli cooperation while pointing to the excellent bilateral relations with Turkey.[52]

The second most important part of Turkish-Israeli military cooperation is weaponry and hardware development. In late 1996 Israeli Aircraft Industries gained a contract against international competition for upgrading fifty-four Turkish F-4 fighter jets worth U.S.$632 million and more recently won a bid to upgrade forty-eight Turkish F-5s in a U.S.$80 million project. This will include increased firepower and maneuverability as well as improvement of vision and electronics. The project has started in Israel and will be finished in the Turkish air force's repair center at Eskişehir, which means that considerable technology transfer to the Turkish military industry is involved.[53]

Accompanying the upgrading of the F-4s is the purchase of 200 Israeli Popeye I standoff missiles by the Turkish air force as well as plans for the common production of hundreds of Popeye II missiles with a range of 150 kilometers. These can also be used in Turkey's F-16s. The states also signed a memorandum of understanding concerning the joint development and production of a medium-range antitactical ballistic missile system after the

United States rejected the inclusion of Turkey in the U.S.-Israeli development of Arrow ATBMs.[54]

Turkey has expressed interest in Israel's Phalcon early warning aircraft, unmanned air vehicles, special fences, and radar control systems to seal off its borders with Iraq and Syria, and the Galil infantry rifle to replace the G-3s Turkey presently uses. Israel Military Industry, with its Merkava III battle tank, is among the bidders for Turkey's U.S.$4.5 billion project to coproduce hundreds of state-of-the-art tanks to replace the aging Turkish equipment.[55] With all these projects, Israel is about to become Turkey's main military industrial partner. This development is sought by Turkey's military leadership, which is looking for alternatives to the United States and west European partners in procurement and coproduction in order to get rid of the political conditionality concerning human rights, the Kurdish issue, and so forth that is often attached to that cooperation.

Finally, Turkish-Israeli military cooperation also involves military training. The Israeli air force has regular access to bases in central Anatolia to train pilots in long-range flying over mountainous land, which is impossible in Israel but would be necessary in missions against Iran. Although details of the training agreement are not published, it is widely believed that Israeli pilots also use the possibility of flying close to Iran, Syria, and Iraq to gather intelligence. Turkish F-16s regularly train for antimissile reactions, electronic warfare, and combat fighting in Israel's Negev desert making use of Israel's advanced training technology.[56] Besides mutual air force training, the Turkish and Israeli navies have held joint exercises in international waters close to the Syrian coast to coordinate search-and-rescue procedures. In January 1998 they were joined by U.S. naval forces in a trilateral maneuver.

While economic cooperation and political traffic between Turkey and Israel have proceeded smoothly, military cooperation became controversial in Turkey and between Turkey and the Arab states. From the very beginning, not only Syria, Iran, and Iraq but also more moderate Arab states vehemently criticized the "nascent alliance," as they characterized Turkish-Israeli cooperation.[57] Repeated Turkish assurances that this cooperation was not directed against any third party and was only one agreement among many others Ankara had signed, including many with Arab countries, could not calm down Arab anxieties and anger. At a ministerial meeting in Cairo in March 1998 the Arab League again expressed its concern over Turkish-Israeli military cooperation and asked Turkey to review its policy. The league also criticized Ankara for its water policy concerning the Euphrates and Tigris Rivers, which is regarded as damaging Syrian and Iraqi interests.[58]

Even stronger concerns have been voiced by Syria and Iran, which feel directly threatened by the cooperation. Possibly in reaction to Turkey's advances toward Israel, Syria moved to improve its frozen relations with Iraq and kept up ties with Iran. Turkey and Israel view Iran with suspicion because of Tehran's involvement in Middle East terrorist activities, from which Turkey and Israel have suffered. Furthermore, Iran's weaponry buildup, especially in medium- and long-range missiles, and its potential nuclear capabilities deeply concern Turkish and Israeli security circles.[59] Even without explicit defense agreements, which do not seem very likely, the military cooperation can serve as a strengthened security belt for both. Israel's position in an eventual military exchange with Iran would be considerably improved if it could make use of the Turkish connection, whereas the fruits of the envisioned procurement and military coproduction programs would further Turkey's deterrent capabilities against eventual Iranian threats in a military conflict, however unlikely.

Turkey also has to see to it that its interests do not become victims of an Israeli-Syrian peace agreement.[60] Ankara is especially concerned that after such an event Syria may be tempted to turn its military potential against Turkey to realize its claim on the Turkish province of Hatay, the former Sanjak of Alexandretta, which Damascus had to cede to Turkey under French pressure in 1939. Furthermore, Syria could try to enforce its position in the water dispute by military threats after having been relieved of its military precaution measures against Israel, or there could even be a Syrian-Israeli understanding of trading their common water problem with respect to the Jordan river against American-backed common pressure on Turkey for giving in to Syrian demands on the Euphrates' water allocation.[61] If its military cooperation with Israel would harden Syria's position concerning the advisability of peace talks, Turkey could not be totally displeased.

Arab criticism has been constantly deemphasized by Turkish governments under pressure from the military leadership. Even during the Islamist interlude of Necmettin Erbakan's premiership, the Refah wing of the government was not allowed to interfere substantially in the emerging cooperation policy, and Erbakan had to swallow his disagreement with that policy, which he had so vehemently voiced when in opposition.[62] Furthermore, many in Turkey's political circles believe that Ankara does not have much reason to care for Arab political feelings because Arab countries have not shown special understanding of or support for Turkey's interests in the past. This holds especially true with regard to the Cyprus issue and compensations for Turkey's losses from the 1991 Gulf War.

There are, however, also those who point out that Turkey, because of its inescapable involvement in Middle Eastern affairs, should be careful not to alienate the Arab countries by developing a one-sided relationship with Israel. This seems also to be the opinion of the Ecevit government. In pursuing its line of a more regionally accentuated foreign policy, Foreign Minister Cem has been visiting various Arab countries to improve relations and calm down Arab concerns of a one-sided Turkish policy in the Middle East.[63]

There is always some tension between a security-focused approach to Middle Eastern affairs, as preferred by the Turkish armed forces, and a more politically inspired approach represented by Turkey's foreign policy elite. The military is mainly guided by considerations of strengthening Turkey's deterrent and defense capabilities against possible hostile military activities from neighboring states plus fighting actual threats to the country's political and territorial integrity. The foreign policy elite normally take into account the broader spectrum of the regional correlation of forces and its possible development. This almost automatically leads to a more reluctant and more balanced policy toward regional developments and regional actors.

The military focus almost inevitably angers neighboring states, who feel threatened by Turkish armament measures, and polarizes regional attitudes, as could clearly be seen by hostile Iranian-Arab reactions to the emerging military cooperation between Turkey and Israel. The political approach, despite many statements to the contrary by its proponents, distances Turkey from issues of regional concern and lessens the country's influence on regional affairs, as can be seen in the minor role Ankara played in the peace process and the lack of influence Turkey has in the hegemonial conflict in the Persian Gulf between Iran and the Arab states.

Both approaches have their merits. As long as the Middle East continues to be dominated by interstate relations mainly driven by considerations of balance of power in which most events are viewed as zero-sum games, a long-term Turkish-Israeli alliance can improve regional stability "by serving as a powerful military deterrent against would-be enemies."[64] This is especially the case if the alliance is backed by the United States, as it has been. Stability can be further improved by military cooperation in contingency planning.

This, however, brings up the delicate question of how far the Turkish military would be ready to engage itself in military eventualities that are not directed at Turkey. Its record indicates great reluctance to do so. Israel has also shown reluctance to become intimately involved in Turkey's security quarrels in the region, be they against the PKK or in water disputes with Syria. This was made abundantly clear by the Israeli government when the Turks had Öcalan expelled from Damascus. The Netanyahu government repeatedly declared that it had nothing to do with Turkey's military threats against Syria. But the Syrian leadership did not dare call Turkey's bluff for fear of a possible Israeli intervention. Therefore, although there are good reasons to expect that Turkish-Israeli military cooperation will not grow into a real alliance, the Arab states still harbor their suspicions. As long as they do, the deterrent potential of the cooperation is functioning.

From the viewpoint of the Turkish military, the rationale for cooperation will be the strengthening of Turkey's capabilities to defend its national interests in the region and in the possible bolstering of Turkish-American relations. Turkish-Israeli cooperation can only be welcomed by the United States as a strengthening of pro-Western elements in the Middle East. This may improve America's inclination to respond positively to Turkish interests in deepening the mutual relationship. If it engages the American Jewish community in supporting Turkish interests, the resistance of other lobbies in Washington could be more easily neutralized.

As to the more political focus on Middle Eastern affairs that is characteristic of important parts of Turkey's political establishment, the main drawback lies in its lack of potential for contributing directly to the resolution of regional political problems. Because political bargaining mainly concentrates on the development of multinational regional regimes for cooperation on various matters, it can fully bring to bear its potential only after the main problems have been solved in principle. As long as the Israeli-Arab conflict and intra-Arab rivalry continue to be the dominant patterns of regional political development, Turkish ideas for intraregional cooperation will be met with verbal consent but will run against strong resistance to implementation. In this respect Turkish-Israeli military cooperation can but heighten Arab suspicion about the real intentions behind Ankara's broader cooperation offers. Consequently, besides certain benefits for Turkey and Israel, the cooperation does not seem to have the potential for a broader impact in overcoming the dominant patterns of regional conflict.

The Looming Problem of Water

Cooperation, or lack thereof, is also the key to dealing with another potential crisis in Turkey's relations with its Arab neighbors: the use of the water in the Euphrates and Tigris basin. Turkey controls the main sources and the upper parts of this water system, which is of utmost importance for the economic development of southeast Anatolia and parts of Syria and of Iraq whose populations are concentrated in the basin.[65] Given the growing populations and the economic development plans of all three for agricultural irrigation and the generation of hydroelectric power, severe problems in water use will soon arise for Syria and Iraq if there is no common water policy.[66] Iraq is planning to extend its irrigated area to 4 million hectares by 2010, Syria may reach 400,000 hectares by 2015, and Turkey is about to extend its irrigable land in the southeast to 1.6 million hectares.[67]

The source of contention between Turkey and its neighbors is the huge development project with which Turkey will turn its southeast into a "paradise." It is called the Southeastern Anatolia Project (Güneydoğu Andadolu Projesi, or GAP), which was started in the late 1970s. GAP is the largest and most ambitious regional development project in the history of the Turkish Republic. With twenty-two dams, nineteen hydropower plants, and 1,000 kilometers of irrigation channels, it is intended to change the economic and the social fabric of nine underdeveloped provinces in Turkey's mainly Kurdish region. "The transformation of the backward local economy from subsistence to commercial agriculture would . . . dilute potential Kurdish national aspirations for an independent homeland."[68] In addition, GAP will increase Turkey's capacity for electric power generation 70 to 80 percent and bring some relief to the country's increasing energy needs.[69] The project has received the highest political priority, which has also meant an immense financial effort undertaken by Turkey because international funds have been sparse in light of the potential for regional conflict associated with the project.[70]

As beneficial as GAP may be for Turkey's economic, social, and political development, it is considered extremely harmful by Syria and Iraq. Although exact calculations are difficult to make because of the volatility of the many variables involved, there are estimates that in its final stage GAP will reduce the Euphrates flow by 30 to 50 percent. This would mean an almost unbearable loss of water for Syria and Iraq. Even taking into account the flow potential of the Tigris would not change the situation very much—with the progress of GAP, Turkey's demand on Tigris water would rise as well. Under optimistic assumptions, "Iraq is most likely to face water shortages within a decade and Syria will do so within twenty to thirty years."[71] This situation may occur even earlier if Turkey does not increase the amount of water it normally releases to its neighbors.[72]

Syria and Iraq are demanding a binding international agreement between the three countries in which the exact amount of water that has to be provided to each of them by the other partners is fixed. Turkey's political elite perceives these demands as an attempt to restrict Turkish sovereignty over the use of its national resources rather than as a useful opening for establishing a cooperation that may lead to a distribution and use of the water that could satisfy the needs of all along the rivers' banks. For its part, Ankara has declared its readiness to look at a cooperative solution but under the condition that

> it is Turkey's natural right to use these water sources according to its necessities and requirements. . . .These two rivers are of vital importance for Turkey. Turkey will continue to take into consideration, as it has always done, in the use of the waters of these two rivers, the situation of the downstream countries. However, Turkey has no obligation to meet all the water needs of the downstream countries.[73]

Turkey's leaders see it as proof of their goodwill that they keep their guarantee of letting pass 500 cubic meters of water per second into Syria, as granted in a protocol in 1987, if Syria takes effective measures against the PKK, which had occurred with the relocation of the PKK headquarters from Damascus to the Beeka Valley. Furthermore, the Turkish government is ready to discuss and solve any practical problem within a committee created in the 1980s in which experts from the three countries meet from time to time to exchange technical expertise on common water problems. Ankara emphasizes that it is an important task for the three countries to search for hydroeconomic and hydrotechnological means for optimal use of the water within the basin. Turkey is of the opinion that the complicated and somewhat ambiguous legal problems of transboundary water courses could also best be approached in that manner. "The complexity of relation between the two legal principles of *reasonable and equitable utilization* of transboundary water courses and *not causing appreciable harm* to beneficiaries should be challenged by means of well-meditated technical approaches."[74]

Turkey declares itself fully ready to cooperate and has proposed a three-stage plan for more rational use of the water—Ankara believes that Syria and Iraq do not use the proper technology to make optimal use of the available water, and consequently both countries put exaggerated demands on the flow. Turkish experts also believe that Syrian and Iraqi land assigned for irrigation is not all suited for that purpose according to internationally agreed classification of soil quality.[75] Turkey's suggestions have been rejected by Syria and Iraq because they do not want any outside interference in their hydropolitics; they want to retain their full sovereignty over their national water policies.

Turkey's cooperative rhetoric has hardly been backed up by substantial moves. Planning and implementing GAP has proceeded without any consultation with Syria or Iraq. Nor are there any starting points in the project for cooperation with regard to hydroeconomics, agriculture, or energy-related use of water. Syrian and Iraqi doubts on the sincerity of Turkish talk of expert cooperation is further nourished by political statements that draw foolish parallels between Arab sovereignty over oil and Turkish sovereignty over water. For instance, former Prime Minister Süleyman Demirel stated during a press conference,

> Neither Syria nor Iraq can lay claim to Turkey's rivers any more than Ankara could claim their oil. This is a matter of sovereignty. We have the right to do anything we like. The water resources are Turkey's, the oil resources are theirs. We don't say we share their oil resources, and they cannot say they share our water resources.[76]

This statement can also be seen as a reply to the Syrian suggestion of developing a commonly agreed formula for sharing the water among the three countries and leaving decisions about the use of each share to the country concerned. For Turkey, this suggestion constitutes an unacceptable infringement on its national sovereignty. It was also for fear of a loss of sovereignty that Ankara did not agree to the Law of the Non-Navigational Uses of International Watercourses adopted by the UN General Assembly in 1997.[77]

The critical element of the water conflict is not a shortage of water but the foreseeable reduction of available water for Syria and Iraq after the completion of GAP, especially its irrigation projects. The available water will also be of lesser quality because of pollution by salts, fertilizers, and insecticides used in Turkish irrigation areas unless Turkey is persuaded to clean up the water. As a consequence, Syria and Iraq fear the crippling of their potential agricultural and energy production. Even Iraq's capacity for oil production could be diminished due to lack of necessary water.[78]

The controversies between Turkey and its neighbors over water are not isolated from other conflicts in their relations and from the regional development of the Middle East. There is a strong link to the Kurdish problem, especially in Turkish-Syrian relations. This has not only been shown by the

1987 protocol on the release of water but on many occasions afterwards. Every time Syria raised the water issue in Arab organizations to ask for support against Ankara, Turkey countered with condemnations of Syrian support for the PKK terrorism and asked for the extradition of PKK chief Öcalan. Syria and Iraq are well aware that Turkey's huge expectations of the GAP project can only come true if peace and stability return to its Kurdish area. Thus there is a constant temptation to feed trouble in southeast Anatolia by direct or indirect support for the PKK as long as Ankara rejects demands for water-sharing measures. In this respect Öcalan's October 1998 expulsion by the Syrian government under Turkish military threat has diminished potential Syrian leverage on Turkish water policy.

What Syria and Iraq fear most is the emergence of Turkey as a regional power because of its command over the water plus the development of a huge economic and energy potential in the GAP area. For Turkey, GAP also means a steep increase in agricultural and energy exports to its Arab neighbors who will be in strong need of such imports if Ankara continues its transnational water policy. What in Turkish political rhetoric (and perhaps even in some Turks' intention) is designed as a huge potential for developing regional economic and political interdependence is perceived as a Turkish straitjacket by Damascus and Baghdad because, as one Turkish official said, "in this region, interdependence is understood as the opposite of independence."[79]

This attitude is also the main stumbling block for the realization of Turkey's various other plans for alleviating the region's midterm water problems. One idea put forward by President Özal during his term as prime minister in the late 1980s would be to pump fresh water from two rivers in southern Turkey via a bifurcated pipeline to the Persian Gulf and the Arab peninsula. This so-called Peace Pipeline Project never developed beyond a feasibility study because of the numerous political problems involved.[80] Turkey's offer to provide fresh water to Israel by transporting it in huge plastic bags not only has met with technical problems but has also had to overcome concerns emanating from the general instability of Turkish-Arab and Israeli-Arab relations.

As the hardening of positions in the peace process has stalled discussion on water issues between Israel and its Arab neighbors, so the continuation of the post–Gulf War situation impedes progress toward a solution of the Euphrates-Tigris water questions. The longer the Iraqi stalemate continues and the more GAP develops, the more complicated will become a solution. Such a development does not work to the advantage of Syria and Iraq because the hydropower plants and irrigation schemes created on the Turkish side will inhibit Turkish flexibility with regard to concessions on water release. Thus an increasing potential for conflict must be expected among the three states of the Euphrates-Tigris basin. This need not necessarily lead to a water war, although under adverse circumstances such a possibility in the next few decades cannot be excluded. However, such a decision would have to be taken by another generation of political leaders who may be more open to ideas of mutual interdependence and multinational regional cooperation than is the case with today's leaders.

Relations with Iran

Turkish-Iranian relations have been characterized by mutual mistrust since the Islamic revolution in Tehran because the two countries "have differing world views and ideologies that are probably impossible to reconcile fully."[81] However, both also have traditions of pragmatic foreign policies that enable them to strive for neighborly relations from which they may derive mutual advantages as long as neither feels threatened by moves of the other. Consequently, depending on which element of the relationship has prevailed, Turkish-Iranian relations have experienced ups and downs in the past twenty years.

With the exception of Erbakan and his followers, the Turkish establishment is convinced that the Iranian government actively supported Islamist movements in Turkey, although Turkish and Iranian versions of Islam have little in common. Turkey's Kemalist state elite noted with some concern the warming of Turkish-Iranian relations during the reign of Islamist Prime Minister Erbakan that culminated in a much publicized visit of Iranian President Ali Akbar Hashemi Rafsanjani to Turkey in December 1996.[82] The coming to power of the more moderate President Mohammad Khatami in 1997 did not lastingly change the Turkish perception of the bilateral relations. Ankara carefully watches the power struggle in Tehran between moderates and hard-liners and still sees forces at work there that try to interfere in Turkey's secular political system. Anti-Turkish remarks by an Iranian official and anti-Turkish demonstrations in reaction to the Kavakçı incident during the inauguration session of Turkey's newly elected parliament in May 1999 (see chapter 5) caused a strong official protest by the Turkish Foreign Ministry and was seen as another sign of persistent anti-Turkish attitudes in official Iranian circles.[83]

Turkish security authorities have repeatedly stated that they can prove Iranian attempts to undermine the secular order of Turkey via furthering

Islamist propaganda and even training and support of Islamist terrorist organizations in Turkey such as the Hizbollah. This has led to mutual extradition of diplomats. In April 1996 eight Iranian diplomats were accused by Turkish security of being involved in terrorist activities after testimony from a captured Turkish Islamist hit man.[84] In February 1997 the Iranian ambassador was forced to leave the country after he had made a public speech during a so-called Jerusalem night event in the Ankara suburb of Sincan in which he openly praised antisecular, fundamentalist positions.[85] As a measure of retaliation, Tehran both times expelled an equal number of Turkish diplomats. The last time, it took a year before both countries were again represented by full ambassadors.

The Turkish military leadership is convinced that the Iranian government, notwithstanding repeated declarations to the contrary, shows no determination to prevent the PKK from establishing temporary bases on the Turkey-Iran border where its fighters prepare for terrorist actions and receive medical treatment. Military officials in Ankara have accused Iran of not implementing agreements on common measures to control the border against PKK activities, thus directly undermining Turkey's domestic security.[86] This suspicion did not calm down even after the replacement of Rafsanjani by Khatami, which had been welcomed by the political elite in Ankara and had led to a marked thaw in political relations. More recently there have again been intelligence reports in Ankara that Iran stepped in as a main supporter of the PKK after Öcalan's expulsion from Syria. Osman Öcalan, Abdullah's younger brother and one of the PKK's leading field commanders, is said to have his main base in the Iranian border area.[87]

The Turkish military is also concerned about Iran's activities involving missile technology and weapons of mass destruction. The successful test of a medium-range Chehab-3 missile in July 1998 that could reach large parts of Turkey reminded the Turkish military of the country's insufficient antimissile capabilities in a region where aquisition of medium-range missiles seems to be a common element of armament programs.[88] The evolving Iranian potential, which may soon be complemented by the even more advanced Chehab-4, gains its full threatening meaning if one takes into account continuous rumors about Iranian efforts to develop a nuclear weapons capability.[89]

Turkish security circles follow with great unease Russian support for the finalization of the Iranian nuclear complex near Busheer. It is assumed that the transfer of technology involved in this project could provide Tehran with the means to produce military nuclear material. Although one need not assume that Iran's armament endeavors are directed at Turkey but serve a more general strategic purpose in the competition for hegemony in the Persian Gulf area as well as a deterrent against a perceived Israeli threat, Ankara's military cannot ignore these developments in a neighboring country.

Political and security concerns of Turkey's leading circles with respect to Iran are to some extent balanced by cooperative efforts in economic relations. These relations boomed in the 1980s during the war between Iran and Iraq when Turkey successfully established itself as an important economic partner for both. Relations experienced an equally steep decline after the end of the war when political and ideological differences received greater weight in Turkish-Iranian relations. However, economic contacts remained stable on a lower level, especially because of Turkish interest in energy deliveries from Iran.

In this respect it was as much coincidence as conscious policy that led Turkey's newly installed Islamist Prime Minister Necmettin Erbakan, during his first tour abroad in August 1996, to conclude the famous Iranian gas deal that caused so much uproar in American political circles.[90] Erbakan took the chance of finalizing a long-prepared agreement, worth U.S.$23 billion, for the supply of a large amount of Iranian natural gas to Turkey over the subsequent twenty-three years, including the construction of the necessary pipelines, only days after President Clinton had signed the Iran-Libya Sanctions Act that threatened to impose a ban on any foreign company that would invest more than U.S.$40 million a year in the Iranian or the Libyan oil and gas industries.[91] At one stroke Erbakan could demonstrate his care for Turkey's energy need, emphasize the sincerity of his policy of Islamic brotherhood toward Iran, make a show of firm political principles toward his domestic followership, and give a slap in the face to the United States. Since then, work on the project has continued, although somewhat slowed down after Erbakan was turned out of office in June 1997.[92] Iranian gas deliveries that were expected to start sometime in 1999 will most likely not materialize before 2000.

Although Erbakan got some criticism for his timing, the deal as such was never seriously questioned in Turkey. It was considered a necessary step to preserve the country's energy security, and in this regard American embarrassment could not induce Turkey to fall in line with the U.S. policy of double containment. In Ankara, Iran is regarded as an important economic partner not only for its energy potential but also as a conduit for Turkish trade relations with the Central Asian states. As long as instability prevails in the Caucasus, Iran provides the main access route for land-based Turkish transportation to the new republics. Turkey has also improved its railway connection with Iran since Tehran opened a new line to link up with the Turkmen railway network in May 1996. This connection will constitute the only functioning railway of the "new Silk Road" until plans for a trans-Caspian ferryboat-based railway connection can be realized. Consequently, transportation regulations are important to Turkish-Iranian official economic relations because Turkey is also the basic outlet for Iranian overland trade with Europe.

Turkish-Iranian economic relations, especially with respect to energy, are somewhat clouded by links to regional policy in the Caspian region that emerged after the collapse of the Soviet Union. Turkey and Iran compete for political and economic influence, although this competition has never become as sharp as many observers had predicted in the early 1990s.[93]

One potential issue of contention is Azerbaijan, with which both countries have relations based on history and kinship. Because more Azeris live in northern Iran than in Azerbaijan proper, Tehran is concerned about potential irredentism that could lead to a larger secessionist movement in northern Iran. Instigation for such a development could come from Turanist forces in Azerbaijan that might find support in pan-Turanist circles of Turkey. The 1992–93 Elchibey government in Azerbaijan with its overt pro-Turkish and covert all-Azeri policy gave a warning signal to Tehran. Since then, Iran has joined Russia in its effort to keep Turkish influence at bay in Baku. On the one hand Iran tries to establish itself as a promising partner for the Azeri leadership under President Haydar Aliyev, and on the other hand it tries to keep the Nagorno-Karabakh conflict going by taking the Armenian side, thus contributing to the continuation of difficulties for Turkey's position in the Caucasus.

Iran also poses a potential threat to Turkey's aspirations of becoming the "natural" conduit for Caspian oil and, probably, gas to the world market via the Baku-Ceyhan pipeline project. These plans would suffer a severe blow if Iran would become an active player, which at present is mainly prevented by the U.S. government's continuing policy of isolating Tehran internationally.[94] The moment the policy of double containment is relinquished, Turkey's chances of tapping Caspian energy would be seriously weakened. Relinquishment would also improve Tehran's chances of becoming a general outlet for Central Asian trade because "Iran, without having to depend on Turkey, has the potential to connect Central Asia to world markets."[95] For this to happen, however, Iran would have to match Turkey's flourishing economic relations with the Central Asian states, which would not be easy, given Iran's economic inferiority to Turkey.

Turkey's actively seeking American support for the realization of the Baku-Ceyhan project, although mainly driven by Turkish national political ambitions concerning Central Asia and the Caspian Basin, is another confirmation for the Iranian leadership that Turkey is an agent of the United States in the region, working against the natural interest of all regional states except Israel. Therefore, Tehran has expanded its political and economic ties with Moscow to slow down developments that would go in Turkey's and America's favor.

This linking of bilateral relations to regional and even international considerations is an element that Turkish-Iranian relations have in common with all of Turkey's Middle Eastern relations. Ankara will have to develop a comprehensive plan for its Middle East policy. But this is hardly possible considering the contradictory factors that characterize these linkages. For example, the improvement of relations with Israel, especially in military matters, automatically harms Turkish-Syrian, Turkish-Iranian, and more general Turkish-Arab relations. Considerably improving relations with Tehran and Baghdad for the sake of alleviating the domestic and transborder pressures of the Kurdish problem would create serious problems in relations with Washington and would also be viewed with suspicion by Israel. Ankara thus seems condemned to a balancing act of its various involvements in the Middle East and cannot have a credible chance of autonomously drawing the lines of the development in the region unless it hurts some of its own national interests.

CHAPTER NINE

The Balkans: Old Challenges, New Opportunities

Like central Asia, the Balkans has been a region in which possibilities of active Turkish engagement have been limited for decades because of the cold war system. "In a sense, Turkey has never really had a chance to develop 'normal' relations with most of the Balkan states since their integration into the Soviet empire over forty years ago."[1] Tensions and conflicts with Greece that started in the mid-1950s further complicated Turkey's relations with the region.[2] But in contrast to Turkey's relations with Central Asia, there were relations with the Balkan states during the cold war. Turkey always favored bilateral relations as good as possible with the Balkan states and was an active supporter of the limited efforts to establish some type of regional political cooperation that started toward the end of the 1980s.

Thus it was natural that after the end of the cold war, the demise of the Soviet Union, and the breakup of the former Yugoslavia, Turkey sought to improve existing links and establish itself more prominently in the Balkans, from which the Ottoman Empire had been expelled in the nineteenth century by violent national liberation movements that were often supported by European powers.[3] The Ottoman retreat from the Balkans was accompanied by several waves of Balkan migration to the Turkish mainland, the last of which took place in the aftermath of World War I. Today, a considerable part of Turkey's population, perhaps 10 percent of the overall population, has family bonds with various parts of the Balkans.

There are also people of Turkish origin living in certain parts of the Balkans, and the much larger group of Balkan Muslims shows some signs of affiliation with Turkey as the heir to the Ottoman Empire.[4] In the early 1990s this led to a revival of the concept of *dış Türkleri* (Turks abroad) as an important part of Turkey's regional foreign policy. The fate of Turkish people abroad and the Balkan Muslim population became a general concern and one justification for Turkish foreign policy engagement.[5] However, Turkish governments have rejected pursuing a neo-Ottoman policy in the sense of overt or covert expansionism into the region. Balkans policy has always been regarded by Ankara's decisionmakers as a natural expression of existing geographic, historical, and cultural links.[6]

The upheavals in the region since the early 1990s have caused a lively and sometimes highly emotional debate in Turkey's media that could not be neglected by the political policymakers. Ankara's policy of defining and pursuing Turkish national interests in the Balkans has had to maintain a balance between often exaggerated and interventionist public expectations, limited national means of action for creating stability on Turkish terms, constraints on the design and implementation of multinational regional architectures emanating from the conflict-ridden regional political pattern, and the necessity to keep Turkish policy in line with the policies of its Western allies.

Turkey's recent more active Balkans policy has not only been driven by domestic forces reacting to regional crises. As a Turkish analyst has said, "The Balkans are a strategic link between Turkey and western Europe. . . . Two and a half million Turkish citizens live in western Europe and more than half of Turkish foreign trade is conducted with that region."[7] This constitutes a strong Turkish interest in Balkan developments, especially in securing regional stability for the sake of guaranteeing easy and unhindered land access to western Europe. Furthermore, as long as Turkey's foreign policy hierarchy is led by the country's interest in a lasting and irrevocable integration into the political, economic, and security framework of the emerging new European order, developments in the Balkans will continue to attract significant attention of Ankara's leading political and military circles.

Stability in the Balkans also ranks high in Turkey's foreign policy priorities because of severe spillover from any Balkan unrest. Thus the transition after the breakup of the Warsaw Pact has been carefully monitored in Ankara, and Turkey has tried to gear its Balkan policy toward stabilizing the new regimes, either by developing extended bilateral ties and supporting multinational efforts to improve regional cooperation or by joining international endeavors at conflict resolution and peacekeeping in the region.

What Ankara most urgently seeks to prevent is a spillover of strains and violent clashes in and among successor states to the former Yugoslavia to the more southern parts of the Balkans. There is a strong concern that if the Former Yugoslav Republic of Macedonia (FYROM) becomes involved in existing conflicts, Greece, Bulgaria, and Turkey would almost inevitably be dragged into the fighting.[8] This could begin another Balkans war, which none of the major regional states wants.[9]

Intense bilateral relations with frequent visits by state dignitaries and top military personnel between Ankara and the new democracies have become routine. A network of bilateral agreements underpins political, military, and economic cooperation. The gradual establishment of bilateral and multilateral free trade zones is progressing. All this has helped Turkey establish itself as an important power in the region. The position is, however, far from being dominant.

All the Balkan democracies show a prominent political and economic orientation toward the core of Europe, with Slovenia, Bulgaria, and Romania looking for membership in the European Union. Albania, Croatia, and FYROM hope to upgrade their relations with the EU to that status in a few years. Slovenia, FYROM, Bulgaria, and Romania are equally eager to join Poland, Hungary, and the Czech Republic in the eventual eastward extension of NATO. Even on the rather limited scale of its economic and political engagement within the provisions of the Europe Agreements or the preaccession strategy, the European Union is the most important external economic force in the Balkans.[10] This was confirmed after the Kosovo war in summer 1999 when the European Union was assigned the major role in the postwar reconstruction within the framework of the Stability Pact for Southeastern Europe.

Good relations with Turkey have to be put into that context and are sought for various reasons. First, lasting stability in the Balkans cannot be reached without Turkey, just as it cannot be secured without Greece and Serbia. Second, Turkey can be useful in promoting the Balkan countries' interest in NATO membership because Ankara may hope that these countries' growing relations with the European Union may also work in the interest of Turkey's membership aspirations. It should, however, be clear for all of them that neither Turkey's voice nor that of the Balkan countries will be decisive.

Bilateral and multilateral regional efforts may be useful in qualifying for more intense integration with the European Union and as an interim arrangement if integration would take longer than expected. Military cooperation can help to reduce existing concerns and strengthen mutual confidence. Finally, expanded regional economic relations and cooperation open markets for Turkey's rapidly developing industry and business and enable the fragile Balkan economies to profit from the development of this regional growth center. These convergent interests constitute the basis on which Turkey can weave a network of cooperative relations with the Balkan countries, Greece and Serbia being the exceptions for the time being.

Coping with the Post-Yugoslavia Legacy

At the end of the cold war, Turkey was among those states that strongly advocated keeping Yugoslavia together. It was only under the impact of developments within Yugoslavia and the ensuing recognition of Croatia, Slovenia, and Bosnia-Herzegovina by the European Union and its member states that Ankara decided in February 1992 to recognize all breakaway states of the former Yugoslavia.[11] This immediately brought Turkey into confrontation with the Serbian leadership under Slobodan Milošević, which pretended to be the only proper heir to Tito's state. Tensions with Greece were also increased by the recognition of FYROM under its chosen name of Republic of Macedonia, which was interpreted by Athens as supporting unwarranted Macedonian claims on Greek status and territory.

Subsequently, Turkey's policy toward the countries of the former Yugoslavia predominantly sought to support the interests of the Muslim population of the region, which in Turkish eyes was heavily threatened by Serbian and Croatian expansionist policies and was not sufficiently noticed by the Western states. Such concerns were expressed as early as May 1992 when deputies, especially those from the Islamist Welfare Party but also from the Motherland Party, claimed in a debate in the Turkish Grand National Assembly that the West and the European Union were reluctant to take action against the Serbs to give "the Serbs time to purge the Balkans of Muslims."[12]

Reluctant to answer urgent requests of the Bosnian government for bilateral military aid, the Turkish government undertook permanent although futile efforts at convincing its Western allies to support lifting the UN arms embargo on the former Yugoslavia in favor of the Bosnian Muslims.[13] Turkey's representatives were more successful in shaping the position of the Organization of the Islamic Conference (OIC) to that effect. Ankara also pondered the idea of direct Western military intervention against the Serbs of Bosnia-Herzegovina.[14]

The futility of the attempts at creating an early forceful and effective international response to what Turkey regarded as Serbian aggression against a core group of Balkan Muslims led to growing disappointment of the Turkish public. As the crisis in Bosnia escalated to war and as news of Serbian atrocities against the Muslim population multiplied, accusations grew in the Turkish media that the West, especially the Europeans, was applying double standards. Muslim Iraq had been forcefully and mercilessly punished, but Christian Serbia was allowed to get away with its genocidal policy.[15]

The West's inconclusive policy concerning the war in Bosnia-Herzegovina became a strong ingredient of a general Turkish suspicion that the Europeans were clandestinely following a policy of keeping Muslims and Muslim states out of Europe. This public opinion would experience a strong revival after the EU summit meeting in Luxembourg in December 1997 rebuffed Turkey's bid to join the European Union.

In contrast to the enraged reactions of the public, the Turkish government accepted the extreme difficulties that were part of achieving any lasting termination of the fighting in Bosnia-Herzegovina, especially of using international military force.[16] Nevertheless, Ankara continuously urged its Western allies to take a decisive stance to bring about a quick end to the war. In December 1992 the Turkish parliament authorized the government not only to deploy Turkish troops to the UN-led peacekeeping operation in Somalia but also to Bosnia if the UN Security Council should authorize international measures.[17]

But it took until May 1993 before a Turkish squadron of F-16s was deployed to the Italian air base at Vicenza to support the NATO operations for enforcing the no-fly zone over Bosnia.[18] And it took another year before the United Nations accepted Turkey's offer to participate in the activities of the UN force monitoring the peacekeeping in Bosnia. The Turkish contingent of 1,500 soldiers was stationed in the region of Zenica in Central Bosnia to monitor a Muslim-Croat disengagement, thus not running the risk of becoming involved in possible clashes between Serbs and Bosnians. The Turkish military participation in UN-led activities was met with objections from Serbia and strong criticism from Greece. Both tried to insinuate that such a move was a decisive step for reestablishing Turkey as a dominant power in the Balkans and thus revitalizing the Ottoman legacy there.[19]

Such a judgment may be justified from a narrow regional view, especially if influenced by Athens's experience of long-standing Greek-Turkish controversies. In an international perspective, however, there can be no doubt that Turkey performed only a marginal role in the (mis)management of the Bosnian war by the international community. Despite its sometimes belligerent rhetoric, Ankara carefully avoided any single-handed activities in support of the Bosnians' case and always aligned its policy with the overall framework created by the moves of its major Western allies and the UN Security Council. Even if Ankara voiced disappointment over or disagreement with certain steps taken or plans proposed by the United Nations and the major powers, it did not disengage from the mainstream international policy on Bosnia. This behavior was conditioned by the realization in official circles in Ankara of Turkey's inadequate means to pursue any unilateral approach to the Bosnian war.

The Turkish government was instrumental in shaping the policy of the Muslim group of states as represented by the OIC. In various declarations the large majority of OIC members urged a more pronounced anti-Serbian international policy but refrained from developing a special Islamic approach and policy. The OIC contact group of which Turkey was a leading representative normally kept continuous relations with the international contact group in the preparation and the conduct of the various international conferences that tried to find a way to end the war.

Turkey's policy on the war was dominated by the idea that only the establishment of a military balance between the Serbs and the Bosnians would create the conditions for ending the war on terms that would protect the political and physical subsistence of the Bosnian Muslims. Thus Turkey's argument for lifting the UN arms embargo in favor of the Bosnians or carrying out decisive international military actions against the Serbian side or both. This position put Turkey in opposition to its European allies and temporarily also created discord with the American administration. Only when developments on the ground in the first half of 1995 led to decisive allied military reactions during which continuous NATO air strikes severely damaged the Serbian military infrastructure including its command and control facilities, did Ankara feel a belated justification of its policy.[20] In this sense the Turks can claim to have made an important contribution toward getting to the Dayton Peace Agreement of November 1995.

The establishment of a convincing military balance between Serbs and Bosnians is also a main feature of Turkey's post-Dayton policy. Ankara is convinced that only such a balance can prevent a reignition of military confrontation between the two after an eventual termination of the SFOR (Stabilization Force) mission. Consequently, Ankara is the main partner in the U.S.-initiated "equip and train" program for the Bosnian Federation

Army: the United States provides military equipment and Turkey takes over the training. According to Hajrudin Somun, the former Bosnian ambassador to Ankara, around 300 Bosnian soldiers come to Turkey every three months.[21] These activities can be regarded as a continuation of Turkey's role as a secret conduit, in breach of the UN arms embargo, for providing arms to the Bosnian side with American consent during the time of conflict.[22] Ankara also keeps its contingent of about 1,000 troops within the 34,000-strong international peacekeeping force of the SFOR.

With the normalization of the Balkan situation after the Dayton Accords, the Turkish government also sought to reestablish working relations with Belgrade because Ankara believes that the Serbian-dominated Federated Republic of Yugoslavia should be reintegrated into normal international relations in order not to create an outcast in a region so politically sensitive.[23] The crisis over the predominantly Albanian-inhabited province of Kosovo, however, led to a serious setback of such ideas.

The violent clashes between the Serbian special police, sometimes supported by ordinary military, and the guerrillas of the Albanian Kosovo Liberation Army (KLA), which led to many victims and widespread refugee movement among the civilian Albanian population of the province, posed delicate political problems for Turkey. For obvious reasons it does not favor dismembering existing states by separatist movements, but it cannot tolerate the suffering of the predominantly Muslim Albanian population.

Therefore Ankara strongly condemned the continuous harassment of the Albanians by the Serbian rulers. It joined its European and American allies in their high-level efforts to convince President Milošević to stop violent actions in Kosovo and settle the conflict by compromise with the political representatives of the Albanian population there.[24] When the violence continued and Milošević turned down the international advice for a peaceful compromise, Ankara supported stronger international measures against the Serbs. The Turkish leadership even advocated the intervention of an international peace force to prevent a repetition of the Bosnian war and declared its readiness to take part in such an action.[25] When in support of the Holbrooke mission, NATO started preparations in October 1998 for air strikes against Serbia, Turkey declared its readiness to contribute to such an operation with eighteen F-16 fighter jets.[26] At the same time, Turkey's political leaders made clear that such an intervention was not to lead to a separation of Kosovo from the Federated Republic of Yugoslavia but to a full restoration of Kosovo's autonomy within the republic. Of special concern was the security of the estimated 20,000-strong Turkish community in Kosovo.

There could be no doubt that after the breakdown of the international efforts for a peaceful solution of the Kosovo crisis in the Rambouillet talks in February 1999, Turkey would fully participate in NATO's military actions against Serbia. Eleven Turkish F-16 fighter jets stationed in Italy participated in the strikes from the beginning, although the Turkish government declared that its jets were only used in defensive operations. When NATO activities escalated, Turkey declared its readiness to provide air bases for the missions. The planes would, however, have to circumvent the Greek airspace due to Athens's refusal to give overflight authority.[27] In order not to unduly stress Serbian and Greek sensitivities, NATO refrained from stationing Turkish ground troops in Macedonia or from upgrading the Turkish presence in Albania, although Ankara offered the deployment of 1,000 troops.

Turkey also accepted a considerable share, up to 26,000, of Kosovar refugees, many of whom joined relatives who had long been living in Istanbul and İzmir. Turkish authorities also established refugee camps in Albania, Macedonia, and the northwestern Turkish province of Kırklareli near the Bulgarian border. It is estimated that 10,000 to 15,000 Kosovars sought refuge in Turkey, where they were welcomed without any complication.[28] In this respect Turkey's policy contrasted positively with that of many European countries, which only reluctantly fulfilled their pledges. And since the beginning of violent clashes in the Yugoslav province, wounded KLA fighters have been treated in Turkish private hospitals, mainly with the support of Turkey's large Albanian diaspora.[29]

A grave concern for Ankara was the possibility of a spillover of the Albanian independence movement from Kosovo to other parts of the Balkans, especially FYROM and the Sandjak of Novi Pazar in the Federated Republic of Yugoslavia that have large Albanian minorities. This would have drawn Albania into a stronger engagement when it preferred an officially low-key response, its strong sympathies and hidden material support for the Kosovo Albanians notwithstanding. Under such circumstances, the danger of a larger Balkan war involving Macedonia, Greece, and Bulgaria would have become a reality from which Turkey could hardly have abstained. Consequently, Ankara strictly adhered to the restoration of autonomy within the boundaries of the Federated Republic of Yugoslavia and rejected any idea of independence for an Albanian Kosovo.

This argument is fully compatible with the general Turkish foreign policy of keeping existing borders in the Balkans and solving ethnic problems within these borders. Although interested in a more prominent regional role, Ankara has no interest at all in being drawn into the domestic intricacies of almost any Balkan state because it realizes that it would not be able to impose single-handedly a solution from the outside. This position also explains why the Turkish government largely refrained from politically exploiting Greece's reluctance in taking the position of the Western institutions, which favored military intervention in Kosovo. Ankara did not want to increase tensions in the region by openly condemning the Greek pro-Serbian public attitude.[30] In addition, Turkey's own unsolved Kurdish question dictates utmost restraint with regard to the support of ethno-nationalistic movements.

Turkey is very much in favor of a lasting negotiated settlement of all Balkan issues that could become the source of future instability. To prevent such a possibility, the government seeks to establish cooperative relations with all Balkan states and promote multinational regional plans that will further stability.

It has to be noted, however, that the Americans and the European governments who designed the political resolution of the Kosovo war within the framework of the G-8 did not plan for a prominent Turkish role in the Kosovo peace force (KFOR) that has to control the Serbian retreat from and the refugees' return to the province. Turkey provides only a small contingent of troops in the KFOR in the German-controlled sector of Kosovo. Neither have there been indications of a special Turkish participation in the overall G-8 activities for the preparation of the postwar situation in Kosovo. The strong regional approach that Foreign Minister Cem initially wanted to be given to the Southeast European Stability Pact had to take second place behind the "European orientation" that was the essence of the German-sponsored version of the pact.[31] This was not least the political preference of the majority of Balkan states, which prefer the European Union to become the strongman of the region instead of Turkey. One might conclude from this that the leading Western powers do not think it appropriate to drag Turkey too intimately into the process of establishing a Balkan peace, although they also acknowledge that such a process cannot be established without Turkish participation.

Refurbishing Bilateral Relations

Since the end of the cold war Ankara has tried to develop and improve its relations with all countries around the Black Sea, especially with Bulgaria and Romania. Extended and warm relations have been established with

Albania and FYROM, which tend to look at Turkey as a support in the region. Turkey's special role in upgrading the Muslim military capability of Bosnia-Herzegovina has already been mentioned. In addition, Ankara participates in the economic and social rehabilitation and development of the war-torn country. Relations with Croatia and Slovenia have also improved considerably, with Croatia being regarded by Ankara as an important factor in Bosnia.[32] This has been emphasized by six official meetings of the presidents of the two countries since 1993. In general, the Balkans has been the region most intensely traveled by Turkey's leading political representatives in the past eight years and where Ankara has developed a close net of bilateral relations backed up by continuous efforts at establishing multilateral cooperation in crucial political and economic areas.

Turkey's relations with Albania are based on the Friendship and Cooperation Agreement signed in 1992, which was bolstered during an official visit to Tirana in February 1993 by President Özal's offer of large-scale aid for economic development and infrastructure improvement. Turkish economic and humanitarian aid slowly began to flow, accompanied by generous support in education. A considerable number of Albanian students study in Turkey with Turkish grants, and a Turkish high school opened in Tirana in early 1993, financed by a Turkish educational foundation.[33] The signing of a declaration on the construction of a trans-Balkan highway linking Istanbul with the Albanian port of Durres by the presidents of Turkey, Bulgaria, FYROM, and Albania in New York in October 1995 was a first step to improve the infrastructure requirements for intra-Balkan trade. Besides, the highway would offer Turkey a comfortable land connection to the Adriatic Sea, circumventing Greece.[34] More important, however, has been the growing military cooperation between Turkey and Albania that has resulted in the training of Albanian military personnel by Turkish experts and first steps toward cooperation in military production.

But all these efforts have largely been ruined by the outbreak of political violence in Albania in early 1996 that could only be terminated by the temporary stationing of an international protection force of 6,000 troops in which Turkey participated with a contingent of 850.[35] Since then Albania has hardly been able to recover its domestic stability. Turkish hopes of enlarged cooperation had to be adapted accordingly and were reduced to reconstruction aid. In addition, it became obvious that Albania does not regard Turkey as a special ally but looks more to the established European organizations to generate support for its economic and political development.

Turkey's relations with FYROM are still marked by the fact that Ankara was the first government to recognize the new state under its chosen name and to open an embassy there. Turkey attaches much importance to its relations with Skopje, as can be seen by the large number of bilateral agreements that have been concluded and by continuing high-level political visits between the capitals. Given its large Albanian minority, continuing tensions with Serbia, vocal nationalistic political opposition, and still uneasy relations with Greece and, to a certain degree, Bulgaria, FYROM's stability is a crucial factor for overall Balkan stability in Turkey's view.

Besides first steps in the direction of close military cooperation between Ankara and Skopje and a continuous political dialogue on Balkan developments, bilateral relations in other areas have not gained momentum.[36] Turkey supports the Macedonian interest in NATO membership as it does that of Bulgaria and Romania.[37] Such a step is regarded as a stabilizing element in the region and would help close the geographical gap between NATO member Turkey and the European core countries of the alliance. In this regard, Turkish interest in NATO membership for other Balkan countries is mainly an indirect means of securing and strengthening its own link with the rest of Europe in the emerging European security policy architecture.

This is also one rationale behind the Turkish-Bulgarian bilateral relations. Bulgaria is one of Turkey's most important Balkan neighbors, if not the most important. This is a tremendous development if one remembers the severely strained relations at the end of the 1980s when Sofia attempted enforced "Bulgarianization" of its large Muslim population, many of whom are of Turkish origin. In summer 1989 more than 300,000 Muslims emigrated to Turkey to escape the pressure from the communist Bulgarian government.[38] Bulgaria was also regarded as one of the main communist supporters of illegal terrorist organizations, the activities of which had contributed to undermine Turkey's domestic stability in the late 1970s.

This picture quickly changed after the fall of Bulgaria's communist leadership. As early as December 1991 first steps at easing the tension on Turkey's western border were taken when the military leaders of both countries signed a document on confidence-building measures that included an exchange of information, cooperation in military training, and a promise to refrain from holding military exercises within fifteen kilometers of the common border.[39] This cooperation has been constantly reinforced since then. Today Turkey's and Bulgaria's chiefs of staff hold regular meetings, and both armies have withdrawn considerable troops and heavy weaponry from the border area. Both have also been driving forces behind the creation of a common intervention-peacekeeping force of the Balkan armies, the creation of which has been agreed on in principle. Even competition between Turkey and Bulgaria with regard to the stationing of the force's headquarters did not really harm the good military relations.[40]

Political relations improved in the same manner. Regular meetings at the highest political level have become common and normally include an exchange of views on all critical issues of Balkan developments. At various times Turkey and Bulgaria have joined their efforts in directing appeals to the international community for the termination of the Bosnian war or the Kosovo unrest. Ankara and Sofia have also undertaken efforts at correcting their image as main conduits for illegal drugs or for easy money laundering. To this end they signed a trilateral agreement with Romania at the presidential level in April 1998 for jointly combating terrorism, organized crime, money laundering, drug trafficking, and human and arms smuggling. Police forces and other relevant state institutions will closely cooperate in regard to these matters.[41]

Concerns over the fate of Bulgaria's Turkish population have calmed down after the political party of this group, the Movement for Rights and Freedom, was accepted as a legitimate force in Bulgaria's new political landscape. The party was important in bringing noncommunist governments to power after the turn to democracy.[42] Bulgaria would like to see a stronger Turkish economic engagement in areas where its Turkish population is concentrated to help relieve the depressed economic and social situation there.

Development of more intense economic relations has mainly been prevented by Bulgaria's endemic economic weakness, which has been exacerbated by the slow progress of economic transformation due to the country's political instability. Mutual trade stands at U.S.$550 million, not including the nonregistered "suitcase trade" and will be boosted by the planned Turkish-Bulgarian Free Trade Area as part of a trilateral free trade area including Turkey, Bulgaria, and Romania to be established between 2000 and 2005.[43] More than 1,000 mainly small Turkish companies are presently operating in Bulgaria. Their investment, however, is a mere U.S.$35 million. Some of Turkey's large industrial and business conglomerates are interested in the new Bulgarian privatization drive as well as in infrastructure projects. Major progress has been impeded, so far, by difficulties with financing, market access, and an underdeveloped Bulgarian banking system.

Relations with Romania were relatively relaxed during the cold war because of Romania's special role within the Warsaw Pact system of keeping its distance from Moscow. After the fall of the Ceaucescu regime, relations improved with at least yearly regular meetings of the presidents of both countries. Their interests coincide with regard to Romania's bid for NATO membership and both countries' drive to become EU members. Bucharest has overtaken Ankara with the European Council's Luxembourg decision of December 1997 to include Romania in the second group of candidate countries for EU membership.

Trade volume stands at U.S.$750 million, which puts Turkey fifth among Romania's trading partners. Some 4,000 Turkish businesses make the country the seventh-largest foreign investor in Romania, although the vast majority are small businesses. With its huge Black Sea port of Constanta, Romania is very much interested in the development of transport infrastructure, especially roll on–roll off ferryboats, between Turkish and Romanian ports.

Black Sea and Other Economic Cooperation

Complementary to its bilateral relations with Balkan states, Turkey is supporting the creation of multilateral regional political and economic cooperation plans. The Black Sea Economic Cooperation (BSEC) project stands out as the most comprehensive and ambitious regional economic cooperation effort so far.[44] More recently, the revival of all-Balkan political cooperation efforts could lead to a welcome complement of the economic endeavor to reinstate the Black Sea as a hub of trade, transport, communication, and tourism.

Founded in 1992 the BSEC includes Turkey, Bulgaria, Albania, Greece, Romania, Moldova, Ukraine, Russia, Georgia, Azerbaijan, and Armenia.[45] The composition of its membership shows that former Turkish President Özal, the driving force behind its creation, had more in mind than narrow regional economic cooperation. His vision was of a larger region than the littoral states of the Black Sea and stretched via the Balkans in the direction of the Mediterranean on the one side and via the Caucasus toward Central Asia on the other. The BSEC region can be regarded as an important link between Europe and Central Asia. However, given its actual status as a nascent economic international organization and the many obstacles to improving cooperative relations between some of its members, the BSEC still has a long way to go until it can fulfill such a function.[46]

The BSEC is designed to promote cooperation among the participants "in the fields of economics, including trade and industrial cooperation, of science and technology and of the environment" by way of developing and carrying out projects of common interest in economic and technical areas.[47] The participants have agreed to establish a free trade zone among them by 2010. Action has been slow so far, although the establishment of a BSEC Trade and Investment Bank in Thessaloniki in July 1997 may help boost the financing of common infrastructure and industrial projects. The bank is supposed to cooperate closely with the London-based European Bank for Reconstruction and Development (EBRD), the so-called East Europe Bank.

Because nine of its eleven member states are economies in transition, and rather poor ones as well, quick results from cooperation look unlikely: difficulties and obstacles easily arise in transforming command to market economies.[48] The often mentioned large economic potential of the BSEC with a future market of 300 million people and vast resources is hard to realize. Lack of appropriate infrastructure is a serious impediment to more rapid and wider cooperation. Thus emphasis is laid on improving the telecommunication network, connecting the national electricity grids, or constructing a ring road around the Black Sea and improving port facilities to improve trade relations. Most of these projects, which undoubtedly would boost trade among BSEC members, are still in the planning phase, although small steps have been taken here and there.

The BSEC aims at transcending economic functional cooperation: its founding documents explicitly relate to the principles of "the CSCE documents to which they all [the member states] subscribe."[49] These include the Helsinki Final Act and follow-up CSCE documents and particularly the Charter of Paris for a new Europe as a way for the peaceful settlement of existing disputes among members. And a lot of disputes have overshadowed relations between BSEC members in the recent years: the endemic tensions between Turkey and Greece, the conflict between Armenia and Azerbaijan over Nagorno-Karabakh, persisting Armenian-Turkish disputes, and Russia's problems in the Caucasus.

Under such circumstances it can be regarded as a success that the BSEC has not only survived but functioned rather smoothly in institutional terms. In just five years an institutional framework has been created for five summit meetings of heads of states or governments, biannual meetings of foreign ministers, regular meetings of a Parliamentary Assembly comprising delegates of the member countries' parliaments, expert groups for the preparation of projects, the Business Council gathering representatives of organized private business, and the Permanent International Secretariat in Istanbul for the coordination of activities. With a more functional orientation the Trade and Investment Bank, the Statistical and Economic Information Center in Ankara, and the Black Sea Studies Center in Athens have been created.[50] Turkey has provided financial and material support, although the funding of the organization now is based on members' contributions.

BSEC institutions and meetings, especially at the level of the foreign ministers, offer welcome opportunities for political talks among members. These have been used by representatives of conflicting member states to sound out possibilities for mending fences. Regular face-to-face communication within BSEC institutions could help improve confidence among members if the overall political situation is conducive. But the BSEC can contribute to the stabilization in the region only insofar as the benefits of functional cooperation are not frustrated by latent or open conflicts in the Balkans or the Caucasus. Contrary to expectations in official Turkish circles, there are no convincing indications that BSEC cooperation has or would directly contribute to conflict resolution or regional stabilization.[51] It is, however, remarkable how little regional or bilateral conflicts have hindered its development.

Turkey's motives for founding and promoting the BSEC are manifold. For Özal this was another step in realizing his conception of Turkey as the primary regional economic and political power. This interest has been carried on by his successors, and for the Ecevit government the BSEC is an important element in its vision of Turkey as the main actor in Eurasia in the next century. The institution also links Turkey to the emerging new European order built on an expanded European Union and NATO. Thus the demands of pro-European circles in Turkey that the European Union develop closer relations with the BSEC.[52] The institution is also expected to further Turkey's EU membership application along with those of Bulgaria and Romania by improving these countries' development. Another motive is Turkey's interest in a stable neighborhood between itself and the rest of Europe and between itself and Central Asia. As long as the BSEC is considered conducive to this end, Turkey will continue to support it.

The last motive is also behind Turkey's engagement in the revival of Balkan cooperation. These endeavors have led since 1996 to regular yearly meetings of the foreign ministers of all Balkan countries, at which they discuss cooperative solutions for problems of regional economic and political development. The fragility of this undertaking became clear at the meeting in Istanbul in June 1998 when disputes over Kosovo almost broke up the conference. This was prevented only by omitting the subject from the final declaration and dealing with it in a side statement signed by six of the eight participating states.[53]

In a similar manner the first Balkan summit meeting of heads of state and governments convened by Greece on Crete in November 1997 carefully avoided substantial language on any of the simmering conflicts, restricting itself to a more general appeal to peaceful and cooperative conflict resolution mechanisms to be applied by the feuding states. The bilateral meetings on the sidelines of the official summit proved no more fruitful in defusing tensions or producing compromises, as was shown by the ineffective meeting between the Greek and Turkish prime ministers. Costas Simitis and Mesut Yılmaz only reiterated the well-known and unreconcilable national positions on the issues.[54]

The second Balkan summit in the Turkish Mediterranean town of Antalya in October 1998 was overshadowed by the American efforts at resolving the Kosovo crisis. Turkey could only declare the meeting a political success after Milošević had given in to Holbrooke's and NATO's pressure so that the inclusion of the Kosovo issue, in a fairly balanced language, in the final declaration of the summit meeting became possible. Despite serious differences about Kosovo, the heads of governments agreed to accelerate work on the institutionalization of the summit platform that perhaps could take place at the Romanian port city of Constanta in late 1999.[55]

The most concrete result so far of general Balkan cooperation is the decision of six countries and Italy to establish a common Balkan peace force. This is the outcome of the meeting of ministers of defense of the Balkan countries in Skopje end of September 1998.[56] Turkey was one of the driving forces behind the agreement. It is, however, only the first step toward setting up an effective common military unit comprising contingents from Turkey, Greece, Bulgaria, Romania, FYROM, Albania, and Italy. Operational steps have yet to be taken. And then it remains to be seen if the force will ever fulfill real peacekeeping tasks in the Balkans.

The political positions of participating states on what should be done with respect to existing and some potential violent conflicts in the region differ considerably as, for instance, differences in Greek or Turkish reactions to the war in Bosnia or the war over Kosovo have clearly shown. How, under such circumstances, common military steps, even restricted to peacekeeping activities, could be agreed upon by all participating states and how a common command could act effectively are questions the answers to which can only be given by future developments. But the agreement that the force shall operate under mandates from the United Nations and the Organization for Security and Cooperation in Europe, with NATO providing assistance and guidance, may help avoid potential controversies.

The short history of the new common military element is full of open and hidden rivalry between Turkey and Greece and Bulgaria's demands for a special position that do not augur well for the future of the undertaking.[57] It may, however, be taken as a good omen that Greece and Turkey have been able to overcome their differences with regard to the location of the headquarters of the new unit in order not to jeopardize the whole endeavor. Headquarters will be rotated every four years among member states. The first location is Plovdiv, Bulgaria. The looming danger of an exploding Kosovo and resulting pressure from the other partners and from the U.S. government, which strongly backed the plan, may have been decisive in enabling the Turkish-Greek compromise. Still, none of the participating states suggested using the Balkan peace force to carry out the Kosovo agreement.

Turkish Balkan policy will always be tainted by considerations of possible repercussions on relations with Greece, and the status of these relations will have consequences for the functioning and development of multilateral regional plans, at least until a lasting reconciliation has been reached between the two. Such Balkan dynamics is, however, far from the creation of opposing "axes" such as Orthodox and Islamic. Balkan politics is too complex and multileveled for such simple analytical or political constructs to be useful for understanding events. It is just as misleading for an analysis of Balkan developments only to look at the outstanding events and most obvious forces—the Bosnian or Kosovo wars, the Serbian leadership, U.S. government special envoys, the contact group, the G-8. Besides these, which easily catch the attention of the international public, there are less spectacular forces driven mainly by Turkey, Greece, and others that may be as decisive for the long-term shaping of the Balkan political landscape as are the more prominent, crisis-related international activities in the region.

CHAPTER TEN

Relations with Greece and the Cyprus Problem

PERHAPS THE STRONGEST CONTINUITY in Turkey's foreign relations after the end of the bipolar international system has been in relations with Greece and its attitude toward the Cyprus problem.[1] If there is a change at all, it would be a growing Turkish assertiveness in this aspect of its foreign policy. Both bilateral relations and Cyprus, meanwhile, have become endemic conflicts that carry the potential of disrupting the strategic situation in the eastern Mediterranean if not properly managed. Neither Turkey nor Greece has shown resolve to propose compromises that may lead to a lasting settlement. To the contrary, with regard to Cyprus the Turkish position has hardened, which does not augur well for a rapprochement in other relations with Greece. Both sides continue to take an assertive and determined stance in relations with one another, a stance that sometimes is not free from belligerence. But there is no Turkish intention of unlimited escalation, nor is there a Greek policy of upsetting the precarious balance in the Aegean. Still, although the likelihood of war between Turkey and Greece is small, it could happen at any time.

The Background: History and Psychology

Turkey's relations with Greece cannot be fully understood unless one takes into consideration the historical heritage.[2] In Greece as well as in Turkey, the relationship between the two countries is perceived as being loaded with traumatic historical experiences. These touch directly and very fundamentally upon the nature of their national identities.[3]

Modern Greece bases its national identity to a large extent on the Hellenic and Byzantine past in Asia Minor, which had mostly ended by the time of the Turkish (Ottoman) conquest of Anatolia, and the successful struggle against the Ottoman yoke, which in the Turkish view is coterminous with the acceleration of the decline of the Ottoman Empire. The Republic of Turkey owes its existence, among other things, to a war of independence in which Greek occupation troops in western and central Anatolia were the main enemy. What is for the Turks the birth of their state is for the Greeks the "Anatolian catastrophe" and the definite end of some kind of neoimperial ideology, the *megali idea.* Thus each modern state links its very existence and an important part of its national identity to events that have been disastrous for the other.

This perception of one's own history and the common history as well as the understanding of respective national identities has strongly influenced the current relationship. Normally, this situation is reinforced on both sides by such "agencies of socialization" as schools, media, and the academic community. "What makes the attempt to attenuate the mutual perceptions about the past more difficult is that they are continuously fed by present events, tensions, confrontations, threats of war, etc."[4] Consequently, Turkish-Greek relations are characterized more by mutual distrust and by a deterrent political behavior than by mutual trust and cooperative endeavors.

The image of the other as the archenemy is easy to invoke during bilateral tensions. The public can be rallied around the defense of national interests and national unity in disputes with the Aegean adversary. Attempts to compromise can be denounced as treason to the national cause. It is this politico-psychological background, this mixture of historical events and collective images, which have been created by biased perception and tradition that have to be taken into account in any effort to understand Turkey's policy toward Greece and Greek reactions toward that policy.

It would be simplistic to reduce Turkish-Greek relations to mutual distrust and distorted images that could be healed by redrawing the collective mind maps. However important this may be, there are serious political and security interests at stake that follow from the special geographic location of the neighboring states bordering on the Aegean Sea and from the strategic location and ethnic composition of Cyprus.

Intervention and support from the outside causes problems as long as third parties are not accepted as neutral and helpful advisers or mediators by both sides. The experience of American and EU intervention in Turkish-Greek affairs is proof of this. The membership of both Greece and Turkey in NATO and the strong military relationship both countries have with the United States have proved to be of only limited, and sometimes mixed, value with regard to a solution of bilateral conflicts, as have been both countries' strong links to the European Union.[5] Nevertheless, Ankara and Athens have constantly vied for Western understanding and support of their just cause against the adversary. "Western influence on the bilateral relations of Greece and Turkey is evident, and the salience of external factors shaping the domestic and foreign policies of the two countries is comparable, if not identical."[6]

Both states have asked for and received considerable allied military aid and arms, which continue to flow. Much of this material, ideally thought to improve both countries' ability to contribute to Western defense, was also used to arm against the perceived military threat from the other side of the Aegean, a feeling much more pronounced in Greece than in Turkey. The Greek armament program can only be rationally explained as military insurance against the Turkish threat. Turkey's large armament provisions are not directly aimed at Greece. But such features of Turkey's program as the aquisition of air-refueling capacity and airborne warning and control system (AWACS) spy planes can be interpreted as an endeavor to leave a strictly defensive posture and gain a limited capacity of strategic power projection. Together with Turkey's inclination to militarily bolster its foreign policy activities, this development could lead to understandable Greek concern with regard to the Aegean and eastern Mediterranean situation.

Turkish Policy on Issues Disputed in Relations with Greece

Turkish-Greek disputes and Turkish policy toward Greece focus on Aegean affairs and possible ways of resolving existing conflicts.[7] These disputes, although simmering since the 1950s, were aggravated with the Turkish invasion of northern Cyprus in 1974. At least since then, Greece has been convinced of Turkey's expansionist intentions toward the whole Aegean and eastern Mediterranean region, whereas Ankara views the development of the conflict primarily as a Greek attempt to enclose Turkey by a "Greek lake" and thus considerably hamper its regional maneuverability.

The Cyprus problem as well as the presence of national minorities—a tiny Greek one in Istanbul, where the important Ecumenical Patriarchate of the Orthodox Church is located, and a larger (and still growing) Muslim one in Thrace, most of whom regard themselves as Turks (irrespective of their ethnic origin as Turks, Pomaks, or Roma)—have become other salient features of the Turkish-Greek conflict. These matters all involve complicated ethnic, political, and legal problems and are closely linked to each other but display clearly distinguishable features and dynamics.[8] Turkish policy concerning relations with Greece always maintains the overall picture of the issues. This does not, however, impede Turkish governments from designing special policies for each.

Turkey's policy toward Greece is predominantly aimed at keeping "the basic balance struck between the two nations by the Lausanne Treaty," as understood by Ankara.[9] This balance, in Turkey's view, is expressed in the treaty's intention "to grant limited areas of maritime jurisdiction to the coastal states and leave the remaining parts of the Aegean to the common benefit of Turkey and Greece."[10] Turkey rejects any Greek claim of sovereignty over the whole Aegean, whatever form or "disguise" this may take. Turkey does not want to have its maritime communication links between the northern (Marmara) and western (Aegean) parts and the southern (Mediterranean) parts of the country interrupted by Greek territory. Furthermore, as a coriparian, Turkey demands an equal share in the Aegean. This is basically a political view of the situation, and so Turkey has been insisting on a political solution to the bilateral conflicts through negotiations between the two sides.

For Greek authorities of any political shade this Turkish argument comes close to a denial of the geographic continuity of Greece in the Aegean because the country here is constituted by hundreds of dispersed islands, many of which are located close to the Turkish shore. A discussion with Turkey of issues related to Greek territorial integrity is out of the question for any politician in Athens. Thus Greeks perceive quarrels with Turkey as mainly legal problems concerning the proper interpretation of international legal texts that regulate the Aegean. If there are any disputes at all, which is constantly denied by Greek governments, with the single exception of the delimitation of the continental shelf, these should be settled by recourse to the International Court of Justice (ICJ) in The Hague.

The major disputes focus on the continental shelf and its distribution between the two countries and on the delimitation of Greece's territorial waters. Turkey denies the applicability of the main international conventions concerning the delimitation of the continental shelf.[11] It has not become a party to the conventions and asks for a negotiated distribution of the Aegean shelf among the two countries, which would attribute a considerable part of the shelf to Turkey. Although Greece accepted negotiations on the issue in the 1970s, it later changed its position and now favors a settlement by the ICJ.[12]

Closely linked to the problem of the continental shelf is the question of delimiting Greece's territorial waters, which presently stand at 6 nautical miles (nm). However, in application of the UN Convention of the Law of the Sea of 1982, Greece has stated its right to extend its territorial waters to 12 nm, although for the time being it would abstain from exercising this right. Turkey regards this as unacceptable because such a move would turn the Aegean into a Greek lake and severely restrict Turkey's naval maneuverability by reducing the amount of high seas from the present 49 percent to a mere 19.7 percent and at some points effectively interrupt the high sea area by linked rings of territorial water around the Greek islands.[13]

After the ratification of the 1982 convention by the Greek parliament on May 31, 1995, the Turkish Grand National Assembly passed a resolution on June 8 in which it declared its hope that the Greek government would abstain from extending the territorial waters but conferred "all the necessary authority, including military measures, to the Government of the Republic of Turkey to protect and defend the vital interests of Turkey in such an eventuality."[14] This has been the strongest expression so far of Turkey's often repeated intention to go to war with Greece in case of an expansion of Greek territorial waters to 12 nm. It is also the first and only threat of war between two NATO states.

Subordinated to these core disputes but no less difficult are the other Aegean issues about which Turkey and Greece have serious disagreements.[15] Turkey, with legal arguments, does not accept Greece's national airspace of 10 nm around its territory, and Turkish military airplanes constantly enter the airspace up to the 6 nm conceded by the Turks, thus provoking continuous Greek protests against Turkish violations.[16] Such incidents are often accompanied by dogfights between Turkish and Greek fighter jets, which always risks the possibility of a military accident because the aircraft are often equipped with armed weapons.

The same problem occurs with Turkey's rejection of Greece's practice in managing the Athens flight information region (FIR),which in Ankara's view constitutes an abuse of purely technical regulations to illegally establish Greek sovereignty claims over the Aegean for military flights. Complying with Greek demands of notifying FIR Athens of flights would, in the Turkish view, lead to an intolerable Greek interference in Turkish military exercises over the open sea. Disputes about flight control of civil air traffic in the Aegean ended in 1980 when Turkey withdrew its protest.[17]

Similarly, NATO air control in the Aegean has been unsettled since 1980 when, after Greece returned to military integration with the alliance, no Turkish-Greek agreement on the division of the military air control over the Aegean could be reached. Turkey rejects the return to the pre-1974 situation valid until Greece's withdrawal from the military integration as a response to NATO's "inadequate" reaction to Turkey's invasion of northern Cyprus. Since 1980 the establishment of a Greek national air command, COMSEVENATAF, in Larissa has been prevented by the Turkish-Greek disagreement over military air control matters.[18] Only after protracted discussions within NATO's institutions could a new allied command structure for the southeastern command be established before the Washington summit for the celebration of NATO's fiftieth anniversary in May 1999. NATO foresees commands in Larissa and İzmir where officers from Turkey and Greece, respectively, will serve.

Although superficially of a technical nature, all these disputes have political cores: who is to govern the Aegean and to what extent? This becomes even more evident when one considers Turkey's complaints about the militarization of the eastern Aegean islands and the Dodecanese islands by Greece. According to Ankara these islands have to be kept demilitarized because of international legal texts regulating their status. Some analysts in Turkey judge these Greek measures, undertaken since the mid-1960s, as an attempt to change the balance of power by denying Turkish warships "the ability to maneuver in a large area in the middle of the Aegean."[19] Thus in the 1970s Turkey established a "Fourth Army" located on the Aegean coast and equipped with a large number of landing craft. For Greece, Turkey's allegations and its military moves are completely unwarranted and constitute another proof of Ankara's expansionist intentions. The ongoing Turkish-Greek quarrel on this matter has time and again restricted NATO's functioning in the Aegean area.[20]

Three times—1974, 1976, and 1987—the Aegean disputes escalated to nearly a military confrontation between Turkey and Greece, but each time they calmed down fairly quickly because of political intervention of NATO partners, especially the United States. The events started Turkish-Greek endeavors for a reconciliation that resulted in the Berne Agreement of 1976 and the Davos process of 1988 for management of the situation, although no substantive solution could be reached. Later the agreements were more or less put on the back burner by both sides because neither was ready or able to develop the necessary political momentum to devise workable and effective compromise formulas.

The Kardak-Imia Crisis

The same pattern could be observed in the most recent serious Turkish-Greek confrontation in the Aegean, the so-called Kardak-Imia crisis of 1996.[21] After a Turkish cargo vessel ran aground near these twin islets in the southeast Aegean in late December 1995, a diplomatic controversy erupted between Ankara and Athens about possession of the rocks. Almost a month later the story was hijacked by some nationalistic media in Greece and Turkey and blown to such a proportion that both governments had to publicly react in uncompromising defense of their national interest. Navy units were deployed around the islets and Greek and Turkish frogmen took positions on different rocks to back the respective territorial claims. The Turkish prime minister, Tansu Çiller, tried to capitalize on the situation for domestic political purposes by showing special resolve to militarily counter any Greek attack on Turkish soil. In Athens, political uncertainty in the wake of PASOK's (the Panhellenic Socialist Movement—the leading Greek Social Democratic Party) recently solved internal dispute about the succession to the late Andreas Papandreou as prime minister led to handling of the crisis by members of the government who were described by a Greek commentator as "a group of actors that compete with one another on stage for the lead role."[22] Military confrontation seemed imminent when telephone intervention by President Clinton and other leading American politicians in Athens and Ankara, backed by diplomatic moves of NATO Secretary General Javier Solana and of senior EU member states, diffused the tension almost overnight. Both sides withdrew their forces and pledged a return to the status quo.[23]

Although superficially the Kardak-Imia crisis looked like just another round in the mutual Turkish-Greek policy of brinkmanship, it introduced a new element into the inventory of disputes: for the first time, Turkey had denied Greek ownership of Aegean islets. This claim was elaborated in the aftermath of the crisis with Ankara's contention that the ownership of hundreds or thousands of small islands and islets in the Aegean is unclear because they have never been the subject of international legal agreements nor is there a clearly delineated demarcation of maritime boundaries between Turkey and Greece. Thus since early 1996 Turkey has been talking of so-called grey areas in the Aegean over which Greece illegally claims sovereignty.[24]

Athens categorically rejects this contention, pointing to the regulations in the Treaty of Lausanne of 1923, the Montreux Convention of 1936, and the Treaty of Paris of 1947. These agreements and related documents as well as decades-long practice to which Turkey mostly complied until the 1970s include detailed regulations to establish a precise enough demarcation of maritime boundaries between Greece and Turkey without leaving grey areas. For Athens the latest Turkish move is an indication of Ankara's intention to revise the situation created by the Treaty of Lausanne.

Athens was especially alarmed over a Turkish effort within NATO to exclude the island of Gavdos (southwest of Crete) from a NATO exercise in May 1996 because its ownership, Turkey claims, is disputed. Greece is of the opinion that Gavdos's status was clearly established by the Treaty of London of 1913, in which Turkey renounced all sovereign rights over Crete. It fits well into Athens' perception of Turkey's military-backed policy of revising the Treaty of Lausanne that in a report prepared by the Turkish War Academy and leaked to the press in July 1996, the grey area argument was restated and added to that was a legal claim of Turkish ownership of any Aegean island up to 6 nm from the Turkish coast, which would, for instance, bring the Greek resort island of Kalymnos under Turkish sovereignty.[25]

Greece strongly protested the new Turkish attitude concerning "the unresolved territorial status of Aegean islands" and sought to garner international support for its protest. With regard to Kardak-Imia, it was backed by Italy, which had ceded the Dodecanese islands to Greece in the Treaty of Paris of 1947 and, somewhat hesitantly, by the United States. Stronger reactions came at the European level: the European Parliament issued a strong condemnation of Turkey's behavior, and Greece effectively blocked any EU financial assistance for Turkey that was foreseen within the framework of the newly established customs union that came into effect on January 1, 1996.

To keep relations with Turkey going by at least partially overcoming this Greek blockade, the EU's Council of Ministers, on Greek insistence, issued a declaration on July 15, 1996, in which it stated that relations between Turkey and the European Union should be guided by respect for international law, international agreements, and the sovereignty and territorial integrity of EU member states. Furthermore, the council called "for the avoidance of any action liable to increase tensions; the use or threat of force, for instance." And it suggested that the case of Imia should be submitted to the International Court of Justice.[26] This declaration was met with Turkish indignation; Ankara refused to specify if it would commit itself to these principles. Nevertheless, the council could release some of the money foreseen for Turkish projects within the framework of the EU's new Mediterranean policy.

In hindsight this decision was another example of bad compromise born of the helplessness of the European Union, which was caught between Greece's constant policy of blocking an improvement in Turkey-EU relations and the interest of the other member states in at least partial progress of that relationship. Greece could transform its national position into an EU position that would lastingly burden the EU's relationship with Turkey, whereas the release of some million ECUs by the council was later blocked by the European Parliament due to its strong criticism of Turkey's human rights record, especially with regard to the Kurds.[27]

Meanwhile, mainly inspired by American intervention and pressure, Athens and Ankara had started trying to find new ways for reconciliation, especially after a declaration of Prime Minister Mesut Yılmaz on March 23, 1996, that Turkey had not only offered a comprehensive discussion of all bilaterally disputed issues but was also ready to contemplate solutions by way of international third-party arbitration, including the jurisdiction of the ICJ.[28] Developments were, however, hampered by domestic political problems in both countries: Simitis's struggle to establish himself firmly on top of his party and government, including early elections in late 1996, on the one hand, and Turkey's growing infighting between secularists and Islamists after the establishment of Erbakan's coalition government in June 1996, on the other. In addition, the U.S. government had to take into account likely repercussions of its activities, such as alienating the Greek vote, on the presidential elections of November 1996.[29] The announcement of the Republic of Cyprus in January 1997 to buy S-300 antiaircraft surface-to-air missiles from Russia as well as ongoing Greek discriminations against its Muslim population in eastern Thrace also contributed to slowing down the international efforts at creating a favorable climate for Turkish-Greek understanding.

Therefore it almost came as a surprise to the public of both countries when the Turkish and Greek foreign ministers, İsmail Cem and Theodoros Pangalos, in a meeting hosted by U.S. Secretary of State Madeleine Albright at the fringe of the Madrid NATO summit meeting, signed a statement on July 8, 1997, in which both sides agreed on some fundamental principles for the conduct of bilateral relations. In this statement, which had been established through heavy diplomatic efforts of the U.S. administration before the summit, both sides agreed to good neighborly relations, respect for each other's sovereignty, respect for the principles of international law, respect for each other's legitimate and vital interests in the Aegean, a commitment to refrain from unilateral acts, and a commitment to settle disputes by peaceful means and without the use of force or threat of force.[30]

Implementation of these principles has proved difficult because both sides have firmly kept to their baselines for approaching a solution of bilateral conflicts. The rapid deterioration of the Cyprus problem after the EU's confirmation of its firm intention to open negotiations with the Republic of Cyprus in 1998 on entering the union and the exclusion of Turkey from the EU's list of candidates for membership has further contributed to the hardening of Turkey's position.[31]

Turkey continues to suggest a package approach in which bilateral discussions and later negotiations should seek compromise on all disputed issues. Greece stands firmly on its position that a solution to the division of the continental shelf between the countries should be brought about by a commonly agreed ruling of the ICJ and, if at all, a step-by-step approach could be used for other disputed issues, the existence of which Athens continues to deny. Witness to this rigidity of both sides are the two fruitless meetings of the Turkish and Greek prime ministers during the Balkan summits on Crete in November 1997 and in Antalya in October 1998.

Turkey has continued to display its well-known mixture of conciliatory and threatening rhetoric as well as conciliatory and agressive actions toward Greece. The Turkish government of Mesut Yılmaz twice sent letters to Athens in early 1998 proposing five points of common action to start Turkish-Greek reconciliation. First, both countries should identify the outstanding issues. Second, they should formalize the Madrid Declaration of July 1997. Third, they should develop and implement a package of confidence-building measures as suggested by NATO Secretary General Solana. Fourth, both governments should convene the group of eminent personalities that had been established on the suggestion of the EU term president to sort out bilateral points of contention. Fifth, for a discussion of these proposals the foreign ministers of both countries should meet in Ankara or Athens before the end of March 1998.[32] These were rejected by the Simitis government. But straying from his conciliatory tone, Prime Minister Yılmaz accused Athens of hostile intentions and warned it "to stay away from the heavy responsibility of possible negative developments" in a declaration issued after the second Greek rejection of Turkey's proposals.[33]

The former Turkish chief of General Staff, General I. Hakkı Karadayı, in one of his farewell messages, accused the Greek military of plotting a limited war against Turkey in the Aegean that would further alienate Turkey from the West and from Europe especially. However, at the same time, Turkish and Greek officers under the guidance of NATO Secretary General Solana tried to establish formulas for the implementation of confidence-building measures in military matters, which had been agreed upon in principle by both sides in 1989. These measures have been deemed necessary by NATO's top military institutions to establish the new command structure in the alliance's southeastern region.[34]

Turkish concerns about Greece's policy toward it have also been influenced by the Greek position with respect to Turkey's Kurds. Greek politicians of all shades, including single members of various governments, have shown open sympathy for the Kurdish cause. This often included sympathy for and a certain support of the PKK. Although the Greek government always denied Turkish allegations of an official cooperation with the PKK, parts of the Greek parliament expressed solidarity with the organization, and the Greek authorities did nothing to prevent the establishment of an ERNK (National Liberation Front of Kurdistan) office in Athens that could be regarded as a quasi-official representation of the PKK. For the Turkish authorities, it was clear that Greece also provided material support for the PKK, including the training of fighters in Greek camps near Lavrion. According to official Greek statements, these were nothing but camps for Kurdish refugees who had fled repression in Turkey's southeast.[35] Turkish authorities and the public regarded these activities as a continuing Greek assault on the country's integrity that could only harden Ankara's position in bilateral relations.

The Turkish allegations against Athens proved to contain an element of truth when it became obvious that members of the Greek government and foreign policy officials had been involved in sheltering Öcalan after his departure from Italy. Turkey's President Süleyman Demirel called Greece a "rogue state" and asked the West to put it on the same list with Iraq, Lybia, and Iran. Ankara demanded that Athens officially declare the end of its support for the PKK or it would face the same Turkish reaction as Syria had in October 1998. The Turkish government froze all talks with Athens about confidence-building measures and started an international campaign to reach a political condemnation of Greece by the European Union and the UN. Domestic pressure on the Greek government also increased when the Greek public was strongly disappointed that authorities had not been able or willing to protect the PKK leader. In a fence-mending operation, Prime Minister Simitis sacked Foreign Minister Pangalos along with other high officials who had been implicated in the Öcalan operation. A clear American and European indication that they would not support the harsh Turkish line against Greece, although they clearly condemned the Greek government's training of PKK fighters and especially the sheltering of Öcalan, took the steam out of Turkish-Greek tensions. Athens developed a conciliatory approach toward Ankara, which was mainly orchestrated by the new foreign minister Georgios Papandreou, who is known for his soft approach to Greek-Turkish relations.[36] In July 1999 bilateral talks of foreign ministry officials on noncontroversial issues started a process of improving the climate in Turkish-Greek relations. Backed by several meetings of their foreign ministers, the officials continued their talks in autumn 1999. It is, however, far too early to speculate about a breakthrough in Turkish-Greek relations unless the dialogue covers the controversial issues as well.

Certain preliminary conclusions can be drawn from this mixed picture. First, Ankara is not ready to compromise on its stance that Turkey has a right to exercise sovereignty over some part of the Aegean beyond its coastal waters. Because the legal foundation of this claim seems somewhat weak, Turkey prefers political negotiation. Second, most of Turkey's political and military elite are insensitive to Greek perceptions of Turkish behavior, especially its aggressive rhetoric and openly displayed military strength. Admittedly, the rhetoric has always been duly reciprocated, and sometimes been provoked, by Greek officials; former Foreign Minister Pangalos stuck out in that respect because of his often undiplomatic way of talking about Turkey. But if such verbal aggressions on Turkish policy might have been annoying to Ankara's leadership, they could hardly be taken as serious threats given Turkey's military superiority.

Third, time and again, Turkey has felt frustrated by Greece's policy of blocking smooth relations between Turkey and the European Union, to which Ankara reacts with an affirmation of its uncompromising approach in bilateral relations. Fourth, as long as this situation does not change, any agreement on procedural steps to overcome differences with Greece are but an indication that Turkey does not want to sever ties with Athens and that it is sensitive to the international environment of the Turkish-Greek conflict. These overtures should, however, not be taken as a sign of Turkish readiness for compromise unless they are accompanied by new suggestions for resolving substantive elements of the conflict. Fifth, unless the international framework of the Turkish-Greek conflict changes fundamentally—that is, its link with European politics on the one hand and U.S. global political interests on the other remains strong—there is little probability that Turkey will escalate the conflict beyond manageability. At the same time, this international environment is also a factor in perpetuating the conflict because Europe and the United States carefully avoid alienating either opponent. This behavior reinforces each side in its perceptions of being right and of being able to elicit Western support for the case against the adversary.

Turkey's Policy on Cyprus: A Hardening of Positions

Turkey's recent policy on Cyprus has been mainly driven by reactions to the new situation on and around the island that evolved because of the EU's intention to start accession negotiations with Cyprus and because of Greek Cypriot attempts to strengthen limited military capabilities, especially by buying Russian-made S-300 air defense missile systems.[37] These developments prompted reactions that made clear that Ankara's overriding interest concerning Cyprus is to preserve the favorable strategic position it obtained by the 1974 military invasion and the stationing of 30,000 troops with heavy weaponry in the north of the island. If this should finally lead to a lasting division of the island, Turkey would not deplore it.

Ankara considers Cyprus the cornerstone of security for Turkey's southern rim and a key element in the defense of southern Anatolia. This includes the security of the oil traffic that may go out of the Bay of Iskenderun after a full resumption of oil delivery through the Iraq-Turkey twin pipeline or after the possible new flow to Turkey's Mediterranean shore from the Caspian basin.[38] For all these reasons, Cyprus must not be controlled by a hostile country, which would, in Ankara's view, be almost automatically the case if the situation on Cyprus would be settled according to Greek Cypriot intentions. Greece's encirclement of Turkey, as perceived by Turkish political and military leadership, should by no means be extended toward the eastern Mediterranean.

Because of this attitude, Ankara reacted harshly to Greek Cypriot plans to aquire the S-300 missile system by threatening a military reaction if the missiles were deployed.[39] The resolve was emphasized by military maneuvers in northern Cyprus that allegedly were training troops to destroy the missiles. Turkish authorities also stopped and searched an Egyptian vessel that passed through the straits because they suspected it of carrying parts of the missile system. And Ankara undertook, without success, various demarches in Moscow to induce a Russian retreat from the deal.[40]

The imminent danger of military action on Cyprus, which would automatically spill over into a Greek-Turkish military conflict, alarmed the U.S. government. Washington entered into heavy diplomatic activity to restrain Turkey and bring about a Greek Cypriot retreat from the deal. After repeated Greek Cypriot postponements of the date of delivery from autumn

1997 to late 1998, American efforts were finally successful when, in December 1998, Athens convinced Republic of Cyprus President Glafcos Clerides to agree to allow Greece to take charge of the missiles, which would be stationed on Crete. This decision caused some political irritation among Greek Cypriots but was met with satisfaction in Ankara, although there was some concern about stationing the S-300s on Crete. This action, Turkey believed, could further complicate the already intricate situation in the Aegean.[41]

Nevertheless, Ankara could feel confirmed in the resolute and more assertive approach toward the Cyprus problem in general that it had developed over the preceding three to four years. Turkey's Cyprus policy met with little domestic political resistance or resistance from Turkish Cypriot circles. The political leadership in the north of the island, especially its president, Rauf Denktaş, is more interested in consolidating its self-declared Turkish Republic of Northern Cyprus and gaining international recognition of some sort than in overcoming the division of the island by way of a political compromise with the Greek Cypriot leadership of the Republic of Cyprus, which represents the only internationally recognized government for the whole island. Denktaş is bound to elicit as much Turkish support as possible because Turkey is the only state that officially recognizes his republic. This makes Turkish Cypriot opposition to Turkey's policy impossible, even if it were deemed sensible by some Turkish Cypriot politicians, as seems sometimes to be the case.

Denktaş's hesitant reaction to any proposed compromise on the Cyprus problem has been strengthened by the Greek Cypriots' plans for a solution that would lead to restoration of the pre-1974 dominance.[42] The incompatibility of the Turkish and Greek Cypriot interests has been proved time and again by the fruitless efforts of UN secretary generals during the past twenty-odd years to bring about a solution.[43] The failure of UN-sponsored attempts to put into practice the bicommunal, bizonal federation that had been the solution agreed to in 1977 by Greek Cypriot leader Archbishop Makarios and President Denktaş suggests that it may be as little realistic and viable as was the framework of the 1959–60 Zurich-London agreements on which the independence of Cyprus was based.

The main factor hardening Turkey's position toward Cyprus since the early 1990s has been the EU's Cyprus policy.[44] On July 3, 1990, the government of the Republic of Cyprus applied for membership in the European Union, which elicited an immediate protest from Turkey and the Turkish Cypriot leadership, who argued that such a move was unconstitutional and illegal under the Zurich-London agreements, which do not allow any union of Cyprus and another state. For the Turkish side, the Greek Cypriot move was equal to asking for union with Greece via the European Union.[45]

Turkish protest was repeated in 1993 when the EU declared Cyprus in principle eligible for membership but delayed a more definitive answer to 1995. In the meantime, Brussels wanted to evaluate the efforts of both Cypriot communities to reach a solution to the division of the island under the auspices of the UN secretary general. The Turkish government declared in a letter from Foreign Minister Hikmet Çetin to the president of the Council of the EU, Belgian Prime Minister Willy Claes, "The Commission's opinion on the Greek Cypriot application for membership in the European Communities contravenes both international law concerning 'Cyprus' as a whole, and the basis of the efforts to reach a settlement of the Cyprus problem."[46]

The course of events was changed after the fall of the iron curtain in Europe. By mid-1994 it had become clear that the European Union would eventually have to accept applications for membership from the newly established democracies in central and eastern Europe. Under pressure from the Greek government, the European Council meeting in Corfu decided in June 1994 that "the next phase of enlargement of the Union will involve Cyprus and Malta."[47]

Turkey's disapproval became especially evident in March 1995 when the Turkish foreign minister, Murat Karayalçın, envisioned Turkish countermeasures in case of the opening of accession negotiations between the EU and Cyprus. These had been decided to take place six months after the end of the intergovernmental conference for the revision of the Maastricht Treaty sometime in late 1997 or early 1998. The decision of the EU's Council of Ministers accompanied the conclusion of the customs union between Turkey and the EU. It had to be taken by the council to get Greek consent to the customs union decision. Karayalcın declared:

> Turkey for her part is determined to see to it that her rights and obligations emanating from the 1960 treaties are kept intact. Turkey will continue to be politically and legally opposed to the membership of Cyprus, in whole or in part, before her own accession to the EU as a full member like the other guarantor power [Greece]. Turkey disagrees with the decision taken by the Council on the membership negotiations of Cyprus. . . . In such an undesirable eventuality, Turkey will be left with no option but to take steps towards achieving a similar integration with the Turkish Republic of Northern Cyprus.[48]

The EU was of the opinion that the accession negotiations constituted a catalytic element to bring about a solution on Cyprus, which it would prefer to have been concluded before accession of the island to the Union. But the EU also denied a Turkish right of veto to any element of EU enlargement policy. To this, Turkish Prime Minister Erbakan declared in December 1996 that "the South of Cyprus cannot join the EU without the permission of Turkey; if it does so, the integration of the Turkish Republic of Northern Cyprus into Turkey will be carried out as quickly as possible."[49]

On January 20, 1997, Turkish President Demirel and Turkish Cypriot leader Denktaş issued a joint declaration in which they not only reiterated the intention of establishing stronger links between the Turkish states but also declared that the start of accession negotiations between the European Union and Cyprus would lead to "the complete abolition of the framework and parameters for a solution which have emerged during the negotiating process in Cyprus."[50]

Between the two rounds of direct talks between Denktaş and President Clerides that took place in July and August, Turkey and the Turkish Republic of Northern Cyprus issued a joint statement on July 20 in which they declared their readiness for the gradual implementation of measures for economic and financial integration as well as partial integration in security, defense, and foreign policy. This statement was followed by the establishment of an association council between Turkey and Northern Cyprus on August 6, 1997.[51]

The EU's December 1997 refusal to incorporate Turkey into the list of candidate countries with which it would start accession negotiations in a foreseeable future not only led to a severe breakdown in EU-Turkey relations but also brought an end to the Turkish Cypriots' readiness to engage in international UN-sponsored talks to overcome the Cyprus deadlock. This was reaffirmed after the official opening of accession negotiations on March 28, 1998. Turkish Foreign Minister Cem warned the European Union "to evaluate its future steps very carefully before it is too late and before the Greek Cypriot administration paves the way towards another war on the island."[52] U.S. efforts to broker a solution on Cyprus, undertaken by President Clinton's special envoy, Richard Holbrooke, in spring 1998 could not thaw the ice.[53] Later in the year Washington concentrated its efforts more on preventing the stationing of the S-300s and less on breaking the deadlock of the Cyprus problem proper.

With full support from Ankara, Denktaş declared that he would only return to the negotiating table with his Greek Cypriot counterpart after the

Turkish Republic of Northern Cyprus had been recognized as an equal partner to the talks. This position was outlined in detail in a plan on August 31, 1998, in which he proposed a "Cyprus Confederation" of two equal Cypriot states that are strongly linked by special treaties with their respective "mother countries." The Cyprus Confederation could become an EU member given the consent of both parts. Turkey should be endowed with full rights and obligations of an EU member state with respect to the Cyprus Confederation until it would itself accede to the European Union.[54] With this plan, which in essence was nothing but a clarification of what he had always thought to be the substance of a Cyprus settlement, the Turkish Cypriot leader formally abandoned the official common ground for the internationally sponsored search for a settlement, the formula of a bizonal, bicommunal federated state on Cyprus.

Given the strong and symbiotic relationship between Turkey and Northern Cyprus, one can assume that Ankara fully endorsed this plan even if it had not been one of its drafters. It perfectly fits into the more nationalistic and assertive approach to foreign policy that has become dominant in Ankara's political circles, especially after Bülent Ecevit and his DSP took the reins of Turkish foreign policy. Its realization would create almost the best of all worlds for Turkey: The actual division of Cyprus would be confirmed; Turkey's influence over the Turkish part of the island would be strengthened; Turkey would have one foot in the door of the European Union by its special status with regard to the Cyprus Confederation; and Turkey's eventual membership in the EU would become much more likely—and be it just for the sake of ending the artificial status as a "partial member," as foreseen in Denktaş's proposal. No wonder that Greece immediately rejected the plan and that the European Union did not officially comment on it. Since then the situation on and around Cyprus has stagnated, not least because the Öcalan matter and the Kosovo war captured the attention of the international and regional entities. After the dissolution of the S-300 threat, Cyprus again drifted out of international attention.

This state of affairs can by no means be regarded as satisfactory by the international community, especially Turkey's Western allies. The probable accession to the EU of a still-divided Cyprus risks aggravating conflicts on the island and between Turkey and Greece. The most likely further formalization of the Turkish Republic of Northern Cyprus's integration into Turkey, which could turn the Green Line into a real border, as well as the further decrease of Turkey's chance to ever become a member of the EU pose the danger of unraveling the alliance's fabric in the region. Even if Greece and the European Union would comply with the lasting division of the island as a consequence of the accession of the Republic of Cyprus to the EU, the action would further Turkey's alienation from Europe and the West. Such a development would not be without consequences for the future of the Greater Middle East as well as that of the Balkans.

CHAPTER ELEVEN

Europe: Still the "Desired Land"?

NEWLY ARISEN ISSUES notwithstanding, the relationship with the European Union remained Turkey's most important foreign policy concern in the 1990s. This is not surprising given the pattern of close relations that links Turkey to the rest of Europe, especially the European Union. But recently a growing number of voices have been calling for a reevaluation of Turkey's European links with the aim of widening its foreign policy orientation and getting rid of the obsession with EU membership. Nevertheless, the vast majority of Turkey's politically conscious public sticks to the goal of EU membership. "For businessmen, EU membership means increased economic opportunity. For human rights activists, it means assurance of greater democratization. But for the establishment and Ataturkists of all stripes, EU membership has been a civilization issue, an existential issue, and a matter of historical affirmation."[1]

The European Union is that part of the world into which Turkey today is most strongly integrated, although it is not a member of the EU. The customs union with the EU covers half of Turkey's trade relations: in 1998 about 50 percent of Turkish exports went to Europe and about 52 percent of imports came from there.[2] These figures can be taken as being roughly representative of the magnitude of trade relations between the two over the past twenty years, with a short exception in the early 1980s when trade relations with Middle Eastern countries overshadowed trade with the European Union. As to direct foreign investment in Turkey, the EU's share is 67.5 percent of total foreign capital approved, and the EU countries account for 46 percent of the companies with foreign capital. The European Union is the area where most Turkish firms abroad are located and where most Turks outside Turkey live—close to 3 million people, nearly 5 percent of Turkey's total population.[3]

Given this, it is to be expected that most Turks traveling abroad also go to European destinations, and Europeans are by far the largest group of tourists who visit Turkey. Unlike earlier times, Turkish migrants living in Europe can maintain strong and extensive personal links to their country of origin by frequent visits with flights of two to four hours. This tends to make the migrant population in EU member states an extension of Turkey in western Europe, especially because these Turks are still not very well integrated into their new home countries.

This holds especially true for Germany where about 75 percent of all Turkish citizens in Europe live.[4] Germany is also Turkey's most important economic partner within the EU, covering almost half of Turkey's trade with the fifteen members and providing the bulk of European direct foreign investment in Turkey as well as the large majority of tourists going to Turkey.[5] It is, then, fully justified to regard German-Turkish relations as the core of Turkey's relations with the European Union. The development of this bilateral relationship is as crucial for EU-Turkey relations as is the Turkish-Greek one.

Besides the strong economic and social integration, there are close political bonds between Turkey and Europe. The most prominent is the Association Agreement, including the customs union, with the the European Union, followed by NATO membership, and the association status in the Western European Union (WEU). Turkey is also a member of the Council of Europe, the Organization for Security and Cooperation in Europe (OSCE), and other politically relevant European institutions. Turkey's most important business associations and trade unions are members or associate members of their European umbrella organization, as are political parties of the center-right and center-left. Thus Ankara's relations with the EU have been influenced as much by political and strategic factors as by economic developments. With the intensification of the country's drive for a eventual membership in the European Union, cultural and religious considerations have increasingly been added to the picture, pointing to Turkey's disputed European identity as perceived by the Turkish elite and the other European countries.

This strong European orientation of Turkish foreign policy has, however, come under attack. The disappointment of short-sighted expectations of the benefits of the customs union with the EU and even more so the decision of the European Council in Luxembourg in December 1997 not to include Turkey in the list of candidate countries for EU membership have led to widespread political disappointment in Turkey. The freeze in political relations with Europe that has been imposed by the government since early 1998 has consolidated this attitude.

Voices are raised on the religious right and the nationalist left that the European Union will never accept Turkey as a member and that under the new international constellation after the end of the East-West conflict, a wide range of alternative orientations is offered to Turkey that are equally apt to fulfill the country's historical mission and political aspirations. In this view, shared by the Virtue Party (FP) and to a large degree by Bülent Ecevit's Democratic Left Party (DSP), Turkey should concentrate its foreign policy efforts at becoming a regional center in the emerging Eurasian political reality and a bridge between Europe and the regions to its east and southeast. Such a policy does not negate Turkey's European identity and the goal of close political links with the European Union but adds to it elements that seem to better fit the political geography, social history, and evolving political culture of contemporary Turkey as well as the political necessities of global political and economic development.

As a consequence Turkey's policy toward the European Union, which normally is equated with Europe, although Europe has a broader meaning, has lost some of its momentum and direction.[6] The "European vocation" remains the top priority for the Turkish business elite, the military leadership, and the traditional political elites that still dominate Turkey's politics, but foreign policy has come more under the influence of nationalist circles that cautiously seem to feel their way toward a new outlook that is less Europe-centered. One should remember that this was also the case in the late 1970s when Ecevit was at the helm of Turkish foreign policy as prime minister of some short-lived governments. He froze relations with the European Economic Community and tried to develop a multidirectional foreign and security policy that would cautiously loosen links with the West.[7] It is unclear how far his renewed attempt in that direction is but an interlude in Turkish foreign policy in reaction to special political circumstances or whether it indicates the beginning of a lasting deviation from Turkey's long-established European policy.

The Background: Identity, Politics, and Economic Development

Relations with the European Union are seen by most Turkish political and business elites in a context that goes far beyond foreign policy considerations. They perceive the identity of the modern Turkish nation-state as directly affected by these relations. For them, it is a matter of Turkey's being recognized as a member of the West and as a European state. EU membership, they believe, is synonymous with the acknowledgement of the standards of contemporary Western civilization for Turkey. Simultaneously, the ultimate success of the Kemalist revolution would be confirmed.[8] These elites normally point out that Turkey has been part of European politics for centuries and has established an unequivocal European identity. As Özdem Sanberk, the former undersecretary of Turkey's Ministry of Foreign Affairs and Turkish ambassador to London, said,

> Turkey always has been a major part of the European System since the earliest times. . . . A Europe without Turkey is inconceivable. . . . So, when we look at the problems of Turkey and the European Union, whatever some European leaders may think, we are looking at an intra-European problem, not an external one.[9]

Next to this overriding factor of Turkey's "naturally" belonging to Europe, there are other political motivations behind the country's drive toward Europe. One is the rivalry with Greece. Considering the deep conflicts between the littoral states of the Aegean Sea, Turkey takes particular care in its foreign policy that in its relations with third countries it enjoys the same status as Greece. Thus, after the Greek application for association with the EEC in 1959, the Turkish application was a logical consequence.[10] It is especially deplored in Ankara that Greece uses its position as a member of the EU in a manner that could keep Turkey apart from western Europe, and without the other members of the EU being able or willing to effectively prevent Greece from doing so.

Another motive concerns security interests. These constituted the chief reason that, after World War II, by accepting the offer of the Truman Doctrine, Turkey incorporated itself into the Western security system.[11] Because of the developing East-West antagonism and superpower rivalry, this move led to Turkey's integration into the Western economic system as well. The country's political and economic development was dependent on these ties, which initially were concentrated exclusively on the United States. As Turkey became disappointed in the United States, above all in the American position in various stages of the Cyprus crisis (the "Johnson letter" of 1964, the arms embargo after 1975) and the neglect of Turkish security interests by the United States in the course of the détente of the late 1960s and early 1970s, Ankara turned more toward Western Europe.

The country began to see itself more clearly as an element of the European part of NATO and at the same time looked for compensation for the reduced aid from the United States. Ankara's disappointment deepened when more recently it saw itself largely bypassed in the slow and cumbersome European efforts to develop some kind of European Union security policy within the framework of European integration. Nevertheless, Turkey's national security remains strongly dependent on its inclusion in the overall Western security policy and defense framework. This includes maintaining strong security links with the European allies.

In addition to political motives, economic interests are important in relations with western Europe. Primarily, it is a question of safeguarding trade relations. The European Union is the major export market for the Turkish agricultural and industrial products. The continuing supply of capital goods from the EU, which is necessary for the Turkish economic development and modernization, is another imperative of the country's trade policy. The possibility of free movement of Turkish workers to Europe, which was in principle established in the Association Agreement of 1963, has been deemphasized in recent years as it has become clear that its realization would not be feasible under the present high unemployment in Europe.[12] Nevertheless, in principle it is a welcome instrument to take the pressure off Turkey's own labor market, which suffers under structural unemployment. As a by-product, labor force migration would also secure a certain inflow of foreign exchange in workers' remittances.

What is more important under present circumstances, however, is guaranteeing a constant and large flow of direct foreign investment from west European firms. This would compensate for the still insufficient national rate of savings and would assist in obtaining know-how and technology that Turkey needs for the continued modernization of its economy. Unlike the early period of relations, the financial aid granted by the EU through the association's Financial Protocols is no longer of special financial significance because of the rapid economic development Turkey has undergone. Its symbolic political significance, however, has grown out of proportion as a result of the deteriorating political climate between Turkey and the European Union. Besides being accepted as a candidate for EU membership in name, the defreezing of EU financial aid under the customs union agreement has in Turkish eyes become the litmus test of the EU's willingness and ability to treat Turkey as an equal.

This complex pattern of Turkey's European vocation and identity as well as political and economic interests constitutes the background against which Ankara's policy toward the European Union has to be analyzed. It is against this background that the rationality of the sometimes seemingly irrational Turkish behavior and attitudes of its European policy can be discerned. The country's European partners often overlook or disregard this more psychological aspect of Turkish relations, so that their policies, even if in European eyes well intended, may fail to meet Turkish expectations. Of course, the Turks often have difficulties understanding that what for them is an issue of the highest national priority for most European politicians constitutes a problem of cost-benefit relations in realizing certain important political interests.

The Customs Union: Final Step toward Membership?

After the Council of Ministers temporarily rejected Turkey's application for membership in February 1989, Ankara's relations with the EU, which at the time was still called the European Community, staggered along for years without any definite direction.[13] The EC was absorbed with preparing the internal reform proposal that led to the Treaty of Maastricht in 1992, the most far-reaching revision of the original Treaty of Rome, and by its endeavors to contribute to European restructuring after the end of the cold war.[14]

Brussels restricted its efforts to offering Turkey some packages of measures for a comprehensive cooperation that should lead to closer relations and finally to the establishment of a customs union between the EC and Turkey, as had been foreseen in the Association Agreement of 1963.[15] The realization of these measures was, however, impeded by constant Greek resistance against the release of any financial aid to Turkey, as had also been foreseen by the association's obligations. Furthermore, Greece could pressure its partners to accept a common political position stating the effects of the Cyprus problem on EU-Turkey relations. This formula became standard language in official EU declarations concerning relations with Turkey. Ankara strongly condemned this formula, which it regarded as a clear violation of an EC commitment that bilateral Turkish-Greek conflicts should have no impact on the European-Turkish relations that had been undertaken by the European Commission in the late 1970s within the context of Greece's entry into the European Community.

However, the slow course of relations with Brussels did not prevent Ankara from developing a growing interest of its own in stronger ties with Europe as it began to realize the consequences of the changes in Europe after the cold war. Turkey was not at all interested in loosening its European ties as an indirect consequence of the EU's growing preoccupation with central and east European states and speeded up its efforts at fulfilling its obligations to establish a customs union within the association framework. Bringing about a customs union had become the overriding imperative of Turkey's European policy by 1993–94.

The European Union met with considerable difficulties in realizing this goal because Greece strongly opposed such a development unless it would lead to some Turkish concessions in Greek-Turkish disputes. Finally it gave in under the pressure of its EU partners when they conceded to open accession negotiations with Cyprus six months after the end of the intergovernmental conference that would prepare a revision of the Treaty of Maastricht deemed necessary to enable the EU to start enlargement toward the central and east European states. Thus on March 6, 1995, Turkey and the EU finally signed an agreement within the association framework that established the customs union by January 1, 1996.[16]

With this step Turkey entered a new phase in its economic development policy: after an import substitution policy that dominated Turkey's development during the 1960s and 1970s, and the export orientation that characterized the 1980s and early 1990s, Ankara is about to apply a framework for its future economic development that is mostly influenced by global market forces. This change necessitates a new economic strategy: whereas import substitution industrialization aimed at creating an internal market and export-oriented industrialization led to a diversification of markets, the new framework requires a strategy that has been called productivity-oriented institution building. "Its pivotal components could be described as *market deepening* and *institutional modernization.*"[17]

The implementation of the customs union meant that trade in manufactured goods between Turkey and the European Union was no longer hampered by customs duties of any kind nor by quantitative restrictions or measures having an equivalent effect. For Turkey, this meant bringing down to zero the low level of customs protection against EU exports and abolishing all extra levies on them, which at the end of 1994 still had the combined effect of an overall protection level of about 12 percent. In addition, within five years Turkey would have to adapt to EU legislation its own legal instruments relating to barriers to trade such as technical norms, standards, and sanitary rules in industrial production. The EU had to abolish nontariff barriers to trade in textiles and clothing. Today, there is complete free trade in manufactured goods between Turkey and the European Union.

The requirements of the customs union go far beyond that of a free trade arrangement because trade with countries that are not members of the European Union is also covered by the regulations. Here the Turkish economy has to face greater changes than those in its relations with EU members. It not only has to adopt the common customs tariff of the EU in its trade with third countries but also has to apply to that trade the rules of the EU's commercial policy and to implement its measures. This means an alignment of Turkey's commercial policy with the preferential trade regimes that the European Union has concluded with many developing countries in the third world, the Mediterranean region, and central and eastern Europe until the end of 2000.

In a midterm perspective the customs union will be accompanied by another round of structural change for Turkish industry as a result of increased international competition. This will particularly affect medium to small companies that do not produce foreign-patented goods and work without foreign private capital participation. For them "much will depend . . . on whether the Turkish government will be able to follow efficient and appropriate policies in the future that will facilitate the transformation and adaptation of the economy," as a Turkish analyst observed.[18]

Despite the continuous endemic instability of domestic politics that for a long time has prevented the establishment of a sound economic policy, Turkish industry has mastered the challenges of the customs union remarkably well. The steep rise in the country's trade deficit with the European Union that occurred in 1996 cannot totally be attributed to the customs union, although the dismantlement of trade barriers in favor of the EU naturally led to an initial surge in imports from Europe.[19] This effect was evened out in the following years. The growth of Turkish imports from and exports to the EU was almost balanced in 1997 and showed a significant export growth and import decline in 1998, which led to a considerable drop in Turkey's trade deficit with the EU.[20] Although not all Turkish hopes concerning an improvement of trade with the European Union materialized, neither did exaggerated fears about the impact of overwhelming European competition on the Turkish market.

The pressure for restructuring the Turkish economy has been further intensified by the legal measures that accompany the trade-related regulations of the customs union decision. Turkey had to institute legal reforms concerning economic matters according to EU rules.[21] These included comprehensive legislative and administrative measures for the protection of intellectual, industrial, and commercial property rights. Furthermore, the competition rules of the EU's internal market, based on articles 85, 86, 92, and 93 of the European Community Treaty, had to be applied to the customs union until January 1, 1998. To this end Turkey adopted a national antitrust law and established a national authority to enforce competition rules. All plans of state aid have to be reported to the Brussels authorities and so will any new instances of aid granted to a company or a group of enterprises. The European Union will reciprocate and inform Turkey on all relevant aid granted by its member states. Both sides have the right to raise objections to aid that in their opinion violates EU law.

The goal of all stipulations regarding state aid, rules of competition, state monopolies, and trade defense instruments is to establish a guarantee against unfair competition within the customs union that is comparable to the one existing in the EU's internal market. The combination of rulings on technical barriers to trade, the reform of laws on competition, and opening government procurement markets is a clear indication that the customs union comes close, so far as industrial products are concerned, to including Turkey in the EU's internal market—without, however, making the country institutionally a part of that market. With the customs union, not only is Turkey's economic integration into the EU considerably upgraded but its integration into the legal sphere of the EU has been intensified with regard to economic and trade law.

To facilitate the adaptation of Turkish industry to the new conditions of the customs union, the EU has pledged to grant financial aid within the framework of renewed financial cooperation. This consists of various elements: a five-year aid program financed by EU budgetary contributions totaling ECU375 million; additional European Investment Bank (EIB) loans that could reach a ceiling of ECU750 million over the same period; and further access, according to the eligibility of projects presented, to special funds provided by the EU under the framework of its Redirected Mediterranean Policy for structural investments in energy, the environment, transport, and communications. Furthermore, upon Turkey's request the European Union may examine the possibility of additional medium-term macroeconomic financial assistance if it is linked to the implementation of economic programs approved by the International Monetary Fund. In total, the EU declared itself ready to support with an estimated ECU1.5 billion the restructuring of Turkey's economy to better adapt to the conditions of the customs union.

The March 6, 1995, decision, however, falls short of what was originally foreseen in the documents of 1963 and 1970 as the substance of the final stage of association. There is still no free trade in agricultural produce because Ankara has not taken the measures that would make the basic regulations of the EU's common agricultural policy applicable to Turkey's national agricultural policy. But for this to happen is not imaginable without Turkey's full membership in the EU. Otherwise Turkey alone would be burdened with the financial consequences of such a move, which would overstretch the country's financial resources. Progress in agricultural trade remains dependent on further negotiated mutal preferences. In addition to agriculture, provision for the free movement of labor, services, and capital is not included in the customs union, nor is the right to establish a profession as a foreigner. With the exception of the free movement of capital, toward which Turkey has already taken many steps, these matters probably will remain pending for the time being. Free movement, which is connected with the movement or lasting settlement of people, is regarded by the EU as an extremely critical issue and is one of the main reasons for its reluctance concerning eventual Turkish membership.

Notwithstanding these omissions, the customs union decision made Turkey the nonmember country that institutionally is most strongly integrated with the EU. Being part of the customs union allows for the strongest possible economic integration short of membership. This has been further strengthened by the creation of a free trade area for steel products under the European Coal and Steel Community Treaty and more reciprocal concessions in agricultural trade, both of which have been agreed on since 1996.

To underline the overall importance that the European Union has attached to improving its relations with Turkey, the Association Council of March 6, 1995, also decided to enlarge economic, industrial, technical, and political cooperation. These include more or less the areas that are part of the EU's cooperation with central and eastern European states under the framework of the Europe Agreements.[22]

Of special importance was the proposal of a high-level political dialogue that has been created for a regular exchange of information and opinion on all matters of common interest. Under this plan, the president of the European Council, the president of the European Commission, and the chief of state or government of Turkey are to meet once a year. The foreign ministers of the EU's troika and Turkey will meet twice a year, as will the political directors of the respective foreign services.[23] These meetings are complemented by consultations among experts at the level of the Common Foreign and Security Policy (CFSP) working groups and regular information to the Turkish government concerning the results of meetings of the European Council, the Council of Ministers of the European Union, and the Political Committee of the CFSP. A framework for a comprehensive and continuous political dialogue has therefore been created. If both sides have the political will to do so, this could be used for an intensive exchange of views on the many difficult problems that tend to separate Turkey and the EU politically.

Turkey's great interest in establishing the customs union became evident during 1995. When the European Parliament showed reluctance to endorse the agreement because of what it thought to be still an unsatisfactory level of democracy and human rights protection in Turkey, Ankara mobilized all resources to overcome the resistance. Domestically, it put considerable pressure on parliament to pass legislation for a reform of the 1982 constitution that had been pending for months because the parties could not reach the necessary compromises. This reform was to lead to wider political participation.[24] The government also managed to soften article 8 of the Anti-Terror Law that had previously led to the prosecution and imprisonment of many journalists and other people for "crimes of thought"—propagating separatism, which meant supporting Kurdish nationalism or terrorism. Pressure from the military prevented complete abolition of article 8, so the authorities still have been prosecuting "crimes of conviction."

Externally, the government undertook great efforts to garner all the support of European political circles that it could get. Prime Minister Tansu Çiller and Foreign Minister Deniz Baykal approached every EU government and important politicians in the EU countries to ask for their support in convincing the European Parliament. Baykal's efforts in adressing his fellow German and British social democrats together with endeavors of Israel's Prime Minister Shimon Peres finally led to a reluctant consent of the Socialist Group of the parliament. This was crucial in securing the necessary majority for the endorsement of the customs union agreement on December 13, 1995.

By the beginning of 1996 there was a good chance for closer EU-Turkey relations. This would not be easy because it had become clear that the two understood different political meanings of membership in the customs union. For Turkey it was the final step to membership in the EU that would have to be approached in line with the provisions of article 28 of the 1963 Association Agreement.[25]

This became clear during the campaign for the early elections that had been called by the coalition government of Çiller and Baykal for December

24, 1995. In her attempt at preventing the fundamentalist Welfare Party from increasing its vote, Çiller styled the endorsement of the customs union agreement by the European Parliament as a question of confirming Turkey's secular Western orientation by implying to the electorate that the customs union would open the door to EU membership.[26] In early December, Turkey's public was plunged into a customs union hysteria, giving the impression that the country's very existence depended on the EP's decision. This led to an unfortunate overpoliticization of the issue.

This was even more so because for the EU members, customs union membership meant reaching an elevated level of relations the future of which should remain open. The EU was still not ready to interpret the Association Agreement as a teleological undertaking aimed at eventual Turkish membership in the EU. Nevertheless, on January 1, 1996, prospects for further improvement in political relations between both sides looked good despite the election defeat of Mrs. Çiller.

The Luxembourg EU Council of December 1997 and After

These prospects did not materialize. Only one month after the start of the customs union, the Kardak-Imia crisis, which met both the new Greek prime minister, Costas Simitis, and the Turkish political leaders under difficult domestic political circumstances, led to a new hardening of Greece's position toward EU-Turkey relations. The conclusion of a financial protocol foreseen in the context of the customs union agreement was blocked by Greek veto, and the EU declaration of July 15, 1996, which asked Turkey to accept international legal arbitration by the International Court of Justice according to Greek demands, further burdened relations with Turkey. When later in the year the situation on Cyprus deteriorated because of Greek Cypriot riots that resulted in the death of two Greek Cypriots who had transgressed the Green Line into the Turkish sector, Greek-Turkish relations were back to their level of carefully managed conflict that comes close to cold war. Turkey-EU relations also could not prosper as some might have hoped when the customs union agreement came into effect.[27]

The pro-European circles in Turkey saw with growing irritation that their country was being outraced by central and east European states in its attempt to become an EU member. Eastern enlargement and the accession of Cyprus seemed to have gained priority over Turkey's long-standing European vocation. Since the second half of 1996, Turkey's policy toward the European Union had been focused on convincing it that it had to include Turkey in the next round of enlargement. This was clearly expressed by Deputy Prime Minister and Foreign Minister Çiller before her meeting with EU representatives in Dublin in December 1996:

> There are three reasons, why Turkey will participate in the next round of EU enlargement: We are the first country to have signed an agreement that foresees accession. We are the only candidate which is already a member of NATO and we are also the only country to have reached the customs union stage of integration which took effect one year ago.[28]

The Turkish position was, however, somewhat handicapped because only half the Erbakan-Çiller coalition government—the DYP and its leader, Foreign Minister Çiller—was really interested in EU membership. Necmettin Erbakan and his Refah Party never made a secret of their reluctance to agree to an eventual Turkish accession, mainly for ideological reasons. This brought the secular faction within the government under an additional and partially self-created pressure of proving to the Turkish people that the country's future was with Europe and that this was accepted and supported by the Europeans. The domestic political function of the issue of EU membership became even more accentuated than was commonly the case.

The uneasy situation of Turkey's Europeanists led to a Turkish policy that was characterized more by attempts at publicly pressuring the EU into concessions than by skillful and discrete diplomatic persuasion. "Turkey . . . tends to regard itself and plays as an outsider rather than acting its role as an insider."[29] To a certain extent the harsh Turkish approach might also have been influenced by Ankara's impression that its claims toward the European Union were fully backed by the U.S. administration. The deterioration of security in the eastern Mediterranean after the Kardak-Imia crisis and the Greek Cypriot announcement of the S-300 deal with Russia convinced the Americans that a stronger Turkish inclusion into the EU was necessary to keep the country on a Western track.[30]

Foreign Minister Çiller and other Turkish officials did not even refrain from creating an explicit linkage between Turkey's consent to an eventual eastward enlargement of NATO and entrance into the EU.[31] "The logic behind this move, according to officials in Ankara, is that NATO expansion in Europe is part of the overall integration process under way on this continent, with the alliance representing the security aspect and the new EU memberships representing the political and economic aspects."[32]

The aggressive Turkish diplomacy toward the EU contributed to increasing concern in European circles about the future of relations with an ally that was deemed to be of strategic importance. Turkey's stance in the eyes of EU circles was additionally complicated by the country's inability to initiate the EU's recommended internal reforms because of rising tensions between secularists and Islamists. These led to greater political influence of the military, and where Europeans would have liked to see an amelioration of human rights policy, an increase in authoritarian tendencies could be realized.

European politicians delivered enough material to nurture Turkish suspicion about its vanishing chances of becoming an EU member. Public (and scholarly) discussion about EU enlargement concentrated on eastward enlargement thus leaving out Turkey (and Cyprus). Turkey was regarded as more a nuisance than an integral element of the new European political and security architecture. Finally, leading European Christian Democrats stated after a meeting in Brussels on March 4, 1997, that European integration was a civilizational project in which a Muslim country like Turkey could have no place.[33] This confirmed Turkey's long-standing suspicion that Europe's policy toward it was driven by motives other than contractual obligations entered into in 1963.

This impression could only partially be corrected by the EU's official reaffirmation of Turkey's eligibility for membership as had been stated in the conclusion of the EC's Council of Ministers answer to Turkey's application for membership in 1989. Furthermore, the EU declared that Turkey would be judged according to the same objective criteria that were to be applied to the applications of the east and central European states. However, the Europeans continued to point to the fact that Turkey was not in a position to fulfil these criteria, mainly for political reasons.[34]

Turkey regarded the report of the European Commission on enlargement that was presented in mid-July under the title *Agenda 2000: For a Stronger and Wider Union* as completely unsatisfactory.[35] Turkey's exclusion from the group of countries with which the commission proposed to start accession negotiations was regarded as a "mistake."[36] Foreign Minister İsmail Cem declared: "It is not just and it is not objective." But he also added that the commission's decision should not be exaggerated in an "obsessive manner" and that it would not be the end of Turkey, which was an important country with great economic dynamism. Nevertheless Turkey's officials felt that their country had not been evaluated according to the same criteria as other applicants.[37] The presentation by the European Commission of a special program beyond the state of customs union for developing relations with Turkey apart from all other applicants, without, however, making a clear reference to membership, is an indication that this Turkish suspicion was not completely unfounded.

Despite occasional repetitions by Cem that Turkey "was not obsessed with EU membership," Turkish diplomatic activities in the following months concentrated on changing the EU's position as had been manifested in *Agenda 2000* and accompanying documents. On the one hand, Ankara tried to relay the message to Brussels that the inclusion of Cyprus in the first group of applicants would almost automatically end all efforts to look for a compromise solution to the Cyprus problem as envisioned by the latest UN-sponsored bilateral talks between Rauf Denktaş and Clerides.[38] On the other hand Turkish officials undertook many diplomatic efforts to bolster the pro-Turkish position of the French government, which would have liked to have included Turkey in some way in the group of candidates, and to overcome British reluctance and, most important, German resistance against this move. Ankara also tried to garner as much U.S. support for its case as it could, and during the autumn of 1997 American diplomats and officials were keen to convince EU politicians that they had to include Turkey among the candidates for membership.

The Turkish prime minister, Mesut Yılmaz, was sure a breakthrough had been reached concerning German resistance when Chancellor Helmut Kohl declared during an official visit by Yılmaz to Bonn in late September 1997 that he supported a later membership and asked for Turkey's own contribution to reach that goal. Germany would assist within the limits of its possibilities.[39] The Turkish prime minister was convinced that these remarks meant German consent to Turkey's equal treatment with all other applicants, but the German chancellor and his government meant only to confirm the established German line that Turkish membership should happen one day, when the necessary conditions had been fulfilled. For reaching this stage the EU should apply a different strategy for Turkey than for the east and central European countries.[40] Therefore, the German government did not like to term Turkey a candidate.

This misunderstanding should have proved fatal for German-Turkish and Turkey-EU relations when the European Council of Luxembourg on December 13, 1997, decided not to include Turkey officially in the list of candidate states but put it in a category of its own as an applicant for which a special "European strategy" should be devised to bring about later membership. The only place Turkey was put on an equal footing with the other eleven applicant countries was with regard to the convening of a European Conference in which the EU wanted to regularly discuss with the heads of state of all eleven candidates plus Turkey problems of common interest that would not be directly related to the matter of EU enlargement.[41]

Although this was the most favorable mention so far at the level of the European Council on Turkey's future in the EU's development, the Luxembourg decision was met with utmost disappointment in Turkey and flatly rejected by the Yılmaz-Ecevit government. In an official statement on December 14 the Turkish government saw some positive elements in the Luxembourg summit's declaration, but it declared the text "unacceptable" for the following reasons:

—Turkey has not been evaluated within the same framework, the same well-intentioned approach, and objective criteria as the other candidate countries.

—Most of the points that had been put forward as new and positive steps for Turkey were in fact the commitments undertaken and not implemented for many years by the EU.

—Partial, prejudiced, and exaggerated assessments were made about Turkey's internal structure and its foreign policy, including Cyprus.

—With these erroneous approaches, attempts had been made to impose unacceptable political conditions that had concealed intentions.[42]

This reaction was not so much caused by the EU's rejection of beginning accession negotiations with Turkey but by Ankara's expectation of different treatment. What the Turks had hoped for was equal treatment, being named a candidate and being included in one of the categories established for the candidate countries. What nobody in Turkey could understand was why the country had not been put on equal footing at least with such weak candidates as Bulgaria or Romania. The Turks did not perceive themselves as having been put into another special category of candidate but as having been put behind all others, in fact as having been decoupled from the enlargement process. For Ankara, this was the proof that different criteria had been applied to Turkey, and these could only have been cultural and religious ones.

The Turkish government also flatly rejected the invitation to the European Conference, which Ankara considered a tricky device to make it accept Greece's position concerning bilateral disputes as well as the candidacy of the Republic of Cyprus, which for Turkey was but "the Greek Cypriot administration."[43] Ankara's rejection also made clear that it was not interested in what it saw as a palliative undertaking that had little to do with Turkey's real political interests. When the Turkish prime minister did not show up for the first European Conference in London in March 1998 but instead visited some Central Asian republics, another device the EU had developed for keeping Turkey on track proved useless.

The idea of the European Conference had been hijacked by the Turkish problem in 1997 because it had been invented in spring 1996 by France in German-French discussions about the best way of starting the eastern enlargement after it had become clear that not all central and east European applicants were equally ready for the start of accession negotiations. The conference was conceived as a multilateral forum for a visible demonstration of the accession perspective of all ten central and east European applicants. Within the German government this idea was a compromise between those who favored a common start with an ensuing differentiation (*Startlinien-Konzept*) and those who advocated beginning the process only with those applicants that were deemed ready. In these discussions Turkey was not considered at all; it was only included after the EU members realized that they had to deal with Turkey in the preparation of the eastward enlargement process. Then Germany and other member states succeeded in downgrading the conference to a mere protocol event with almost no political substance.[44]

Ankara was also deeply disappointed by the EU's readiness to include Cyprus as a candidate with whom accession negotiations should be opened early. Turkey did not hesitate to denounce such a move as illegal and to repeat its intention of closer integration between Turkey and the Turkish Republic of Northern Cyprus (TRNC). Rauf Denktaş declared that any further UN endeavors to bring about a dialogue between the two communities was dead and asked the EU representative on Cyprus to leave the Turkish Cypriots alone. A federation on Cyprus was regarded possible only after the recognition of the TRNC.[45]

In the following months the Ecevit part of Turkey's new secular coalition government put much more emphasis on the treatment of Cyprus in the Luxembourg decision than on the treatment of Turkey itself. Ecevit had declared some days after the EU summit that Turkey could well exist without EU membership, although Ankara would never give up this goal even after having been so unfairly treated.[46]

The situation deteriorated further when Prime Minister Yılmaz declared the comprehensive political dialogue between Turkey and the EU terminated and even threatened that Ankara would withdraw its application for membership if the EU was not ready to reverse its decision on the next European Council in Cardiff in early summer 1998. He ostensibly tried to play the American card during his visit to Washington in the immediate aftermath of Luxembourg when he accused the EU of discriminating against Turkey for religious reasons and mentioned especially the German chancellor, whom he accused of wanting to turn the EU into a Christian club.[47]

Some weeks later in the run-up to the European Conference, Yılmaz repeated his accusations against Germany and accused the Kohl government of following a policy of *Lebensraum*, a geopolitical conception of the Nazi regime, with its open support of the EU's eastern enlargement. In this way Germany was "to divide Europe between Bulgaria and Turkey."[48] Implicitly this meant that in Yılmaz's view Germany feared Turkish political competition in the longer run.

Although the British EU presidency tried to thaw the ice in the first half of 1998, Ankara remained firm in its rejection of reestablishing political relations with the EU. It continued, however, close bilateral relations with the most important member states apart from Germany. Political ties were never really severed, although the Turkish government experienced some severe disappointments in this strategy.

First, it had to realize that the United Kingdom could not overcome mainly Greek resistance against any improvement of EU-Turkish relations. The European Council of Cardiff in June 1998 could do no more than confirm the elements of the Luxembourg summit without any improvement in those aspects that had been so severely criticized by Turkey.[49] In the meantime the process of enlargement had been started without Turkey. The EU instruments for preparing candidates for later membership had been put into place and differed considerably from those foreseen for Turkey. These instruments had not even become part of the *acquis* of the association by the time of the Cardiff European Council meeting because of the continuous Greek veto against the providing any financial means for a substantial "European strategy" for Turkey. According to the European Commission, without that money the implementation of the program would be impossible.

Ankara also had to swallow a condemnation by the Socialist-led majority of the French National Assembly of the Ottoman treatment of Armenians during World War I. This abruptly ended the honeymoon in Turkish-French relations that had developed in the wake of Turkey's condemnation of Germany.[50] And when the Italian government proved unable to prevent a meeting of the so-called Kurdish parliament in exile—a PKK-dominated attempt to attract international support for the Kurdish cause—in September in Rome, another candidate for fostering the Turkish case in the EU was lost.[51] Turkey's strategy of bilaterally organizing its relations with Europe to change the EU's position thus did not show the expected results.

Relatively unimpressed by Turkey's complaints and pressures, the European Union continued with the policy announced in Luxembourg. The Council of Ministers asked the European Commission to propose a more elaborate plan for the European strategy and asked it to find a way of circumventing Greek obstruction of financial aid to Turkey. The commission presented the asked-for proposals against Greek resistance. In its initial operational proposals for the European strategy in March 1998, the commission developed a wide range of practical cooperation measures that aimed at improving the functioning of the customs union and extending EU-Turkey cooperation into areas that had been proposed by the EU for years but failed to materialize due to political problems of the relationship. The commission carefully refrained from touching these political problems in its proposals. It made clear, however, that implementation of the prosposals would necessitate providing the financial means foreseen for the support of Turkish industry in the customs union framework.[52]

In October 1998 when the commission proposed some ways of realeasing money for programs in Turkey without the necessity of Greek consent, the government in Athens announced that it would appeal to the European Court of Justice if the EU Council of Ministers should approve the proposals.[53] Athens also criticized the first progress report on Turkey, in which the commission evaluated Turkish efforts to reach the conditions for the eventual opening of membership negotiations, as being too soft and forthcoming toward Ankara.[54] Athens tried to counter this by distributing a report of its own in which Turkey was heavily criticized for the well-known shortcomings of its internal situation and its agressive foreign policy, especially with Turkish-Greek relations and Cyprus.[55] The European Parliament deleted any provisions for financial aid to Turkey from the budget of 1999. Thus by late autumn 1998 the European Union was still without a working European strategy for Turkey. As had been the case on earlier occasions, the EU showed itself unable to implement a comprehensive and substantial strategy for improving Turkish-European relations because of problems with Greece.

The Turkish government reacted to the EU's behavior by continuing its rejectionist rhetoric while cautiously starting to cooperate. It presented a proposal of its own for upgrading the European strategy that was regarded partly as a response to the commission's initial operational proposals and partly as a widening of its scope. Ankara especially admonished the slow start of financial cooperation and stated that "it is up to the EU itself to find ways of overcoming the obstacles that are due to EU institutions or member states." It also pointed to the necessity of improving the decisionmaking and consultation mechanism within the association to enable the institution to fully fulfill its function of preparing Turkey for later membership.[56]

The Turkish initiative did not lead to much movement in EU-Turkey relations because the position in Brussels and among the EU member states did not change. Preoccupied by domestic problems such as the dissolution of Mesut Yılmaz's coalition government in November 1998, the protracted attempts of various politicians to form a new government, the run-up to the early elections of April 18, 1999, and, above all, the capture of the PKK leader, Abdullah Öcalan, the Turkish government also gave little attention to relations with the EU. There was even less incentive to do so because of the new strains in Turkish-European relations that were caused by Italy's refusal to extradite the PKK leader to Turkey and Greek complicity in hiding him from Turkish prosecution.

Nonetheless, the German EU presidency tried to give new momentum to relations with Ankara in spring 1999. The new German government of social democrats and Greens that had come to power in the national elections of October 1998 changed the German approach to Turkey's eventual EU membership by accepting the country's status as candidate without, however, giving up the established European conditions for the start of entrance negotiations. A proposal of the German EU presidency to the European Council meeting in Cologne in June 1999 to change the EU's position toward Turkey met with Greek and Scandinavian resistance and was finally dropped from the presidency's "conclusions" about the meeting.[57]

Turkey reacted in a mixed way to this German-European move. In an exchange of letters between Prime Minister Bülent Ecevit and German Chancellor Gerhard Schröder, the Turkish government acknowledged the existence of the EU criteria for membership of any European country but made clear that it was not ready to accept European interference in the "southeastern problem."[58] Concerning the nonresult of the Cologne EU summit meeting, the Turkish foreign ministry stated that "the EU's discriminatory policy toward Turkey has not changed. Therefore, no one should expect Turkey to alter its approach to its relations with the EU."[59] Although the German move indicated a substantial change in Bonn's approach to EU-Turkey relations, it would have mainly meant a change in EU language without giving up the political fundamentals of the EU position. A slow return to normalcy in Turkey-EU relations cannot be excluded, although this development could be brought to an abrupt end any time by internal political developments in Turkey, which may again confirm European suspicions of the country's political "backwardness," or by some careless political moves of the EU that may again awake Turkey's political sensitivity.

An improvement in Turkey's relations with the European Union will not only depend on some policy changes on the European side. Turkey will have to constructively address those problems that Europeans time and again have mentioned as a hurdle for quick and early EU membership: domestic human rights violations, treatment of the Kurds, shortcomings in the democratic structure, conflict with Greece, and the Cyprus problem. The Turkish government will have to give up its practice to make the Europeans believe that announcements of fundamental reforms in democracy and human rights are reforms in substance. And it will have to develop and sustain a policy of conciliation with Greece that is marked by some substantial Turkish concessions in exchange for Greek ones. There are serious doubts that the coalition government of Bülent Ecevit will be able and ready to move in that direction.

Above all, however, Turkey's Western-oriented elites have to start a domestic debate that openly addresses the question of what EU membership would really mean for Turkey and its society, because much of Turkey's emotional behavior with regard to EU relations results from widespread public misconceptions of the European Union and its political rationality. The Turkey-EU Affairs Investigation Commission of the Turkish parliament put this problem in a nutshell in its report *Relations between Turkey and the European Union* by stating, "The question of how the transfer of sovereignty to EU institutions will be compatible with our traditions needs to be addressed."[60]

The neglect of this discussion so far makes it easy for Turkey's governing politicians to put the blame for the disappointing state of affairs on the Europeans and to divert public attention from Ankara's own deficiencies in solidly managing the relationship. If there has been a Turkish discussion of the matter, it has been characterized by a growing reluctance to accept what is seen as European interference into Turkish sovereign affairs. Thus one may conclude that what Turkey wants is a platonic membership in the EU and not a real one.

CHAPTER TWELVE

Turkey in the Western Security System: Asset or Liability?

TURKEY'S PLACE in the Western security system has changed considerably since the end of the cold war. Uncertainty prevails in many respects and its dissipation will not be easy and will need time. In the days of the global strategic confrontation between East and West, Turkey was the pivotal element of NATO's southeastern flank. It contributed to the policy of credible deterrence in the European theatre, and its national security was guaranteed by its inclusion in the alliance.

Today, there is no longer a viable European theatre of NATO, and direct military threats to Turkey have been greatly diminished. Ankara and its allies are facing a new security policy environment that has been described "as a period of transition and transformation that calls for reorientations and new architectures."[1] In this new order Turkey is being challenged to find a place. For its allies and partners this will decide whether it will continue to be an asset of Western security policy or if and to what extent it may become a liability. This question may be answered in a different manner by Turkey's American and European allies.

In Ankara the question may arise for the first time as to whether the strong link to the Western security system can still be regarded as an undisputable asset or if it may become a liability to the country's security interests. A general feeling of risk and uncertainty has arisen because of the increased intricateness of the new constellations of conflict in the country's immediate neighborhood, many of which have direct repercussions on its security. Additionally, NATO's search for a new role, strategy, and organization has been creating a certain uneasiness in Turkish security policy circles about the real political and military value of the country's existing alliance bonds. A feeling has been growing that this alliance is only of limited value for guaranteeing military security against the new risks the country is facing.

So far the Turkish security policy establishment does not see a viable alternative to continuing the existing security relationships. There are no new comprehensive alliances or other security structures that could effectively replace the existing ones, nor will Turkey be able to reach a status of security self-sufficiency in the near future. Its political and economic strength will remain weak with respect to single-handedly developing a national security capacity that would enable it to meet all relevant challenges. In addition, its military and political elite stick to the firm conviction that the continuation of the Kemalist Westernization of Turkey does not allow a loosening of ties with the Western security system.

As a result of this complicated situation, the Turkish military leadership and its civilian followers in the government apply a multitrack strategy that does not block any option for the medium term. First, Turkey has undertaken strong efforts to develop and strengthen its national military and industrial capabilities for guaranteeing its national security. For this purpose the military leadership has developed a program for a comprehensive overhaul and modernization of the armed forces amounting to US$150 billion in the next thirty years.[2]

Ankara is well aware of the necessity of foreign support and cooperation for reaching this goal. The improved military-industrial cooperation with Israel has to be seen in this perspective, given a growing European reluctance in continuing defense aid to and military-industrial cooperation with Turkey and the continuing uncertainty over the American ability to fulfill its respective commitments toward the country because of recurrent disagreements between the administration and Congress.

Ankara has tried to keep its links with the existing institutional framework of Western security policy as close and comprehensive as possible. NATO remains the central pillar for the country's inclusion in the Western network. Consequently, Ankara shows a certain reluctance to approve a too quick comprehensive institutional, organizational, and political overhaul of the alliance, including its enlargement toward the east. The Turks show a special reluctance to Europeanizing NATO that would entail a marked reduction of the American role in the alliance.[3]

At the same time, Ankara is eager to be fully included in the emerging more independent European security structures that seem to evolve in connection with the reformed European Union. It is sometimes unclear if the Turkish drive toward EU membership is a result of its security policy interests or if its security policy advances to Europe are but another instrument for reaching EU membership. Turkish officials and politicians contend that the country has to be included in the European Union because of the comprehensive character of the new European security architecture of which they want to be an integral part. In their view, European security includes a military and an economic-social part, the former mainly being provided by an enlarged NATO and the latter by the enlarged European Union.[4]

One problem with its attitude toward the post–cold war transition of the European and transatlantic security framework is that Ankara has political goals and ad-hoc policies with regard to its special interests but has failed to develop ideas as to how the new framework should be structured. There is no Turkish "grand strategy" that would comprehensively describe the country's place in the new architecture. This cannot come as a surprise. The volatile and sometimes chaotic domestic political situation with its rapid changes of governments of different ideological outlook and composition has not favored developing sound national strategies of whatever kind. Thus the power of definition concerning its pressing security policy challenges remains with the military leadership, which tends to be conservative in its decisions.

In doing so it follows the general Western approach to revising the allied security framework that is characterized by careful adaptation of existing structures and organizations and not by a new grand design. What has been conspicuously absent from the European mainstream of discussions about restructuring Europe after the end of the cold war, however, is where and how Turkey should fit into the new European security architecture. All plans and discussions about a common security policy element of the reformed European Union that would eventually also include elements of common defense and that would be the backbone of a more autonomous European participation in the allied security structure have completely left out considerations about Turkey's role, implicitly leaving the answer to the "Turkish problem" to the United States, as had been the case for most of the cold war.

For Ankara the question of how the coming European security architecture would be developed and what could and should be Turkey's place is of paramount importance. The answer will ultimately decide whether Turkey can continue with its established multinational security policy or whether the Turkish leadership has to make stronger efforts at developing specific national concepts for dealing with the country's security challenges. Developing a more national approach toward security matters need not necessarily mean severing ties with the alliance, but it would lead to a stronger accent on a specific national policy plus, perhaps, a reduction of Turkey's role in the alliance to that of a special relationship with the United States.[5]

To find an answer to the question regarding Turkey's place, some connected matters have to be addressed. What are Turkey's security risks and how do these risks and interest fit into the Western and European risk perception and definition of security interests? What will be the likely institutional evolution of the Western security system and what is and what could become of Turkey's place within this system? What is Turkey's likely contribution to the realization of changing Western and European security interests? What is the Western security system's likely contribution to the realization of Turkey's security interests?

Perceptions of Security Risk

With the end of the Soviet Union there is no longer a commonly felt, clearly defined security threat to Europe. It is no longer clear to European citizens against whom to prepare for collective defense. This also holds true for most European states individually, with a few exceptions in the former Yugoslavia and perhaps the Baltic republics where Russia is still considered a threat to national independence. Another exception is the Aegean and eastern Mediterranean where Greece feels seriously threatened by Turkey and has made preparations in its national defense strategy.

In general, however, military precautions of European states are now taken against not very well defined security risks. The debate about NATO's reform and the arguments put forward in some European states in the discussions about national military restructuring strengthen the impression that contemporary military security policy is not about traditional national defense but much more about military-backed intervention in conflicts outside NATO's area that may somehow affect Europe's security.

In addition, the concept of security has broadened to include a variety of risks that could undermine the stability of Europe's nations and societies. A list of such risks, commonly agreed upon by all twenty-seven countries of the Western European Union, includes armed conflicts of a limited nature deriving from unsettled border disputes or ethnic strife; the proliferation of weapons of mass destruction and their means of delivery, especially in the Middle East and South Asia; international terrorism, organized crime, drug trafficking, and uncontrolled illegal immigration; and environmental risks deriving from either modern industrial plants, transportation of dangerous substances, or military-related environmental damage. From a special future-oriented perspective one could add "information war" or "cyberwar" to this list.[6]

These security risks can be seen in the violent conflict in the former Yugoslavia and its resulting enforced large refugee movements to other European states. The weakening and sometimes total breakdown of public order furthers the spread of networks of organized crime that thrive on illegal immigration, drug trafficking, and arms smuggling. Southern European states confront uncontrolled illegal immigration from the southern Mediterranean. Together with the fear of increased numbers of violent Islamic fundamentalist groups, such immigration was an important reason for the sharpened political awareness of NATO and the Western European Union with respect to the southern Mediterranean.[7] Some states in the greater Middle East enjoy special attention from the Europeans because of their proven or assumed capability of aquiring or developing weapons of mass destruction and the delivery means that could pose a threat to some parts of southern Europe. Iran, Iraq, and Libya are especially mentioned.[8]

A special feature of many of these security risks is their nonmilitary or mixed military-civilian character. Consequently, military means or threats of military force are mostly applied to reach political goals, as has been the case in trying to make Saddam Hussein comply with UN resolutions or inducing Slobodan Milošević to change his policy toward Kosovo. Another growing application of military means in and around Europe is peacekeeping or peace enforcement operations after a (normally provisional) settlement of acute conflict has been reached by sometimes military-backed political processes. All these are characterized by a less clear mission for the use of military force than had been the case during the era of strategic bloc confrontation. The demands on European armies' force structures, operational concepts, and even strategies have changed accordingly.

Another feature of these new security risks is their transnational nature. They have a strong tendency to transgress national borders or to easily spill over from their sources. Thus there is a strong conviction among European governments that these challenges can best be met by international cooperative efforts that should be undertaken and organized by common security policy institutions. Besides military initiatives such as peacekeeping and peace enforcement, other measures of conflict prevention by proactive policies range from nonproliferation treaties over export control regimes to international charters for environmental protection.

To make these regimes effective, there must be cooperation-minded participants, which in the European view can best be guaranteed by stable democratic political systems that are open to the outside world. The promotion and preservation of such systems becomes an important element of modern security policy. It is from this perspective that the European Union and the Council of Europe get their special meaning for modern European security policy. It is also from this perspective that strengthening democratic regimes and economic prosperity in Europe's neighborhood becomes imperative. The larger the family of functioning stable democracies in Europe and its vicinity, the easier and more effective the European attempts to cope with security challenges.

The drive to construct Europe's new security architecture based on functionally complementary and mutually reinforcing institutions such as NATO, the European Union, the Organization for Security and Cooperation in Europe (OSCE), and the Council of Europe is justified by this fundamental guideline. From this also follow the attempts to create a cooperative network with the states in Europe's neighborhood to the east and south. The creation of the Euro-Mediterranean Partnership within the so-called Barcelona Process as well as the EU's partnership and cooperation agreements with Russia and other members of the Commonwealth of Independent States are justified by security policy considerations as are the more militarily defined undertakings within NATO's Partnership for Peace (PfP) program.[9]

Turkey's security policy agenda only partially overlaps this main European one. Ankara generally shares the European security policy position, as can be deduced from its unconditional consent to the WEU document on European security. There can be no doubt that the new security risks also affect Turkey and that the country is important in confronting them.

Turkey is directly involved militarily and politically in peacekeeping efforts in the former Yugoslavia and the Transcaucasus. It is also involved in European activities to combat drug trafficking and illegal immigration. One of the main international drug highways runs through its eastern regions to Europe, and Turkish authorities are crucial in efforts to intercept the traffic.[10] Illegal migration from the Middle East and South Asia often takes maritime routes starting from Turkish harbors and ending in Greece or

Italy. The growing influx of Kurdish refugees from northern Iraq into Italy caused a political row between Rome and Ankara in early 1998.[11]

Even preventing ecological damage has become an element of Turkey's security policy: avoiding a human and environmental catastrophe in Greater Istanbul has become an important argument for Ankara's choice of bringing Caspian oil to the world market via the Baku-Ceyhan pipeline. This matter, of course, is clearly dominated by Turkish and American geostrategic interests that far surpass oil economics.[12]

Another modern security risk, international terrorism, affects Turkey and its relations with its alliance partners in a special manner. For the vast majority of Turks the PKK constitutes one of the most dangerous international terrorist organizations, one that intends to destroy the country's territorial integrity. The Turkish public and political leadership are especially disappointed with main Western allies' handling of the PKK. Western support for Turkey's policy of a relentless military fight against the terrorists in Turkey and across the border in Iraq has been considered too little and evasive. NATO's repeated official declarations of readiness to combat international terrorism seem empty words when PKK terrorism receives substantial support.

European public and sometimes even official condemnations of serious human rights violations that have accompanied Turkish military activities in the southeastern provinces or European criticism of Turkish military incursions into northern Iraq as a violation of Iraq's national sovereignty have led Turkey's public to believe that the Europeans are not ready to display practical allied solidarity if protecting Turkey's national security were necessary.[13] Actions such as the repeated disruption of German defense aid as a reaction to Turkish military measures in fighting Kurdish terrorism have been cited as proof of Europe's attitude. Turkey's public and diplomatic quarrel with Italy over the extradition of the captured PKK leader Abdullah Öcalan is viewed as another sign of lack of solidarity if not of hidden sympathy with Turkey's enemies.[14] The more sympathetic position of the Clinton administration has provided small solace for Ankara because it has also revealed a deep rift between America and European allies within NATO with regard to the design of allied policies toward Turkey.

But there is reason to believe that the bonds with the West created by Turkey's NATO membership and other institutional relations with Europe have limited the Western criticism of military action against Kurdish terrorism to mostly verbal condemnations and some minor, more symbolic political reactions. After all, there is a great difference between Western reactions to Turkish activities against the separatist Kurds and reactions to what the Serbian regime of Milošević has done to crush what it regarded as a violent Kosovar-Albanian separatist movement undermining the territorial integrity of the Serbian part of the Federated Republic of Yugoslavia. The difference between what is regarded as political hypocrisy and differentiated political behavior sometimes seems very small and to a large extent depends on what friends and allies a country has.

Because of Kurdish terrorism, Turkey does not share as clearly the general European feeling of relief from direct threats to national security. It continues to be in a complicated security situation, although the development of the situation has often been influenced by its own politics. The threat of a military confrontation between the two blocs has, of course, vanished, but other immediate security risks have arisen or existing ones have intensified.[15]

Although it is no longer a systemic adversary, Russia still causes more security concerns for Turkey than for any European country. Admittedly, there is no longer a direct Russian military threat. In addition, Russia has become an interesting market for Turkish products and even more so for Turkish construction companies. And Turkey relies heavily on Russia for its growing imports of natural gas. But Russia's continuing involvement in violent Caucasian and Transcaucasian conflicts holds out the possibility of Russian-Turkish conflicts, given the links that bind Turkey to many countries in the region.[16] The history of the Chechnian uprising in late 1994 bears witness to the possibility.[17] And Russian troops continue to be stationed at Turkey's borders with Georgia and Armenia. Turkey is especially concerned about what it regards as a one-sided Russian approach to the conflict over Nagorno-Karabakh, which has important political and security implications for Turkey given its strained relations with Armenia and its ethnically buttressed friendly relations with Azerbaijan.[18] Ankara's uneasiness has further been fueled by Russia's success at achieving some change in the Conventional Forces in Europe (CFE) Treaty regulations about the amount of military forces and equipment in the flank zones.[19] The concerns have been only superficially calmed by the agreement reached in various bilateral and multilateral negotiations between Ankara, Moscow, and Washington within the OSCE framework that tried to find rules for the Russian forces in the southern flank of the CFE that took care of Turkish concerns.[20]

There is also a Turkish-Russian rivalry concerning the mapping of oil and gas pipelines in the Caspian region and Turkmenistan. The mapping is a matter of strategic importance for the development of the region. It is also linked to the unstable situation in the Black Sea area: would the Turkish Straits be open for the expected oil traffic if pipelines would mainly end up in the Russian harbour of Novorossiisk?

The unsolved problem of pipeline routing overshadows cooperative relations with Russia that have been established within the framework of the Black Sea Economic Cooperation project. In addition, Turkey could eventually be dragged into a Russian-Ukrainian struggle over the sovereignty of the Russian naval bases on the Crimean peninsula. This matter has so far been only superficially resolved through agreements between Kiev and Moscow. Turkey is indirectly linked to Crimean developments through ethnic kinship with the Crimean Tatars that are striving for greater political autonomy from Ukraine.[21] Renewed Russian-Ukrainian disputes over the bases would induce unrest among the Russian population on the peninsula and could spill over into Crimean Tatar circles, which would try to profit from the unstable situation to advance their cause. Under such circumstances Ankara would have to resist domestic pressures to help the Tatar "cousins," a demand that if followed could seriously damage relations with both Ukraine and Russia.

Turkey's concerns about Russian political goals in the region have been extended by Moscow's refusal to scrap the S-300 deal with Cyprus, which was regarded as a highly destabilizing act in the tension-ridden eastern Mediterranean and Aegean.[22] If one further takes into account that Ankara has good reason to believe in some Russian support for the PKK, it becomes clear that many in Turkey's security policy circles view Russian activities in Turkey's neighborhood with utmost suspicion. There is widespread belief that Moscow still wants to undermine Turkey's domestic stability and external security. Turkish-Russian relations can be characterized as "a sort of Cold Peace."[23]

One has to take into consideration these problems to understand Turkey's concerns about NATO enlargement and the establishment of a special relationship between Russia and the alliance. Ankara is not at all interested in the creation of lasting tensions in Western-Russian relations that may spill over into Russian-Turkish relations. But it is strictly opposed to any Western concessions toward Russia that may result in greater Russian maneuvering room in the CIS countries, especially in the Caucasus.[24]

It is not only its different position in relation to Russia that distinguishes Turkey's security policy from the policies of most of its European partners and allies. The equally serious security problems on Turkey's southeastern borders have already been dealt with.[25] The Kurdish unrest and its regional repercussions especially give rise to security concerns. Turkey's assertive attitude and resulting behavior toward its neighboring states with regard to the Kurdish threat have angered both Baghdad and Damascus and burden the future of bilateral relations. Even if Öcalan's capture by the Turkish authorities should finally lead to the disintegration of the PKK, this need not mean the end of Turkey's problem with the Kurds and of its neighbors' involvement, especially if its intransigent position on water use does not change. The complex and tension-ridden bilateral relations between Ankara and Baghdad or Damascus will most likely continue to give the Turkish leadership ample occasion for security concerns.

These special security risks in the Middle East seem to exist outside the European security policy orbit, although their repercussions cannot completely be neglected by the Europeans, given their security interest in a stable regional neighborhood. Thus Turkish Middle East policy has to be an element of European concern and overall political planning.

Another problem of Turkish security policy of much more direct concern to other European states is the tensions with Greece and about Cyprus.[26] In the past these tensions have been contained by mutual restraints by both Greece and Turkey that have been strongly motivated by their NATO membership and the direct influence of the alliance, especially the United States. But the internal functioning of NATO has often been seriously hampered by the Greek-Turkish conflict.

This conflict also gives rise to doubts about the assumption that the alliance's self-perception as an organization for guaranteeing the collective security of all members by means of common defense and shared political values is really applicable to the whole NATO area or if it only fits the Atlantic core.[27] Alliance members threatening each other with military actions cannot be regarded as examples of common defense or shared values. The loss of a common threat to NATO definitely has further loosened the already precarious cohesion on its southeastern flank. However, the NATO membership of both adversaries and its general political implication of being part of the more comprehensive Western system still seems to constitute a threshold in the bilateral conflict that neither Ankara nor Athens wants to transgress.

The problem has gained a special European security dimension with the start of the European Union's accession negotiations with Cyprus. This action has led to a further separation of the island's population and could lead to a lasting rift in Turkey's relations with the rest of Europe if no solution is found before membership in the EU takes effect. The disputes over Cyprus pose the possibility of seriously damaging the efforts to create a stable European security architecture. An increase in Greek-Turkish tensions on the island with the possibility of military actions would almost automatically spill over into a general Greek-Turkish military confrontation. This would affect all of southeastern Europe and the eastern Mediterranean region and would lead to a total disintegration of the alliance in this area. This in turn would most likely not occur without serious consequences for the developments in the greater Middle East.[28]

Although the often heard statement that Turkey's security situation is a nightmare is a tremendous exaggeration, one cannot deny the country's special security situation in the alliance's European context. Ankara faces many more and more precisely defined security risks than its European allies. This situation asks for different security policy endeavors by the Turkish state and also raises the question of allied contributions to strengthen Turkey's security stability. However, Ankara's national approach to security problems often complicates allied, especially European, support.

Turkey's security policy is characterized by a certain ambivalence. For the regional context, Ankara favors a multilateral, negotiation-oriented policy in which it seeks to secure its national interest by cooperation with its allies.[29] If, however, immediate national security concerns are involved, Turkish diplomatic policy takes on a certain rigidity and one-dimensionality with regard to means. Inflexible persistence on what Ankara thinks is a rightful and legitimate position, often in combination with open or disguised military threat, conveys the image of a regional bully. This posture is a direct result of the two principles that have been guiding Ankara's understanding of national security policy: "protection of territorial and national integrity, and defence of legitimate rights, sovereignty and freedoms."[30]

Considering these principles, Turkey's recent security policy seldom conveys the image of a country that believes in nonviolent conflict resolution and international multilateralism. Instead, it can be considered as following the principles of the realist approach in international relations, believing in the balance of power and the pursuit of national interests at the cost to other states if necessary. Under the present regional circumstances, Turkey can successfully follow such a policy because, with the exception of Russia, there is no nearby rival it has to fear militarily.

Such a national security policy, however, does not fit well into the overall European development characterized by multinational and multidimensional security policy organizations. The emerging European security architecture requires restraint in the pursuit of national interests and asks for countries to engage in compromises for the sake of strengthening the common interest. Such a political approach is nothing new or unusual for Turkey because these are the established principles that have guided the political and institutional development of the existing Western security system for five decades. The application of these principles seems, however, to become more difficult in a security policy environment that has lost the disciplining function of the old strategic antagonism between highly armed and ideologically separated blocs.

Turkey and the Evolving European Security Architecture

Turkey's special security situation and its response pose problems for constructing a new European security architecture. Although already strongly incorporated in the existing architecture, Turkey feels bypassed in shaping a new order for the European continent. As a high Turkish officer has said,

> Unfortunately, the new European strategic concept is based on a fairly narrow-minded framework. Europe . . . has decided that the Alliance's primary strategic goal should be the enhancement of security in central Europe. . . . The mistake is in the shortsighted approach when determining the new security borders of Europe. The basic elements, such as the economic and social dimensions and the political stability within the security concept, are being ignored. . . . By ignoring the important contribution a secular, democratic, and modern Turkey can make to international security and stability, the West is denying it an opportunity to fully integrate with Europe.[31]

Additionally, Ankara seems not yet to have found the most effective political way to influence the process.

Turkey has been a cherished member of NATO since the early days of the alliance, which in all likelihood will remain the backbone of European security as long as transatlantic relations remain the strongest element of American interests in Europe. Turkey participates, although somewhat reluctantly and in the background, in adapting the alliance to the new international environment. It has a reserved attitude toward NATO enlargement, not only because of the clear rejection by its allies of the link it has tried to establish between NATO expansion and EU expansion but also because of concerns about the definition of NATO's future relation with Russia.

Furthermore, Turkey is affected by the organizational restructuring of NATO's Southern European Command and the future regional command in the eastern Mediterranean and Aegean Sea. For some time this restructuring has caused the Turkish leadership concern for safeguarding participation in NATO's new command structure.[32] Still, Ankara is ready without any reservations to participate in alliance tasks beyond collective defense, as can be seen by its participation in all NATO activities in the post-Yugoslavia wars and its active engagement in making the Partnership for Peace program a success in the newly independent states of Central Asia. The newly established PfP center in Ankara is witness to the Turkish engagement.

It remains to be seen, however, if and how far Turkey is ready to endorse a more general interventionist NATO strategy under American leadership. As can be inferred from its evasive reactions to the latest American attempts at disciplining Saddam Hussein, there may be serious obstacles to its participation in allied engagements in the Middle East, especially when these are based on the formula of interested and willing parties, a formula that increasingly seems to become the operational mode of allied military activities that are, nevertheless, backed by common political decisions of NATO's Atlantic Council.

Whereas Turkey's contribution to the reforming Atlantic alliance is fairly obvious, NATO's contribution to Turkey's security policy concerns is much less so. Looking at Ankara's large and complex security agenda, "one cannot resist asking to what extent its European partners might be sharing Turkey's security concerns. Where would the threshold of Europe's vital interests lie?"[33] The persistent Turkish-European quarrels about security concerns, the Kurdish restlessness, and the challenge of political Islam do not bode well for cooperation on matters such as water distribution in the Euphrates-Tigris basin or conflicts with Armenia over Nagorno-Karabakh. Europe's adversarial attitude toward Turkey with respect to Cyprus and the Aegean disputes has already been mentioned. All this can but lead to the conclusion that Ankara's orientation to the alliance implies an almost exclusive orientation toward the United States as long as Washington, at least rhetorically, supports Turkey's interests in crucial national security problems.

Turkey's involvement in the Organization for Security and Cooperation in Europe, with its fifty-five member states stretching from the United States to Russia, is much less burdened with such difficult questions than its NATO membership. In the OSCE it enjoys full member status and actively participates in such activities as peacemaking efforts in Nagorno-Karabakh or the Vienna negotiations on the adaptation of the treaty on conventional force reductions in Europe.

Turkey has, however, some problems with the norm setting and regime building activities of the organization with respect to protecting human rights and minority rights in the new European political and security system. Together with other European states, it has prevented some more far-reaching results of the OSCE conferences in Copenhagen and Moscow. But there can be no doubt that Ankara is ready to support OSCE missions and efforts to reestablish stability, security, and functioning systems of law and democracy in the former Yugoslavia or in Albania.

From Ankara's perspective the most significant problems of participation in the evolving European security architecture are posed by the unclear relationship with the security policy framework developing around the reformed and enlarged European Union. The Western European Union and the EU's Common Foreign and Security Policy (CFSP) are of special importance.[34]

In the early 1990s the WEU seemed about to become more important in European security policy because of the EU's decision to adopt the organization as the nucleus of its own security and defense policy ambitions by making WEU membership conditional on EU membership.[35] However, developments took a somewhat different course after the crises in the former Yugoslavia and the ensuing disillusionment about Europe's genuine security policy and defense abilities. America's importance in European security affairs and NATO's contribution were confirmed. With the decisions of the Berlin North Atlantic Council meeting in June 1996 to create Combined Joint Task Forces (CJTFs) and establish the European Security and Defence Identity within NATO, the WEU's role for European security affairs became less important and its eventual merger with the European Union less likely.[36]

Given also a certain American interest in a strengthened European security policy, it was decided that the WEU should become the European pillar of NATO and would also be linked to the European Union, thus creating an institutional security policy triangle in Europe. But some important issues remained unresolved, especially the substance of the WEU-EU link as created by the Treaty of Maastricht and more recently confirmed by the Treaty of Amsterdam.

Nevertheless, since the mid-1990s the WEU has seen considerable institutional and organizational growth. Its membership grew to ten after the inclusion of Greece. All WEU members are also EU members and members of NATO. Besides this, six "associate members" (Iceland, Norway, Turkey, the Czech Republic, Poland, and Hungary) are members of NATO but not of the European Union. With this differentiation the EU, from Ankara's perspective, repeated "the historic aberration of according Greece preferential treatment over Turkey . . . this time in the even more sensitive area of security and defence." [37]

Furthermore, there are five "observers" that are members of the European Union but for political reasons chose not to become full members of the WEU: Austria, Denmark, Finland, Ireland, and Sweden. As a consequence of the general opening up to the east, the WEU also took on an east European affiliation of ten "associate partners" in 1994 (Bulgaria, the Czech Republic, Estonia, Hungary, Latvia, Lithuania, Poland, Romania, Slovakia, and, since 1996, Slovenia). The Czechs, Poles, and Hungarians were transferred to the status of associate members after their accession to NATO membership. The large membership in the WEU makes the organization the only forum in which almost all European states with common security concerns can meet and discuss these issues without the presence of either the United States or Russia.

External growth has been complemented by internal organizational diversification and stronger political and operational substance. The original purpose of providing binding collective defense assistance for its members was complemented by the so-called Petersberg tasks in June 1992. They include humanitarian and rescue missions, peacekeeping, and combat assignments in crisis management, including peace enforcement wherever European security is considered at stake. It is in this context that NATO's Combined Joint Task Forces should most often be employed.

The considerably increased political and operational capabilities of the WEU have, however, not cured its main weakness: it has been unable to establish an autonomous European security and defense policy organization to replace the strong dependence on U.S. military assets to conduct larger operations, especially outside Europe. Thus the WEU's potential contribution to European security affairs will remain limited for a long time, even if its member states would undertake the necessary financial and political efforts for overcoming the existing deficiencies, which they seem unwilling to do.

There is therefore ample reason to assume that far into the twenty-first century European security policy will not be effectively transformed into action without involving the United States. This would mean that NATO will generally be the organization that makes important political and operational decisions on Europe's security concerns.[38] The war over Kosovo was a clear confirmation of this assumption.

Turkey is an associate member of WEU and is so far being prevented from becoming a full member because of its nonmembership in the European Union.[39] As an associate member, however, it enjoys all possibilities of participation in WEU activities from the biweekly meetings of the twenty-eight ambassadors and having five officers on duty in the defense planning cell to the participation of Turkish parliamentarians in the WEU Assembly, which meets twice a year. The only exception, although important, is the exclusion from decisionmaking in the WEU Council and the exclusion from the collective defense clause of the WEU Treaty.[40] The problem of possible military conflicts between Turkey and Greece, which is a full member of the WEU, has been solved by a decision that the collective defense clause is not applicable with regard to conflicts between NATO members.

A further dispute about Turkey's inclusion in WEU decisionmaking concerning the eventual activation of Combined Joint Task Forces has also been solved. As far as NATO assets will be involved in CJTFs, Turkey will fully participate in WEU decisionmaking.[41] Anyway, this dispute caused by initial Greek objection against Turkey's participation does not really constitute a substantial problem but is more of a political nature regarding Turkey's status vis-à-vis the other European states. There are only very few cases in which U.S. participation in CJTF decisions is unlikely, because most of the NATO assets for combined joint task forces are U.S. assets. In such cases the real decisionmaking power will not be in the WEU forums.

However, in the months before the Washington NATO anniversary summit meeting in April 1999 Turkey again stressed the necessity of its explicit agreement with any decision of the NATO council concerning the use of alliance assets for European purposes. Ankara enforced a change in the language of NATO's New Strategic Concept in which this right is implicitly acknowledged by a reference to a case-by-case basis for alliance decisions.[42] Furthermore, Turkish diplomats successfully watered down a paragraph in the Washington Declaration of the heads of state and governments with respect to a more independent European role in defense.[43] In both instances Ankara tried to stop what it regarded as the growing exclusion of Turkey from the emerging European Security and Defence Identity, that is from another important area of European political development.

Real problems for Turkey will, however, arise from its associate status in the WEU if plans for a merger of this organization with the EU materialize. Serious discussion of such a development has started with the European Council meeting in Cologne in June 1999.[44] This leap toward creating an independent European security and defense policy decisionmaking center within the European Union had become possible because of a British change of attitude that had been initiated by the new Labour government of Prime Minister Tony Blair.[45] But given the still considerable differences between the EU member states, the realization of such ideas will take time, as will an eventual inclusion of the WEU into the institutions of the EU's Common Foreign and Security Policy.[46] Even greater problems would arise if the WEU would be dissolved and its capacities completely integrated into the European Union. In that event the question of what would happen with members of the WEU family that are not full EU members would have to be answered without creating greater rifts in Europe's security architecture.

The European Union seems ready to move in that direction because it is driven by its three most important member states—Germany, France, and Great Britain. If political decisions about WEU activity would no longer be taken by the WEU Council but by the EU Council of Ministers meeting in the framework of the Common Foreign and Security Policy (CFSP), things would be different. The WEU Council of Ministers, in an attempt to dispel upcoming concerns, declared in November 1995 that in case of a complete integration of the WEU into the CFSP, "the participation of associate members in the further development of the European Security and Defence Identity would have to be maintained and even improved vis-à-vis their present status through, appropriate arrangements to ensure their involvement and association with the CFSP."[47]

However, in light of the EU's categorical refusal to allow nonmembers to participate, even on a partial basis, in its decisionmaking, it remains unclear how such "appropriate arrangements" could be structured to meet legitimate political interests of associate members of the WEU concerning the full participation in all relevant WEU activities. This would, most likely, be even more the case with Turkey, given that Athens anxiously seeks to keep its political advantage in blocking Ankara's integration into the European Union. But eventually becoming associated with the CFSP in addition to being an associate member of the WEU and the EU by the Ankara Agreement of 1963 would most likely be regarded by the Turks as another proof of Europe's unwillingness to fully accept Turkey within its ranks.

Under such circumstances associate members of the WEU could not automatically be expected to comply with political decisions that have been taken without their participation. It remains an open question if, in such a situation, Ankara would use its veto in the Atlantic Council if the use of the CJTF for WEU purposes was required. It has already used the veto threat during the discussion about its full inclusion in WEU decisionmaking about the eventual employment of the CJTF, which Greece tried to block.[48]

Another problem could arise from the possibility that some central and east European states would be granted EU membership before Turkey. Because all of these new EU members would automatically become eligible for WEU membership as well, and most would apply, some former Warsaw Pact members would get preferential treatment in European security affairs over a staunch, long-standing NATO ally. Turkish perceptions that since the end of the cold war Europeans have lost their political interest in their ally would be confirmed. The inclusion of these states in NATO would hardly alleviate Turkish annoyance.

These, for the moment still rather abstract, reflections make clear that there are substantial stumbling blocks on the way to a more elaborated European security architecture that result from a certain marginalization of Turkey. They also point to some serious intellectual flaws in the conceptions. If the Europeans take seriously their strategy of complementing a stable European security architecture by a politically and economically stable regional neighborhood, Turkey and its future relations with the European Union has to be included in the design.

In response Turkey should start a serious domestic debate about the pros and cons of its integration with Europe in security and defense affairs other than by NATO membership. This integration would require Ankara to take a much more "European" approach to defense and security matters. It would have to decide how far it is ready to align its own national threat and risk perception with prevailing European views on such issues as Kurdish restlessness, political Islam, relations with Armenia, or Middle Eastern water distribution. It would be naive of Turkey's people to assume that a stronger alignment with or even complete integration into the EU element of Europe's new security architecture would automatically result in accepting Turkey's views on these issues and making them a priority of autonomous European security and defense planning.

Thus both Turkey and its European allies and partners would profit from seriously beginning to confront the issue of Turkey's inclusion in the emerging European security architecture. This would also help clarify the country's longer-term place in the Atlantic alliance. For the Europeans it should be clear that without a resolution of Turkey's status, Europe's security cannot be sufficiently planned. Ankara should realize that inclusion in the European security architecture has more far-ranging implications than just EU membership. As in all politics, there are no magic formulas for the solution of complex security problems.

PART THREE

European and American Policy toward Turkey

SINCE THE MID-1980S Turkey has been one of the most important political forces in its region. It has shed the status of developing nation and entered the group of countries regarded as emerging markets. Its economy has opened up to international competition and shown one of the most impressive growth rates among the member states of the Organization for Economic Cooperation and Development. It has all potential to continue in this direction if the necessary stable political framework for economic development can be sustained and improved.

Politically, Turkey stands out as one of the few examples of democratic states among the countries of the Islamic world. In its region it is among those states with the longest experience in democracy. However, measured by European yardsticks, Turkey's democracy still shows significant deficiencies resulting from a political culture characterized by values and mechanisms of a closed society.[1] Since the mid-1990s Turkey's democratic development has almost come to a standstill: governmental instability, self-centered party politics, the growth of political Islam, and the reaffirmation of the nationalist and authoritarian elements of Kemalism have contributed to the stasis. If these deficiencies could be overcome, the country's further integration into the emerging new European political architecture would be enormously facilitated.

Turkey's responses to the new foreign and security policy challenges it is confronted with display the elites' growing awareness of the country's potential for influencing the political development in such crucial areas as the Caucasus, the Middle East, the Balkans, and the Black Sea region. Even more important is the growing political will among Turkey's leaders to stand up to these challenges and to take the opportunity to strengthen the country's political influence in the region.[2] This has been made especially clear by Prime Minister Bülent Ecevit in the program of his short-lived one-party minority government of January 1999. This program dealt with Turkey's regional political role in its foreign policy section. This emphasis has been repeated in the government program of Ecevit's three-party coalition government, formed after the early elections of April 1999, where it is stated,

> Turkey's traditional strategic importance and weight has become all the more pronounced as a result of recent developments in the Balkans, Caucasia, Central Asia, Black Sea, Mediterranean region and Middle East. Turkey is now the key player in this axis which might be called the process of "Eurasianization." Our government is resolved to make use of the opportunities and responsibilities of this position of our country to the benefit of our nation.[3]

Because this government is based on a broad majority in parliament, its statement on Turkey's foreign policy objectives can be regarded as representative of the prevailing attitude among the country's political decision-makers.

However, the domestic difficulties of the past years have also affected the country's foreign policy: The continued quarrels between the established parties of the political center and the growing influence of Islamic forces have prevented the development of a national grand strategy for Turkey's future foreign and security policy. The Islamists advocate a nationally based foreign policy that favors closer relations with the Islamic world, so far without any great success. The political and military leadership in Ankara is wavering between a greater emphasis on developing Turkey's capabilities and orientations as a strong nation that mainly follows its national interests and political goals or the more traditional attempt to bind the country into a network of political alliances. Future relations with the United States and the European Union are the crucial variable. Developments in that respect are, however, strongly impeded by Turkey's inability to promote its democratic development.

CHAPTER THIRTEEN

The Current Situation: Policies, Motives and Limitations

EUROPEAN AND AMERICAN policies toward Turkey since World War II have been dominated by strategic considerations. Turkey's relations with its Western partners have profited from its location. Global or regional security interests and orientations of the United States and Western Europe have been the driving force of Western policy and not, as many Turks like to see it, feelings of friendship or a sense of shared destiny, values, or ideology.

During the cold war the convergence of European and American interests in relations with Turkey was greater than it has been since the changes in international politics at the beginning of the 1990s. The NATO-related European and American convergence of interests gave way to more differentiated policies. Americans view Turkey mainly as an aid in containing Iran and Iraq, bolstering the ailing peace process in the Middle East by expanding Turkish-Israeli cooperation, circumventing Russia and Iran in bringing Central Asia's considerable energy resources to market, and other U.S. regional strategic interests. For the Europeans, relations with Turkey kept their strategic value but were defined in more general and imprecise terms, such as the country's function as a bridge to the Islamic world or to Central Asia or as a barrier against the advance of threatening Islamic fundamentalism. This is a consequence of the equally vague way the Europeans tend to define their new security interests more generally: stability, prosperity, and peace in Europe and its neighborhood.

American-Turkish Relations: The Dominance of Strategic Interests

U.S.-Turkish relations have been tested on a number of issues that have left both sides with lingering questions regarding the other's political intent. During the cold war it was clear what the alliance stood for: a common front against the Soviet Union. Yet this did not prevent serious strains from occuring in the relationship.[1] The most important events were Lyndon Johnson's letter of 1964 in which the American president warned the Turkish government against invading Cyprus, and the arms embargo imposed on Turkey between 1975 and 1978 as an American reaction to the invasion and occupation of northern Cyprus in the summer of 1974. Because the fate of the Turkish population on Cyprus is an undisputed national cause in Turkey, the Turks felt let down by their American ally and Turkish reliance on the Americans was severely undermined.[2]

Ankara increasingly regarded American policy toward it as an expression of selfish superpower interests rather than an honest commitment to the defense of Turkey's most salient national interests. And indeed, the various American administrations, not to speak of the U.S. Congress, tended to view Turkey's contribution to the Atlantic alliance always as

> a function of its strategic value [that] as such did not strike a chord deep within the U.S. public and its representative institutions, specifically the U.S. Congress. Unlike most other U.S. allies, Turkey has no strong cultural, historical, emotional, ideological, or even economic ties to the U.S. which could be used to buttress its position.[3]

This situation is of mixed value for the conduct of Turkish-American relations. On the one hand, Ankara need not influence or convince the American public of the appropriateness of this or that American policy concerning Turkish affairs because the American public is not interested in or informed about such issues. Turkish political leaders have only to concentrate on American policymakers, a Washington-based political class that includes a rather closed circle of political decisionmakers and opinion leaders in the administration, Congress, and the media.

On the other hand, it is almost impossible to arouse public support (or rejection) for any political measure concerning U.S.-Turkish relations. Policy formulation and decisionmaking is confined to a small circle that is often vulnerable to the influence of organized ethnic interests. Greek and Armenian political lobbies, for instance, normally do not oppose U.S. policy measures that are favorable for Turkey because of substantial arguments but solely because of their ethnic-national affiliation. Turkey's difficult relations with some of its neighboring states are thus replicated in its relations with the United States via the functioning of the American political process.

Ankara has made considerable efforts to establish a pro-Turkish lobby in Washington. These efforts have shown mixed results. Some former senior American diplomats and political figures have tried their best to promote Turkey's case in accordance with the remuneration the firms they work for get from the Turkish government. Turkish efforts to engage the important Jewish community have not been especially successful. In spite of the growing strategic cooperation with Israel since 1996, the influential American Jewish organizations have been reluctant to display strong support for Turkish concerns, although Jewish support for the Baku-Ceyhan oil pipeline has caused some irritation with the Armenian lobby.

It is against this background that American-Turkish relations have developed.[4] The Gulf War of 1991 marked a turning point in the relationship because it convinced U.S. leaders that Turkey's strategic value for American interests was more to be seen in respect to what came to be called the greater Middle East than in its classic NATO role. Turkey increasingly was regarded as an anchor of stability in a region of growing volatility and was expected to project that stability. This change of focus gave new momentum to the relationship but also brought new problems for American policy.

Turkey came to be regarded as a pivotal state in the geostrategic development of Eurasia, especially the newly independent states (NIS) in the former Soviet south. The United States and Turkey favor the establishment of pro-Western, secular, and, if possible, democratic states in Central Asia and the Caucasus. The U.S. administration furthers this development through bilateral economic cooperation and military assistance within the framework of NATO's Partnership for Peace program. Turkey also strongly engages itself within the NATO framework and has developed intensive bilateral ties with these states over a broad range of political, economic, and cultural issues. Neither Ankara nor Washington seems to be much concerned about the semiauthoritarian structure of the political system in the NIS.

Turkey is of even greater value for American regional strategic interests as the crucial link within the east-west energy corridor, which is promoted by the United States as the best solution for bringing Caspian and Central Asian energy resources to market. The strategic idea is to prevent a reemergence of Russia as the dominant political and military power in the region.[5]

The plan is part of the American strategy of double containment because it also prevents Iran from a stronger engagement in the Caspian region's emerging energy transportation plans.

The American interest perfectly meets Turkey's own interest of establishing itself as a major regional force in relations with the NIS and especially the energy-rich countries of the area. For this to happen, it is necessary to limit Russian influence and to restrain Iranian aspirations with regard to transport routes for oil and gas. Given Turkey's own limited strategic leverage, this can only be accomplished with American support.

However, Ankara may have relied too much on U.S. strategic interest in designing a convincing concept for its own part in the energy corridor strategy. Turkish political leaders underestimated the influence of the international oil companies and consortia in the final decisions on pipeline routing. As a consequence, for some time Ankara failed to put enough emphasis on developing a sound and convincing financial scheme for the Baku-Ceyhan pipeline, although it had been clear early on that the economic viability of this proposition would meet with considerable resistance from consortia.[6]

Turkish leaders relied heavily on political pressure for reaching their goal, but they overestimated the effect of manipulating the regime of the Turkish Straits to restrict tanker traffic and the leverage of the U.S. administration on the oil companies as well as the administration's readiness to bolster American regional strategic goals with significant financial backing. Ankara did not heed carefully enough Washington's early warning that the solution not only had to be strategically rational but also economically feasible and that this part of the deal had to be fulfilled mainly by the regional states through which the pipelines would run; hence Ankara's disillusionment when the project ran into serious difficulties in the late autumn of 1998.

In hindsight it is also clear that the U.S. administration unintentionally sent unclear political signals to Ankara as to what it would contribute to the realization of Baku-Ceyhan and what it expected from Turkey. The complications surrounding the realization of the pipeline project show that despite close and intense collaboration, misunderstandings can arise because of insufficient mutual knowledge. It also shows that American and Turkish strategic culture and their broader political attitudes toward regional issues are not fully congruent.

If the Baku-Ceyhan pipeline project should falter or be postponed for a considerable time because of its bleak commercial prospects, Turkish disappointment could easily express itself in a new wave of anti-American feeling. It would be difficult for its political leaders and especially for the public to understand that even the American government may not be able to enforce its strategic goals on the decisionmaking bodies of international oil firms.

U.S.-Turkish differences are more clearly visible in Middle East policy, although superficially there is a consensus. Washington and Ankara agree that the existing regional balance has to be kept and stabilized under continued domination of Western interests. The rise of any regional hegemonic power must be prevented. The regional spread of weapons of mass destruction must be limited and finally undone. The peace process has to be brought to a successful conclusion. The establishment of a multinational peace and stability-oriented regional network has to be promoted.

But beyond these common general goals, Turkish and U.S. regional policies differ. This is most obvious in attitudes toward the Iraqi regime and the handling of the situation in northern Iraq. Washington wants to oust Saddam Hussein and use a common Kurdish front in northern Iraq for that purpose. The Turkish leadership wants to keep Iraq intact, even at the cost of continuing Saddam's reign, and prevent the establishment of an autonomous Kurdish political entity in northern Iraq, which would be expected to destabilize Turkey's own Kurdish area.[7]

As a consequence, Turkish-American cooperation in dealing with Iraq has often been accompanied by thinly veiled Turkish mistrust of American moves. This became evident again in the aftermath of the accord between the two rival northern Iraqi Kurdish groups that was brought about by American mediation in Washington in September 1998, much to Turkish annoyance because Ankara had been left out of the negotiations.[8] How far apart the American and the Turkish policies concerning Iraq are could also be judged from the cool statement of the Turkish foreign minister after the Anglo-American military strikes against the regime in Baghdad in December 1998. İsmail Cem discussed Turkish concerns about the developments across the border without expressing any sign of understanding, not to speak of sympathy, for the American move.[9] The DSP-led government was, however, realistic enough not to object to the use of İncirlik air base for the continued American air strikes against Iraqi radar stations and planes that violate the no-fly zone over northern Iraq.

Should the recent American moves to organize Iraqi opposition against Saddam prove successful but result in political turmoil in Baghdad because of the inability of the opposition to form a stable new Iraqi regime, a breakaway of the Kurdish provinces in the north is possible. In such a situation Turkey's intervention would be inevitable, most likely upsetting the political geometry of the region. Thus Washington would be well advised to continue its close contact with Ankara in shaping and executing Iraq policy and to develop a clear idea of where and how Turkey should fit in American designs for a political restructuring of a post-Saddam Iraq.

Turkish and American policies especially differ on relations with Iran. Here Ankara works against declared American interests by seeking to keep normal relations with Tehran and to use Iranian resources for satisfying Turkey's growing energy needs. All this clearly contravenes continued American efforts to isolate Iran from international politics. Ankara's policy of normal relations is not a speciality of Turkish Islamists, although the spectacular Iran gas deal that circumvents if not contradicts the Iran-Libya Sanctions Act (ILSA) was concluded during the administration of Turkey's first Islamic prime minister, Necmettin Erbakan from the Welfare Party. But with the exception of the military leadership, which maintains a certain reserve toward Tehran, all Turkish political forces advocate normal relations with the neighbor to the east that serves as another important conduit to the Central Asian region besides the routes that pass through the politically unstable Caucasian states.

Of course, normal relations with Iran also include political differences at times and competition with regard to developments in the Caspian Sea area. However, these would never lead to a policy of total disruption of relations or other forms of containment toward Iran. To keep Turkey as an ally to realize broader U.S. strategic regional interests, Washington does not complain too loudly about Ankara's independent policy toward Iran.

In a similar manner the Turks express their irritation only mildly about U.S. policy toward Syria. "Many [Turkish] decisionmakers tend to believe that the United States is more concerned about gaining Syria's goodwill to obtain its support for the peace process rather than pressing Syria to quit sponsoring terrorism."[10] For Ankara, the Syrian regime has been the most potent supporter of Turkey's most important internal threat, the Kurdish terrorist PKK. Even after Turkey pressured Damascus in October 1998 to oust PKK leader Abdullah Öcalan and officially stop supporting the organization or risk a military invasion of Syrian territory, Ankara is still suspicious concerning the long-term reliability of Syria's commitment.

Furthermore, Turkish political circles fear that America and Israel may put pressure on Ankara to accommodate Syrian requests to share the water of the Euphrates in exchange for Syria's leaving the water resources of the

Golan Heights to Israel within the framework of an overall Israeli-Syrian arrangement. Turkey does not want to become a victim of the peace process in that manner as long as the Turkish military and political elite continue to consider its various disputes with Syria a serious security threat.[11] However, these apprehensions do not influence Ankara's general strong political support of American efforts in achieving peace in the Middle East.

Turkish disappointment with or suspicion of American political moves in the Middle East is usually expressed at home, especially in the media, than in formal diplomatic relations or informal Turkish-American contacts. Here, stressing mutual interests and functioning political cooperation dominates.[12] The concept of a "strategic relationship" is the preferred way to describe American-Turkish bonds.

This is necessitated by Turkey's continuing dependence on American military cooperation in one form or another. Although the traditional form of military aid to Turkey as it had been envisioned in the Defense and Economic Cooperation Agreement (DECA) of 1980 has almost been reduced to insignificance, military sales of American modern equipment to the Turkish armed forces as well as commercial provision of state-of-the-art weapon systems continue to remain an important element in Turkey's efforts to modernize its military. In a somewhat inverse manner, this can be concluded from Turkish complaints over the withholding of American warships and attack helicopters, the delivery of which had been agreed, due to resistance in Congress.[13] The continuing difficulties concerning American weapons procurement for Turkey caused a harsh criticism by the Turkish General Staff in which even a revision of the DECA was not excluded.[14]

There is, then, a certain ambivalence in the attitude of Turkey's military leadership toward Turkish-American relations. Generally, the military has upheld close relations with the U.S. armed forces since Turkey entered NATO. "For Turkish soldiers, members of the U.S. Armed Forces are 'comrades-in-arms,'" as Deputy Chief of the Turkish General Staff General Çevik Bir described the relationship.[15] On certain subjects, however, such as arms procurement, policy on northern Iraq, the development of the Conventional Forces in Europe Treaty, or policy toward Syria, the military leaders are much more cautious in appraising American intentions. This caution cannot be mitigated by the fact that the Department of Defense normally is one of the strongest supporters of Turkish interests within the American administration.

Despite this special strategic relationship, American policy has not been able to diffuse the most dangerous internal threat to the cohesion of the

Atlantic alliance: Turkish-Greek conflicts in NATO's southeastern region. Reconciliation seems almost impossible as long as the U.S. government follows a policy that tries to accommodate both allies. The establishment of the so-called seven-to-ten ratio determining military aid and deliveries of equipment to Greece and Turkey, for instance, did nothing to overcome the existing tensions between the two nor did it contribute to strengthening NATO's military regional effectiveness. It only served to mollify anti-Turkish lobbies in Congress and to uphold more or less well functioning political relations with both countries.

The American administration has been able to prevent any conflict from leading to serious Greek-Turkish military clashes. It has not, however, been able to resolve the countries' long-standing differences, be it with regard to the political issues of sharing sovereignty in the Aegean or the more military-technical issues of NATO's area command structure. The best Washington has been able to achieve have been more or less detailed agreements between Turkey and Greece to seek a peaceful settlement of their disputes. The implementation of these agreements has been cumbersome, and both sides have soon returned to a more threatening posture.

The same can be said of recent American attempts to promote a solution of the intricate Cyprus problem. Even worse, the Clinton administration could not prevent the hardening of the Turkish position after the European Union's decision to start membership negotiations with the government of the (Greek) Republic of Cyprus as the only legal representative of the whole island. Whereas Ankara, in full concurrence with the Turkish Cypriot leader Rauf Denktaş, now insists on prior recognition of the Turkish Republic of Northern Cyprus as a sovereign political state if talks with the Greek Cypriot side on possible solutions to the Cyprus problem are to be reopened, "the United States' goal in Cyprus remains a bicommunal, bizonal federation."[16]

The stalemate in Cyprus talks veils a far-reaching disagreement between Washington and Ankara: Ankara wants the basic international understanding of the problem to be changed in its favor—recognition of two separate and equal political entities (states) on the island—while Washington mainly tries to solve the problem on the assumption that there is only one state on the island with two ethnic communities that live in different zones, each enjoying limited self-governance.

It is not surprising that under these circumstances the Americans have fallen back on proposing measures that could increase security on the island, especially preventing delivery of the Russian S-300 antiaircraft missile systems, and could also serve as starting points for establishing lasting confidence-building measures between the Greek and the Turkish Cypriots.[17] The first was reached by exerting strong pressure on the Greek Cypriots and on Athens; the second has still to be achieved. A broader approach for resolving the Cyprus problem proper seemingly has also been put on the back burner.

Toward the Middle East as well as Cyprus, American and Turkish interests only partially coincide as a result of the growing Turkish self-assertiveness, an outcome of the ongoing political debate in Ankara over the country's long-term general political (re)orientation. This creeping foreign and security policy disconnect between Washington and Ankara can only partially be mended by strong, long-term American diplomatic support for Turkey's ambitions concerning the routing of oil and gas pipelines from the Caspian basin and for still strong ambitions to become a member of the European Union.

The more Ankara is convinced that Turkey has to design its own future based on a more assertive pursuit of its national interests and security requirements, the more problems will arise for American-Turkish cooperation. The renationalization of Turkey's political orientation that is an inescapable side effect of the policy of "reenforced" Kemalism under the leadership of the military and state elites will inevitably also refocus Turkey's foreign policy on a more strictly national agenda, gradually pushing international bonds and commitments into the background. The increasingly parochial Turkish approach to international political affairs will often confront broader American strategic requirements.

EU-Turkey Relations: Ambiguity and Misunderstandings

In the aftermath of the 1980 military coup, Ankara's human rights record and the plight of Turkey's Kurdish minority have become increasingly important in European evaluations of relations with Turkey. With the Helsinki Process, the growing political prominence of the Green parties in some European states, and the greater prominence of the European Parliament in European politics after its first direct election in 1979, political morals and values have taken on more importance in European political discourse. The EU's own ambitions to cross the threshold from a mainly economy-oriented entity to a more political one furthered this development. EU policy and behavior have increasingly been evaluated by political standards instead of mere economic rationality. Consequently, the relations with Turkey changed from the economic focus of the Association Agreement to consider political relations.

This development was accelerated after the end of the cold war when the restraining effect of East-West antagonism ceased to influence European-Turkish relations. Turkey's strategic importance for European security did not vanish, but its definition became more vague than it was when it was the southeastern bulwark of NATO and the barrier against the Soviet drive toward the Mediterranean and the Middle East. The issues that burdened the integration of Turkey and the European Union gained in importance, whereas the political advantages became less clear than they had been before 1989–90.

Since the early 1960s EU-Turkish relations have been determined on the European side by security policy. Under the conditions of the East-West antagonism, Turkey had to be firmly bound to the Western camp to help counter the Soviet threat. Thus the Association Agreement of 1963 (Treaty of Ankara) was mainly concluded by the European Economic Community to maintain an evenhanded political treatment of NATO's two southeastern members, Greece and Turkey. The Europeans, however, lacked the proper means for conducting a relationship that was undertaken mainly for strategic reasons. They were forced to make use of the Association Agreement, trade preferences, and other economic and institutional instruments and capabilities if they were to follow strategic and security policy goals. Consequently, the Association Agreement deals exclusively with establishing a strong and close economic relationship between Europe and Turkey in the form of a customs union. The union is based on an association that could eventually lead to Turkish membership in the European Economic Community (article 28 of the agreement).

Turkey's relationship with the European Union is still characterized by a disequilibrium between its economic and political components. Although the country has become economically the most strongly integrated European nonmember state, its political relationship has remained an insufficient dialogue within the Association Agreement framework. This dialogue has been often hampered by political developments in Turkey, especially after the military coup of 1980, which led to constant strong European criticisms of the state of its democracy, protection of human rights, and treatment of the Kurds.[18] After Greece's entrance into the EU in 1981, political relations deteriorated further because of the conflict between Turkey and Greece and the unsolved problem of the divided Cyprus. The political dialogue often deteriorated into mutual recriminations.

In spite of Europe's slow but continuous development toward a political union culminating in the Treaty of Amsterdam in 1997, this situation has not changed. The European Union is still unable to develop genuine strategic relationships with nonmember countries because it lacks effective common foreign and security policies. This has meant that the EU has never developed a strategic place for Turkey within political conceptions about, for instance, relations with the Middle East, Central Asia, or the Caucasus. European political approaches to relations with the newly independent states of the former Soviet Union, resolving the Caspian basin energy problems, relations with Iran, or coping with the post–Gulf War situation in Iraq have rarely made explicit reference to Turkey. The Association Agreement relationship was never regarded as an element of European strategic foreign policy, although it came into existence for just such a purpose during the cold war.

Because from the very beginning Turkey viewed the relationship with the European Union as politically determined and expected reciprocal treatment from its European partners, disappointment has been inevitable. Turkish authorities correctly were and are of the opinion that the strategic character of its relation with the EU cannot adequately be expressed through economic policy. With no equivalent alternative offer possible by the Europeans because of their foreign and security policy constraints, membership in the EU becomes the only available instrument for the long-term concretization of the strategic core of EU-Turkey relations.

Because of its poor performance in pursuing strategic political interests, the EU has been ambiguous in defining its relationship with Turkey. It was hesitant to declare Turkish membership in the European Union as the long-term goal of relations and shied away from developing a political strategy toward that end. Thus its affirmations of the strategic importance of relations with Turkey became dubious in the eyes of many a Turk.

Turkish policy became obsessed with EU membership, considering any European plans and suggestions at improving the economic integration of Turkey into Europe to be of secondary importance. This attitude was, however, driven more by national, inward-looking motivations of fulfilling the Kemalist vision of Westernization than by an objective interest in being a part of the reshaping of Europe's political destiny. This may explain why, for instance, there has never been wide public debate about the benefits and costs of Turkish membership in the European Union. If being accepted as Europeans is the driving force behind Turkey's membership ambitions, questions of the political and economic consequences of membership, not to speak of the eventual necessary systemic adaptations, are unimportant.

The resulting mutual misunderstanding and lack of sensitivity for the real problems of the other culminated at the meeting of the European Council in Luxembourg in December 1997. Here for the first time the EU sought to express its will to have Turkey as a future member if and when the country fulfills the requirements for membership as previously laid down by the European Council. The EU also declared itself ready to develop a "European strategy" for Turkey toward that end. But it failed to include Turkey in the group of its eleven candidate states, although it made Turkey a separate case for which the same conditions should be applied as were to be applied to the eleven other countries. Furthermore, as a result of Greek resistance, Turkey was not explicitly named a candidate, which for Ankara meant nothing else but the continuation of European ambiguity.

For the Turkish political elite, this was another proof of the EU's unwillingness to treat Turkey like any other European country. The Turkish government took the EU's position as a renewed refusal in disguise of the country's candidacy for membership. It had hoped to be at least included among the candidate countries of central and eastern Europe. So Ankara declared the political dialogue with the EU canceled. In the future it would restrict relations to matters covered by the Association Agreement proper, mainly the functioning and development of the customs union. Political dialogues would only be conducted with individual member states. This position has been maintained because of the EU's inability to change its position on Turkey's "candidacy."[19]

Turkey's drive to be named a candidate instead of being named "eligible" for EU membership tends to be self-deceiving as long as the European Union does not change its position that countries with which it intends to open accession negotiations must fulfill certain conditions. As long as it is convinced that Ankara does not fulfill the political conditions, the EU will not engage in accession negotiations no matter how Turkey is named in EU documents or declarations. Turkey's prospects for membership do not depend on terminology but on Ankara's substantial changes in policy and behavior. Turks would be heavily misled if they were to interpret a change of EU terminology to "candidate" and "candidacy" as a weakening of the EU's position on conditions for opening entry negotiations.

In such a situation the EU cannot expect Turkish cooperation on any political issue that may be of some importance to Brussels, whether its democratic behavior, human rights record, or treatment of its Kurdish population. Even with regard to important regional issues such as lessening tensions in the Caucasus or establishing a zone of peace and prosperity in the Mediterranean area, Turkey can no longer be regarded as a special partner of the EU. There is a clear tendency in the Turkish political elite after Luxembourg to secure the country's strategic interests through increased strategic cooperation with the United States and greater reliance on its own capabilities, although they have to be further developed.

Consequently, EU-Turkey political relations have reached an all-time low. There is no hope that the disequilibrium between Turkey's strongly developed economic integration with Europe and its crippled political integration will be righted in the near future. The EU's difficulties in developing an adequate and effective policy for conducting a strategic relationship with Turkey will persist. Political and social dynamics in Europe and in Turkey tend to further the mutual alienation.

EU members' political attention is increasingly absorbed in preparations for the first round of eastern enlargement. The necessary internal adaptations, including some far-reaching revisions of financial and institutional regulations and negotiation of the terms of accession for the first five central and east European candidates will absorb much of the EU's political resources and their public attention. To this has to be added the continuing need of all member states to cope with the economic and social consequences of globalization. The European Union will remain a predominantly inward-looking political force for the next few years.

Thus relations with Turkey will remain the domain of a few diplomatic and media specialists. For most politicians and the European public these relations will be regarded as a nuisance unless some critical situation should occur, such as Turkish renunciation of the customs union or a military clash between Turkey and Greece.

In Turkey, the struggle between the Kemalists and non-Kemalists will continue because there is no group or politician who can reconcile them. Political volatility and military interference in politics will also continue, as will the generally unsatisfactory regard for human and citizens' rights and attempts to resolve the Kurdish problem. Politicians will use the "EU issue" for domestic political purposes, especially because Turkish critics of European mistreatment of Turkey's ambitions will find ample justification for their arguments in the EU's self-absorbed behavior. As a consequence, Turkish foreign policy will increase its self-centered and assertive tendency, rendering integration into European multinational processes more complicated.

CHAPTER FOURTEEN

The Challenge: Anchoring Turkey in the West

WHAT ARE THE POLICIES that the European Union and the U.S. administration have to follow to further anchor Turkey in the West? What do Turkish political leaders have to do to maintain the country's Western orientation? There are no easy answers to these questions. Because the future course of international relations is still only dimly visible, which factors are important to the answers also remain unclear.

Influencing Turkey's Westernization

In addition to some difficult foreign policy issues, Turkey's domestic affairs have become a serious obstacle for improving EU-Turkish relations. American-Turkish relations have often also been soured by the shortcomings of Turkey's democratic setup. Concerns about the growth of political Islam's anti-Western forces have to be added. Continuing Ankara's use of Western political models for shaping the country's polity has become as urgent as upgrading its democratic standards. Continued Westernization and democratic development is a significant task of both Turkey's political elite and its society. In helping accomplish these tasks, foreign assistance is not totally useless but is always of limited influence. Nevertheless, European and American political circles should try to develop ideas to support Turkey's continuing efforts to develop a Western democratic system.

Strengthening Turkey's Westernizers against their domestic opposition from more Islamic or more nationalist circles or both is difficult because they have not in the past been able to modify the authoritarian tendencies of the Kemalist regime. All efforts to strengthen liberal democratic tendencies have been curtailed if they conflicted with the established Kemalist principles.

The civilian Western-oriented political forces have not been uncompromising advocates of full democratization and liberalization of Turkey's state and society. More often they have bowed to the restrictive demands of the guardians of traditional Kemalism, whether with regard to the Kurdish question or greater freedom of speech or freedom of political association. Thus the domestic politics of Turkey's secularist parties has deepened the European-Turkish cleavage. As long as the military leadership continues to set the tone in Turkey's efforts at Westernization, there is little chance for more fundamental change.

Nevertheless, Western policymakers should openly support those groups that try to modernize Turkey's democracy by advocating structural political and social reforms. These groups are to be found in the Turkish parliament and the mainstream political parties, although they may often be a minority in these institutions. Another task for European and American policy would be to help strengthen those forces in Turkish society that advocate more openness, more real equality, a full application of human and civil rights, broader political participation, and less state and military involvement in the political process.

To improve the chances for such a political engagement, Americans and Europeans should continue to explain to the Turkish political leadership and public that American and European concerns are not foreign interference in Turkey's sovereign domestic affairs but normal political conduct among allies. Especially if it wants to become an EU member, Turkey has to accept continuous thorough evaluation of its domestic affairs by EU institutions. One may doubt the objectivity and fairness of the evaluation process, as Turkish authorities frequently have, but one cannot deny the legitimacy of such behavior.

Western partners should also improve their support for liberal and democratic civil groups that advocate a more open society in Turkey. This includes especially the human rights organizations and political groups that peacefully advocate the political acknowledgement of Turkey's ethnic diversity. Europeans and Americans should, however, concentrate support mainly on those groups that are ready to work on as broad a basis as possible. An approach to human rights or ethnic diversity that is based on ideological preferences or narrow-minded ethnicity normally does not further the establishment of an open society. But Turkey's Western partners should defend the right to freedom of expression and organization even of these groups as long as they do not advocate or practice violence.

An important indirect means of support for Westernization is to multiply organized personal contacts: state scholarships for university students and Turkey's inclusion in the professional and scholarly exchanges of the European Union such as the Leonardo and Socrates programs. Another way to improve awareness and understanding would be to establish bilateral youth exchanges modeled on the successful program of the German-French Youth Office. Turkey and the EU member states should also systematically encourage the mutual establishment of university institutes, chairs, and courses by which knowledge of the partner country is disseminated in a lasting and systematic manner.

Difficult targets for broadening systematic political contacts are political Islam and the Kurds. Although political Islam has to be regarded as a "natural" phenomenon of Turkish society and Turkish political life, its anti-Western and antidemocratic features can best be contained by fully developing liberal democracy and realizing broad economic and social well-being. Because state suppression and criminalization of political Islam would be politically unwise, European and American institutions dealing with Turkey should not refrain from establishing contacts with such an important group. If it is appropriate, they should be included in seminars, symposiums, workshops, and other types of gatherings dealing with contemporary Turkish affairs. It would be politically shortsighted of European and American institutions to neglect representatives of normal political Islam, such as the majority of the Virtue Party leaders. Europeans and Americans should not be more selective than Turkish politicians in this respect. Having normal contacts with representatives of political Islam should, however, be clearly distinguished from supporting their ideologies. This would not be in the long-term interest of Europe and the United States. And, of course, representatives of radical Islamic groups that advocate the abolition of democracy should not be included in any kind of contact.

A matter of equal sensitivity, especially for Turkey's European partners, is the conduct of relations with Kurdish organizations and representatives. There is widespread agreement, even among ardent Turkophiles, that "the Kurdish issue is the most serious medium-term politico-social problem which Turkey faces."[1] This agreement includes the opinion that the way Turkish authorities have dealt with the matter has not led to much alleviation of the problem. In contrast to the Turkish mainstream position, American and European political circles alike contend that only a change of policy could bring about a solution of the Kurdish problem.

Knowing Turkish sensitivity concerning this matter, American and European governments and leading politicians, with some exceptions such as the European Parliament, have been reluctant to put forward ideas for possible solutions. Nor have there been systematic efforts to establish a kind of track two diplomacy, which would bring together Turkish and Kurdish representatives on a semiofficial basis to address the problem.

Some European governments have been reluctant to disapprove of the more or less clandestine activities of the Kurdistan Workers Party (PKK) and its supporters on their territory. What many Turks, including leading politicians, have regarded as support of a terrorist organization, these European governments have thought of as either supporting liberal democratic standards with regard to organizations that have not committed crimes in their country or taking a politically justified opportunity to prevent political violence in their country.

Preventing violence has been especially important for the German government. After serious incidents of PKK-instigated public violence in the early 1990s in various places in Germany, the authorities banned the PKK and supporting organizations in 1993 but concluded a kind of a truce with the PKK leadership according to which the authorities would not voluntarily enforce the ban as long as the PKK would refrain from public action and violent activities in the country.[2] This compromise has also determined the much criticized decision of the German government not to execute the international warrant for Öcalan when the PKK leader was held in Italian custody in Rome in late 1998 and ask for his extradition to Germany where he had been accused of ordering PKK murders of "defectors."

The Europeans' policy on the Kurdish issue, especially the mishandling of the Öcalan affair, has contributed to the deterioration of European-Turkish relations without furthering a solution of the problem. As a change, European authorities should start discreetly establishing a common position favoring informal discussions with Ankara on ways to resolve the Kurdish issue within the borders of Turkey. They should also seek American cooperation to that end. This process should start by using nonofficial institutions that work on the fringes of official political relations. In doing so the Europeans should make clear from the very beginning that for them the PKK or its supporting organizations could not be directly part of the discussions but that Turkey would be expected to accept other, nonradical Kurdish organizations to be eventually included even if these organizations are suspected to have or do, indeed, have some relations with circles close to the PKK.

All efforts to reach a European-Turkish understanding about handling the Kurdish problem in Turkey should refrain from internationalizing the issue. Proposed solutions should be aimed at changing the situation within Turkey's borders and should not carry implications of a regional approach to the problem. Convening an international Kurdistan conference or even an international Kurdistan tribunal would not alleviate the Kurdish problem in Turkey nor the Kurdish problem in general. Ideas for establishing a comprehensive Kurdish state in the region, as they are sometimes put forward by Kurds in European exile, are not realistic. The various states in the Middle East are not ready for such a move, and the Kurds living in the region do not seem prepared.

The only aim of these talks should be to promote a normalization of the treatment of Kurds in Turkey to the level achieved in some EU member states with regard to their minorities. A good starting point could be taking up the initiatives developed by Turgut Özal in the early 1990s that have been dropped by his successors. If the EU member states are honest in their still somewhat vague offer of membership for Turkey when the necessary conditions are fulfilled and in their offer to support Turkey in its efforts to meet the conditions, the beginning of a discreet European-Turkish dialogue on the Kurdish problem is necessary. This would require a realistic European position on the issue and a Turkish understanding that it is lagging behind contemporary Western standards in its policy toward a minority.

All direct and indirect European and American efforts to promote liberal democracy and open society in Turkey would, however, prove futile if they were not accompanied by trustworthy political steps to improve its incorporation into the Western system. Only a policy of continued close alliance and partnership can justify active Western participation in any development of Turkey's political and societal setting that goes beyond normal diplomatic relations. The problem with establishing such a perspective, however, is the difference between European and Turkish, and to a lesser extent American and Turkish, expectations of what the political substance of this alliance and partnership should be.

The Difficulties of Improving the Alliance

It will be difficult to establish a common American-European policy toward Turkey's future function in the Western alliance. The political challenges facing the European Union and the United States differ considerably. Washington has to keep beneficial relations with an important strategic ally; the Europeans have to decide if, when, and under what circumstances they want to or have to incorporate Turkey into the ongoing process of European integration.

The challenge to the United States can be met with a few clearly defined strategic policies that by no means would make Turkey an integral part of American policymaking. The Europeans eventually have to make Turkey a part of their common policymaking, accepting most of its national domestic and foreign policy challenges as an element of common European policymaking. Washington may be asked to evaluate and probably redesign its foreign policy toward an important partner; EU members would be asked to turn one part of their foreign relations into an element of their common internal political process.

The best the U.S. administration and its main European allies could do under such circumstances is to maximize the exchange of information on their policies on Turkey. They should improve the existing consultation mechanisms to reach a common understanding of how best to deal with Ankara and establish a division of labor to keep Turkey within the Western fold. Of course, where appropriate and possible, Washington and the Europeans should follow a common policy.

Seen from Ankara, the picture looks similar. Upgrading Turkish-American relations means refurbishing a very important part of Turkish foreign policy. Becoming a member of the EU would mean exchanging sovereign Turkish foreign policy for a common political process in which Turkish influence over the outcome would often be limited. The Turkish-American special relationship mainly defined by bilateral political needs and alliance considerations would, to a certain extent, become part of the European-American relationship in which Turkey would have to sacrifice some of its national interests for the sake of the common goals of the EU's policy toward Washington. In the longer term this would affect Turkey's role as a special strategic ally helping to realize American regional strategic interests.

There is little Washington can do to improve its bilateral strategic relationship with Turkey, which is already very strong. Some further reduction of trade barriers in sensitive products such as textiles may be possible. But an American-Turkish free trade area does not seem very promising given the geographic distance between the partners. The symbolic political value of such a step would, however, be tremendous. Increasing American direct foreign investment in Turkey is less a concern of Washington than of

Turkish authorities, who need to create political stability to attract more foreign investors.

American political engagement in promoting the Baku-Ceyhan oil pipeline can hardly be expanded, either with respect to securing the cooperation of Caucasian political leaders or backing Turkish concerns regarding the risks of increased tanker traffic through the Turkish Straits. A stronger financial engagement could, however, be contemplated to improve the economic feasibility of the project. This action would depend on the American political resolve to realize the east-west energy corridor in the Caspian basin. Given an expanding global economy, however, it may be unwise in the longer run to try to counter market forces at all costs.

The United States shows considerable support of Turkish interests, especially in the Balkans and the Black Sea region where it encourages establishing a multinational peacekeeping force of the Balkan countries and supports Turkish engagement in implementing the Dayton Accords in Bosnia-Herzegovina and in the train-and-equip program for the Bosnian army. Washinton also encourages Turkish initiatives in the newly independent states of Central Asia, although here one could think of improved American-Turkish cooperation in promoting programs for the economic and political transformation of these countries.

Closer and upgraded American-Turkish political contacts seem necessary in policies toward Iraq. American moves concerning development in the Iraqi Kurdish area seem not to have been sufficiently explained to Ankara. A more intense high-level dialogue about the long-term intentions of American policy toward Iraq in general and the Kurdish area in particular may be helpful to ameliorate Turkish concerns. All efforts at explaining Washington's policy notwithstanding, Turkish understanding of American moves will remain limited as long as Turkey's own approach to the Kurdish question, especially the unfounded suspicions about the intentions of foreign powers regarding Turkey's territorial integrity, remain unchanged. Such irritations in American-Turkish political communication will normally not lead to a weakening of Ankara's support for overall American policy toward the Middle East.

American-Turkish military relations are mainly limited to Turkish arms procurement and the NATO air base at İncirlik where the forces of the Northern Watch operation are stationed. Arms procurement and American support of the modernization of the Turkish armed forces are sensitive issues because of the complicated regional security pattern. Turkey is faced with some threat from its eastern and southeastern neighbors with whom its has a somewhat strained relationship. And there is always the simmering conflict with Greece, the intensification of which is not at all in American or Western interests. The threat from the southeast may suggest a needed improvement of Turkey's military capabilities, but the conflict with Greece would strongly recommend substantive disarmament and arms control. American policy on military aid and arms procurement should deemphasize the principle of equity between Ankara and Athens and instead encourage arms control by carefully limiting its deliveries to either side. Above all, it should seek to disentangle itself from the machinations of ethnic lobbies in Congress.

Turkey is still underequipped to defend against weapons of mass destruction and medium and long-range missiles. The actual and prospective military posture of some of its regional neighbors makes this a real concern for Ankara's military planners. In this respect the delivery of American Patriot antimissile systems would be welcome. But the military's wish for extensive modernization of its main battle tanks and a considerable increase of the number of attack helicopters cannot be regarded as having a purely defensive rationale. These measures would also considerably strengthen Turkey's offensive capacity, especially if combined with a thorough upgrading of command and control capabilities.

American policy on arms procurement and military aid should carefully take into consideration these conflicting goals. Washington should promote Turkey's defensive capabilities where necessary without contributing to an upgrading of its offensive capabilities. It should seek to establish a common understanding on these matters with its European NATO partners and the Israeli government. The regional military balance does not warrant helping Turkey upgrade military capabilities across the board.

Turkey's connection to the Western alliance would be much strengthened if the conflict with Greece could be resolved and not just temporarily managed. Reconciliation with Greece would remove the strongest obstacle against Turkish accession to the European Union. The U.S. administration should continue its efforts to bring about a lasting understanding between Greece and Turkey and to that end should try to establish a common strategy with its main European allies.

Beyond the introduction of confidence-building measures between Athens and Ankara bilaterally or within NATO, the United States and its main European partners should develop ideas about more substantial efforts that could be made by the antagonists to show their readiness for real reconciliation. For instance, the abolition of Turkey's so-called Aegean army could be traded for Greek concessions on the extent of its territorial waters.

Political elites in both countries could be persuaded that it would be in their own long-term best interests to work to achieve a fundamental change in public attitudes toward the Aegean conflict. Given serious restraints on the political maneuverability of European governments because of the influence of Greek EU membership, it would be the continuous task of Washington to take the lead in such political efforts.

Even after the success of moving the S-300 missiles to Crete, America must continue to work toward lasting peace on Cyprus. Otherwise the dangerous confrontation that occurred in early 1997 when the Greek Cypriots announced having ordered the missiles will occur again. Experience has shown that the established proposal to resolve the problem does not carry much prospect of success. Reunification of the island under whatever formula does not seem likely because the different ideas of a unified Cyprus prevailing on each side of the Green Line are irreconcilable. The UN-controlled division backed by a strong Turkish military presence in the north has led to a rather peaceful coexistence of the two antagonistic communities. This suggests that a more permanent solution of the Cyprus problem should be sought by preserving the existing division.

America should try to find ways to consolidate the division for the time being instead of trying to further a rapprochement neither side wants. Discussion of the possibility of reunification should be left until after each community has had the chance to settle in its part of the island without being threatened by political or territorial demands from the other side. Under such circumstances the European Union could speed up the accession of the (Greek) Republic of Cyprus if it had become clear that this would not imply any Greek claim on the Turkish part of the island. The formalization of the status quo would thus fulfill Greek Cypriot expectations of joining the EU without forever foreclosing a later change if the sovereign people of both sides so wish.

Most likely, such a solution would increase Greek-Turkish tensions due to Greek political disappointment. It is therefore important that Ankara take a more flexible position for resolving conflicts over offshore national limits in the Aegean Sea. Turkey will have to accept that the Treaty of Lausanne did not allot it half of the seabed and that generally accepted international conventions in the meantime favor certain Greek claims. Washington and its European allies should convince the Turkish leadership that it has to be more conciliatory toward Athens if it wants to get the Cyprus issue settled according to its interest. Recurrent Turkish recourse to a threat of war cannot be accepted as civil behavior among allies.

The most crucial necessity for firmly anchoring Turkey in the West is to include it in the emerging European political architecture. EU membership and incorporation into the European security framework are of greatest importance. Having Turkey firmly attached to Europe's new political system would greatly contribute to Europe's future security. The European Union would encounter far fewer problems in its southeastern neighborhood if Turkey were at its side instead of being left on its own in a highly instable region. The stabilization of Turkey via its inclusion in the European architecture would also improve Europe's stability.[3]

Such opinions do not go uncontested in Europe. There are voices that simply deny Turkey its European quality, a position echoed in some conservative political circles and that, ironically, very much overlaps the opposition of Turkey's Islamists to the country's joining the European Union.[4] Another position claims that Turkish membership would overload the EU and thus has to be postponed into an unknown future. It is especially argued that European security concerns would be enlarged to include domains that are not of direct security policy interest to Europe, such as the water dispute between Turkey and its neighbors.[5]

Such discussions notwithstanding, the European Union has made clear since the Luxembourg meeting that Turkey's accession is accepted as a real possibility if the country is ready to fulfill the conditions established by the European Council of Copenhagen in 1993 for the membership of the central and east European democracies. Furthermore, the EU has offered Turkey a comprehensive and—to all understanding—open and adaptable program of cooperation to realize Turkey's membership, the "European strategy." However, the EU has not been ready or able to revise its decision to exclude Turkey from the group of eleven countries named "candidates" and with which the EU either opened accession negotiations in spring 1998 or has declared its readiness to open negotiations in the future. Such an official declaration does not exist with regard to Turkey.

The reason for such reluctance can most likely be found in the political circumstances that distinguish the Turkish situation from the situations of other prospective members: the conflict with Greece, including the Cyprus problem, and Turkey's democratic deficiencies, especially with regard to the Kurds. The first complex can be seen as an objective obstacle for membership because, given the necessity of unanimous consent of EU members to the accession of any new state, a Greek veto of membership is to be expected as long as the Greek-Turkish conflict continues. How difficult Greek resistance against any improvement in EU-Turkey relations is to overcome was experienced by President Clinton before the European Council meeting of Cardiff in June 1998, when he in vain tried to convince Greek Prime Minister Costas Simitis to back a British proposal for Turkey's eventual integration into the EU.[6] The Kurdish question has aquired such a prominent place in the saga because of the European Parliament's insistence on it, which is an outcome of political pressure developed by Kurdish exile groups and their sympathizers in various EU member states. Because no EU enlargement is possible without the final consent of the parliament, a solution to the problem is critical.

Turkey has made it clear that it does not want to join the EU on the basis of Brussels' conditions. Ankara sees the conditions as they concern the Kurdish problem and relations with Greece, including the Cyprus issue, as an unfair imposition of special prerequisites that are not imposed on other candidate countries in a similar manner. Turkey is not ready to sacrifice positions that are dear to its national honor for the sake of EU membership. As it has been stated in the fifty-seventh government's program:

> Turkey's full membership in the European Union is its right emanating from history, geography and international treaties. We shall endeavour to realize Turkey's aim of full membership in the European Union with equal rights and status as other members. Turkey will assume its rightful place in the integration process in Europe and while doing this, it will go on protecting its national rights and interests meticulously. In this regard, we shall carefully monitor and exploit all opportunities and developments which may accelerate our relations with the European Union. Turkey will adopt a determined approach aimed at enjoying full and equal footing in political and economic European and Transatlantic institutions and formations as well as those related to security and defence.[7]

As political circumstances in the majority of the EU member states stand, integration will be difficult to achieve without some major Turkish political concessions that Ecevit's three-party coalition government does not seem ready to make nor that the Turkish public is adequately prepared to accept. As long as Turkey remains convinced that its membership is a matter of granting it its "right," Ankara will continually run into problems in its relations with the European Union. Brussels will hardly be able to change its position on the conditions of an eventual Turkish entry.

Even if fourteen member states were ready to relent, continued Greek resistance would suffice to keep the status quo in EU-Turkish relations.

How firm Greece is on its position can easily be deduced from Athens's stubborn resistance even against any EU move to release some of the money owed to Turkey as an accompaniment of the customs union. Most likely, Turkish entry will not come about in the forseeable future, since Ankara, on its side, is equally impeded from changing its position because of the prevailing nationalistic drive in its politics.

Without a chance of EU membership soon, without even an EU commitment to open accession negotiations, with the Greek-Turkish conflict continuing, and with little hope for a solution of the Cyprus conflict, relations between the European Union and Turkey are doomed to deteriorate further. Under these circumstances the EU and its main member states should do everything possible to maintain the existing bonds with Turkey. They should consolidate and expand the customs union to its fullest. The European Commission should expand its staff dealing with Turkey to ensure the smooth functioning of the proposed institutions and procedures. EU-Turkish relations within the relatively narrow borders of the customs union should become habitual for both sides as quickly as possible. Moreover, the commission and some important member states should continue their effort to find ways to circumvent Greek resistance against the implementation of financial cooperation within the customs union framework.

Germany, Great Britain, and France should take into account the question of Turkey's place within the developing European security policy framework. Especially if an EU membership is not immediately likely, Turkey should not be relegated to the fringe of Europe's security organization nor should the problem be left completely to the Atlantic alliance. Ankara's expected gradual political alienation from the rest of Europe should not be complemented by an equally gradual removal from Europe's common security policy endeavors.

There are countervailing forces to a rapid and complete Turkish split with Europe. These forces are mainly the result of existing strong links between Turkey and Europe on all levels of their relationship. In addition, it will not be easy for Turkey to develop an alternative to its Western orientation. The disappointing results of Erbakan's attempts to establish some kind of Islamic foreign policy are witness to this. Another indication of the difficulties of finding convincing alternative foreign and security policy designs is the continuation of Turkey's endeavors to become accepted as a candidate by the European Union despite all the rebuffs it has had to suffer. Even those politicians in Turkey for whom EU membership is not an obsession, as Foreign Minister İsmail Cem said, do not contemplate a complete and radical break with Europe.

There are thus good reasons to assume that Turkey will remain in the Western fold but probably on a different basis than has been the case over the past forty-five years. It will be the task of American and European policymakers to adapt to this situation. Adaptation may be easier for Washington because as a reflex of a growing retreat from Europe, the Turkish leadership will seek closer ties with the United States. It remains to be seen if America can stand up to this expectation. For the Europeans the main task will be to avoid unnecessary strains in their changing relations with Turkey. Existing bonds have to be cultivated, and any chance to improve relations has to be taken. Perhaps a greater differentiation in the EU's integration process after the next round of enlargement may offer new opportunities to bring a changing Turkey closer to a changed European Union.

Notes

Preface

1. *A National Security Strategy for a New Century* (White House, May 1997), p. 22.

2. "Declaration of the European Union Presidency on Customs Union with Turkey," *Agence Europe*, Document 1924 (Brussels, February 28, 1995), p. 2.

3. See, for instance, Graham E. Fuller and Ian O. Lesser, with Paul B. Henze and J. F. Brown, *Turkey's New Geopolitics: from the Balkans to Western China* (Westview Press, 1993); and Kemal Kirişçi, "The End of the Cold War and Changes in Turkish Foreign Policy Behavior," *Foreign Policy* (Ankara), vol. 17 (1993), pp. 1–43.

4. Remarks of Graham E. Fuller at a roundtable in Istanbul in May 1997; see *At the Crossroads of Geo-politics: Turkey in a Changing Political Environment* (Hamburg: Körber-Stiftung, 1997), p. 32. (Minutes of the 109th Bergedorfer Gesprächskreis, Istanbul, May 24–25, 1997.)

Part One

1. It should be noted that the term Kemalism is not of Turkish origin but has been invented by foreign analysts of modern Turkey. The Turkish equivalent that has been introduced accordingly is *Atatürkçülük*.

2. The Kemalist principles of republicanism, populism, laicism or secularism, nationalism, etatism, and revolutionism or reformism, after their codification by the Republican Peoples Party in the early 1930s, were symbolized by arrows to demonstrate their forward-oriented power. In 1937 these principles were incorporated into Turkey's constitution. See Udo Steinbach, *Die Türkei im 20. Jahrhundert. Schwieriger Partner Europas* (Bergisch Gladbach: Gustav Lübbe Verlag, 1996), pp. 139–44.

3. See, for instance, M. Hakan Yavuz, "Search for a New Social Contract in Turkey: Fethullah Gülen, the Virtue Party and the Kurds," *SAIS Review*, vol. 19 (Winter-Spring 1999), pp. 114–43.

Chapter One

1. On Mustafa Kemal's revolution see Bernard Lewis, *The Emergence of Modern Turkey*, 2d ed. (Oxford University Press, 1968), pp. 323–487.

2. Binnaz Toprak, "The Religious Right," in Irvin C. Schick and Ertuğrul A. Tonak, eds., *Turkey in Transition: New Perspectives* (Oxford University Press, 1987), p. 224.

3. Lewis, *Emergence of Modern Turkey*, pp. 262–79.

4. Turhan Feyzioğlu, "Atatürk's Rational, Scientific and Realistic Approach to the Modernization of Turkey," in Turhan Feyzioğlu, ed., *Atatürk's Way* (Istanbul: Otomarsan, 1982), pp. 1–74.

5. For an example of this interpretation by one of the ideologues of Kemalist tradition see Enver Ziya Karal, "The Principles of Kemalism," in Ali Kazancığıl and Ergun Özbudun, eds., *Atatürk: Founder of a Modern State* (London: C. Hurst, 1981), pp. 11–35.

6. Binnaz Toprak, "Civil Society in Turkey," in Augustus Richard Norton, ed., *Civil Society in the Middle East*, vol. 2 (E. J. Brill, 1996), p. 107. In this sense populism is a reflection of the Islamic idea of *umma*, but it also shares some commonality with the organic ideas of society developed by the fascist ideologies of the time. It does, however, carry a democratic connotation by alluding to the will of the people as the basis of the republican regime.

7. Ayşe Kadıoğlu, "The Paradox of Turkish Nationalism and the Construction of Official Identity," *Middle Eastern Studies*, vol. 32 (April 1996), pp. 177–93.

8. Christian Rumpf, *Das türkische Verfassungssystem* (Wiesbaden: Harrassowitz Verlag, 1996), p. 101.

9. The Turkish idea *lâiklik* can be translated as either *laicism* or *secularism*. In the European context laicism means the strict separation of state and church(es), whereas secularism means the result of the vanishing of religious elements, norms, and rites from society. This distinction is difficult to apply to Sunni Muslim societies because of the lack of established institutions of religion, that is Islamic "churches". For Turkey, the term secularism is normally applied to designate the special Kemalist way of separating politics (state) and religion (Islam). For the special meaning of the term as applied to Turkish circumstances see Rumpf, *Das türkische Verfassungssystem*, pp. 105–13.

10. The other two principles of Kemalism, etatism and revolutionism or reformism, have been of minor importance, although the first served to justify strong state intervention into economic policy. The second, in Turkish *inkılâpcılık*, is meant to indicate the moving character of the Kemalist revolution that never can be regarded as completed; the principle never became instrumental for Kemalist politics.

11. Erik J. Zürcher, *Turkey: A Modern History* (New York: I. B. Tauris, 1994), pp. 173–83; and Feroz Ahmad, *The Making of Modern Turkey* (Routledge, 1993), pp. 57–59.

12. Lewis, *Emergence of Modern Turkey*, p. 270.

13. Ministry of Education, *A Speech Delivered by Mustafa Kemal Atatürk 1927* (Ankara: Başbakanlık Basımevi, 1981).

14. Metin Heper, *The State Tradition in Turkey* (Beverley: Eothen Press, 1985).

15. Şerif Mardin, "Center-Periphery Relations: A Key to Turkish Politics?" *Daedalus*, vol. 102 (Winter 1973), pp. 169–90.

16. Rumpf, *Das türkische Verfassungssystem*, pp. 100–13.

17. "Turkish Hearths Open Center in Balgat," *Turkish Daily News Electronic Edition*, July 21, 1997 (www.turkishdailynews.com [August 1999]).

Chapter Two

1. Cem Behar, "Recent Trends in Turkey's Population," in Çiğdem Balım and others, eds., *Turkey: Political, Social and Economic Challenges in the 1990s* (E. J. Brill, 1995), pp. 97–106, especially pp. 97–98.

2. Behar, "Recent Trends," p. 98.

3. For more information on Turkey's "successor generation" see Istanbul Mulkiyeliler Foundation Social Research Center, *Turkish Youth 98: The Silent Majority Highlighted* (Ankara: Konrad Adenauer Foundation, 1999).

4. William Hale, *The Political and Economic Development of Modern Turkey* (St. Martin's, 1981), pp. 86–253.

5. Saadet Oruç, "Ankara Rushes to Meet Its Growing Energy Need," *Turkish Daily News Electronic Edition*, December 16, 1997 (www.turkishdailynews.com [August 1999]).

6. Anne O. Krueger and Okan H. Aktan, *Swimming against the Tide: Turkish Trade Reform in the 1980s* (San Francisco: ICS Press, 1992), pp. 34–39, give a concise overview of the various policy measures taken in that period. For a more elaborate analysis see Sübidey Togan and V. N. Balasubramanyam, eds., *The Economy of Turkey since Liberalization* (St. Martin's, 1996).

7. See the interview with Tosun Terzioğlu, president of the Scientific and Technical Research Council of Turkey (TÜBİTAK), "On Anatolian Tigers with TÜBİTAK President Tosun Terzioğlu," *Turkish Daily News Electronic Edition*, May 12, 1997.

8. Ziya Önış, "The State and Economic Development in Contemporary Turkey: Etatism to Neoliberalism and Beyond," in Vojtech Mastny and R. Craig Nation, eds., *Turkey between East and West: New Challenges for a Rising Regional Power* (Boulder, Colo.: Westview Press, 1996), p. 173.

9. *OECD Economic Surveys, 1991–1992: Turkey* (Paris: OECD, 1992), p. 111.

10. "Building a Concensus for Structural Reform," *OECD Economic Surveys, 1996–97: Turkey* (Paris: OECD, 1997), pp. 48–63.

11. "Year Ends in the Middle of a Crisis," *Briefing* 1224, December 28, 1998, pp. 32–33.

12. Ziya Önış, "The Political Economy of Export-Oriented Industrialization in Turkey," in Balım and others, eds., *Turkey: Political, Social, and Economic Changes*, pp. 117–29; and Öniş, "State and Economic Development," pp. 162–73.

13. Since November 1987, when Turgut Özal called early elections because of a lost public referendum that brought back into politics all political leaders who had been banned from political activity after the 1980 military coup, Turkey has experienced

eleven governments, six of them fairly weak coalition governments and three minority governments.

14. "Inflation Steals almost 30 Percent of Buying Power in Turkey," *Turkish Daily News Electronic Edition*, December 3, 1997.

15. *OECD Economic Surveys, 1996–97: Turkey*, pp. 49–52.

16. Michael Matting, "Nicht einmal ein Stück Brot," *Die Zeit*, September 26, 1997, p. 34; and "7.5 Million Living on the Edge of Starvation in Turkey," *Turkish Daily News Electronic Edition*, March 14, 1998.

17. Neslihan Öztürk and Metin Demirsar, "Turkey's SSK Hospitals Teeter on the Verge of Collapse," *Turkish Daily News Electronic Edition*, August 15, 1997; and "SSK Deficit to Reach $25.5 Billion in 2025," *Turkish Daily News Electronic Edition*, June 21, 1999.

18. According to news reports, in the 1990s unstructred development of state agencies created considerable disorder in the public sector with various agencies often having almost identical responsibilities in economic affairs, creating many problems for private entities. "Disorder in the Public Sector Increases," *Turkish Daily News Electronic Edition*, April 21, 1998.

19. "Peaceful Civil Disobedience Proves Frightening to Regime,"*Briefing* 1131, February 24, 1997, pp. 6–7.

20. "The Susurluk Incident," *Turkish Daily News Electronic Edition*, January 7, 1997.

21. Binnaz Toprak, "Civil Society in Turkey," in Augustus Richard Norton, ed., *Civil Society in the Middle East*, vol. 2 (E. J. Brill, 1996), p. 117.

22. M. Akıf Beki, "Non-Governmental Organizations Awake to the New Century," *Turkish Daily News Electronic Edition*, July 22, 1996.

23. Heidi Wedel, "Ansätze einer Zivilgesellschaft in der Türkischen Republik—Träger der Demokratisierung oder neue Eliteorganisation?" in Ferhad Ibrahim and Heidi Wedel, eds., *Probleme der Zivilgesellschaft im Vorderen Orient* (Opladen: Leske and Budrich, 1995), pp. 113–34.

24. Jilian Schwedler, "Introduction: Civil Society and the Study of Middle East Politics," in Jilian Schwedler, ed., *Towards Civil Society in the Middle East? A Primer* (Boulder, Colo.: Lynne Rienner, 1995), pp. 3–7.

25. Gülistan Gürbey, "Politische und rechtliche Hindernisse auf dem Weg der Herausbildung einer Zivilgesellschaft in der Türkei," in Ibrahim and Wedel, eds., *Probleme der Zivilgesellschaft*, pp. 95–111.

26. For an example see *1994 Turkey Human Rights Report* (Ankara: Human Rights Foundation of Turkey, 1995).

27. As investigations by parliament's Human Rights Commission have shown, there is evidence of the continuation of systematic torture in some police departments and prisons in the southeastern provinces. See, Mustafa Erdoğan, "Systematic Torture Is Evident . . ." *Turkish Daily News Electronic Edition*, April 3, 1998.

28. See *Briefing* 1188–92, April 20–May 18, 1998, for the events surrounding the capture of Şemdin Sakık, former second in command of the PKK and the repercussions of his leaked allegations on Turkey's internal and external situation.

29. See especially the annual *Country Reports on Human Rights Practices* published by the Bureau of Democracy, Human Rights, and Labor of the U.S. Department of State (www.state.gov/www/global/human_rights/hrp_reports_mainhp.html [July 1999]); and

Human Rights Watch, *World Report* (www.hrw.org/worldreport99/europe/turkey.html [July 1999]).

30. Erdinç Ergenç, "Equation of Environment and Energy," *Turkish Daily News Electronic Edition*, June 3, 1996.

31. Raşıt Gürdilek, "Stepping across the Threshold," *Turkish Daily News Electronic Edition*, January 30, 1997.

32. For instance, twenty years after its inception the huge Southeast Anatolian Project (GAP) that nears completion in a few years has now been included in the state's environmental measures with the signing of an environmental protocol in April 1998 by the state ministers responsible for the project and the environment; see *Turkish Daily News Electronic Edition*, April 22, 1998.

33. "SOS Signals from the Environment," *Turkish Daily News Electronic Edition*, March 23, 1998; and Esra İdil, "Promising Efforts but Major Environmental Problems Persist," *Turkish Daily News Electronic Edition*, June 5, 1998.

34. Yeşim Arat, "Politics and Big Business: Janus-Faced Link to the State," in Metin Heper, ed., *Strong State and Economic Interest Groups: The Post-1980 Turkish Experience* (Walter de Gruyter, 1991), pp. 135–47.

35. Bülent Tanör, *Perspectives on Democratisation in Turkey* (Istanbul: TÜSİAD, January 1997).

36. "Ain't Gonna Work on Tansu's Farm No More," *Briefing* 1143, May 26, 1997, pp. 6–7.

37. Esra İdil, "An Outline of Television and Radio Broadcasting in Turkey," parts 1 and 2, *Turkish Daily News Electronic Edition*, May 5 and 6, 1998.

38. See Günter Seufert, *Politischer Islam in der Türkei. Islamismus als symbolische Repräsentation einer sich modernisierenden muslimischen Gesellschaft* (Stuttgart: Franz Steiner Verlag, 1997), pp. 142–48, 391–415.

39. Oya Baydar, ed., *Trade Unions in Turkey* (Istanbul: Friedrich Ebert Vakfı, 1997), pp. 132–43.

40. "RTUK after New Sanctions on Broadcasting Companies," *Turkish Daily News Electronic Edition*, April 13, 1998.

41. Nilüfer Göle, *The Forbidden Modern: Civilization and Veiling* (University of Michigan Press, 1996).

42. Sirin Tekeli, "Les Femmes, Vecteur de la Modernisation," in Stéphane Yerasimos, ed., *Les Turcs: Orient et Occident, Islam et Laïcité* (Paris: Éditions Autrement, 1994), pp. 138–57.

Chapter Three

1. On the military interventions of 1960, 1971, and 1980, see William Hale, *Turkish Politics and the Military* (Routledge, 1994), pp. 104–36, 175–93, and 231–56. Because the events of spring 1997 have not so far been analyzed comprehensively, one has to rely on press reports for the main facts.

2. Together with the new Party Law, the names of more than 700 politicians who were banned from politics were published in the *Official Gazette;* see *Briefing* 428, May 2, 1983, p. 13.

3. İlter Turan, "Political Parties and the Party System in Post-1983 Turkey," in Metin Heper and Ahmet Evin, eds., *State, Democracy and the Military: Turkey in the 1980s* (Walter de Gruyter, 1988), pp. 63–80, esp. pp. 73–75; and Heinz Kramer, *Das neue politische System der Türkei,* Working Paper AZ 2374 (Ebenhausen: Stiftung Wissenschaft und Politik, 1983), pp. 52–62.

4. Üstün Ergüder, "The Motherland Party, 1983–1989," in Metin Heper and Jacob Landau, eds., *Political Parties and Democracy in Turkey* (I. B. Tauris, 1991), pp. 152–69.

5. Demirel felt personally deceived by Turgut Özal, whom he had entrusted with designing the fundamental economic policy reform program of January 1980 when Özal actively cooperated as deputy prime minister with the military after the September coup that brought Demirel's political career to a temporary halt. The actual party leaders, Mesut Yılmaz of ANAP and Tansu Çiller of DYP, are deeply divided over their desires for leading an eventually merged center-right party.

6. On the intervention of the military in the formation of a government after the 1995 elections see "Reasons for ANAP-RP Breakdown Questioned," *Briefing* 1081, March 4, 1996, pp. 3–5.

7. The Populist Party (Halkçı Parti, or HP) founded by the military merged with the Social Democracy Party (Sosyal Demokrasi Partisi, or SODEP) led by Erdal İnönü, the son of Atatürk's second man and successor İsmet İnönü, to form the Social Democratic Populist Party (Sosyal Demokrat Halkçı Parti, or SHP) in 1985. In 1995 this party merged with its revived rival, the (new) Republican People's Party of former SHP secretary general Deniz Baykal, who was the only rival to Ecevit in the Turkish center-left political camp until the defeat of the CHP in the 1999 elections.

8. Alan Makovsky, "Turkey's Nationalist Moment," *Policy Watch* 384, April 20, 1999.

9. For an account of the political crisis that led to the coup see Clement H. Dodd, *The Crisis of Turkish Democracy* (Beverley: Eothen Press, 1983); Mehmet Ali Birand, *The Generals' Coup in Turkey: An Inside Story of 12 September 1980,* trans. by M. A. Dikerdem (Washington: Brassey's Defense, 1987); and Lucille W. Pevsner, *Turkey's Political Crisis: Background, Perspectives, Prospects,* Washington Papers 110 (Washington: Center for Strategic and International Studies, 1984).

10. Ahmet Evin, "Demilitarization and Civilianization of the Regime," in M. Heper and A. Evin, eds., *Politics in the Third Turkish Republic* (Boulder, Colo.: Westview Press, 1994), pp. 23–40.

11. A special case in point is the short-lived experience of the New Democracy Movement (Yeni Demokrasi Hareketi, or YDH) created by the young businessman Cem Boyner that gained a certain international prominence as a modern political force but proved unable to attract the electorate in the 1995 elections. For the programatic outlook of the party, see Cem Boyner, *Die Türkei am Scheideweg* (Stuttgart: Robert Bosch Stiftung, 1996).

12. Ersin Kalaycıoğlu, "Elections and Party Preferences in Turkey: Changes and Continuities in the 1990s," *Comparative Political Studies,* vol. 27 (October 1994), pp. 402–24.

13. Ersin Kalaycıoğlu, "The Logic of Contemporary Turkish Politics," *Middle East Review of International Affairs (MERIA) Journal,* vol. 1, no. 3 (September 1997) (www.biu.ac.il/SOC/besa/meria [July 1999]).

14. İlter Turan, "The Oligarchic Leadership of Turkish Political Parties: Origins, Evolution, Institutionalization and Consequences," Koç University Working Paper 1995/19, Istanbul, 1995.

15. However, the practice of luring away deputies from their original party by promising material or political rewards in order to change governments or undermine the stability of an adverse party had started much earlier. For instance, in 1978 Bülent Ecevit formed a majority government on the basis of twelve deputies who had defected from Süleyman Demirel's Justice Party. See Nicole Pope and Hugh Pope, *Turkey Unveiled: Atatürk and After* (London: John Murray, 1997), p. 133.

16. "Military: Won't Tolerate Moves Aimed at Eroding Image," *Turkish Daily News Electronic Edition*, March 21, 1998 (www.turkishdailynews.com [August 1999]).

17. "Attention Focused on Military Again," *Turkish Daily News Electronic Edition*, March 13, 1998; and Kemal Balcı, "Civilians vs. Military," *Turkish Daily News Electronic Edition*, March 19, 1998.

18. Stephen Kinzer, "The Battle for Secularism Moves to a Turkish Court," *International Herald Tribune*, April 6, 1998, p. 8.

19. For this purpose the military had declared in April 1997 a change in the country's national defense concept by giving priority to the national and territorial integrity and the domestic threat to the fundamentals of the republic—in other words, by putting on equal footing the fight against the separatist Kurdish PKK and Islamic fundamentalism. Hayri Birler, "Tolerating Fundamentalism: PKK Amounts to Republic's Suicide, Army Says," *Turkish Daily News Electronic Edition*, April 30, 1997.

20. İlter Turan, "The Military in Turkish Politics," *Mediterranean Politics*, vol. 2 (Autumn 1997), pp. 123–35.

21. İlnur Çevik, ". . . And the Military Breaks Its Silence," *Turkish Daily News Electronic Edition*, January 6, 1999. For the events that led to Yılmaz's resignation see William Hale, "In Deep Trouble," *World Today*, vol. 55 (January 1999), pp. 22–25.

22. Such criticism can be found, for instance, in the *Democracy Report* of TÜSİAD; see *Perspectives on Democratisation in Turkey* (Istanbul: Turkish Industrialists' and Businessmen's Association, 1997), pp. 87–90.

23. Turan, "Military in Turkish Politics," p. 135.

24. Metehan Demir, "Erbakan Signs $600 mn Israeli Deal to Modernize Turkish F-4s," *Turkish Daily News Electronic Edition*, December 6, 1996.

25. David Eshel and Selçük Emre, "Turkey, Israel to Cooperate in Missile Defence System," *Jane's Defence Weekly*, April 29, 1998, p. 3.

26. Gerd Höhler, "Panzer müssen nicht mehr rollen," *Frankfurter Rundschau*, April 27, 1998, p. 2.

27. Metehan Demir, "Military Bridges Foreign Policy Gap," *Turkish Daily News Electronic Edition*, May 11, 1998.

28. Christian Rumpf, *Das türkische Verfassungssystem* (Wiesbaden: Harrassowitz Verlag, 1996), p. 180.

29. "Freedom of Thought on Trial," *Turkish Daily News Electronic Edition*, June 5, 1998.

30. The procedures of these special criminal courts for civilians are run by military personnel. Rumpf, *Das türkische Verfassungssystem*, pp. 209ff and 264ff.

31. Rumpf, *Das türkische Verfassungssystem*, pp. 205–11, comes to the conclusion "that in such a system justice all too often fails" (p. 211).

32. European Court of Human Rights, *Incal vs. Turkey*, case no. 41/1997/825/1031, Strasbourg, June 9, 1998 (www.dhcour.coe.fr/eng/PRESS/emay-june98.html#INCAL

[July 1999]); also quoted in Hugh Poulton, "The Turkish State and Democracy," *International Spectator* (Rome), vol. 34 (January-March 1999), pp. 47–62.

33. For details see Ayla Ganioğlu, "Ocalan Trial Will Be Concluded by Civilianized DGM," *Turkish Daily News Electronic Edition*, June 20, 1999; and *Briefing* 1247, Ankara, June 21, 1999, p. 7.

Chapter Four

1. İsmet G. İmset, *The PKK: A Report on Separatist Violence in Turkey (1973–1992)* (Ankara: Turkish Daily News, October 1992), is the most comprehensive account of PKK development up to the early 1990s. For an analysis of the PKK see also Henri J. Barkey and Graham E. Fuller, *Turkey's Kurdish Question* (Lanham, Md.: Rowman and Littlefield, 1998), pp. 21–60.

2. Kemal Kirişçi and Gareth M. Winrow, "The International Dimension of the Kurdish Question," in *The Kurdish Question and Turkey: An Example of Trans-state Ethnic Conflict* (Portland, Ore.: Frank Cass, 1997), pp. 157–82.

3. Barkey and Fuller, *Turkey's Kurdish Question*, pp. 97–132.

4. Henri J. Barkey, "Turkey's Kurdish Dilemma," *Survival*, vol. 35 (Winter 1993–94), pp. 51–70; and Gülistan Gürbey, *Auf der Suche nach einer Lösung der Kurdenfrage in der Türkei: Optionen und Hindernisse*, report 4/1995 (Fankfurt: Hessische Stiftung Friedens- und Konfliktforschung, 1995), pp. 9–10.

5. Kirişçi and Winrow, *Kurdish Question*, p. 113.

6. Ümit Cizre Sakallıoğlu, "Kurdish Nationalism from an Islamist Perspective: The Discourses of Turkish Islamist Writers," *Journal of Muslim Minority Affairs*, vol. 18 (April 1998), pp. 73–89. *Kurdish question* is a literal translation of the Turkish *Kurt sorunu*, which is used to describe what is officially called the *Southeastern problem.*

7. For examples see Hugh Poulton, "The Turkish State and Democracy," *International Spectator* (Rome), vol. 34 (January-March 1999), pp. 56–58.

8. For examples of this "dirty war" see İmset, *PKK*, passim.

9. Kirişçi and Winrow, *Kurdish Question*, p. 130.

10. "The Migration Commission Report," *Briefing*, 1181, February 23, 1998, p. 7, quoting a report of the Migration Commission of the Turkish parliament. An abridged version has been published in German by Dialog-Kreis, ed., *Parlamentarier der Türkei durchbrechen Tabu in der Kurdenfrage* (Idstein: Meinhardt Text und Design, July 1998).

11. Kemal Kirişçi, "Erzwungene Migration in der Türkei," *Südosteuropa-Mitteilungen*, vol. 37 (1997), pp. 176–81.

12. It is impossible to establish the exact number of Kurds living in Turkey because the Turkish population census has not included questions concerning the mother tongue since 1965. Furthermore, it is difficult to define exactly who is a Kurd because of the results of the Turkish policy of assimilation and the usual difficulties in establishing clear boundaries for ethnic conceptions. Using the 1965 census data, Servet Mutlu estimated the number of Kurdish speaking persons among Turkey's population for 1990 to be 7 million. Today, the number of about 10 million Kurds in Turkey mostly goes unchallenged in public discussion. For further information see Servet Mutlu, "Ethnic Kurds in Turkey: a Demographic Study," *International Journal of Middle East Studies*, vol.

28 (November 1996), pp. 517–41. On the question of defining a Kurd, see also Kirişçi and Winrow, *Kurdish Question*, pp. 24–26.

13. İmset, *PKK*, p. I.

14. Christian Rumpf, "Minderheiten in der Türkei und die Frage nach ihrem rechtlichen Schutz," *Zeitschrift für Türkeistudien*, vol. 6 (1993), pp. 173–209.

15. Kirişçi and Winrow, *Kurdish Question*, pp. 94–105.

16. Michael M. Gunter, *The Kurds in Turkey: A Political Dilemma* (Boulder, Colo.: Westview, 1990), pp. 11–56.

17. Lale Yalçın-Heckmann, *Tribe and Kinship among the Kurds* (Frankfurt am Main: Peter Lang, 1991). For political consequences of this situation see Gunnar Wiessner, "Grundfragen aktueller politischer und militärischer Entwicklungen in den kurdischen Provinzen der Türkei," *Orient*, vol. 38 (1997), pp. 289–310.

18. Bruce Kuniholm, "Sovereignty, Democracy and Identity: Turkey's Kurdish Problem and the West's Turkish Problem," *Mediterranean Politics*, vol. 1 (Winter 1996), pp. 353–70.

19. For details see Henri J. Barkey, "The People's Democracy Party (HADEP): The Travails of a Legal Kurdish Party in Turkey," *Journal of Muslim Minority Affairs*, vol. 18 (April 1998), pp. 129–38.

20. Barkey, "People's Democracy Party," p. 131.

21. Philip Robins, "The Overlord State: Turkish Policy and the Kurdish Issue," *International Affairs*, vol. 69 (October 1993), pp. 665–70.

22. Nimet Beriker-Atiyas, "The Kurdish Conflict in Turkey: Issues, Parties and Prospects," *Security Dialogue*, vol. 28 (1997), 439–52, esp. p. 446f; and "The Writer, the Prime Minister, and the PKK," *Briefing* 1103, August 12, 1996, pp. 1, 5–6.

23. David McDowall, *A Modern History of the Kurds* (I. B. Tauris, 1996), pp. 115–50. The Treaty of Sèvres has become an important point of reference in the argumentation of Turkish nationalists who suspect Turkey's western allies of following a hidden agenda for the dismemberment of the republic by advocating that Turkey's Kurds be granted special rights. Even president Süleyman Demirel, in spring 1995, spoke of a western "conspiracy" against Turkey in that respect. See Kirişçi and Winrow, *Kurdish Question*, p. 209f.

24. Heidi Wedel, "Binnenmigration und ethnische Identität—Kurdinnen in türkischen Metropolen," *Orient*, vol. 37 (1996), pp. 437–52; and Gülistan Gürbey, *Auf der Suche nach einer Lösung der Kurdenfrage in der Türkei: Optionen und Hindernisse*, report 4/1995 (Frankfurt am Main: Hessische Stiftung Friedens-und Konfliktforschung, 1995), pp. 14ff.

25. Kirişçi and Winrow, *Kurdish Question*, p. 121.

26. Beriker-Atiyas, "Kurdish Conflict in Turkey," p. 445f; and Kirişçi and Winrow, *Kurdish Question*, pp.149–51.

27. For a more detailed discussion of these ideas see Kirişçi and Winrow, *Kurdish Question*, pp. 183–207; and Barkey and Fuller, *Turkey's Kurdish Question*, pp. 179–220.

28. İmset, *PKK*, p. I.

29. Beriker-Atiyas, "Kurdish Conflict in Turkey," p. 439.

30. Kirişçi and Winrow, *Kurdish Question*, p. 124f.

31. For an overview of the project and its aims see Ali İhsan Bağış, *Southeastern Anatolia Project: The Cradle of Civilization Regenerated* (Istanbul: Gelişim Yayınları and Interbank, 1989); Ahmet Şahinöz, "Le Projet de l'Anatolie du Sud-Est: une nouvelle source alimentaire en Méditerranéen Orientale," in Ali İhsan Bağış, ed., *Water as an*

Element of Cooperation and Development in the Middle East, pp. 109–27 (Ankara: Hacettepe University and Friedrich-Naumann Foundation in Turkey, 1994); and Servet Mutlu, "The Southeastern Anatolia Project (GAP) of Turkey: Its Context, Objectives and Prospects," *Orient*, vol. 37, no. 1 (1996), pp. 59–86.

32. Mahmut Bali Aykan, "Turkey's Policy in Northern Iraq, 1991–1995," *Middle Eastern Studies*, vol. 32 (October 1996), pp. 343–66. See also chap. 8 in this book.

33. Kirişçi and Winrow, *Kurdish Question*, pp. 161–67.

34. Barkey and Fuller, "Turkey's Kurdish Question," pp. 70–72; and Kirişçi and Winrow, *Kurdish Question*, p. 148f.

35. Tim Weiner, "U.S. Helped to Catch Kurdish Leader," *International Herald Tribune*, February 22, 1999, p. 1.

36. For details, see "Revelations of the Century?" *Briefing* 1245, June 7, 1999, pp. 17–18; "Is There More Than Meets the Eye to the 'Case of the Century?'" *Briefing* 1246, June 14, 1999, pp. 10–12; "Öcalan Gives Political Defense," *Briefing* 1248, June 28, 1999, pp. 14–15; and "Turkey Sorts Out Reaction to Verdict," *Briefing* 1249, July 5, 1999, pp. 9–13.

37. Robert W. Olson, *The Emergence of Kurdish Nationalism and the Sheik Said Rebellion, 1880–1925* (University of Texas Press, 1989), pp. 91–127; see also Martin M. van Bruinessen, *Agha, Scheich und Staat* (Berlin: Edition Parabolis, 1989), pp. 379–433.

38. Orhan Kilercioğlu, "Reflections on Apo's Capture," *Turkish Daily News Electronic Edition*, February 23, 1999 (www.turkishdailynews.com [August 1999]).

39. Martin van Bruinessen, "Shifting National and Ethnic Identities: The Kurds in Turkey and the European Diaspora," *Journal of Muslim Minority Affairs*, vol. 18 (April 1998), pp. 39–52.

40. "From Spaghetti Westerns to Macoroni Southeasterns—Italy 'Disappoints,'" *Briefing* 1212, October 5, 1998, p. 19.

41. Poulton, "Turkish State," pp. 59–61.

42. This scandal erupted in November 1996 as a consequence of a car accident near the small town of Susurluk in which a former deputy chief of Istanbul's state security department, an important Kurdish tribal chief and DYP deputy, and a famous nationalist mafia killer sought by Interpol were revealed to have been in the same car. An attempt of the DYP minister of interior, Mehmet Ağar, to cover up failed and led to his resignation and that of the head of the national state security department. Various investigations undertaken into the scandal by a parliamentary commission, a special state prosecutor, and journalists give strong support to the assumption that in the mid-1990s a network of leading politicians, high-ranking state security officials, probably some high-ranking military, and nationalist mafia killers had been established to get rid of persons who were regarded as supporters of the separatist Kurdish forces but also to topple Azerbaijan's president Haidar Aliyev. "Susurluk: A Year of Fading Dreams," *Briefing* 1165, October 27, 1997, pp. 5–8; and "Will the State Ever Be Cleansed?" *Briefing* 1178, Ankara, January 26, 1998, pp. 5ff.

43. İmset, *PKK*, pp. 105–20; and Wiessner, "Grundfragen aktueller politischer und militärischer Entwicklungen," pp. 298ff.

44. One of the main defendants in the Yüksekova gang trial, Fatih Özhan, a former member of the police force's special team, revealed that there are five gangs operating in the Yüksekova area of Hakkâri province that had been engaged in drug smuggling, murder, and kidnapping; see Mustafa Erdoğan, "PKK Informer Alleges More State-Gang

Links," *Turkish Daily News Electronic Edition*, June 2, 1998; see also "Gang Convicted, But Senior Officials Still at Large," *Briefing* 1210, September 21, 1998, p. 6.

45. Beriker-Atiyas, "Kurdish Conflict in Turkey," p. 451.

46. See, for instance, William Safire, "In Victory, Turkey Must Show Magnanimity toward the Kurds," *International Herald Tribune*, February 19, 1999; Graham E. Fuller, "Handle Ocalan Arrest with Care," *Los Angeles Times*, February 18, 1999; or Faruk Şen, "Voraussetzung wäre eine stabile Regierung," *Frankfurter Allgemeine Zeitung*, April 17, 1999, p. 8.

Chapter Five

1. Nilüfer Göle, "Secularism and Islamism in Turkey: The Making of Elites and Counter-Elites," *Middle East Journal*, vol. 51 (Winter 1997), pp. 46–58, esp. pp. 53–57.

2. Some Western analysts try to picture the actual Turkish situation in just that simplistic manner. This approach has the advantage of pointing to a danger in the political development of Turkey. However, it also tends to foreclose avenues of a more differentiated democratic development that would constructively take into account the Islamic reality of Turkey. See Bassam Tibi, *Aufbruch am Bosporus: Die Türkei zwischen Europa und dem Islamismus* (Munich and Zürich: Diana Verlag, 1998); and Shireen T. Hunter, *Turkey at the Crossroads: Islamic Past or European Future,* CEPS Paper 63 (Brussels: Centre for European Policy Studies, 1995).

3. Turhan Feyzioğlu, "Secularism: Cornerstone of the Turkish Revolution," in Turhan Feyzioğlu, ed., *Atatürk's Way* (Istanbul: Otomarsan, 1982), pp. 209–12; and Mehmet Ali Ağaoğulları, *L'islam dans la vie politique de la Turquie* (Ankara: Ankara Üniversitesi, 1982), pp. 32–35.

4. Paul Dumont, "Disciples of the Light: The Nurju Movement in Turkey," *Central Asian Survey*, vol. 5, no. 2 (1986), pp. 33–60, esp. p. 38f.

5. İlkay Sunar and Binnaz Toprak, "Islam in Politics: The Case of Turkey," *Government and Opposition*, vol. 18 (Autumn 1983), p. 421.

6. Ümit Cizre Sakallıoğlu, "Parameters and Strategy of Islam-State Interaction in Republican Turkey," *International Journal of Middle East Studies*, vol. 28 (1996), pp. 231–51, esp. p. 236.

7. Sencer Ayata, "Patronage, Party, and State: The Politicization of Islam in Turkey," *Middle East Journal*, vol. 50 (Winter 1996), p. 41.

8. In this view real laicism, in the sense of institutionally separating state and religion, in Turkey would mean the separation of the *diyanet* from the state—that is, its likely dissolution—leaving the organization of religious life for the Sunni Muslim to the various orders and communities or to other institutions that are organized around mosques, as long as there would be no nationwide voluntary organization of Islam in Turkey, which is unlikely to be established.

9. Karin Vorhoff, *Zwischen Glaube, Nation und neuer Gemeinschaft: Alevitische Identität in der Türkei der Gegenwart* (Berlin: K. Schwarz, 1995).

10. For details see "Authorities Set to Excuse Sivas Holocaust," *Briefing* 945, July 5, 1993, p. 3; and "Coalition and Regime Withstand Sivas Anger," *Briefing* 946, July 12, 1993, pp. 3–6.

11. For an account of the Gazi incidents see Aliza Marcus, "Should I Shoot You? An Eyewitness Account of an Alevi Uprising in Gazi," *Middle East Report*, vol. 26 (April-June 1996), pp. 24–26.

12. "Alawis Get TL 425 Bn Assistance from the Budget," *Turkish Daily News Electronic Edition*, December 2, 1997 (www.turkishdailynews.com [August 1999]).

13. Rainer Hermann, "Die drei Versionen des politischen Islam in der Türkei," *Orient*, vol. 37 (March 1996), pp. 35–58.

14. Ely Karmon, "Radical Islamic Political Groups in Turkey," *Middle East Review of International Affairs (MERIA) Journal*, vol. 1 (January 1998) (www.biu.ac.il/SOC/besa/meria [August 1999]).

15. Binnaz Toprak, "Islamist Intellectuals: Revolt against Industry and Technology," in Metin Heper and others, eds., *Turkey and the West: Changing Political and Cultural Identities* (I. B. Tauris, 1993), pp. 237–57.

16. Differentiation between orders (*tarikatler*) and communities (*cemaatlar*) is not always easy to establish. Orders, in general, are historic organizations of Turkish folk Islam and have existed for centuries in Anatolia. They are hierarchically organized with various levels of spiritual and organizational competence and are led by a sheik as the spiritual and organizational leader. Their members distinguish themselves by certain rites or modes of dressing. Religious communities are of a much younger date and often derive from an order. Their organization very much resembles that of the orders with regard to hierarchy. The leader of a community normally is not considered a sheik, although his spiritual and organizational leadership is as firm and undisputed.

17. Şerif Mardin, "The Nakşibendi Order in Turkish History," in Richard Tapper, ed., *Islam in Modern Turkey*, pp. 121–42; and Dumont, "Disciples of the Light," pp. 33–60.

18. Nilüfer Narlı, "Tarikats and Cemaats in Turkey," *Turkish Daily News Electronic Edition*, January 24, 1997.

19. Sunar and Toprak, "Islam in Politics," p. 427.

20. A former president of the directorate, Lütfü Doğan, even advocated the reinstatement of *Shar'ia* law in 1976 and had to be reminded by the president of the state that such an opinion was a criminal offense. See Karl Binswanger, "Islamischer Fundamentalismus und türkischer Nationalismus," n.d.

21. Ayata, "Patronage, Party, and State," p. 48.

22. Dumont, "Disciples of the Light," p. 57.

23. Bahattin Akşit, "Islamic Education in Turkey: Medrese Reform in the Late Ottoman Times and Imam-Hatip Schools in the Republic," in Richard Tapper, ed., *Islam in Modern Turkey: Religion, Politics and Literature in a Secular State* (I. B. Tauris, 1991), pp. 145–70, esp. pp. 146–52.

24. Rainer Hermann, "Fethullah Gülen—eine muslimische Alternative zur Refah-Partei?" *Orient*, vol. 37 (December 1996) pp. 619–45; and M. Hakan Yavuz, "Search for a New Social Contract in Turkey: Fethullah Gülen, the Virtue Party and the Kurds," *SAIS Review*, vol. 19 (Winter-Spring 1999), pp. 114–43, esp. pp. 119–26.

25. "Controversy over Education Reform Heightens," *Turkish Daily News Electronic Edition*, July 30, 1997.

26. See the interview on education reform given by Minister of National Education Hikmet Uluğbay in Sirma Even, "Raising the Individual of the 21st Century with Equal Educational Opportunity for All," *Turkish Daily News Electronic Edition*, September 1,

1997. There is some relevance to this argument because empirical research shows that the inclination of voting non-Islamist depends to an important degree on the period of time voters have been exposed to secular education; see Ersin Kalaycıoğlu, "The Logic of Contemporary Turkish Politics," *Middle East Review of International Affairs (MERIA) Journal*, vol. 1 (September 1997) (www.biu.ac.il/soc/besa/meria [July 1999]).

27. Ayata, "Patronage, Party, and State," p. 43.

28. Şerif Mardin, "Center-Periphery Relations: A Key to Turkish Politics?" *Daedelus*, vol. 102 (Winter 1973), pp. 169–91.

29. Howard A. Reed, "Revival of Islam in Secular Turkey," *Middle East Journal*, vol. 8 (1954), pp. 267–82; and Bernard Lewis, "Islamic Revival in Turkey," *International Affairs*, vol. 28 (1952), pp. 38–48.

30. Sakallıoğlu, "Parameters and Strategy of Islam-State Interaction," pp. 236–42.

31. For details of this development see Ağaoğulları, *L'Islam dans la vie politique*, pp. 145–242.

32. "Campaign Secularism," *Briefing* 1227, January 18-25, 1999, pp. 14–15.

33. Nilüfer Narlı, "Moderate against Radical Islamicism in Turkey," *Zeitschrift für Turkeistudien*, vol. 9 (1996), p. 45.

34. Sami Zubaida, "Turkish Islam and National Identity," *Middle East Report*, vol. 26 (April-June 1996), pp. 10–15.

35. İhsan D. Dağı, "Islam, Politics and the Welfare Party," *Dış Politika/Foreign Policy*, vol. 19, nos. 3–4 (1995), pp. 17–28; and Ayata, "Patronage, Party and State," pp. 44ff.

36. Sunar and Toprak, "Islam in Politics," p. 432.

37. Sakallıoğlu, "Parameters and Strategy of Islam-State Interaction," p. 242.

38. Dagmar Zeller-Mohrlok, *Die Türkisch-Islamische Synthese: Eine Strategie zur Kanalisierung innen-politischer und wirtschaftlicher Konflikte der Türkei in den 80er Jahren* (Bonn: Holos Verlag, 1992).

39. "Campaign Secularism," *Briefing* 1227, January 18–25, 1999, p. 14. For a more differentiated discussion of the Turkish Islamic synthesis within the reemergence of Turkish political Islam, see Günter Seufert, *Politischer Islam in der Türkei. Islamismus als symbolische Repräsentation einer sich modernisierenden muslimischen Gesellschaft* (Istanbul: Franz Steiner Verlag, 1997), pp. 182–202.

40. Uğur Mumcu, *Rabıta* (Istanbul: Cumhuriyet, 1987); and Christian Rumpf, *Laizismus und Religionsfreiheit in der Türkei* (Ebenhausen: Stiftung Wissenschaft und Politik, 1987), pp. 133–57. *Rabıta* is the Turkish name of the Muslim World League.

41. Günter Seufert, *Café Istanbul: Alltag, Religion und Politik in der modernen Türkei* (Munich: Verlag C. H. Beck, 1997), p. 66.

42. Sakallıoğlu, "Parameters and Strategy of Islam-State Interaction," p. 247.

43. Ronnie Margulies and Ergin Yıldızoğlu, "The Political Uses of Islam in Turkey," *Middle East Report*, vol. 18 (July-August 1988), pp. 12–18; and Nilüfer Narlı, "The State, Religion and the Opposition in Turkey," *Zeitschrift für Türkeistudien*, vol. 4 (1991), pp. 27–43, esp. pp. 37–41.

44. He even avoided openly attacking the education reform of 1997 but found a clever way to adapt to it by adding primary schools to his existing lycees, thus circumventing the limits on teaching religion in the middle schools. Gülen's schools now offer a religious-oriented education from elementary school to the secondary level.

45. For instance, in an interview with the Turkish press, he compared the ousting of

the Erbakan-led coalition government by the military and other public forces to "cutting a gangrenous organ with the surgeon's knife" and stated that "the country has retreated from the edge of a cliff"; Uğur Akıncı, "Fetuallah Gülen: Go to Elections while Refah Is Sued," *Turkish Daily News Electronic Edition*, August 30, 1997.

46. In the same interview Gülen declared democracy "the most reasonable form of governance" for Turkey; Akıncı, "Fetuallah Gülen."

47. In February 1998 Gülen even visited Pope John Paul II in Rome to promote an interreligious dialogue among Christianity, Judaism, and Islam; "Gülen Says Meeting with Pope Fruitful," *Turkish Daily News Electronic Edition*, February 12, 1998.

48. "Refah Flails as New Social Project Wends Its Way," *Briefing* 1179, February 9, 1998, pp. 4–5.

49. "Revelations Hurt Gülen, Prosecutor Demands Punishment," *Turkish Daily News Electronic Edition*, June 21, 1999.

50. See also "Judgement Day for Fethullah Gülen," *Briefing* 1247, June 21, 1999, pp. 11–14.

51. "Islamic Capital, or Just Plain Capitalist?" *Briefing* 1229, February 8, 1999, pp. 9–11.

52. Z. Öniş, "The Political Economy of Islamic Resurgence in Turkey: The Rise of the Welfare Party in Perspective," *Third World Quarterly*, vol. 18 (September 1997) pp. 743–66, esp. pp. 757–61.

53. Seufert, *Politischer Islam in der Türkei*, pp. 395–402.

54. Rumpf, *Laizismus und Religionsfreiheit*, pp. 117–32.

55. Erhan Öztürk, "The Turban from Past to Present," *Turkish Daily News Electronic Edition*, December 25, 1998.

56. Michael E. Meeker, "The New Muslim Intellectuals in the Republic of Turkey," in R. Tapper, ed., *Islam in Modern Turkey*, pp. 189–219.

57. Heinz Kramer, "Die türkischen Wahlen vom 24.12.95," *KAS-Auslandsinformationen*, vol. 12 (1996), pp. 3–26.

58. Such a way of proceeding is not at all alien to Western countries if one remembers, for instance, the McCarthy era in the United States or the German policy of legally banning all communist organizations until the late 1960s. In more recent times, however, the habit of fighting deviant political positions by political instead of administrative means has been widely accepted in the West.

59. "The Refah Party Gets to Work on Secularism within the Civil Service," *Briefing* 1100, July 22, 1996, p. 1.

60. For details see Philip Robins, "Turkish Foreign Policy under Erbakan," *Survival*, vol. 39 (Summer 1997), pp. 82–100. The conspicuous neglect of Central Asia in RP foreign policy raises doubts about the validity of the thesis of "neo-Ottomanism" as the basic political concept of Turkish Islamists that recently has been developed by Bassım Tibi; see *Aufbruch am Bosporus*, passim.

61. Kemal Balcı, "Southeast Plan Cut, Security Tightened," *Turkish Daily News Electronic Edition*, August 29, 1996; Balcı, "Erbakan Unveils Southeast Plan," *Turkish Daily News Electronic Edition*, September 13, 1996; and Burhanettin Duran, "Approaching the Kurdish Question via *Adil Düzen*: An Islamist Formula of the Welfare Party for Ethnic Coexistence," *Journal of Muslim Minority Affairs*, vol. 18 (April 1998), pp. 111–28.

62. Ayla Ganıoğlu, "RP at a Crossroads," *Turkish Daily News Electronic Edition*, February 1, 1997.

63. Carol Migdalovitz, *Turkey's Unfolding Political Crisis*, CRS report 97-462 (Congressional Research Service, April 11, 1997), pp. 11-13.

64. "When the Campaign Agenda Becomes the Real Agenda," *Briefing* 1128, February 3, 1997, pp. 8–10.

65. November 10, 1938, the date of Atatürk's death, is commemorated with public ceremonies every year.

66. For a detailed discussion of these matters see "Army Delivers Calm for the Holidays," *Briefing* 1129, February 10, 1997, pp. 1, 4–7.

67. "Recommendations of the State Council Meeting and Comment," *Briefing* 1133, March 10, 1997, p. 4.

68. Metehan Demir, "Military Watchdog Group Monitors Spreading Fundamentalism," *Turkish Daily News Electronic Edition*, June 14, 1997

69. Heinz Kramer, *Türkei: Die Rückkehr zur Normalität* (Bonn: Friedrich-Ebert-Stiftung, 1997), pp. 2–4; and Ayşen Hiç Gencer, *Political and Economic Challenges Facing the New Turkish Government* (Ebenhausen: Stiftung Wissenschaft und Politik, 1998), pp. 9–13.

70. Metehan Demir, "Government and Armed Forces Should Work Cooperatively against Fundamentalism," *Turkish Daily News Electronic Edition*, September 13, 1997.

71. ". . . And They Closed Refah," *Turkish Daily News Electronic Edition*, January 17, 1998, and "RP Closure Decision Takes Effect," February 23, 1998.

72. Even Hüsamettin Cindoruk, a former close aid to President Demirel and chairman of the Democratic Turkey Party that was a partner in Mesut Yılmaz's three-coalition government, believed there was not sufficient legal evidence for abolishing the Welfare Party. "Cindoruk: Constitutional Court Made a Very Narrow Comment," *Turkish Daily News Electronic Edition*, February 25, 1998.

73. "Virtue Party Founds Group in Parliament," *Turkish Daily News Electronic Edition*, February 24, 1998.

74. Kemal Balcı, "Growing Pains in Virtue Not Over," *Turkish Daily News Electronic Edition*, May 16, 1998.

75. Alparslan Esmer, "Differences May Lead to Split in Virtue," *Turkish Daily News Electronic Edition*, May 27, 1998.

76. "Rectors' Committee: 'Wearing a Headscarf Is a Crime,'" *Turkish Daily News Electronic Edition*, March 14, 1998.

77. Stephen Kinzer, "The Battle for Secularism Moves to a Turkish Court," *International Herald Tribune*, April 6, 1998, p. 8.

78. "Anti-Terror Branch after Green Capital," *Turkish Daily News Electronic Edition*, April 22, 1998.

79. "DGM Demands MÜSİAD's Closure," *Turkish Daily News Electronic Edition*, May 25, 1998.

80. "MÜSİAD Chairman's Prison Term Postponed," *Turkish Daily News Electronic Edition*, April 23, 1999.

81. "Commission Endorses Bill Imposing Limitations on Mosque Construction," *Turkish Daily News Electronic Edition*, April 23, 1998; and "New Precautions Taken against Islamic Sects," *Turkish Daily News Electronic Edition*, May 7, 1998.

82. "RTÜK: Misuse of Religious Sentiments Is Unacceptable," *Turkish Daily News Electronic Edition*, March 24; and "HYK Discusses Technical Side of Struggle against

Fundamentalist, Separatist Broadcasting," *Turkish Daily News Electronic Edition*, April 4, 1998.

83. İlnur Çevik, "Are They Religious People or Extremists?" *Turkish Daily News Electronic Edition*, March 30, 1998.

84. Kemal Balcı, "Political Islam at the Focal Point of Politics," *Turkish Probe*, no. 311 (December 27, 1998) (38.242.79.170/past_probe/date.htm [August 1999]); and İlnur Çevik, ". . . And the Military Breaks Its Silence," *Turkish Daily News Electronic Edition*, January 6, 1999.

85. Alan Makovsky, "Turkey's National Moment," *Policy Watch*, no. 384 (April 20, 1999).

86. "Prosecutor Files Closure Case against Virtue," *Turkish Daily News Electronic Edition*, March 23, 1999.

87. For details of the events see "Merve and Her Scarf Prompt Application for Fazilet Closure," *Briefing* 1241, May 10, 1999, pp. 3, 6–7; and "Politicians 0; Justices 1," *Briefing* 1242, May 17, 1999, pp. 10–11.

88. Öniş, "Political Economy of Islamic Resurgence in Turkey," pp. 749–53.

89. Melih Yürüsen and Attila Yayla, *Die türkische Wohlfahrtspartei* (Sankt Augustin: Konrad-Adenauer-Stiftung, February 1997), pp. 35–49.

90. Seufert, *Politischer Islam in der Türkei*, p. 327.

91. Öniş, "Political Economy of Islamic Resurgence in Turkey," p. 755.

92. Türkei-Programm der Körber-Stiftung, *Religion—ein deutsch-türkisches Tabu?/ Türk-Alman ilişkilerinde din tabu mu?* (Hamburg, 1997), p. 117.

93. Philip Robins, "Political Islam in Turkey: The Rise of the Welfare Party," *JIME Review*, no. 28 (Spring 1995), p. 71.

94. Hakan Aslaneli, "Municipal Inspectors Split," *Turkish Daily News Electronic Edition*, August 5, 1997.

95. For details of Welfare's local policies see Uğur Akıncı, "The Welfare Party's Municipal Track Record: Evaluating Islamist Municipal Activism in Turkey," *Middle East Journal*, vol. 53 (Winter 1999), pp. 75–94.

96. Seufert, *Café Istanbul*, p. 148.

97. Heidi Wedel, "Politisch inszenierte Privatheit gegen 'Staatsfeminismus': Frauen in islamistischen Bewegungen der Republik Türkei," in Brigitte Kerchner and Gabriele Wilde, eds., *Staat und Privatheit* (Opladen: Verlag Leske + Budrich, 1997), p. 297–303.

98. Wedel, "Politisch inszenierte Privatheit," p. 301.

99. These were the conservative journalist Nazlı Ilıcak, a pronouncedly modern woman; Ankara professor of international relations Oya Akgönenç; and the computer engineer and devout Muslim Merve Kavakçı, who should become famous for the "turban scandal" that she provoked in parliament.

100. Seufert, *Politischer Islam in der Türkei*, p. 321–23.

101. Seufert, *Politischer Islam in der Türkei*, pp. 267–476.

102. Contrary to common belief, eastern Anatolia has not only recently become a "Welfare area" due to reactions to the state policy of martial suppression. It was already a "religious-politico" stronghold in the 1970s for the MSP; see Ağaoğulları, *L'Islam dans la vie politique*, pp. 303–09.

103. Metin Heper, "Islam and Democracy in Turkey: Toward a Reconciliation?" *Middle East Journal*, vol. 51 (Winter 1997), p. 45.

104. Jenny B. White, "Pragmatists or Ideologues? Turkey's Welfare Party in Power," *Current History*, vol. 96 (January 1997), pp. 28–29.

Chapter Six

1. The issues of democratic transformation and consolidation of democracy have generated a special branch in the discipline of comparative politics in which scholars try to develop a generally applicable body of explanation for these processes. The debate can be followed in detail in the *Journal of Democracy.* More recent attempts to summarize the state of the art can be found in Juan J. Linz and Alfred Stepan, *Problems of Democratic Transition and Consolidation: Southern Europe, South America and Post-Communist Europe* (Johns Hopkins University Press, 1996); and Laurence Whitehead, ed., *The International Dimension of Democratization: Europe and the America* (Oxford University Press, 1996).

2. George S. Harris, "The Role of the Military in Turkey in the 1980s: Guardians or Decision-Makers?" in Metin Heper and Ahmet Evin, eds., *State, Democracy and the Military: Turkey in the 1980s* (Walter de Gruyter, 1988) , pp. 177–200.

3. On exclusion see Charles Taylor, "The Dynamics of Democratic Exclusion," *Journal of Democracy*, vol. 9 (October 1998), pp. 143–56.

4. Menderes Çınar, "Rebuilding the Center: Mission Impossible?" *Private View*, vol. 1/2 (Autumn 1997), pp. 72–78.

5. Morton Abramowitz in a remark at the 109th Round Table, "Bergedorfer Gesprächskreis," 24–25 May, 1997, in Istanbul; see Körber-Stiftung, ed., *At the Crossroads of Geo-politics: Turkey in a Changing Political Environment* (Hamburg, 1997), p. 88.

6. Ergun Özbudun, "Turkey: How Far from Consolidation?" *Journal of Democracy*, vol. 7 (July 1996), p. 127.

7. Heinz Kramer, "Die türkischen Wahlen vom 24.12.1995," *KAS-Auslandsinformationen*, vol 12 (1996), pp. 3–26.

8. Ersin Kalaycıoğlu, "The Logic of Contemporary Turkish Politics," *Middle East Review of International Affairs (MERIA) Journal*, vol. 1 (September 1997) (www.biu.ac.il/SOC/besa/ meria [August 1999]).

9. See, for instance, "Yılmaz and Cindoruk Seal the Deal," *Briefing* 1198, June 29, 1998, pp. 1, 4–5.

10. "RP Extends Conditional Support to Presidential System," *Turkish Daily News Electronic Edition*, September 19, 1997 (www.turkishdailynews.com [August 1999]).

11. A noteworthy exception from the mainstream of the state elite's approach to Turkey's pressing political problems has been the speech of Necdet Sezer, chief justice of the Constitutional Court, at the court's thirty-seventh anniversary on April 27, 1999, in which he vehemently emphasized the necessity of drastic legal reforms to strengthen Turkey's democratic performance, especially with regard to the guarantee of freedom of expression. For details see "Sezer: Thought Crimes Have No Place in a Democracy," *Briefing* 1240, May 3, 1999, pp. 10–12; and Fehmi Koru, "Yes Sir, We Have Honorable Judges, Too . . ." *Turkish Daily News Electronic Edition*, April 28, 1999.

Part Two

1. Alan Makovsky, "The New Activism in Turkish Foreign Policy," *SAIS Review*, vol. 19 (Winter-Spring 1999), pp. 92–113.

2. Mehmet Öğütçü, "'Surgical Operation' to Heal Turco-Syrian Rift," *Turkish Daily News Electronic Edition*, October 8, 1998 [August 1999]).

3. Öğütçü, "Surgical Operation."

4. See, for instance, Hüseyin Bağcı, "Turkey's Foreign Policy in a Changing Strategic and Regional Environment," *Informationen zur Sicherheitspolitik*, no. 5 (*Die Türkei und Europa*) (Vienna: Militärwissenschaftliches Büro, Bundesministerium für Landesverteidigung, February 1998), pp. 20–32; and Ziya Öniş, "Turkey in the Post-Cold War Era: In Search of Identity," *Middle East Journal*, vol. 49 (Winter 1995), pp. 48–68.

5. As regards the DSP, this approach is a continuation of Ecevit's "multidimensional foreign policy" of the 1970s, which at the time put more emphasis on "Third Worldism" and opening up toward the Soviet Union. For details see Michael M. Boll, "Turkey's New National Security Concept: What It Means for NATO," *Orbis*, vol. 23 (Fall 1979), pp. 609–31.

6. For details see "Coalition Government Programme: Programme of the 57th Government, Presented to the Turkish Grand National Assembly by Prime Minister Bülent Ecevit" June 4, 1999 (www.byegm.gov.tr/57hukumet/programme.htm [July 1999]).

Chapter Seven

1. See Heinz Kramer, "Will Central Asia Become Turkey's Sphere of Influence?" *Perceptions*, vol. 1 (March-May 1996), pp. 112–27; and Bilal N. Simşir, "Turkey's Relations with the Central Asian Turkic Republics," *Turkish Review: Quarterly Digest*, vol. 6 (Summer 1992), pp. 11–15.

2. Elkhan E. Nuriyev, "The Ongoing Geopolitical Game in the Caucasus and the Caspian Basin: Towards War or Peace?" Lecture at the Center for Russian and Eurasian Studies of the Monterey Institute of International Studies, February 18, 1999 (www.cns.miis.edu/cres/nuriyev.htm [July 1999]).

3. For a comprehensive account of the development of Turkey's relations with the new republics in Central Asia up to the mid-1990s see Garreth M. Winrow, *Turkey in Post-Soviet Central Asia* (London: Royal Institute of International Affairs, 1995); and Philip Robins, "Between Sentiment and Self-Interest: Turkey's Policy toward Azerbaijan and the Central Asian States," *Middle East Journal*, vol. 47 (Autumn 1993), pp. 593–610.

4. Mehmet Öğütçü, "Religious 'Bias' in the West against Islam: Turkey as a Bridge in Between," *Dış Politika/Foreign Policy*, vol.18 (1994), pp. 87–119, esp. pp. 105–08.

5. See Hakkan Kirimli, "Turkey and the Turkic World: A Reappraisal," paper prepared for the conference on The Central Asian Region: Potential Conflicts and Perspectives, Ebenhausen, November 9–11, 1994, p. 6f.

6. See Gareth M. Winrow, "Turkey and the Newly Independent States of Central Asia and the Transcaucasus," *Middle East Review of International Affairs (MERIA) Journal*, vol. 1 (July 1997) (www.biu.ac.il/SOC/besa/meria [July 27, 1999]).

7. "First Summit of Turkic Leaders Opens in Ankara," *Turkish Daily News*, October 31, 1992.

8. Robert S. Greenberger, "Baker Is Wooing Central Asian Republics," *Wall Street Journal*, February 14, 1992, p. A8.

9. See Duygu B. Sezer, "Turkey's Grand Strategy Facing a Dilemma," *International Spectator* (Rome), vol. 27 (1992), pp. 17–32.

10. Ola Tunander, "A New Ottoman Empire? The Choice for Turkey: Euro-Asian Centre vs. National Fortress," *Security Dialogue*, vol. 26 (1995), p. 414.

11. The most prominent example of this new geopolitics of Eurasia is Zbigniew Brzezinski, *The Grand Chessboard: American Primacy and Its Geostrategic Imperatives* (HarperCollins, 1997), esp. pp. 30–56. Until recently a Caspian basin area defined by a set of common features did not exist. This geopolitical region emerged after the demise of the Soviet Union. It is basically defined by the dynamics and commonalities that spring from the search of the new republics of Azerbaijan, Turkmenistan, Kazakhstan, Georgia, and to some extent Armenia to establish outlets for the energy resources of the area and attract international investments independently of Russian decisions. See Friedemann Müller, *Machtpolitik am Kaspischen Meer* (Ebenhausen: Stiftung Wissenschaft und Politik, 1999), pp. 9–13.

12. İsmail Cem, "Turkey: Setting Sail to the 21st Century," *Perceptions*, vol. 2 (September-November 1997), pp. 5–12. Even more certain of Turkey's Eurasian future is the preface to a booklet published by the Turkish Ministry of Foreign Affairs in July 1998. Foreign Minister Cem stated: "Contemporary Turkey aspires to be the leading economic and political actor in Eurasia." *Turkey and the World, 2010–2020: Emergence of a Global Actor* (Ankara: DIVAK, 1998), p. 3.

13. Bess Brown and Elizabeth Fuller, *Die Türkei und die muslimischen Republiken der ehemaligen Sowjetunion*, Internal Studies 84/1994 (Sankt Augustin: Konrad-Adenauer-Stiftung, 1994), pp. 17–18.

14. *Turkish Daily News*, May 4, 1992.

15. See Stephen Blank, "Energy, Economics, and Security in Central Asia: Russia and Its Rivals," *Central Asian Survey*, vol. 14 (1995), pp. 373–406. For a more balanced analysis of Russian interests in the region see Stephan de Spiegeleire, "Russian Responses to Possible EU Policy Initiatives in the Caucasus," in Friedemann Müller and Claude Zullo, eds., *The European Union and the Caucasus Region: Oil, Interests, and Influence*, SWP-S 427 (Ebenhausen: SWP, 1998), pp. 101–22, esp. 103–15.

16. For details see Suha Bölükbaşı, "Ankara's Baku-Centered Transcaucasia Policy: Has it Failed?" *Middle East Journal*, vol. 51 (Winter 1997), pp. 80–94.

17. Nuriyev, "Ongoing Geopolitical Game."

18. Although first, perhaps politically motivated, assumptions about the dimension of the Caspian oil reserves have been considerably questioned, there is no doubt that the region's contribution to the world energy market of the twenty-first century will at least amount to the size of the North Sea oil reserves. Thus it may well be exaggerated to talk of a new Kuwait, but one cannot neglect the Caspian's contribution to world energy in the decades to come. International Energy Agency (IEA), *Caspian Oil and Gas: The Supply Potential of Central Asia and Transcaucasia* (Paris, 1998); and Amy Myers Jaffe and Robert A. Manning, "The Myth of the Caspian 'Great Game': The Real Geopolitics of Energy," *Survival*, vol. 40 (Winter 1998-99), pp. 112–29.

19. See Temel İskit, "Turkey: A New Actor in the Field of Energy Politics?" *Perceptions*, vol. 1 (March-May 1996), pp. 58–82.

20. William Hale, "Turkey: Economic Issues and Foreign Policy," London, 1997, pp. 8–9. See also "Trans-Caspian Gas: Whoever Dares, Wins," *Turkish Probe Electronic Edition*, no. 326 (April 11, 1999) (http://38.242.79.170/past_probe/date.htm [August 1999]).

21. www.gasandoil.com/goc/news/ntc84429.htm [December 1999].

22. İskit, "Turkey: A New Actor," pp. 68–70.

23. For an overview of the complicated pipeline game in the Caspian Sea region see Geoffrey Kemp and Robert E. Harkavy, *Strategic Geography and the Changing Middle East* (Washington: Carnegie Endowment for International Peace and Brookings Institution Press, 1997), pp. 131–53; and Müller, *Machtpolitik am Kaspischen Meer*, pp. 18–20.

24. Müller, *Machtpolitik am Kaspischen Meer*, p. 19.

25. İskit, "Turkey: A New Actor," p. 79.

26. For details see Suha Bölükbaşı, "The Controversy over the Caspian Sea Mineral Resources: Conflicting Perceptions, Clashing Interests," *Europe-Asia Studies*, vol. 50 (May 1998), pp. 397–414, esp. pp. 404–05.

27. For details of the political and security risks concerning the future development of the region see S. Neil MacFarlane and Claude Zullo, "Petroleum and Politics in the Caucasus: New Wine in Old Bottles?" in Müller and Zullo, eds., *European Union and the Caucasus Region*, pp. 21–46; Vicken Cheterian, "Oil, Pipelines, and Security in the Caucasus," in Müller and Zullo, eds., *European Union and the Caucasus Region*, pp. 47–57; and Ariel Cohen, "Ethnic Conflicts Threaten U.S. Interests in the Caucasus," Heritage Foundation Backgrounder 1222, September 25, 1998, provided by *Turkistan Newsletter*, October 2, 1998 (www.euronet.nl/users/sota/turkistan.htm [October 1998]).

28. Michael Lelyveld, "Caucasus: U.S. Military Presence in Caspian Appears Inevitable," Radio Free Europe/Radio Liberty, February 4, 1999 (www.rferl.org [August 1999]); *Turkish Daily News Electronic Edition*, January 31, 1999 (www.turkishdailynews.com [August 1999]); and Nuriyev, *Ongoing Geopolitical Game*.

29. The slump in oil prices that appeared in 1998, and the downward revision of estimated oil reserves in the Caspian area, especially in Azerbaijan, made Baku-Ceyhan less economically attractive. As long as uncertainty prevails as to whether Azerbaijan will produce enough oil in the long term or whether oil from other sources could be added to the Azerbaijani oil to fill the projected pipeline, the AIOC remains reluctant to make a final decision on the main exporting pipeline. See, Thomas Goltz, "Back in Baku: Watching a Boom Go Bust," *Washington Quarterly*, vol. 22 (Summer 1999), pp. 67–87; Bhusan Bahree, "Turkey Wants Caspian Oil Pipeline," *Wall Street Journal*, November 9, 1998; and Charles Recknagel, "1998 in Review: Slump in Prices Could Delay Caspian Oil Boom," Radio Free Europe/Radio Liberty, December 17, 1998.

30. Ambassador Richard Morningstar, special advisor to the president and secretary of state for Caspian basin energy development, address at Kent State University, November 23, 1998 (www.state.gov/www/policy_remarks/1998/981123_mrngstar_caspian.html [August 1999]).

31. Stephen Kinzer, "Caspian Pipeline Tug-of-War: Washington Favors Geopolitics over Economics," *International Herald Tribune*, November 11, 1998, p. 10.

32. "Europe Said Interested in Pipeline Skirting Iran," *Turkistan Newsletter*, February 25, 1998.

33. "U.S. Interests in the Central Asian Republics," testimony of Robert W. Gee,

assistant secretary of energy for policy and international affairs before the Subcommittee on Asia and the Pacific of the House International Relations Committee, 105 Cong, 2 sess, February 12, 1998. Appeared in *Turkistan Newsletter*, February 18, 1998.

34. Yasemin Dobra-Manco, "US Officials at TDA Conference Express Unprecedented Support for Turkey and Baku-Ceyhan Pipeline," *Turkish Daily News Electronic Edition*, May 29, 1998.

35. See Winrow, "Turkey and the Newly Independent States."

36. Uğur Akıncı, "PCF Report: Baku-Ceyhan Pipeline Is Bad Choice," *Turkish Daily News Electronic Edition*, May 19, 1998.

37. "Guarded Optimism over Pipeline Issue," *Briefing* 1192, May 18, 1998, pp. 13–14.

38. "Turkish Caspian Policy Paying Dividends," *Briefing* 1183, March 9, 1998, p. 14; and "Sense and Consistency for Baku-Ceyhan," *Briefing* 1190, May 4, 1998, p. 15.

39. "Aliyev: 'Final Decision on Baku-Ceyhan Has Been Made,'" *Turkish Daily News Electronic Edition*, November 1, 1998.

40. "Caspian Oil . . . Maybe in the Next World, Maybe Earlier," *Turkish Probe Electronic Edition*, no. 326 (April 11, 1999); and Michael Lelyveld, "Azerbaijan/Turkey: Obstacles Remain in Pipeline Policy," Radio Free Europe/Radio Liberty, April 20, 1999.

41. Bülent Gökay, "Caspian Uncertainties: Regional Rivalries and Pipelines," *Perceptions*, vol. 3 (March-May 1998), p. 61. "The Bosphorus and the Dardanelles are not crude oil pipelines," declared Turkish Foreign Ministry spokesman Necati Utkan when he outlined that, according to Turkish data, 4,248 tankers had passed through the Bosphorus in 1996; see Orya Sultan Halisdemir, "Turkey: Straits not Crude Oil Pipeline," *Turkish Daily News Electronic Edition*, November 27, 1997.

42. Orya Sultan Halisdemir, "IMO Committee: 1994 Straits Act," *Turkish Daily News Electronic Edition*, November 22, 1997; Halisdemir, "IMO Asks Turkey to Abolish Straits Act," November 26, 1997; and Halisdemir, "Turkey," November 27, 1997.

43. See Erkaya's interview on the issue in Saadet Oruç, "The Czars Are Dead But Their Dreams Are Still Alive," *Turkish Daily New Electronic Edition*, April 29, 1998.

44. Orya Sultan Halisdemir, "IMO to Debate Turkey's Policy on the Straits," *Turkish Daily News Electronic Edition*, May 19, 1999.

45. Yasemin Dobra-Manco, "SMITHSONIAN calls Bophorous a Disaster Waiting to Happen," *Turkish Daily News Electronic Edition*, December 15, 1998.

46. James M. Dorsey, "Back Oil Firms to Keep Turkey Strong," *Wall Street Journal*, February 11, 1999, p. 8; and Michael Lelyveld, "Caspian: Politicians Warn Oil Producers of Dangers Ahead," Radio Free Europe/Radio Liberty, November 24, 1998.

47. Jaffe and Manning, "Myth of the Caspian 'Great Game,'" pp. 117–18.

48. *Turkistan Newsletter*, December 11, 1998.

49. Martha Brill Olcott, "The Caspian's False Promise," *Foreign Policy*, no. 111 (Summer 1998), pp. 95–113.

50. See Uğur Akıncı, "Baku-Ceyhan Gets Mega-Boost from US," *Turkish Daily News Electronic Edition*, November 21, 1997.

51. "Turkish-Turkmen Natural Gas Pipeline Agreement Signed," *Turkish Daily News Electronic Edition*, May 22, 1999.

52. Atila Eralp, "Facing the Challenge: Post-Revolutionary Relations with Iran," in Henri J. Barkey, ed., *Reluctant Neighbor: Turkey's Role in the Middle East* (Washington: United States Institute of Peace Press, 1997), pp. 93–112.

53. Nezihi Çakar, "A Strategic Overview of Turkey," *Perceptions*, vol. 3 (June-August 1998), pp. 5–15.

54. Turkish Ministry of Foreign Affairs, *Relations with the Central Asian Republics* (www.mfa.gov.tr/grupa/ae/asian.htm [August 1999]); and Erol Manisalı, "Turkey's Economic Relations with the Caucasus and Asian Turkish Republics," *Foreign Policy*, vol. 21 (1997), pp. 65–75.

55. See Turkish International Cooperation Agency, *Annual Report 1995* (Ankara, 1994ff).

56. According to Boric Shikhmuradov, Turkmenistan's minister of foreign affairs, Turkish industry was instrumental in establishing the new Turkmen textile industry; Uğur Akıncı, "Turkmen FM: Turkey Is One of the Main Pillars of Our Independent Development," *Turkish Daily News Electronic Edition*, October 8, 1997.

57. See, for instance, Jonathan Rugman, "The East Is Ours, Say Turkish Dreamers," *Observer*, March 1, 1992; or Nuri Eren, "The Turkic Republics and the Contributions of Turkey," *Turkish Daily News*, July 20, 1992.

58. Turkish International Cooperation Agency, "Development of Trade between Turkey and Central Asian Republics," Ankara, November 1997; and "Turkey's Foreign Trade by Principal Sectors, Country and Commodity Groups, 97–98 and 98–January 99," *Briefing* 1233, March 8, 1999, pp. 36–37. These figures are based on preliminary results of official statistics; they do not include "unofficial trade."

59. Hale, *Turkey: Economic Issues*, p. 5.

60. If one takes GDP as an indicator of market size and economic potential, one has to realize that the combined GDP of the three energy-rich Caspian states, Azerbaijan, Kazakhstan, and Turkmenistan in 1996 of U.S.$ 23.4 billion was about that of Bremen, the smallest of Germany's Länder. Friedemann Müller, "The Influence of Petroleum on Stability in the Caspian Region," in Müller and Zullo, eds., *European Union and the Caucasus Region*, pp. 86–97, esp. p. 87.

61. Büşra Ersanlı Behar, "Rediscovering Multidimensionality: Turkey's Quest for Partnership with the Turkic Republics," *Private View* (Istanbul), vol. 1 (Winter 1997), pp. 60–64.

62. See, for instance, the interview of the Turkmen foreign minister with *Turkish Daily News Electronic Edition*, October 8, 1997, in which he stated that these schools "are contributing to our nation-building process."

63. Winrow, "Turkey and the Newly Independent States."

64. "Bursa Hosts Turks from the Adriatic to the Great Wall of China," *Turkish Daily News Electronic Edition*, March 21, 1998.

65. In May 1998 the directorate organized the third Islamic Council of Eurasia, which gathered forty-eight religious dignitaries of "moderate" Muslim background from the Balkans, the CIS, including the Russian Federation, and Turkey. These regular meetings are intended to reduce the influence of extremist religious Islamic organizations and states in the "Turkic world." "Third Eurasian Council Held in Ankara," *Turkish Daily News Electronic Edition*, May 26, 1998.

66. Bölükbaşı, "Controversy over the Caspian Sea," pp. 408–12.

67. For details see Svante E. Cornell, "Turkey and the Conflict in Nagorno Karabakh: A Delicate Balance," *Middle Eastern Studies*, vol. 34 (January 1998), pp. 51–72.

Chapter Eight

1. Soli Özel, "Of Not Being a Lone Wolf: Geography, Domestic Plays, and Turkish Foreign Policy in the Middle East," in Geoffrey Kemp and Janice Gross Stein, eds., *Powder Keg in the Middle East: The Struggle for Gulf Security* (Washington: American Association for the Advancement of Science, 1995), p. 164.

2. Duygu Bazoğlu Sezer, "Turkey's Political and Security Interests and Policies in the New Geostrategic Environment of the Expanded Middle East," Occasional Paper 19 (Washington: Henry L. Stimson Center, 1994), pp. 2–5.

3. Özel, "Of Not Being a Lone Wolf," pp. 167–71.

4. Sabri Sayarı, "Turkey: The Changing European Security Environment and the Gulf Crisis," *Middle East Journal*, vol. 46 (Winter 1992), pp. 9–21, esp. pp.16–20.

5. Gülnur Aybet, "Turkey in Its Geo-Strategic Environment," in Royal United Services Institute for Defence Studies, London, ed., *RUSI and Brassey's Defence Yearbook 1992* (Washington: Brassey's, 1992), p. 100.

6. Bilge Criss and Pinar Bilgin, "Turkish Foreign Policy toward the Middle East," *Middle East Review in International Affairs (MERIA) Journal*, vol. 1 (January 1997), (www.biu.ac.il/ SOC/besa/meria [August 1999]).

7. See also the lecture "Turkey and the Middle East: Policy and Prospects," given by Oğuz Çelikkol, a high official from the Turkish Ministry of Foreign Affairs, to The Washington Instutute for Near East Policy, Washington, April 6, 1998; (www.washingtoninstitute.org/media/celikkol.htm [August 1999]).

8. For a discussion of Özal's policy in the Persian Gulf crisis of 1990 see Philip Robins, "Turkish Policy and the Gulf Crisis: Adventurist or Dynamic?" in Clement H. Dodd, ed., *Turkish Foreign Policy: New Prospects* (Huntingdon: Eothen Press, 1992), pp. 70–87.

9. William Hale, "Turkey, the Middle East and the Gulf Crisis," *International Affairs*, vol. 68 (October 1992), pp. 679–92, esp. p. 686.

10. There had already been use of Turkish bases for U.S. activities in Middle Eastern crises such as the rescue of American personnel from Lebanon in 1982, but Turkey had always been eager not to become involved in direct military activities.

11. For an explanation of domestic motives of Özal's approach, see Nicole Pope and Hugh Pope, *Turkey Unveiled: A History of Modern Turkey* (London: John Murray, 1999), pp. 198–244.

12. Özel, "Of Not Being a Lone Wolf," p. 170.

13. Sayarı, "Turkey: The Changing European Security Environment," p. 14.

14. Kemal Kirişçi, "Provide Comfort and Turkey: Decision Making for Refugee Assistance," *Low Intensity Conflict and Law Enforcement*, vol. 2 (Autumn 1993).

15. Ronald Ofteringer and Ralf Bäcker, "A Republic of Statelessness," *Middle East Report*, vol. 24 (March-June 1994), pp. 40–45; and Isam al-Khafaji, "The Destruction of Iraqi Kurdistan," *Middle East Report*, vol. 26 (Fall 1996), pp. 35–38, 42.

16. The history of this rivalry is described at some length by David McDowall, *A Modern History of the Kurds* (I. B. Tauris, 1996), pp. 302–91.

17. Sheri Laizer, *Martyrs, Traitors and Patriots: Kurdistan after the Gulf War* (London: Zed Books, 1996), pp. 123–36. This division also roughly coincides with the linguistic division among Kurmanji- and Surani-speaking Kurdish tribes, the two main Kurdish dialects of northern Iraq.

18. Mahmut Bali Aykan, "Turkey's Policy in Northern Iraq, 1991–1995," *Middle Eastern Studies*, vol. 32 (October 1996), pp. 343–66, esp. p. 357.

19. Quoted by Kemal Kirişçi, "Turkey and the Kurdish Safe-Haven in Northern Iraq," *Journal of South Asian and Middle Eastern Studies*, vol. 19 (Spring 1996), p. 31. This function even included providing Barzani and Talabani with Turkish diplomatic passports.

20. For details see Michael M. Gunter, "The KDP-PUK Conflict in Northern Iraq," *Middle East Journal*, vol. 50 (Spring 1996), pp. 225–41.

21. "Operation Queried at Home and Abroad," *Briefing* 1034, March 27, 1995, pp. 8–11; "First Troops Out after Week of Diplomacy," *Briefing* 1036, April 10, 1995, pp. 8–10; and "Operation over; Border Security Talks Continue," *Briefing* 1040, May 8-15, 1995, pp. 3–4.

22. Henri J. Barkey, "Kurdish Geopolitics," *Current History*, vol. 96 (January 1997), pp. 1–5.

23. Harvey Sichermann, "America's Alliance Anxiety: The Strange Death of Dual Containment," *Orbis*, vol. 41 (Spring 1997), pp. 223–40, esp. pp. 236–38.

24. F. Stephen Larrabee, "U.S. and European Policy toward Turkey and the Caspian Basin," in Robert D. Blackwill and Michael Stürmer, eds., *Allies Divided: Transatlantic Policies for the Greater Middle East* (MIT Press, 1997), pp. 143–73, esp. pp. 153–54. See also "Operation Provide Comfort," *Turkish Daily News Electronic Edition*, December 27, 1996 (www.turkishdailynews.com [August 1999]); and Raşıt Gürdilek, "US Emerges Chief Loser from Kurd Fight," *Turkish Daily News Electronic Edition*, January 15, 1997.

25. "UN Approves Start of Oil-for-Food Deal," *Turkish Daily News Electronic Edition*, December 10, 1996.

26. Metehan Demir and Saadet Oruç, "Turkish Army's Annual Spring Clean in N. Iraq," *Turkish Daily News Electronic Edition*, May 26, 1997.

27. Harun Kazaz, "Final Statement of the Leaders' Meeting September 17, 1998," *Turkish Daily News Electronic Edition*, October 5, 1998; and Alan Makovsky, "Kurdish Agreement Signals New U.S. Commitment," *Policy Watch*, no. 341 (September 29, 1998).

28. İlnur Çevik, "US on the Iraqi Kurdish Accord: Give Us the Benefit of the Doubt," *Turkish Daily News Electronic Edition*, September 30, 1998. For an American attempt to remove Turkish concerns see "Welch Worldnet 'Dialogue' on Northern Iraq Accord," *USIS Washington File*, October 19, 1998 (www.usia.gov/regional/nea/gulfsec/welch101.htm [August 1999]).

29. Ministry of Foreign Affairs, "Statement Made by İsmail Cem, Foreign Minister, on the Special Security Meeting Held between Turkey and Syria," Ankara, October 20, 1998; (www.mfa.gov.tr/grupb/ba/baa98/october/02.htm [August 1999]). For an analysis of the events see Alan Makovsky, "Defusing the Turkish-Syrian Crisis," *Middle East Insight* (January-February 1999), pp. 15–16; and Gülistan Gürbey, "Die türkisch-syrische Krise: Nur eine Kriegsdrohung?" *Südosteuropa-Mitteilungen*, vol. 38 (1998), pp. 349–59.

30. Saadet Oruç, "Political Missiles Open a New Page in Turkish Policy on Iraq," *Turkish Daily News Electronic Edition*, January 23, 1999.

31. *Turkish Daily News Electronic Edition*, January 31, 1999.

32. Saadet Oruç, "Öcalan Overshadows Tariq Aziz's Visit," *Turkish Probe*, no. 319 (February 21, 1999).

33. Harun Kazaz, "Turkey's Reaction to Iraqi Opposition Visit Not Understood in Washington," *Turkish Daily News Electronic Edition*, May 27, 1999.

34. Statement by a Turkish diplomat of the Foreign Ministry in October 1997, quoted in Alain Gresh, "Turkish-Israeli-Syrian Relations and Their Impact on the Middle East," *Middle East Journal*, vol. 52 (Spring 1998), pp. 194–95.

35. Aykan, "Turkey's Policy in Northern Iraq," pp. 352–62.

36. A striking example of this attitude was allegations by Deputy Prime Minister and Foreign Policy Coordinator Bülent Ecevit during the Iraq crisis in early 1998 in which he suspected Great Britain of having a covert intent to set up a separate state in Kurdish northern Iraq; see "Ankara Meets on Crisis Agenda on Brink of Sustained US Strike," *Turkish Daily News Electronic Edition*, February 18, 1998.

37. See, for instance, "Regional Security Plan—Proposal of the Democratic Left Party for Replacing the 'Operation Provide Comfort,'" paper presented to the Turkish public by the party chairman Bülent Ecevit on April 15, 1996.

38. Mahmut B. Aykan; "Turkish Perspectives on Turkish-US Relations Concerning Persian Gulf Security in the Post–Cold War Era: 1989–1995," *Middle East Journal*, vol. 50 (Summer 1996), p. 353.

39. There are even voices to be heard in Turkish political circles that "unemployment [in the southeast] is increasingly feeding the activities of the Kurdistan Workers Party (PKK)."; Mehmet Ali Birand, "Is There a New Role for Turkey in the Middle East?" in Henri J. Barkey, ed., *Reluctant Neighbor: Turkey's Role in the Middle East* (Washington: United States Institute of Peace Press, 1996), p. 174. In this view Turkey's "terrorist problem" is mostly caused by the U.S.-led Iraq policy of the international community.

40. For details see "Turkey Poised for Gulf Explosion," *Briefing* 1179, February 9, 1998, pp. 8–10; and "Foreign Plots and a Little Paranoia," *Briefing* 1180, February 16, 1998, pp. 12–13.

41. Birand, "Is There a New Role for Turkey?" p. 174.

42. For a comprehensive discussion of Turkish-Iraeli relations since the late 1980s see George E. Gruen, "Turkey and the Middle East after Oslo I," in Robert O. Freedman, ed., *The Middle East and the Peace Process: The Impact of the Oslo Accords* (University Press of Florida, 1998), pp. 169–212.

43. Nadia E. El-Shazly, "Arab Anger at New Axis," *World Today*, vol. 55 (January 1999), pp. 25–27, esp. p. 27.

44. İlnur Çevik, "Turkey-Israel Forge Closer Ties," *Turkish Probe*, no. 170 (March 15, 1996), p. 16; Çevik, "Turkey Gets Its Way at the Anti-Terrorism Summit," *Turkish Probe*, no. 170 (March 15, 1996), p. 17; and Burak Bekdil, "Turkey, Israel Move Closer to Customs Pact," *Turkish Probe*, no. 170 (March 15, 1996), p. 24. The Free Trade Agreement was complemented by an agreement to prohibit double taxation and another to promote and protect investments. For the military cooperation agreement see Raşıt Gürdilek, "What's So Wrong with Some Mutual Back-Scratching?" *Turkish Probe*, no. 174 (April 12, 1996), p. 10.

45. Saadet Oruç, "Turkish Trade via Israel to the United States Expected to Boost Export Volume," *Turkish Daily News Electronic Edition*, January 5, 1999.

46. Alparslan Esmer, "Israel-Turkey Business Council: Hoping to Bridge Two Countries," *Turkish Daily News Electronic Edition* (Israel supplement), September 8,

1998; and "Turkey's Foreign Trade by Selected [Sectors] and Countries in January-December, 1998," *Briefing* 1233, March 8, 1999, p. 37.

47. Metin Demirsar, "Israeli Tourists Flock to Turkey", *Turkish Daily News Electronic Edition* (Israel supplement), September 8, 1998.

48. Michael Eisenstadt, "Turkish-Israeli Military Cooperation: An Assessment," *Policy Watch*, no. 262 (July 24, 1997).

49. See "Ambassador Kandemir: Turkey May Allow Israel to Retaliate against Iraq," *Turkish Daily News Electronic Edition*, February 21, 1998.

50. Saadet Oruç, "Will Jordan Become the Third Party in Turco-Israeli Partnership?" *Turkish Daily News Electronic Edition*, June 4, 1998.

51. Saadet Oruç and Metehan Demir, "Growing Turkish-Jordanian Military Ties Worry Arabs," *Turkish Daily News Electronic Edition*, April 23, 1998.

52. Uğur Akıncı, "King Hussein: No Plans to Join Turkish-Israeli Military Cooperation," *Turkish Daily News Electronic Edition*, March 20, 1998.

53. Saadet Oruç, "Turkish-Israeli Ties on the Eve of the 21st Century (Part 1)," *Turkish Daily News Electronic Edition*, December 3, 1997.

54. David Eshel and Selçük Emre, "Turkey, Israel to Co-operate in Missile Defence System," *Jane's Defence Weekly*, April 29, 1998, p. 3.

55. Metehan Demir, "Turkey, Israel to Hold Strategic Talks in May to Evaluate Threats," *Turkish Daily News Electronic Edition*, April 22, 1998.

56. Alparslan Esmer, "No S-300 Missiles in Israel's Negev Desert," *Turkish Daily News Electronic Edition*, July 15, 1998.

57. Daniel Pipes, "A New Axis: The Emerging Turkish-Israeli Entente," *National Interest*, no. 50 (Winter 1997–98), p. 38.

58. "Arab League: Turkey Should Review Its Cooperation with Israel," *Turkish Daily News Electronic Edition*, March 27, 1998.

59. For an assessment of Iran's capabilities in weapons of mass destruction see W. Seth Carus, "Iranian Nuclear, Biological and Chemical Weapons: Implications and Responses," *Middle East Review of International Affairs (MERIA) Journal*, vol. 2 (March 1998) (www.biu.ac.il/SOC/besa/meria [August 1999]).

60. Şükrü Elekdağ, "2½ War Strategy," *Perceptions*, vol. 3 (March-May 1996), pp. 51–52.

61. Gresh, "Turkish-Israeli-Syrian Relations," pp. 192–96; and Gruen, "Turkey and the Middle East," pp. 193–95.

62. In late 1996 Prime Minister Erbakan tried in vain to stall an agreement on upgrading Turkish F-4 fighter planes by the Israeli Aircraft Industries. He was regularly left out of the political process according to a high-ranking military official, who shortly before the end of the Refahyol coalition asked the Turkish press, "Since when, up to now, has the Prime Minister played a role in the decision-making process in relations with Israel?" Metehan Demir, "Erbakan's Remarks over Maneuvers with Israel Stir Controversy," *Turkish Daily News Electronic Edition*, May 15, 1997.

63. Alparslan Esmer, "Caught in Mideast Quandary," *Turkish Probe*, July 12, 1998.

64. Pipes, "New Axis," p. 38.

65. For geographical, hydrological, and economic details of the Euphrates-Tigris basin see Nurit Kliot, *Water Resources and Conflict in the Middle East* (Routledge, 1994), pp. 100–72.

66. With respect to the Tigris, Iran, too, is of importance because of its control of some tributaries such as the Lesser Zab. Until now, this has not caused any problems in Iranian-Iraqi relations. That could change, however, if Tehran would begin using the waters of the Lesser Zab for irrigation or hydroelectric energy, thus curtailing the amount of Tigris water available to Iraq.

67. John Kolars, "Managing the Impact of Development: The Euphrates and Tigris Rivers and the Ecology of the Arabian Gulf—A Link in Foreign Tri-Riparian Cooperation," in Ali İhsan Bağış, ed., *Water as an Element of Cooperation and Development in the Middle East* (Ankara: Hacettepe University and Friedrich-Naumann-Foundation, 1994), pp. 129–53.

68. Murhaf Jouejati, "Water Politics as High Politics: The Case of Turkey and Syria," in Barkey, ed., *Reluctant Neighbor*, p. 133.

69. For an overview of the project see Servet Mutlu, "The Southeastern Anatolia Project (GAP) of Turkey: Its Context, Objectives and Prospects," *Orient*, vol. 37 (March 1996), pp. 59–86; and John F. Kolars and William A. Mitchell, *The Euphrates River and the Southeast Anatolia Development Project* (Southern Illinois University Press, 1991), pp. 18–76.

70. For instance, after Syrian complaints the World Bank decided not to become involved in financing the Atatürk Dam and its related Urfa tunnel system for the irrigation of the vast Harran plain south of Urfa. Turkey had to shoulder the financing for this core element of the project largely by itself. Given Turkey's severe budgetary problems, GAP runs constantly behind schedule. For details see Greg Shapland, "Policy Options for Downstream States in the Middle East," in J. A. Allan and Chibli Mallat, eds., *Water in the Middle East: Legal, Political and Commercial Implications* (New York: Tauris Academic Studies, 1995), pp. 310–11.

71. Kliot, *Water Resources and Conflict*, p. 148.

72. Some damage to Syrian agriculture occurred when Turkey stopped or greatly reduced the flow of Euphrates water in 1990 and 1991 while filling the Atatürk Reservoir. Although Turkish authorities argue that the average amount of water over a period of some months did not fall below the guaranteed level, the actual reduction caused environmental and production harm to agriculture on the Euphrates' banks; see Philip Robins, *Turkey and the Middle East* (London: Pinter Publications for the Royal Institute of International Affairs, 1991), pp. 90–94.

73. Minister of State Mehmet Gölhan in his opening speech of an international conference on Middle Eastern water issues in Ankara, 1993; see "Water as a Factor of Cooperation and Development in the Middle East," in Bağış, ed., *Water as an Element of Cooperation*, pp. 9, 12.

74. Özden Bilen, "A Technical Perspective on Euphrates-Tigris Basin," in Bağış, ed., *Water as an Element of Cooperation*, p. 95.

75. Department of Regional and Transboundary Waters, *Water Issues between Turkey, Syria and Iraq* (Ankara: Ministry of Foreign Affairs, 1996).

76. Quoted in John Bulloch and Adel Darwish, *Water Wars: Coming Conflicts in the Middle East* (London: Victor Gollancz, 1993), pp. 74–75. Similar remarks by other Turkish officials are quoted in Hasan Chalabi and Tarek Majzoub, "Turkey, the Waters of the Euphrates and Public International Law," in Allan and Mallat, eds., *Water in the Middle East*, pp. 208–09.

77. United Nations, General Assembly, Doc. A/51/869. For a Turkish view see Bülent

Olcay, "The Euphrates-Tigris Watercourse Controversy and the 1997 Convention on the Law of the Non-Navigational Uses of International Watercourses," *Dış Politika/Foreign Policy*, vol. 21 (1997), pp. 48–81.

78. Thomas Naff, "Sources of Potential Conflict in the Persian Gulf: The Water Factor," in Kemp and Gross Stein, eds., *Powder Keg in the Middle East*, pp. 295–318.

79. Quoted in Jouejati, "Water Politics as High Politics," p. 146.

80. Kliot, *Water Resources and Conflict*, pp. 131–33.

81. Tschanguiz H. Pahlavan, "Turkish-Iranian Relations: An Iranian View," in Barkey, ed., *Reluctant Neighbor*, p. 76.

82. "Iranian President Arrives in Ankara," *Turkish Daily News Electronic Edition*, December 20, 1996; and "Iran-Turquie: une relation qui s'affirme," *Le Figaro*, December 23, 1996, p. 4.

83. "Turkey Toughens Stance on Iran," *Turkish Daily News Electronic Edition*, May 17, 1999.

84. Nazlan Ertan, "Take Back Your Spies," *Turkish Probe*, no. 174 (April 12, 1996), pp. 8–9.

85. Semih D. İdiz, "Crisis with Iran," *Turkish Daily News Electronic Edition*, March 5, 1997.

86. Ayşe Karabat and Metehan Demir, "Ankara Skeptical of Iranian Proposal against PKK," *Turkish Daily News Electronic Edition*, June 20, 1997; and "L'armée turque accuse Téhéran," *Le Figaro*, March 26, 1997.

87. "Turkish Officials Suspect Iran and Greece Are Cooperating to Help PKK," *Turkish Daily News Electronic Edition*, May 26, 1999.

88. Geoffrey Kemp and Robert E. Harkavy, *Strategic Geography and the Changing Middle East* (Washington: Carnegie Endowment for Peace and Brookings, 1997), pp. 265–94.

89. Carus, "Iranian Nuclear, Biological and Chemical Weapons."

90. John Barham, "Erbakan's Visit to Iran Irks US," *Financial Times*, August 9, 1996, p. 4; Steven Erlanger, "New Turkish Chief's Muslim Tour Stirs U.S. Worries," *New York Times*, August 10, 1996, p. 1; and Philip Robins, "Turkey's Links with Iran Are No Cause for Panic," *International Herald Tribune*, August 27, 1996, p. 8.

91. "'The Gas Deal with Iran Should Not Be Politicized' Experts Say," *Turkish Daily News Electronic Edition*, August 14, 1996; and "Gas Pipeline Alarms U.S.," *Middle East Economic Digest*, August 23, 1996, p. 7.

92. American embarassment over the project also calmed down, and in summer 1997 Washington not only gave its consent to another gas pipeline project with which Turkmen gas would be transported to Turkey through Iran but also encouraged the American Unocal company to participate in the construction of the Turkish leg of the Turkish-Iranian gas deal. See Saadet Oruç, "Turkey's BOTAŞ, US UNOCAL Company to Cooperate for the Transportation of Iranian Gas," *Turkish Daily News Electronic Edition*, June 28, 1997; and Uğur Akıncı, "State Department Supports Turkmen-Iran-Turkish Gas Line," *Turkish Daily News Electronic Edition*, July 30, 1997.

93. Bruce Pannier, "Turkey and Iran in Former Soviet Central Asia and Azerbaijan: The Battle for Influence That Never Happened," *Perspectives on Central Asia*, vol. 2 (April 1998), pt. 1 (www.cpss.org/casianw/perca0498.tx [August 1999]); and (May 1998) pt. 2 (www.cpss.org/ casianw/perca0598.txt [August 1999]).

94. Patrick Clawson, "Iran and Caspian Basin Oil and Gas," *Perceptions*, vol. 2 (December 1997-February 1998), pp. 17–27.

95. Pahlavan, "Turkish-Iranian Relations," p. 85.

Chapter Nine

1. Graham E. Fuller, "Turkey in the New International Security Environment," in F. Stephen Larrabee, ed., *The Volatile Powder Keg: Balkan Security after the Cold War* (American University Press, 1994), p. 142.

2. Although strongly related to the general developments in the Balkans and Turkey's policies, the Greek-Turkish relations and conflicts, including the conflict over Cyprus, are discussed separately in chapter 10.

3. For details see Stanford J. Shaw and Ezel K. Shaw, *History of the Ottoman Empire and Modern Turkey*, vol. 2: *Reform, Revolution, and Republic: The Rise of Modern Turkey, 1808–1975* (Cambridge University Press, 1977).

4. See R. Craig Nation, "The Turkic and Other Muslim Peoples of Central Asia, the Caucasus, and the Balkans," in Vojtech Mastny and R. Craig Nation, eds., *Turkey between East and West: New Challenges for a Rising Regional Power* (Boulder, Colo.: Westview, 1996), pp. 112–24; and Hugh Poulton, "Playing the Kinship Card in the Balkans," *Transition*, vol. 2 (June 14, 1996), pp. 16–20.

5. Gareth Winrow, *Where East Meets West: Turkey and the Balkans* (London: Alliance Publishers for the Institute for European Defence and Strategic Studies, 1993), pp. 22–28.

6. For a comprehensive evaluation of the Ottoman legacy see Maria Todorova, "The Ottoman Legacy in the Balkans," in L. Carl Brown, ed., *Imperial Legacy: The Ottoman Imprint on the Balkans and the Middle East* (Columbia University Press, 1996), pp. 45–77. On "neo-Ottomanism," see F. Stephen Larrabee, "Turkey and the Balkans: Toward Neo-Ottomanism?" in *Internationales Umfeld, Sicherheitsinteressen und nationale Planung der Bundesrepublik*, Teil C, *Unterstützende Einzelanalysen* (Ebenhausen: Stiftung Wissenschaft und Politik, February 1993), pp. 143–57; and Ali Fuat Borovalı, "Post-Modernity, Multiculturalism and Ex-Imperial Hinterland: Habsburg and Ottoman Legacies Revisited," *Perceptions*, vol. 2 (December 1997-February 1998), pp. 122–34.

7. Duygu Bazoğlu Sezer, "Turkey in the New Security Environment in the Balkan and Black Sea Region," in Mastny and Nation, eds., *Turkey between East and West*, p. 81.

8. Former Yugoslav Republic of Macedonia is the name to which Skopje agreed as a provisional compromise to increase international recognition and secure its UN membership. Although initial conflicts with Greece over the name and the constitution could be settled via American mediation, a final settlement of the issue of the official name is still pending.

9. Constantine P. Danopoulos, "Turkey and the Balkans: Searching for Stability," in Constantine P. Danopoulos and Kostas G. Messas, eds., *Crises in the Balkans: Views from the Participants* (Boulder, Colo.: Westview Press, 1997), p. 215.

10. See George Stubos, *Economic Restructuring and Integration in the Balkans: Dilemmas, Hopes and Rational Expectations*, OP97.17 (Athens: Hellenic Foundation for European and Foreign Policy [ELIAMEP] Online Publications, 1997) (www.eliamep.gr/publications/op/op9717.pdf [August 1999]).

11. "Türkei erkennt Nachfolgerepubliken Jugoslawiens an," *Nachrichten aus der Türkei* (Bonn: Turkish Embassy, February 14, 1992), pp. 2–3.

12. "Turkish Parliament Condemns 'Massacre' of Muslims in Bosnia-Hercegovina," *BBC Summary of World Broadcast*, ME/1380, May 14, 1992.

13. Ali Fuat Borovalı, "The Bosnian Crisis and Turkish Foreign Policy," *Dış Politika/Foreign Policy*, vol. 18 (1993), pp. 74–87.

14. Mahmut B. Aykan, *Turkey's Role in the Organization of the Islamic Conference: 1960–1992: The Nature of Deviation from the Kemalist Heritage* (Vantage, 1994), pp. 150–58.

15. Ömer Erzeren, "Türkei: 'Bomben auf serbische Stellungen,'" *Die Tageszeitung*, August 11, 1992, p. 7.

16. Alan Cowell, "Turkey Faces Moral Crisis over Bosnia," *New York Times*, July 11, 1992, p. 4.

17. "Die Türkei beschloss die Entsendung von Soldaten nach Somalia und Bosnien-Herzegowina," *Nachrichten aus der Türkei* (Bonn: Turkish Embassy, December 11, 1992), p. 1.

18. Greece denied overflight permission for the Turkish fighter planes and the accompanying transport planes because of opposition to any Turkish military involvement in the international handling of the Bosnian war. Athens feared that such an involvement could bolster Turkey's general presence in the Balkans to the detriment of Greek regional security interests. Greece viewed Turkey's activities in the region, especially the growing bilateral relations with FYROM and Albania as well as the support for the Bosnian Muslims, as an attempt to create an "Islamic arc" in the Balkans to separate Greece from its European partners. Yannis Valinakis, "Greek Security Policy in the Perspective of CFSP," in Heinz-Jürgen Axt, ed., *Greece and the European Union: Stranger among Partners?* (Baden-Baden: Nomos Verlag, 1997), pp. 199–240, esp. pp. 203–12.

19. Helena Smith, "Greek Fury at Plan for Turk Peace Force," *Guardian*, March 24, 1994, p. 12.

20. On Western military reactions see Marie-Janine Calic, *Krieg und Frieden in Bosnien-Hercegovina* (Frankfurt am Main: Suhrkamp Verlag, 1996), pp. 242–48.

21. Sirma Evcan, "Bosnian Ambassador and Mrs. Hajrudin Somun: 'We Can Never Say Good-bye to Turkey,'" *Turkish Daily News Electronic Edition*, April 11, 1998 (www.turkishdailynews.com [August 1999]); and Colin Woodard, "Building Up Bosnia's Army," *Transition* (November 1, 1996), pp. 52–53.

22. John Pomfret, "U.S. Allies Fed Pipeline of Covert Arms to Bosnia," *Washington Post*, May 12, 1996, p. A1.

23. "Turkey and Serbia Begin to Normalize Ties," *Briefing* 1091, May 20, 1996, p. 10.

24. "Cem Conveys President's Message to Milosevic," *Turkish Daily News Electronic Edition*, March 9, 1998.

25. "Demirel Urges Action on Kosovo, Pledges Turkish Participation," *Turkish Daily News Electronic Edition*, July 28, 1998.

26. "Eighteen Turkish Jets to Be Ready for Kosovo Intervention," *Turkish Daily News Electronic Edition*, October 13, 1998.

27. Sibel Utku, "Yugoslavia Protests over Enhanced Turkish Role in NATO Strikes," *Turkish Daily News Electronic Edition*, May 19, 1999; and "Military Approves NATO Use of Bandirma and Balikesir Bases," *Turkish Daily News Electronic Edition*, May 27, 1999.

28. Sibel Utku, "Kosovars Flee to Turkey," *Turkish Daily News Electronic Edition*, March 25, 1999; and Hakan Aslaneli, "Starting New Lives in Istanbul," *Turkish Daily News Electronic Edition*, April 13, 1999.

29. Sibel Utku, "Wounded KLA Guerillas Treated in Turkey," *Turkish Daily News Electronic Edition*, May 17, 1999.

30. For details see "Kosovo Reincarnates Ecevit's Pan-Slavic, Pan-Orthodox Phobia," *Briefing* 1237, April 12, 1999, pp. 14–16.

31. See "Ankara Remains Confused," *Briefing* 1238, April 19, 1999, pp. 16–17.

32. Yüksel Söylemez, "An Overview of Turkish-Croatian Relations," *Dış Politika/Foreign Policy*, vol. 19 (1995), pp. 15–35.

33. "Albanien und die Türkei," *Nachrichten aus der Türkei* (Bonn: Turkish Embassy, July 23, 1993), pp. 3–4.

34. "Turkey Leads the Way for Trans-Balkan Highway," *Turkish Daily News*, October 24, 1995.

35. Paul Kubicek, "Albania's Collapse and Reconstruction," *Perceptions*, vol. 3 (March-May 1998), pp. 117–33; and Metehan Demir, "Turkey to Be Responsible for Northern Albania with 850 Troops," *Turkish Daily News Electronic Edition*, April 16, 1996.

36. On military cooperation see Ümit Enginsoy, "Turkey to Give F-5s to Macedonia," *Defense News*, July 13, 1998, p. 7.

37. "FM Cem Stresses Importance of Macedonia's NATO Membership," *Turkish Daily News Electronic Edition*, April 21, 1998.

38. Nicole Pope and Hugh Pope, *Turkey Unveiled: Ataturk and After* (London: John Murray, 1997), pp. 202–05.

39. Winrow, *Where East Meets West*, p. 14.

40. Kelly Couturier, "Turkey Assuming Lead Peacekeeping Role," *Washington Post*, July 16, 1998, p. A25.

41. Sibel Utku, "Turkey, Romania, Bulgaria Agree to Fight Crime, Expand Economic Ties," *Turkish Daily News Electronic Edition*, April 17, 1998.

42. Sabine Riedel, "Die türkische Minderheit im parlamentarischen System Bulgariens," *Südosteuropa*, vol. 42 (1993), pp. 100–24; and Emil Mintchev, "Die politische Organisierung der bulgarischen Türken—neue Erfahrungen, neue Herausforderungen," *Zeitschrift für Türkeistudien*, vol. 10 (1997), pp. 51–54.

43. Utku, "Turkey, Romania, Bulgaria."

44. For a comprehensive overview see Yannis Valinakis and Sergei Karaganov, "The Creation and Evolution of the BSEC: An Assessment," in Thanos M. Veremis and Dimitrios Triantaphyllou, eds., *The Southeast European Yearbook, 1997–98* (Athens: ELIAMEP, 1998), pp. 243–91.

45. Selim İlkin, "Les tentatives de coopération économique de la Turquie et la zone de coopération économique en Mer Noire," *Cahiers d'études sur la Méditerranée orientale et le monde Turco-Iranien—CEMOTI*, no. 15 (1993), pp. 51–75.

46. At the summit meeting of BSEC members in Yalta in June 1998 the cooperation plan was officially transformed into a regional international organization; "Regional Cooperation Given a Boost," *Briefing* 1195, June 8, 1998, p. 13.

47. "Summit Declaration on the Black Sea Economic Cooperation," Istanbul, June 25, 1992 (www.die.gov.tr/turikish/BSEC/toplanti.htm#1 [August 1999]).

48. For an analysis of transition problems at the level of enterprises see Charalambos

Vlachoutsicos and Panagiotis Liargovas, "Barriers to the Transition of Enterprises in BSEC Countries from Central Plan to Market Economy," in *Southeast European Yearbook, 1997–98*, pp. 293–318.

49. "The Bosphorus Statement," Istanbul, June 25, 1992 (www.turkey.org/turkey/politics/bsec/bsec8.htm [August 1999]); see also Summit Declaration, points 1 and 9.

50. See Ines Hartwig, "Die Schwarzmeerwirtschaftskooperation—Strukturen regionaler Zusammenarbeit in Südosteuropa," *Integration*, vol. 19 (January 1996), pp. 49–57; "The BSEC Structure" (www.turkey.org/turkey/politics/bsec/bsec3.htm [August 1999]); and "The BSEC in Action" (www.turkey.org/turkey/politics/bsec4.htm [August 1999]).

51. See Ercan Özer, "The Black Sea Economic Cooperation and Regional Security," *Perceptions*, vol. 2 (September-November 1997), pp. 76–106.

52. See Yasemin Dobra-Manco, "Economic Development Holds Key to Stability in the BSEC Region," *Turkish Daily News Electronic Edition*, April 23, 1997; and Ercan Özer, "The Black Sea Economic Cooperation and the EU," *Perceptions*, vol.1 (September-November 1996), pp. 72–86.

53. "Istanbul Fails to Pin Down Milosevic," *Briefing* 1196, June 15, 1998, p. 12.

54. "Zwiespältiges Ergebnis des ersten Balkangipfels," *Neue Zürcher Zeitung*, November 5, 1997, p.3.

55. Sibel Utku, "Yugoslavia Joins Balkan Nations in Common Position on Kosovo," *Turkish Daily News Electronic Edition*, October 14, 1998.

56. "Bildung einer Friedenstruppe für Südosteuropa," *Neue Zürcher Zeitung*, September 29, 1998, p. 5.

57. See "Turkey Agrees with Four Balkan Nations to Set Up Deployment Force for Region," *Turkish Daily News Electronic Edition*, March 20, 1998; "Macedonia Emerges as Strong Option for Station of Planned Balkan Force," March 24, 1998; and "Multinational Peace Force Set Up," May 25, 1998.

Chapter Ten

1. For a comprehensive account of Turkish-Greek relations until the end of the 1980s, see Tozun Bahcheli, *Greek-Turkish Relations since 1955* (Boulder, Colo.: Westview, 1990).

2. The following considerations were first developed in Heinz Kramer, "Turkey's Relations with Greece: Motives and Interests," in Dimitri Constas, ed., *The Greek-Turkish Conflict in the 1990's: Domestic and External Influences* (St. Martin's, 1991), pp. 57–72. For a more elaborate analysis of the sociopsychological components of Turkish-Greek relations see Vamık D. Volkan and Norman Itzkowitz, *Turks and Greeks: Neighbours in Conflict* (Huntingdon, Cambridgeshire, U.K.: Eothen Press, 1994).

3. Byron Theodoropoulos, "Perception and Reality: How Greeks and Turks See Each Other," in Thanos M. Veremis and Dimitrios Triantaphyllou, eds., *The Southeast European Yearbook, 1997–98* (Athens: Hellenic Foundation for European and Foreign Policy [ELIAMEP], 1998), pp. 45–52.

4. Theodoropoulos, "Perception and Reality," p. 46–47.

5. See Theodore A. Couloumbis, *The United States, Greece and Turkey: The Troubled Triangle* (Praeger, 1983); and Richard Haass, "Managing NATO's Weakest Flank: The United States, Greece and Turkey," *Orbis*, vol. 30 (Fall 1986), pp. 457–73.

6. Şükrü S. Gürel, "Turkey and Greece: A Difficult Aegean Relationship," in Canan Balkır and Allan M. Williams, eds., *Turkey and Europe* (Pinter Publishers, 1993), p. 167.

7. For a comprehensive overview see Suha Bölükbaşı, "The Turco-Greek Dispute: Issues, Policies and Prospects," in Clement H. Dodd, ed., *Turkish Foreign Policy: New Prospects* (Cambridgeshire, U.K.: Eothen Press, 1992), pp. 27–54. For a representative Greek view with special emphasis on legal problems see Christos Rozakis, "An Analysis of the Legal Problems in Greek-Turkish Relations 1973–1988," *Yearbook 1989: Special Issue: Southeastern Europe* (Athens: Hellenic Foundation for European and Foreign Policy, 1990), pp. 193–251.

8. For the minority issue from the Greek perspective see Hellenic Republic, Ministry of Foreign Affairs and Ministry of Press and Mass Media, *European Perspectives: Economic & Foreign Policy Issues* (Athens, n.d.), pp. 104–11. The Turkish perspective can be found in Turkish Ministry of Foreign Affairs, *Foreign Affairs—Turkish Minority of Western Thrace* (www.mfa.gov.tr/grupa/ac/acd/minor.htm [August 1999]); and Turkish Ministry of Foreign Affairs, *Foreign Affairs—Turkey's Religious Tolerance* (www.mfa.gov.tr/grupa/ac/ace/default.htm [August 1999]).

9. Şükrü Elekdağ, "2 ½ War Strategy," *Perceptions*, vol. 1 (March-May 1996), p. 40.

10. Turkish Ministry of Foreign Affairs, *Turkish-Greek Relations: Aegean Problems;* (*www.mfa.gov.tr/grupa/ad/ade/adea/default.htm* [August 1999]).

11. See Renate Platzöder and Wolfgang Graf Vitzthum, eds., *Seerecht—Law of the Sea: Textausgabe* (Baden-Baden: Nomos, 1984), pp. 58–63, 122–27.

12. For details see Heinz-Jürgen Axt and Heinz Kramer, *Entspannung im Ägäiskonflikt? Griechisch-türkische Beziehungen nach Davos* (Baden-Baden: Nomos, 1990), pp. 13–23.

13. Turkey pretends not to be the only country that would reject such a Greek move. All countries of the Black Sea and of the Danube whose naval links of communication mainly go through the Aegean Sea after having passed the Turkish Straits allegedly share Turkey's position. See Semih D. İdiz, "Greek Aegean Claims Start Hitting Rocks Bigger Than Turkey's 'Casus Belli,'" *Turkish Daily News Electronic Edition*, December 11, 1996 (www.turkishdailynews.com [August 1999]).

14. Elekdağ, "2 ½ War Strategy," p. 42.

15. For the Greek position on the disputed issues see *Hellenic Republic, European Perspectives: Economic & Foreign Policy Issues*, pp. 39–46; and Thanos Veremis, "The Ongoing Aegean Crisis," *Thesis*, vol. 1 (Spring 1997), pp. 22–32.

16. The Turkish argument that sea limits and airspace are identical according to international habits is shared by the United States. According to the former spokesman of the Department of State and American ambassador to Greece, Nicolas Burns, this has been " a consistent position for many years." İdiz, "Greek Aegean Claims."

17. Axt and Kramer, *Entspannung im Ägäiskonflikt*, pp. 24–27.

18. This was foreseen in the so-called Rogers Plan for Greece's reintegration into NATO's military structure. International Institute for Strategic Studies, *Prospects for Security in the Mediterranean*, part 1, Adelphi Papers 229 (London, 1988), p. 87.

19. Elekdağ, "2 ½ War Strategy," p. 38.

20. Petros N. Stagos, "Le différend Gréco-Turc au sujet de la position de l'île de Lemnos dans le dispositif de l'OTAN," in Semih Vaner, ed., *Le différend Gréco-Turc* (Paris: L'Harmattan, 1986), pp. 183–98.

21. Kardak is the Turkish name of the uninhabited rocky islets in the Dodecanese

area; its Greek ownership has been disputed by Ankara. Imia is the Greek name of the rocks. For details of the crisis and its aftermath see Ekavi Athanassopoulou, "Blessing in Disguise? The Imia Crisis and Greek-Turkish Relations," *Mediterranean Politics*, vol. 2 (Winter 1997), pp. 76–101; Krateros Ioannou, "A Tale of Two Islets: The Imia Incident between Greece and Turkey," *Thesis*, vol. 1 (Spring 1997), pp. 33–42; and Turkish Ministry of Foreign Affairs, *The Kardak Dispute*; (www.mfa.gov.tr/grupa/ad/ade/aded/default.htm [August 1999]).

22. P. Evthymiou, "They Left the War to the (TV) Channels," *To Vima*, February 4, 1996, quoted by Ekkehard Kraft, "Die griechisch-türkische Krise um die Felseninsel Imia Ende Januar 1996," *Südosteuropa*, vol. 45 (1996), p. 770.

23. Nazlan Ertan, "Turco-Greek Ties Hit Rock Bottom," *Turkish Probe*, no. 165, February 2, 1996, pp. 10–13; and "U.S. to Seek Peace in Aegean after Islet Crisis," *Briefing* 1078, February 5, 1996, pp. 5–6.

24. Turkish Ministry of Foreign Affairs, *Turkish-Greek Relations: Aegean Problems.*

25. *Frankfurter Allgemeine Zeitung*, August 9, 1996, p. 2; and Veremis, "Ongoing Aegean Crisis," p. 30.

26. "Declaration Adopted by the 15 Ministers of Foreign Affairs of the EU at the Last General Affairs Council," Council of Ministers of the European Union, Brussels, July 15, 1996, in *European Perspectives*, p. 78.

27. Semih D. İdiz, "1996, a Year of Qualitative Changes in Ties with the West," *Turkish Daily News Electronic Edition*, January 14, 1997.

28. For details see Turkish Ministry of Foreign Affairs, *Turkey's Aegean Peace Process Initiative*; (www.mfa.gov.tr/grupa/ad/ade/adec/Peace1.htm [August 1999]).

29. See Athanassopoulou, "Blessing in Disguise?" pp. 88–95.

30. See "Greek-Turkish Relations: The Madrid Joint Declaration," *Thesis*, vol. 1 (Summer 1997), pp. 44–45; and "Ankara Cautiously Optimistic after Turco-Greek Agreement," *Turkish Daily News Electronic Edition*, July 10, 1997.

31. See chapter 11 on Turkey's EU relationship.

32. Turkish Ministry of Foreign Affairs, "Information Note Concerning the Proposals Made by Turkey To Greece on 12 February 1998 about a Process of Peaceful Settlement of Problems over the Aegean between the Two Countries, 12 February 1998," (www.mfa.gov.tr/grupa/ad/ade/adec/08.htm [August 1999]); and "Press Statement Regarding the Turkish Goverment's Proposals to Greece (12.03.1998)," (www.mfa.gov.tr/grupa/ad/ade/adec/13.htm [August 1999]).

33. "Statement by Prime Minister Mesut Yılmaz Concerning Relations with Greece," Ankara, April 30, 1998.

34. "Turkey and Greece Agree to Fully Implement CBMs," *Turkish Daily News Electronic Edition*, June 5, 1998; and "NATO-Sponsored Turco-Greek Meetings on CBMs Continue," *Turkish Daily News Electronic Edition*, July 29, 1998.

35. For details see Turkish Ministry of Foreign Affairs, "Greece and PKK Terrorism (I)," Ankara, February 1999 (www.mfa.gov.tr/grupe/eh/terror/greecebk/default.htm [August 1999]); and "Greece and PKK Terrorism (II)" (www.mfa.gov.tr/grupe/eh/eh05/default.htm [August 1999]).

36. For details see Hasan Ünal, "Caught Red-Handed, This Time Athens May Face Difficulties," *Turkish Probe*, no. 326, April 11, 1999; "Ankara's Stance toward Athens Justified, But Misguided in Long Run," *Briefing* 1234, March 15, 1999, pp. 20–21; and

"Der griechisch-türkische Konflikt spitzt sich zu," *Neue Zürcher Zeitung*, March 4, 1999, p. 1.

37. For an overview of the official Turkish position with regard to Cyprus, see Turkish Ministry of Foreign Affairs, *Cyprus Issue* (www.mfa.gov.tr/grupa/ad/add/default.htm [August 1999]).

38. Andreas Andrianopoulos, "The Long Arms of Oil Interests," *Transitions*, vol. 4 (June 1997), p. 36.

39. See Turkish Ministry of Foreign Affairs, "Recent Greek Cypriot Attempts to Purchase Missiles from Russia and the Resulting Danger for the Peace and Stability in Cyprus" (www.mfa.gov.tr/grupa/ad/add/fuze.htm [August 1999]).

40. For details see Madeleine Demetriou, "On the Long Road to Europe and the Short Path to War: Issue-Linkage Politics and the Arms Build-up on Cyprus," *Mediterranean Politics*, vol. 3 (Winter 1998), pp. 38–51.

41. See Turkish Ministry of Foreign Affairs, "Press Conference by Foreign Minister Ismail Cem on the S-300 Issue, December 30, 1998" (www.mfa.gov.tr/grupa/ad/add/30.htm); and "Gurel: S-300s Tension in the Region Will Continue," *Turkish Daily News Electronic Edition*, January 2, 1999.

42. For an overview of the Greek Cypriot position see "Outline Proposal of the Cypriot Government for the Establishment of a Federal Republic and for the Solution of the Cyprus Problem," in Hellenic Foundation for European and Foreign Policy, *Yearbook 1989*, pp. 291–304.

43. For an overview see Clement H. Dodd, *The Cyprus Imbroglio* (Cambridgeshire, U.K.: Eothen Press, 1998), pp. 34–60; and Suha Bölükbaşı, "The Cyprus Dispute and the United Nations: Peaceful Non-Settlement between 1954 and 1996," *International Journal of Middle East Studies*, vol. 30 (1998), pp. 411–34.

44. See Dodd, *Cyprus Imbroglio*, pp. 61–74, 112–16; and Neill Nugent, "Cyprus and the European Union: A Particularly Difficult Membership Application," *Mediterranean Politics*, vol. 2 (Winter 1997), pp. 53–77.

45. See Ministry of Foreign Affairs, "The Cyprus Question within the Context of Membership to the EU," Ankara, 1997. This paper contains a collection of all important official Turkish reactions to EU moves with respect to the accession process of Cyprus. See also Salahi Sonyel, "Reactions in the Turkish Republic of Northern Cyprus to the Application by the Greek Cypriot Administration of South Cyprus for Membership of the European Union," in Heinz-Jürgen Axt and Hansjörg Brey, eds., *Cyprus and the European Union: New Chances for Solving an Old Conflict?* Südosteuropa Aktuell 23 (Munich: Südosteuropa-Gesellschaft, 1997), pp. 151–58.

46. Ministry of Foreign Affairs, "Cyprus Question," p. 6. For the EU's position see "Commission Opinion on the Application by the Republic of Cyprus for Membership, Conclusions," in Axt and Brey, eds., *Cyprus and the European Union*, pp. 244–46.

47. "Conclusions of the Presidency of the European Council meeting in Corfu on June 24-25, 1994," *Agence Europe*, June 26, 1994, p. 10.

48. Ministry of Foreign Affairs, "Cyprus Question," p. 10.

49. Ministry of Foreign Affairs, "Cyprus Question," p. 13.

50. "Joint Declaration of the Presidents of the Republic of Turkey and the Turkish Republic of Northern Cyprus," Ankara, January 20, 1997 (www.mfa.gov.tr/grupa/ad/add/rusmis9.htm [August 1999]).

51. "Agreement between the Government of the Republic of Turkey and the Government of the Turkish Republic of Northern Cyprus on the Establishment of an Association Council," Lefkoşa, August 6, 1997 (www.mfa.gov.tr./grupa/ad/add/doc5.htm). See also Dodd, *Cyprus Imbroglio*, pp. 101–07.

52. "Turkey Warns of Cyprus Escalation as EU Starts Eastward Enlargement," *Turkish Daily News Electronic Edition*, March 31, 1998. For an overview of the general Turkish reaction see Hüseyin Bağcı, "Turkish Reaction to the EU Approach," in Susanne Baier-Allen, ed., *Looking into the Future of Cyprus-EU Relations* (Baden-Baden: Nomos Verlag, 1999), pp. 39–50.

53. "Holbrooke: No Breakthrough in Cyprus Talks," *Turkish Daily News Electronic Edition*, April 6, 1998; "EU Becomes Target of Turkey and Holbrooke's Criticism over Deadlock in Cyprus," *Turkish Daily News Electronic Edition*, May 6, 1998; and Elizabeth Gleick, "Mission Impossible," *Time*, May 18, 1998.

54. Ministry of Foreign Affairs, "Call for Peace from Turkish Side: Rauf Denktaş Proposes Confederation in Cyprus," August 31, 1998 (www.mfa.gov.tr/grupa/ad/add/305.htm). See also "New Discussion on Cyprus: Federation vs. Confederation," *Turkish Probe*, no. 295, September 6, 1998.

Chapter Eleven

1. Alan Makovsky, "Turkey's Faded European Dream," in *The Parameters of Partnership: Germany, the U.S. and Turkey* (Washington: American Institute for Contemporary German Studies, 1998), p. 57.

2. Figures are taken from "Turkey's Foreign Trade by Principal Sectors, Country and Commodity Groups," *Briefing* 1233, March 8, 1999, p. 36. For a detailed assessment of EC-Turkey trade relations see Canan Balkır, "Turkey and the European Community: Foreign Trade and Direct Foreign Investment in the 1980s," in Canan Balkır and Alan M. Williams, eds., *Turkey and Europe* (Pinter, 1993), pp. 100–39.

3. "Enterprises with Foreign Capital Operating in Turkey," *Briefing* 1227, January 18-25, 1999, p. 34.

4. For the situation with respect to Germany see Heinz Kramer, "The Institutional Framework of German-Turkish Relations," in *Parameters of Partnership*, pp. 10–31.

5. Hans-Joachim Vergau, "Turkey and Germany as Economic Partners," *Turkish Daily News Electronic Edition*, October 3, 1998 (www.turkishdailynews.com [August 1999]).

6. The difference between the concepts of Europe and the European Union is discussed in a somewhat broader framework in the contributions to *Grenzfall Europa/Avrupa'nın ince eşiğinde* (Hamburg: Edition Körber Stiftung, 1999).

7. For details see Heinz Kramer, *Die Europäische Gemeinschaft und die Türkei: Entwicklung, Probleme und Perspektiven einer schwierigen Partnerschaft* (Baden-Baden: Nomos, 1988), pp. 61–74; and Didier Billion, *La Politique Extérieure de la Turquie* (Montreal: L'Harmattan, 1997), pp. 161–260, esp. pp. 179–98.

8. For a general survey of the Western orientation of Turkish foreign policy see Oral Sander, "Turkish Foreign Policy: Forces of Continuity and Change," in Ahmet Evin, ed., *Modern Turkey: Continuity and Change* (Opladen: Leske Verlag, 1984), pp. 115–30. The Kemalist origins of this orientation are especially dealt with by Mehmet Gönlübol, "Atatürk's Foreign Policy: Goals and Principles," in Turhan Feyzioğlu, ed., *Atatürk's Way*

(Istanbul: Otomarsan, 1982), pp. 255–302. This article includes many pertinent quotations from Mustafa Kemal's works.

9. "The Outlook for Relations between Turkey and the European Union after the Cardiff Summit," prepared remarks by Özdem Sanberk, Turkish ambassador to the United Kingdom, Monday, July 20, 1998 (www.washingtoninstitute.org/media/sanberk.htm [August 1999]). For a comprehensive and very prominent argument along these lines see the publication by the late Turkish president Turgut Özal, *Turkey in Europe and Europe in Turkey* (Nicosia, Cyprus: K. Rustem, 1991).

10. See Mehmet Ali Birand, "Turkey and the European Community," *World Today*, vol. 34 (1978), pp. 52–61; and Tozun Bahcheli, "Turkey and the EEC: The Strains of Association," *Revue d'intégration européenne/Journal of European Integration*, vol. 3 (1980), pp. 220–37.

11. For details see Bruce Robellet Kuniholm, *The Origins of the Cold War in the Near East: Great Power Conflict and Diplomacy in Iran, Turkey and Greece* (Princeton University Press, 1980). For a Turkish view see Metin Tamkoç, "The Impact of the Truman Doctrine on the National Security Interests of Turkey," *Dış Politika/Foreign Policy*, vol. 6 (1977), pp. 18–40; and Yuluğ Tekin Kurat, "Turkey's Entry to the North Atlantic Treaty Organization," *Dış Politika/Foreign Policy*, vol. 10 (1983) pp. 50–77.

12. For a short overview see Meltem Müftüler-Baç, *Turkey's Relations with a Changing Europe* (Manchester University Press, 1997), pp. 19–22.

13. For details see Atila Eralp, "Turkey and the EC in the Changing Post-War International System," in C. Balkır and A. M. Williams, eds., *Turkey and Europe* (Pinter, 1993), pp. 32–44; and Mahmut Bozkurt, *Die Beziehung der Türkei zur Europäischen Union* (Frankfurt am Main: Peter Lang, 1995), pp. 100–49.

14. These endeavors are analyzed in Heinz Kramer, "The European Community's Response to the 'New Eastern Europe,'" *Journal of Common Market Studies*, vol. 31 (June 1993), pp. 213–44.

15. The Association Agreement of 1963 and the Additional Protocol to it in 1970 envision the gradual establishment of a customs union for industrial products by 1995. The customs union should be complemented by additional measures in various other economic areas that bring the whole undertaking near to the level of a common market. For details see Kramer, *Die Europäische Gemeinschaft und die Türkei*, pp. 36–40, 47–53.

16. For details see Heinz Kramer, "The EU-Turkey Customs Union: Economic Integration Amidst Political Turmoil," *Mediterranean Politics*, vol. 1 (Summer 1996), pp. 60–75. The following analysis rests on this article.

17. Heiko Körner, "Development Strategies of Turkey in the Customs Union," in Zentrum für Türkeistudien, *Die Türkei in der EU-Zollunion: Empirie—Theorie—Perspektiven* (Münster: LIT Verlag, 1999), pp. 15–21, esp. p. 17.

18. Mükerrem Hiç, "Turkey's Customs Union with the European Union: Economic and Political Prospects," working paper SWP-AP 2926 (Ebenhausen: Stiftung Wissenschaft und Politik, 1995), p. 19.

19. For a provisional analysis of the economic effects of the customs union see the contributions in Zentrum für Türkeistudien, *Die Türkei in der EU-Zollunion.*

20. For details see "Turkey's Foreign Trade by Principal Sectors, Country and Commodity Groups, 96–97, 97–98" *Briefing* 1183, March 9, 1998, p. 29; and *Briefing* 1233, March 8, 1999, p. 36.

21. *Text of Decision No. 1/95 (Customs Union) of the EC-Turkey Association Council of 6 March 1995 on Implementing the Final Phase of the Customs Union* (Brussels, March 6, 1995), articles 29–49.

22. "Association between the European Community and Turkey," *Resolution of the EC-Turkey Association Council*, Brussels, March 6, 1995.

23. "Troika" is official EU jargon for a political representation of the union that is composed of the union's acting president plus the previous and the next one.

24. For a sceptical evaluation of the constitutional changes see Christian Rumpf, *Die Verfassungsänderungen in der Türkei. Ein Schritt nach Europa?* working paper SWP-IP 2927 (Ebenhausen: Stiftung Wissenschaft und Politik, 1995).

25. In article 28 of the agreement it is stipulated that "As soon as the operation of this Agreement has advanced far enough to justify envisaging full acceptance by Turkey of the obligations arising out of the Treaty establishing the Community, the Contracting Parties shall examine the possibility of the accession of Turkey to the Community." According to this wording, there is no legal automaticity for Turkish EU membership as Turkish politicians and officials often contend. However, there can also be no doubt about the final political goal of the Turkey-EU relationship as based on the Association Agreement.

26. Michael Dynes, "Çiller Underlines Islamic Danger in Plea to Major," *Times* (London), November 23, 1995, p. 14.

27. Greece, for instance, blocked more forthcoming language in the statement of the Irish EU presidency during the preparation of the European Council meeting in Dublin in December 1996 by restricting the final wording to the established EU line of argumentation. This was not at all welcome in Ankara. (Personal communication to the author.)

28. *Agence Europe*, December 14, 1996, p. 4a. For an earlier discussion of the issue see Heinz Kramer, *Die Assoziierungsabkommen der EU: Die Türkei und Mittelosteuropa in einem Boot?* (Bonn: Friedrich-Ebert-Stiftung, 1995).

29. Michael Lake, "Turkey and the European Union," in *Parameters of Partnership*, p. 43.

30. See F. Stephen Larrabee, "U.S. and European Policy toward Turkey and the Caspian Basin," in Robert D. Blackwill and Michael Stürmer, eds., *Allies Divided: Transatlantic Policies for the Greater Middle East* (MIT Press, 1997), esp. pp. 151–61. See also Makovsky, "Turkey's Faded European Dream," pp. 60–63.

31. Mrs. Çiller first made remarks to that respect after her meeting with EU representatives after the European Council of Dublin in December 1996 and is said to have reiterated this linkage at her meeting with five colleagues from the large EU member states in Rome at the end of January 1997 where the Europeans tried to improve the climate in relations with Turkey. "Çiller Lays the Cards on the Table," *Briefing* 1122, December 23, 1996, p. 3; *Agence Europe*, January 31, 1997, pp. 2–3; and "Kinkel fordert einen 'fairen Umgang' mit der Türkei," *Frankfurter Allgemeine Zeitung*, January 30, 1997, pp. 1–2. This led also to some strong reactions in Washington; see Uğur Akıncı, "US Puts Full Weight behind Turkey's EU Bid," *Turkish Daily News Electronic Edition*, January 31, 1997.

32. "A Pallative Gathering in Rome," *Briefing* 1128, February 3, 1997, p. 4.

33. Lionel Barber, "EU Group Rebuffs Turkish Entry Push," *Financial Times*, March 5, 1997, p. 2.

34. See the comprehensive report about the unofficial meeting of the EU's ministers of foreign affairs in Apeldoorn, Netherlands; *Agence Europe*, March, 17-18, 1997, pp. 4–5.

35. European Commission, *Agenda 2000: For a Stronger and Wider Union* (Brussels, July 16, 1997).

36. The commission named Hungary, Poland, the Czech Republic, Slovenia, and Estonia, as well as Cyprus and proposed so-called preaccession strategies for all applicant countries except Turkey, for which a special program was envisioned to bring the country closer to the EU by going beyond the customs union relationship, an approach called "customs union plus." See Commission of the European Communities, "Commission Proposes Deepening Relations with Turkey," Press Release, IP/97/652, July 15, 1997; and "Commission Proposes a New Procedure for the Adoption of Certain Implementing Measures Relating to Indirect Taxation," IP/97/653, July 15, 1997.

37. "Turkey Blasts EU Commission over 'Mistaken Decision,'" *Turkish Daily News Electronic Edition*, July 17, 1997.

38. "Verärgerung Ankaras über die Erweiterungspläne der Europäischen Union," *Neue Zürcher Zeitung*, July 24, 1997, p. 3. As was mentioned in the previous chapter, Denktaş first wanted to cancel the second round of talks with Clerides planned for August in Glion, Switzerland, because of the EU's plans as revealed in *Agenda 2000.* However, American, UN, and Turkish persuasion made him change his mind.

39. Ralph Atkins, "Kohl Shift on EU and Turkey," *Financial Times*, October 1, 1997, p. 2.

40. This line had been clearly explained to the Turkish public in an article by the German ambassador to Turkey in the Turkish daily *Milliyet* on August 29, 1997. Mr. Vergau wrote that Turkey's strength and problems were not comparable to those of other applicants. Consequently, an evaluation according to the same criteria as applied to Bulgaria and Slovakia could not automatically guarantee equal treatment of Turkey in procedural and temporal terms. "Turkey does not fit in any group of candidates."

41. For details see Luxembourg European Council, *12 and 13 December 1997 Presidency Conclusions*, points 4–9 and 31–36.

42. *Statement of the Turkish Government Regarding the Conclusions of the Luxembourg Summit* (unofficial translation) (Ankara, December 14, 1997).

43. Makovsky, "Turkey's Faded European Dream," p. 51.

44. See Barbara Lippert, "Der Gipfel von Luxemburg: Startschuß für das Abenteuer Erweiterung," *Integration*, vol. 21 (January 1998), pp. 12–31, esp. pp. 13–14.

45. *Agence Europe*, December 15-16, 1997, p. 6.

46. Remarks made by Ecevit in Güneri Çivaoğlu's political magazine *Durum* of the private television station Kanal D on December 19, 1997, in which the author participated some days after the Luxembourg decision.

47. "Yılmaz Urges EU to Make Its Decision to Turkey by June," *Turkish Daily News Electronic Edition*, December 18, 1997; and "Yılmaz: Kohl diskriminiert die Türkei," *Süddeutsche Zeitung*, December 20-21, 1997, p. 1.

48. John Barham and Quentin Peel, "Turkey Accuses Kohl of 'Lebensraum' Policy," *Financial Times*, March 6, 1998, p. 18.

49. "European Council (Cardiff) June 15 and 16, 1998, Presidency Conclusions," point 68, *Agence Europe*, June 18, 1998; and "Fresh, If Not Glossy, Page Opens with EU," *Briefing* 1197, June 22, 1998, pp. 9–12.

50. Nazlan Ertan, "Turkey Reacts Harshly against French Recognition of 'Armenian Genocide,'" *Turkish Daily News Electronic Edition*, May 30, 1998; and "Time to Reconsider Demirel's Suggestion," *Briefing* 1194, June 1, 1998, pp. 9–12.

51. "From Spaghetti Westerns to Macaroni Southeasterns—Italy 'Disappoints,'" *Briefing* 1212, October 5, 1998, pp. 17–19.

52. European Commission, *European Strategy for Turkey: The Commission's Initial Operational Proposals*, document Com/98/124 final (Brussels, March 4, 1998).

53. Nazlan Ertan, "EU Move to Improve Ties Angers Greece," *Turkish Probe Electronic Edition*, November 1, 1998.

54. European Commission, *Regular Report from the Commission on Turkey's Progress towards Accession*, document Com/98/711 (Brussels, November 4, 1998).

55. Nazlan Ertan, "Greece Launches Offensive against Overtures between Turkey and EU," *Turkish Daily News Electronic Edition*, October 28, 1998; and Ertan, "EU Report: New Base for Ties or Same Old Criticism?" *Turkish Daily News Electronic Edition*, November 6, 1998.

56. Turkish Ministry of Foreign Affairs, *A Strategy for Developing Relations between Turkey and the European Union, Proposals of Turkey* (Ankara, July 17, 1998); (http://www.mfa.gov.tr/ grupa/ad/adc/strategy.htm [August 1999]).

57. For details of the German endeavors see Nazlan Ertan, "The Problem with the EU Summits," *Turkish Probe*, no. 335, June 13, 1999.

58. For details see "Turkey Reaches 'Sanity Stage' in EU Rhetoric," *Briefing* 1246, June 14, 1999, pp. 16–19.

59. Turkish Ministry of Foreign Affairs, "Answer Given by Sermet Atacanlı, Deputy Spokesman of the Ministry of Foreign Affairs to a Question Related to the EU," Press Release, Ankara, June 4, 1999 (www.mfa.gov.tr/grupb/ba/baa99/June/02.htm [August 1999]).

60. Turkish Grand National Assembly, *Relations between Turkey and the European Union: Report of the Turkish Grand National Assembly Investigation Commission: Summary* (Ankara, March 1998), p. 15.

Chapter Twelve

1. Çevik Bir, "Turkey's Role in the New World Order," *Strategic Forum*, no. 135 (February 1998), p. 1.

2. Vural Avar, "The Turkish Armed Forces in 2000 and Beyond," *NATO's Sixteen Nations, Special Supplement on Defence and Economics in Turkey: Pillar of Regional Stability* (1998), pp. 15–23; and Yalçın Burcak, "The Turkish Defence Industry in the 21st Century," *NATO's Sixteen Nations*, pp. 25–32. See also Metehan Demir, "Turkish Defense Industry: A Rising International Star," *Turkish Daily News Electronic Edition*, August 22, 1996 (www.turkishdailynews.com [August 1999]).

3. See Ali L. Karaosmanoğlu, "NATO Enlargement: Does It Enhance Security?" in *Turkey and European Union: Nebulous Nature of Relations* (Ankara: Turkish Foreign Policy Institute,1996), pp. 23–34.

4. Ömür Orhun, "Turkey and the West: Tension within Cooperation," paper prepared for an IISS-SAM conference, "Turkey-NATO Relations after Enlargement," Ankara, 1997. A slightly adapted version has been published as "Turkey, Norway and the U.S. in the New European Security Context," *Dış Politika/Foreign Policy*, vol. 21 (1997), pp. 5–12.

5. See Şadi Ergüvenç, "Turkey: Strategic Partner for the European Union," in *Turkey and European Union*, pp. 1–22.

6. Western European Union, *European Security: A Common Concept of the 27 WEU Countries* (Madrid: Extraordinary Council of Ministers, November 1995), pp. 8–13.

7. Assembly of the Western European Union, *Security in the Mediterranean Region*, Report submitted on behalf of the Political Committee by Mr. de Lipkowski, document 1543 (Brussels, November 1996); and Ian O. Lesser and others, *Nato's Mediterranean Initiative: Policy Issues and Dilemmas*, MR-957-IMD (Santa Monica, Calif.: RAND, 1998).

8. For more details see Ian O. Lesser and Ashley J. Tellis, *Strategic Exposure: Proliferation around the Mediterranean*, MR-742-A (Santa Monica, Calif.: RAND, 1996).

9. For the Barcelona Process see, for instance, the contributions in Richard Gillespie, ed., "The Europe-Mediterranean Partnership Initiative," *Mediterranean Politics*, vol. 2 (September 1996, Special Issue), pp. 1–5; and Roberto Aliboni, "Confidence-Building, Conflict Prevention and Arms Control in the Euro-Mediterranean Partnership," *Perceptions*, vol. 2 (December 1997-February 1998), pp. 73–86.

10. Cahit Uyanık, "PKK Drug Operations, Legal Loopholes Fuel Crime," *Turkish Daily News Electronic Edition*, January 29, 1997.

11. "Human Trade," *Briefing* 1176, January 12, 1998, pp. 7–9; and Council of the European Union, "Illegal Immigration from Iraq and the Neighbouring Region," Press Release 5271/98, Brussels, January 26, 1998.

12. See chapter 7.

13. Şadi Ergüvenç, "Turkey's Security Perceptions," *Perceptions*, vol. 3 (June-August 1998), pp. 32–42.

14. İlnur Çevik, "Some Italians Are Making a Fatal Mistake," *Turkish Daily News Electronic Edition*, November 18, 1998; "Public Anger against Italy Mounts," *Turkish Daily News Electronic Edition*, November 23, 1998; Nazlan Ertan, "EU Warns Turkey against 'Formal Boycott' against Italy," *Turkish Daily News Electronic Edition*, November 25, 1998; and Stephen Kinzer, "Flap Over Kurd Underscores Turkish-European Gulf," *International Herald Tribune*, November 30, 1998.

15. Duygu Bazoğlu Sezer, "Turkey's New Security Environment, Nuclear Weapons and Proliferation," *Comparative Strategy*, vol. 14 (1995), pp. 149–72.

16. Paul B. Henze, "Russia and the Caucasus," *Perceptions*, vol. 1 (June-August 1996), pp. 53–71.

17. Ümit Enginsoy, "Turkey Fears Transcaucasia Will Be Another Yugoslavia," *Turkish Probe*, no. 108 (December 16, 1994), pp. 10–11; Enginsoy, "Turkey Shifts Policy on Chechnya," *Turkish Probe*, no. 110 (December 30, 1994), pp. 11–12; and Enginsoy, "Çiller: Chechnya No Longer Russia's Internal Affair," *Turkish Probe*, no. 112 (January 13, 1995), pp. 12–13.

18. Svante E. Cornell, "Turkey and the Conflict in Nagorno Karabakh: A Delicate Balance," *Middle Eastern Studies*, vol. 34 (January 1998), pp. 51–72.

19. Gülnur Aybet, "The CFE Treaty: The Way Forward for Conventional Arms Control in Europe," *Perceptions*, vol. 1 (March-May 1996), esp. pp. 25–31; and Richard A. Falkenrath, "The CFE Flank Dispute: Waiting in the Wings," *International Security*, vol. 19 (Spring 1995), pp. 118–44.

20. The deputy chief of Turkey's General Staff, General Çevik Bir, declared in February 1998, "Within the context of the Conventional Forces in Europe (CFE) negotiations,

a green light is practically given to prior adversaries to deploy more forces in the Caucasus in exchange for certain concessions in central Europe. By doing so, the risks for Turkey are compounded and the newly independent states are left under political and military pressure." *Strategic Forum*, no. 135 (February 1998), p. 4.

21. For a detailed analysis see Duygu Bazoğlu Sezer, "Balance of Power in the Black Sea in the Post-Cold War Era: Russia, Turkey, and Ukraine," in Maria Drohobycky, ed., *Crimea: Dynamics, Challenges, and Prospects* (Lanham, Md.: Rowman & Littlefield, 1995), pp. 157–94.

22. Duygu Bazoğlu Sezer and Vitaly Naumkin, "Turkey and Russia: Regional Rivals," *Policy Watch*, no. 268 (Washington, September 30, 1997, Special Policy Forum Report).

23. A. Suat Bilge, "Analysis of the Turkish-Russian Relations," *Perceptions*, vol. 2 (June-August 1997), pp. 66–92, esp. p. 92.

24. Semih D. İdiz, "Ankara 'Guarded' on Clinton's NATO Expansion Announcement," *Turkish Daily News Electronic Edition*, October 24, 1996; and Karaosmanoğlu, "NATO Enlargement: Does It Enhance Security?"

25. See chapter 8.

26. See chapter 10.

27. Ronald R. Krebs, "Perverse Institutionalism: NATO and the Greco-Turkish Conflict," *International Organization*, vol. 53 (Spring 1999), pp. 343–77.

28. For details see Heinz Kramer, "The Cyprus Problem and European Security," *Survival*, vol. 39 (Autumn 1997), pp. 16–32.

29. See, for example, "Turkish Defense Policy," speech by H. E. Hikmet Sami Türk, Minister of Defense, Republic of Turkey, to the Washington Institute for Near East Policy, Washington, March 3, 1999; (www.washingtoninstitute.org/media/samiturk.htm [August 1999]).

30. Ergüvenç, "Turkey's Security Perceptions," p. 39.

31. Bir, "Turkey's Role in the New World Order," pp. 1–2, 4. For an overview of the process of restructuring Europe's security architecture, see the contributions in Carl Lankowsky and Simon Serfaty, eds., *Europeanizing Security? NATO and an Integrating Europe*, AICGS research report 9 (Washington: American Institute for Contemporary German Studies, 1999).

32. İlnur Çevik, "Turkey Eyes French-US NATO Command Debate with Concern," *Turkish Daily News Electronic Edition*, December 13, 1996.

33. Ergüvenç, "Turkey's Security Perceptions," p. 41.

34. For an overview see the contributions to Anne Deighton, ed., *Western European Union 1954–1997: Defence, Security, Integration* (Oxford: European Interdependence Research Group, 1997); and Guido Lenzi, ed., *WEU at Fifty: Insiders' Reflections on the Future of WEU after Fifty Years* (Paris: WEU, Institute for Security Studies, 1998).

35. For details see Treaty of Maastricht on the European Union, article J-4 and the Declaration on Western European Union in the Final Act of the Intergovernmental Conference that negotiated the Treaty of Maastricht, in which the envisioned relationship of WEU to NATO on the one hand and to the European Union on the other hand is substantiated.

36. Ministerial Meeting of the North Atlantic Council, Berlin, June 1996, *Final Communiqué*, NATO Ministerial Communiqué M-NAC-1(96)63, points 6–8; and

Stephan De Spiegeleire, "The European Security and Defence Identity and NATO: Berlin and Beyond," in Mathias Jopp and Hanna Ojanen, eds., *European Security Integration: Implications for Nonalignment and Alliances* (Paris: WEU Institute for Security Studies, 1999), pp. 57–99.

37. Turan Moralı, "European Security and Defence Identity and Turkey," *Perceptions*, vol. 1 (June-August 1996), p. 136.

38. The case of the "extraction force" that was created in November 1998 for a possible military rescue of OSCE observers in Kosovo is a striking example of this. Although praised as the first "Europeans only" military force and mission in the context of managing a violent conflict in Europe, its creation was a clear consequence of robust American diplomacy toward Miloşević and the result of deliberations and decisions that took place exclusively within NATO institutions. Consequently, the mission was guided and controlled by NATO's military headquarters.

39. This status has been created by the WEU Council of Ministers' Petersberg Declaration of June 1992 for European NATO states that are not members of the European Union and has been improved by the "Kirchberg Declaration" of May 1994.

40. Moralı, "European Security and Defence Identity and Turkey," pp. 136–37.

41. "WEU Puts Pressure on Greece," *Turkish Daily News Electronic Edition*, April 9, 1997; and "WEU Accepts Turkey in Decision-Making," April 16, 1997.

42. "Turkey Escapes from Last-Minute Isolation," *Briefing* 1240, May 3, 1999, pp. 18–19.

43. "NATO Finds a Mid-Way Formula to Avert Turkish Veto Threat," *Briefing* 1239, April 26, 1999, pp. 22–23.

44. See annex III to the *Conclusions of the Presidency of the Meeting of the European Council in Cologne, June 3–4, 1999*. "Declaration of the European Council and Presidency Report on Strengthening European Common Policy on Security and Defence" is included in this annex. (www.europa.eu.int/council/off/conclu/june99/annexe_en.htm#a3 [August 1999]).

45. Philip Webster, "Britain to Back Defence Role for Europe," *Times* (London), October 21, 1998, p. 1; and Tom Buerkle, "Blair Now Backs EU Defense Arm," *International Herald Tribune*, October 22, 1998, p. 5. For a first evaluation of the EU-related problems of the British initiative see Peter Schmidt, *Neuorientierung in der europäischen Sicherheitspolitik? Britische und britisch-französische Initiativen*, SWP-AP 3088 (Ebenhausen: Stiftung Wissenschaft und Politik, 1999).

46. In March 1997 France, Germany, Italy, Spain, Belgium, and Luxembourg took a common initiative for a stepwise integration of WEU into the EU by presenting a document to the Intergovernmental Conference for the revision of the Treaty of Maastricht. This initiative met with strong resistance from the EU's neutral member states. *Agence Europe*, March 24–25, 1997, pp. 4–5; and Tom Buerkle, "Make the EU a Defense Alliance? Debate Deepens Security Policy Rifts," *International Herald Tribune*, March 28, 1997, p. 5.

47. Quoted in Assembly of the Western European Union, *Organizing Security in Europe: Political Aspects*, Document 1509 (Brussels 1996), p. 42. A similar language can be found in the *Presidency Report* (see note 44).

48. "Çiller Cripples WEU over Greek Blockage of Membership Bid," *Turkish Daily News Electronic Edition*, November 20, 1996.

Part Three

1. Günter Seufert, "Ein parlamentarisches System ohne Demokratie," *Entwicklung + Zusammenarbeit*, vol. 39 (1998), pp. 238–40.

2. Ian O. Lesser, "Turkey's Strategic Options," *International Spectator* (Rome), vol. 34 (January-March 1999), pp. 79–88.

3. *Programme of the 57th Government, Presented to the Turkish Grand National Assembly by Prime Minister Bülent Ecevit, 4 June 1999* (www.byegm.gov.tr/57hukumet/programme.htm [September 1999]).

Chapter Thirteen

1. For an overview of U.S.-Turkish relations during the cold war see, Henri J. Barkey, "Turkish-American Relations in the Postwar Era: An Alliance of Convenience," *Orient*, vol. 33 (1992), pp. 447–64.

2. Paul B. Henze, *Turkey and Atatürk's Legacy: Turkey's Political Evolution, Turkish-US Relations and Prospects for the 21st Century* (Haarlem: SOTA, 1998), pp. 77–90.

3. Barkey, "Turkish-American Relations," pp. 462–63.

4. For an overview see Kelly Couturier, *U.S.-Turkish Relations in the Post Cold War Era* (Istanbul: Friedrich Ebert Foundation, 1997).

5. Kemal Kirişçi, "Turkey and the United States: Ambivalent Allies," *Middle East Review of International Affairs (MERIA) Journal*, vol. 2 (December 1998) (www.biu.ac.il/SOC/besa/meria [August 1999]).

6. See, for instance, various remarks of representatives of oil companies at the 113th Bergedorfer Round Table at Baku, June 1998, as documented in Körber-Stiftung, ed., *Energie und Geostrategie im kaspischen Raum—Akteure, Interessen, Konfliktpotentiale* (Hamburg, 1999).

7. This was again emphasized by the publication of Bülent Ecevit's revised and updated Regional Security Plan in late January 1999; "Ecevit Reveals His Masterpiece: The Updated 'Regional Security Plan,'" *Briefing* 1228, February 1, 1999, pp. 13–14.

8. Harun Kazaz, "What Was Signed between the KDP and the PUK in Washington, and Where It Is Leading," *Turkish Daily News Electronic Edition*, October 5, 1998 (www.turkishdailynews.com [August 1999]); and Alan Makovsky, "Kurdish Agreement Signals New U.S. Commitment," *Policy Watch*, no. 341, September 29, 1998.

9. "Turkey Expresses Concerns over Strike on Iraq" *Turkish Daily News Electronic Edition*, December 18, 1998.

10. Kirişçi, "Turkey and the United States."

11. Şükrü Elekdağ, "2 ½ War Strategy," *Perceptions*, vol. 1 (March-May 1996), pp. 44–52.

12. See, for instance, the speech delivered by Baki İlkin,Turkey's ambassador to the United States, to the Washington Institute for Near East Policy, Washington, September 2, 1998 (www.washingtoninstitute.org/media/ilkin.htm [September 1999]).

13. Metehan Demir, "Cobra Executives Accuse US of 'Shadow Embargo' on Ankara," *Turkish Daily News Electronic Edition*, December 9, 1996; and Philip Finnegan, "U.S. May End Turk, Greek Aid," *Defense News*, January 26-30, 1998.

14. Harun Kazaz, "Turkey Fires a Policy Warning Flare in Washington Conference," *Turkish Daily News Electronic Edition*, May 8, 1999.

15. Çevik Bir, "Turkey's Role in the New World Order," *Strategic Forum*, no. 135 (February 1998), p. 4.

16. Strobe Talbott, "U.S.-Turkish Relations in an Age of Interdependence," Turgut Özal Memorial Lecture delivered at the Washington Institute for Near East Policy, October 14, 1998; (www. washingtoninstitute.org/media/talbott.htm [September 1999]).

17. "U.S. Intensifies Efforts to Reduce Tension in Cyprus," *Turkish Daily News Electronic Edition*, December 12, 1998.

18. For details see Heinz Kramer, *Die Europäische Gemeinschaft und die Türkei* (Baden-Baden: Nomos Verlag, 1988), pp. 84–111; and Mahmut Bozkurt, *Die Beziehungen der Türkei zur Europäischen Union* (Frankfurt am Main: Peter Lang, 1995), pp. 59–71.

19. See, for instance, "Statement Made by the Ministry of Foreign Affairs on the Conclusion of the EU Vienna Summit of 11–12 December 1998," in which it is said that "the EU's failure to put Turkey's application on a legally binding basis" would lead to Turkey's continuation of its strictly bilateral conduct of political relations with EU member states (www.mfa.gov.tr/grupb/ba/baa98/december/05.htm [September 1999]).

Chapter Fourteen

1. Paul B. Henze, *Turkey and Atatürk's Legacy: Turkey's Political Evolution, US Relations and Prospects for the 21st Century* (Haarlem: SOTA, 1998), p. 180.

2. For details see Heinz Kramer, "The Institutional Framework of German-Turkish Relations," in *The Parameters of Partnership: Germany, the U.S. and Turkey—Challenges for German and American Foreign Policy* (Washington: American Institute for Contemporary German Studies, 1998), pp. 19–21.

3. This argument is elaborated by Heinz Kramer, "Ein wichtiger Sicherheitspartner. Die Europäische Union darf die Türkei nicht auf Dauer aussperren," *Frankfurter Allgemeine Zeitung*, May 21, 1997, p. 11; and Kramer, "Europäische Interessen in den Beziehungen zur Türkei," in Erich Reiter, ed., *Österreich und die NATO Die sicherheitspolitische situation Österreichs nach der NATO-Erweiterung* (Graz: Styria, 1998), pp. 417–33.

4. See, for instance, Vittorio Sanguineti, "Turkey and the European Union: Dreaming West but Moving East," *Mediterranean Quarterly*, vol. 8 (Winter 1997); and Sanguineti, "Turkey and the European Union: Fundamentalism or Algerian Syndrome?" *Studia Diplomatica*, vol. 50 (January 1998), pp. 37–59.

5. Matthes Buhbe, "Die Türkei und die Grenzen der europäischen Integration," *Internationale Politik und Gesellschaft*, no. 3 (1998), pp. 157–72.

6. See Michael C. Evans, "European Union Expansion: The Case for the Admission of Turkey," *Strategic Review*, vol. 26 (Fall 1998), pp. 16–21, esp. p. 17.

7. *Programme of the 57th Government, Presented to the Turkish Grand National Assembly by Prime Minister Bülent Ecevit, 4 June 1999* (www.byegm.gov.tr/57hukumet/programme.htm [September 1999]).

Index